Additional Praise for
NO ONE HAD A TONGUE TO SPEAK

"This memorable account of an epic flood is all the more impressive because its authors, one of them the son of a survivor, are so young. Their reporting is painstaking, their stories heartbreaking."
—Anne Fadiman, author of
The Spirit Catches You and You Fall Down

"The anatomy of a perfect storm: not just a South Asian monsoon-driven tragedy killing thousands, but an overall portrait of social, political, historical, and moral corruption and dysfunction. Inspections are missed, planning is chaotic, and the disempowered find themselves squarely in the path of an epic disaster."
—Clark Blaise, coauthor (with Bharati Mukherjee) of
Days and Nights in Calcutta and
The Sorrow and the Terror:
The Haunting Legacy of Air-India 182

"Sandesara and Wooten provide a fresh, engaging account of a horrendous, man-made flood in Gujarat, India. The tale of the Machhu dam disaster highlights the pitfalls of a top-down approach to development, risk mitigation, and long-term recovery, using the words of those who have experienced it. As a globally surgent India marches ahead with its economic growth and comes to terms with its prospects and limitations in the realm of development, these two researchers offer a refreshing, comprehensive, painstaking, and lively account of a defining moment in India's past. From policymakers to common citizens, readers will relish this book's narration and ponder its implications for future disasters."
—Mihir Bhatt, founder of the
All India Disaster Mitigation Institute

No One Had a Tongue to Speak

No One Had a Tongue to Speak

The Untold Story of One of History's Deadliest Floods

Utpal Sandesara & Tom Wooten

Prometheus Books

59 John Glenn Drive
Amherst, New York 14228–2119

Published 2011 by Prometheus Books

Cover image courtesy of Gunvantbhai Sedani
Cover design by Jacqueline Nasso Cooke

Inquiries should be addressed to
Prometheus Books
59 John Glenn Drive
Amherst, New York 14228–2119
VOICE: 716–691–0133
FAX: 716–691–0137
WWW.PROMETHEUSBOOKS.COM

15 14 13 12 11   5 4 3 2 1

Library of Congress Cataloging-in-Publication Data

Sandesara, Utpal, 1986–
    No one had a tongue to speak : the untold story of one of history's deadliest floods / by Utpal Sandesara and Tom Wooten.
        p. cm.
    Includes bibliographical references and index.
    ISBN 978–1–61614–431–9 (hardcover)
    ISBN 978–1–61614–432–6 (e-book)
    1. Floods—India—Morvi. 2. Floods—India—Machchhu River. 3. Disaster relief—India—Morvi. 4. Disaster victims—India—Morvi—Interviews. 5. Flood damage—India—Morvi. 6. Dam failures—India—Morvi. I. Wooten, Tom, 1986– II. Title.

HV610 1979 .M67 S26 2011
363.34'93095475—dc22

                                                                2010054590

Printed in the United States of America

To Ishani and Caroline,
with love,
from your big brothers

A Map of the State of Gujarat

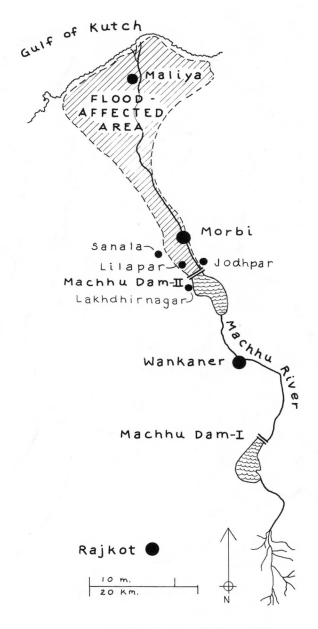

A Map of the Machhu River Valley and Rajkot

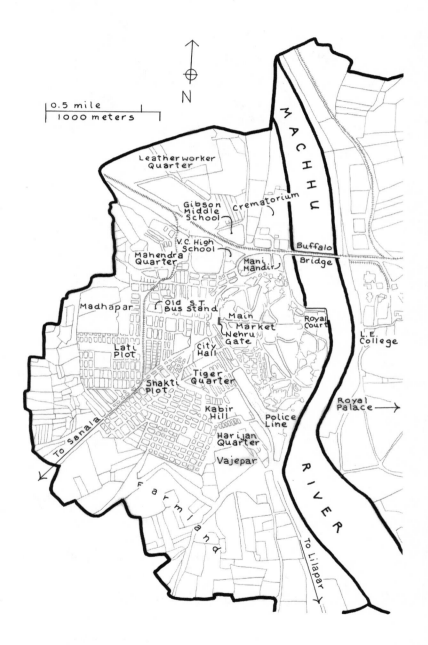

A Map of the City of Morbi

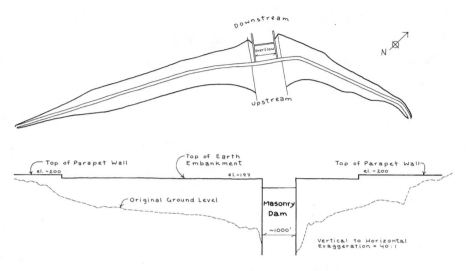

A Diagram of the Original Machhu Dam-II

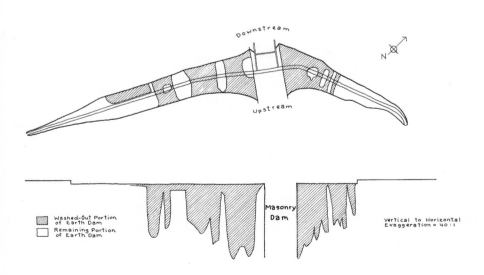

A Diagram of the Damage Incurred by the Machhu Dam-II on August 11, 1979

Contents

Major Characters

CITIZENS OF MORBI AND ITS ENVIRONS

Pratapbhai Adroja
The giddy, friendly proprietor of Ghost Paan, a small tobacco shop in downtown Morbi. Resides in the Mahendra Quarter.

Ratilal Desai
The no-nonsense mayor of Morbi. Owns a small paint factory and resides in the main market area. A Vaniya by jati.

Kanubhai Kubavat
An instructor at Morbi's teaching college. Officiates at a small temple in the Tiger Quarter, where he resides. A Brahmin by jati.

Dhirubhai Mehta
The prosperous owner of Mehta Machinery, an agricultural equipment shop in downtown Morbi. A member of the Rotary Club. A Vaniya by jati.

Gokaldas Parmar
Morbi's representative in the Gujarat legislative assembly. A member of the Congress Party. Resides in Shakti Plot. A member of the poorer Satwara agricultural jati.

Bhagvanji Patel | A farmer and factory owner from the village of Lilapar. A member of the powerful Patel agricultural jati.

T. R. Shukla | The principal of Morbi's arts college. An active member of the Rotary Club. Resides on the Machhu River's eastern bank.

Gangaram Tapu | A strong, charismatic convict incarcerated in Morbi's prison for the murder of a Miyana gangster. Resided in Kabir Hill prior to his conviction.

Khatijaben Valera | A woman of the Valera family, the large Muslim clan that provided music in Morbi's old royal court. Resides between the Harijan Quarter and Vajepar.

CITIZENS OF MALIYA

Husainbhai Manek | A fisherman and salt laborer from Maliya, and a member of the Miyana quom.

Abdulbhai Mor | A shrewd salt factory owner from Maliya, and a member of the Miyana quom.

Jashabhai Samani | A farmer residing on the open land surrounding Maliya, and a member of the Miyana quom.

CIVIL SERVANTS

A. R. Banerjee | The chief government administrator (collector) of Rajkot District, in which Morbi lies.

Dipankar Basu | The spirited, efficient secretary of the Machhu Dam-II Inquiry Commission.

H. K. Khan | An Indian Administrative Service officer who serves as the chief civil servant (secretary)

	in Gujarat's Agriculture Department. Later serves as the special secretary for relief.
Ushakant Mankad	The Home Guard commander for Rajkot District. Resides in the city of Rajkot. A native son of Morbi.
A. C. Mehta	The deputy engineer in charge of the Machhu Dam-II's operation.
J. F. Mistry	The engineer who oversaw the design of the Machhu Dam-II. Later the chief engineer for irrigation projects in Gujarat.
Lakshmanbhai Mohan	The mechanic on the Machhu Dam-II.
Y. K. Murthy	The former chairman of the Central Water and Power Commission and the technical consultant to the Machhu Dam-II Inquiry Commission.
B. J. Vasoya	The engineer who oversaw the construction of the Machhu Dam-II. Later the superintending engineer for the Sardar Sarovar dam project.

STATE-LEVEL POLITICIANS

Babubhai Patel	Gujarat's chief minister. Originally tied to the Machhu Dam-II as the state's public works minister during the dam's construction. A member of the Janata Party. A member of the powerful Patel agricultural jati.
Keshubhai Patel	Gujarat's agriculture minister. A member of the Janata Party. A member of the powerful Patel agricultural jati.
Madhavsinh Solanki	The leader of the opposition in the Gujarat legislative assembly. A member of the Congress Party.

Foreword

Disasters Natural and Unnatural

There is no better place in which to read a book about a disaster—the collapse of a massive dam in Gujarat, India, on August 11, 1979—than in Haiti less than a year after an earthquake leveled much of its capital city on January 12, 2010. These past three decades afford us, perhaps, safe purchase from which to discuss disasters natural and unnatural. The topic has generated a varied literature, from the first-person testimonial to scholarly histories, and *No One Had a Tongue to Speak* sits quite comfortably in between these genres.

So too do its young authors live between worlds shaped by disasters of one sort or another. The Asian tsunami of 2004 and Hurricane Katrina had a great impact on the shared commitment of Utpal Sandesara and Tom Wooten, who together decided early in their college studies to write a book about the rupture of the Machhu dam and its ending or upending of many lives in India— an event that occurred before they were born.

I was lucky enough to teach Sandesara during his first year at Harvard, and to serve as a mentor to him in the years since. But it's not for that reason alone that I was eager to read this book and write its foreword. It's rather that I knew, as these young scholars embarked on this project, that it might be important not for their own intellectual development (which, well under way, was not a great concern) but rather for a world riven by disasters born of human agency.

The obvious distinction between "natural" and "unnatural" disasters, between events like the 2004 tsunami, say, and Chernobyl, is not so obvious at all upon closer inspection. The lines are never clearly drawn. When an entire city in Gujarat is destroyed by the waters once impounded by the Machhu dam, it is easy to conclude that human agency is at the root of the disaster. When a quake suddenly levels a city, it is easy to conclude that Mother Nature is at work. But few observers of Katrina in New Orleans and the Gulf Coast concluded that human agency was not involved in either the region's vulnerability or the inadequacy of relief and reconstructions.

Few observers in post-quake Haiti would submit that reconstruction will be effective without an acknowledgment of the *social* nature of disaster. The country is, alas, a living laboratory on the topic. It's fair to say that almost no country has had a greater struggle with disasters natural and unnatural, and with the fettering and unfettering of human agency, than has Haiti. Storm and fire and flood will always be with us, surely. But as we learned in Haiti in 2008, when four hurricanes lashed the country in the space of a month, it is difficult to control water when human beings have irrevocably altered the environment: deforestation had already rendered the country and its coastal populations vulnerable to the sort of suffering that ensued. For those few Haitians who failed to learn that lesson, it was brutally reiterated little over a year later when an earthquake destroyed much of the capital city and stilled perhaps a quarter of a million voices, including many well known to me, on a single day.

So although Haiti was not foremost in the minds of Sandesara and Wooten when they initiated this project, my experience here is surely why they asked me to write a foreword to their important and arresting book. *No One Had a Tongue to Speak* is the most gripping account I've read of an unnatural disaster. I have long had reason to think about dams. In 1983, between college and medical school, I traveled for the first time to a squatter settlement in central Haiti, and it was there, twenty-seven years later, that I began to read Sandesara's and Wooten's book. That squatter settlement was formed when Haiti's largest river was dammed to build a hydroelectric dam, the people who farmed the fertile valley behind the dam were forced up into the arid hills above them. They received scant or no compensation; in fact, they didn't even receive water or electricity, the promised products of the project.

Over the years, living and working in the settlement, I became obsessed with dams—so much so that a journalist once asked me, "Do you have something against dams?" The answer was no, not at all. In fact, as I write this foreword I am among those politicking for more small hydroelectric dams in Haiti, so that its people, especially the smallholder farmers, will have power to cook and build small businesses and process or preserve their agricultural products. But I learned when still a graduate student that there was, already, a substantial literature about dams—not only their impact on those displaced, but also on the environments damaged or altered by their construction. There was even a literature about the impact of dams bursting.

The human project, it's increasingly clear, amounts to one giant messing with Mother Nature. The arrogance of some in charge of designing and implementing large infrastructure projects is laid bare by Sandesara's and Wooten's book, as it has been in studies of Chernobyl and Haiti.[1] But none of this hubris is of recent vintage. Students of public health know that early efforts to build a canal spanning the Atlantic and Pacific Oceans, across narrow Panama, were met with failure because epidemics of mosquito-borne disease, especially malaria and yellow fever, were fanned by the project—as cholera was fanned in Europe and America by the growth of large cities.[2] These were (to use the

great sociologist Robert Merton's term) "unanticipated consequences of purposive social action"—the result of human agency,
of choices—and spectacular as such.[3] But even when the link
between disaster and human agency is less clear, the causes usually include poor planning or feckless administration. Mike Davis,
in *Late Victorian Holocausts*, makes the point that a number of
great nineteenth-century famines in India and elsewhere occurred
not because monsoons struck becalmed backwaters cut off from
the British Empire, but rather because of policies mandated within
regions tightly and unequally tied to London.[4]

The Gujarat disaster is best read in this light. The destruction
of the city of Morbi recounted in *No One Had a Tongue to Speak*
was not a freak accident so much as an accident waiting to
happen. In one sense, it was a quintessential modern disaster. In
another, it joins a long and growing list with deep roots in what
some would term colonial and neocolonial efforts to bring both
nature and culture under the dominion of centralizing polities.

Since this is also the legitimate project of modernity—with all
its hubris and hope, with its promise and peril—it would be pru-
dent, surely, to learn lessons from the Gujarat tragedy. Sandesara
and Wooten offer us that chance, and theirs will become more
than just another cautionary tale. This account of the Gujarat
disaster might serve as both warning and ethical guidebook for
those of good will who believe in the hope and promise of sustainable, just development, those who spurn the Luddite trap that
rejects all bold (and inherently risky) efforts to live better on this
planet without destroying it.

There are three reasons I believe that my claim—that *No One
Had a Tongue to Speak* needs to become required reading—will
hold true. The first is mundane, almost pedestrian: as the planet
grows more crowded, studies like this one can and should inform
efforts to prevent the noxious, unanticipated consequence of purposive social action. The arc of history is clear: there will be more
events of this sort, not fewer. Regardless of one's take on development (whether one be a grassroots activist or a protagonist of

grand public works), regardless of one's role (victim, critic, pawn, decision maker, obstructionist, or green-lighter), we need to admit that unanticipated consequences will affect us all. We should learn from past mistakes to prepare for unexpected and harmful events, natural and man-made. We don't have much choice on this score, not at this late date in our collective history, because we all need sanitation and food and electricity and safety—freedom from want and also the political freedoms that accompany sustainable development, as the great Amartya Sen has argued in a series of books and studies that should serve as companion volumes to this account from Gujarat.[5]

The second reason this book is important is a bit less obvious; it concerns claims of causality. There is no question that we still don't know enough about the lessons to be drawn from what happened in 1979 in Gujarat. But there is a great deal of dissensus regarding what caused what. This is in part because of lack of documentation, on which I comment more below, but also because disputed claims of causality follow every disaster, whether natural or unnatural. Why did Katrina cause so many deaths in a modern American city? Why were immediate responses to it considered inadequate rather than adequate? In chapter after chapter, Sandesara and Wooten lay bare the anatomies of harm, near and distal, caused by the disaster—from Ratilal Desai cradling the corpse of a drowned child in the main market to Gokaldas Parmar watching his house get swallowed up from a neighbor's roof, from District Collector A. R. Banerjee's relief efforts to Chief Minister Babubhai Patel's frustration amid cycles of accusation paralyzing the state government. Their experiences remind us that although all involved agree that something terrible happened in one region in Gujarat, at a specific time and on a certain day, not everyone agrees about what had caused it. Heavy rains? Incompetent dam operators? Engineering flaws? As the crowded planet and built environment change, as the very climate changes, such contested claims of causality will continue to swell in volume and in content, as noted with regard to less controversial topics such as epidemic disease.[6]

Finally, let me note a third reason this book will endure: it offers humble documentation of a tragedy that, like so many others, was forgotten almost as soon as it happened. So many lives are extinguished on every day of every year, just as so many lives are begun. Most vital events are never registered in the first place, much less noted with respect. But there has long been a natural order of things—that the young are meant to reach old age and children are meant to bury their parents— and events such as the collapse of the Machhu Dam-II (or the Haitian earthquake or Katrina in New Orleans) disrupt the natural order of things. These need to be recorded and shared. Dave Eggers gave us a similar gift when he wrote *Zeitoun*, a book about one middle-class family's experience of Katrina. Given their resources—jobs, shelter, a solid family—they should have been OK. But because Abdulrahman Zeitoun himself fell outside of locally entrenched categories of race and religion (even as he tumbled into other emerging categories), and because Katrina followed 9/11 as national traumas, we are reminded that modern-day disasters are always social.[7]

So it is in this book about the collapse of a dam in Gujarat, 1979. Just as Eggers committed himself to chronicling the travails of the Zeitoun family, whose suffering would have otherwise been "undocumented," and thus missed, so too have Sandesara and Wooten committed themselves to documenting the impact of the dam's collapse on the people of Morbi. Here is a Gujarati analog of *Zeitoun*.

It is also a social history, and explicitly one. In New Orleans, the story was mostly about race and class (and, to some extent, about religion). In Haiti, how one fared in the face of recent disasters was mostly a story of class. But in India, of course, it is about class and caste, gender and religion. Social complexities are confronted more boldly in this book than in most others. *No One Had a Tongue to Speak* would be important even if it were a yeoman's report, even if it were an infelicitous translation of first-person accounts. But it is more than history's first draft: beautifully written, this book is suspenseful, elegiac, and haunting.

Paul Farmer, MD, PhD
Kolokotrones University
Professor, Harvard University;
Chair, Department of Global Health
and Social Medicine,
Harvard Medical School; and
Cofounder, Partners In Health

February 2011
Port-au-Prince, Haiti

Acknowledgments

We hatched the plan for this book on a cold January night in 2005, when we were freshmen in college. In the six years that have elapsed since, hundreds of people have lent us their energy, insights, and advice. The pages you now hold in your hands were shaped by their support and assistance.

For early encouragement and guidance, we are greatly indebted to Steve Bloomfield, Jennifer Leaning, Bill Clark, Sheila Jasanoff, Jill Lepore, Steve Biehl, Bill Fisher, and Gary Krist. For academic backing and administrative support, we thank the Harvard Committee on Degrees in Social Studies, the Harvard Committee on Degrees in History and Literature, the University of Pennsylvania Medical Scientist Training Program, and the University of Pennsylvania Department of Anthropology; in particular, we wish to acknowledge Anya Bernstein, Ted MacDonald, Maggie Krall, Skip Brass, and Philippe Bourgois. This book's development paralleled our own academic and intellectual growth during our time in college, which was greatly influenced by Marshall Ganz, Arachu Castro, Paul Farmer, Sadhana Bery, and Pauline Peters. Finally, our fieldwork in India would have been impossible without the generous financial support of the Harvard South Asia Initiative, the Harvard Asia Center, and the Radcliffe Fellowships program.

After a summer of research in India, we arrived back at Harvard without an academic adviser. Despite his full roster of students, Max Likin agreed to take us under his wing. With humor and patience, he instructed us in the art of storytelling and shepherded our first draft to completion.

This journey has not been easy, and a number of people have supported (and tolerated) us along the way. We send our thanks and love to Jonathan Chow, Yinliang He, Zach Widbin, Laura Togut, Monica Thanawala, Winnie Nip, Jingshing Wu, Mary Brazelton, Virginia Anderson, Jane Cheng, Joy Xi, Kathleen Coverick, Michelle Wile, Tracy Carroll, Aaron Zagory, Joshua Stanton, Kevin Uy, Nate Walker, Chris Hsiung, Ben Wang, Nabil Thalji, James Hui, Tina Ho, Jon Brestoff, Trudy Kao, Dan Leyzberg, Caroline Wooten, Lee Wooten, Jamie Devol, Ishani Sandesara, Nautama Sandesara, and Niranjan Sandesara.

The hospitality of a number of people in India allowed us to carry out an unbelievable amount of research over the span of eleven short weeks in 2006. We are tremendously indebted to Kapilbhai Patel and Meeraben Patel for their hospitality in Ahmedabad and Gandhinagar, and to Bhavanaben Patel, Ramaben Vaishnav, Bharatbhai Vaishnav, Lalabhai Humbal, Rajuben Humbal, and the late Jashwantbhai Humbal in Morbi for their hospitality and cobra-fighting prowess.

Our interviews and archival research would not have been possible without help from Dilipbhai Barasara, Prabhakarbhai Khamar, Mohansinh Jadeja, Manoharsinh Jadeja, Dineshbhai Kundalia, V. Thiruppugazh, Narendrabhai Modi, Hanifbhai Chauhan, Prafulbhai Doshi, Y. K. Murthy, Dhirubhai Mehta, Ratilal Desai, Gokaldas Parmar, Haribhai Panchal, Babubhai Patel, R. A. Mehta, B. R. Shah, Rahul Bhimjiani, Bhaskarbhai Tanna, Pradeep Sharma, A. R. Banerjee, Gokaldas Parmar, Arvindbhai Patel, D. A. Satya, C. K. Nimavat, Harshadbhai

Gohil, Ramilaben Solanki, Prafulbhai Doshi, and the staff of the Harvard Library System. In particular, Dilipbhai's tireless efforts greatly enhanced our fieldwork, and we owe him our deepest gratitude.

A number of organizations also lent us their support. We are indebted to the staff of the Indian Census Bureau office in Ahmedabad; R. T. Kotak, B. B. Patadiya, Atul Mehta, and the staff of the subdistrict and prant offices in Morbi; N. A. Khadia and the staff of the Morbi Irrigation Section Office; the staff of the Rajkot Irrigation Circle; K. B. Shah, D. H. Patel, and the staff of the Gujarat Central Designs Organization; the staff of the Gujarat Legislative Assembly; Manubhai Shah and the staff of the Consumer Education and Research Centre; J. B. Patel and the staff of the Gujarat Irrigation Department; Deepak Bhatt, Jagdish Trivedi, and the staff of the Rajkot Directorate of Information; Mr. Padiyar and the staff of the Gandhinagar Directorate of Information; and the editors and staff of *Phulchhab*, *Akila*, and *Sandesh*.

Mahendrabhai Dave and the Trust of the Morbi Flood Museum hold a special place in our hearts.

For three memorable weeks in Morbi, Ishani and Nautama Sandesara were our adventurous translators and guides. Many stories and characters would have escaped these pages without their indefatigable help.

Watching this manuscript move from a draft to a published book has been tremendously gratifying, and we owe our gratitude to the skilled hands that have helped to shape the final product. Nishubhai Sedani and the royal family of Morbi graciously volunteered their photographs. Jamie Devol prepared the maps and diagrams, and computer edits were provided by Jon McMurry and Matt Conboy. Zach Widbin, Monica Thanawala, and Alice Lee provided extensive and insightful comments on our writing. Rick Balkin worked tirelessly until he found our story a home; as first-time authors, we could not have asked for a more knowledgeable, nurturing, or humorous agent. We give our heartfelt thanks to Mark Hall, Chris Kramer, Jennifer Tordy, and Jade Zora Ballard, who have guided us through the publication process at Prometheus Books with patience, understanding, and enthusiasm.

Finally, and most important, we thank the one hundred forty-eight individuals who shared their stories with us. Their generous, courageous, and forthright narration captivated us for days. Because of them, we left India awestruck, inspired, and determined to complete our work. We hope that we have done them justice in these pages.

A Note to the Reader

All translations from Gujarati sources—written and spoken —are our own. We have taken the liberty of normalizing orthography in excerpts from written material wherever such changes have not altered the meaning or flavor of the original— for instance, replacing "Morvi" with the commonly accepted spelling "Morbi." Where Indian English sources have used Roman transliterations of Gujarati words for which uncontroversial translations exist (such as "subdistrict" for *taluka*), we have made the appropriate changes in the interest of readability. Additionally, frequently used foreign terms (such as *jati* or *paan*) are italicized only at their first occurrences in the book.

We have presented personal names as Gujaratis would recognize them. For most names, this has meant including the respectful suffix *-bhai* (Brother) or *-ben* (Sister); the exceptions are those personal names that already contain an integrated suffix (such as *-ji*, *-das*, *-sinh*, or *-lal*), to which *-bhai* or *-ben* would not normally be added.

When referring to individuals by a single name, we have generally employed the family name. The four notable exceptions are Bhagvanji Patel, Keshubhai Patel, Babubhai Patel, and Khatijaben Valera. We refer to the Patels by their personal names in order to avoid confusion among them. (This is in keeping with the practice of many Gujaratis, who will refer to Patels by their personal names.) We refer to Khatijaben Valera by her personal name in order to enable easy distinction from the other members of her clan.

Prologue

"A Vaniyan of Morbi Goes to the Machhu's Waters"

Morbi, a city on the banks of the Machhu River, was not particularly famous.[1] In fact, it was little known outside Gujarat, the western Indian state in which it lay. To be sure, it had once been the envy of many princes on the subcontinent. After Indian unification and independence, however, it had declined in importance. It was a small city with a colorful royal past, a few notable industries, and a handful of imposing monuments. By the late 1970s, all but the most avid students of the Saurashtra Peninsula's princely history had forgotten the names of Morbi's kings—save one.[2]

For nearly two hundred years, children all over Gujarat had heard the tale of how Jiyaji Jadeja, Morbi's ruler at the turn of the nineteenth century, had wronged one of his subjects. "A Vaniyan of Morbi Goes to the Machhu's Waters"—the song detailing the king's indiscretion—was a standard in every Gujarati folk singer's repertoire. It reminded listeners that indecent behavior often carried grave consequences.

King Jiyaji Jadeja ruled over Morbi from 1790 to 1827.[3] He gained widespread fame for his bravery, his fierceness, and—above all—his insatiable lust. Despite possessing five wives, he

I

often pursued beautiful commoners; fearing for their lives, most submitted.

But on one occasion—an occasion that would live on in the lore of the Gujarati people—a woman resoundingly rebuffed Jiyaji's advances, speaking words that would haunt the kingdom long after his passing.

According to the legend, a Vaniyan (merchant woman) of Morbi set out one morning to fetch water from the Machhu River. Descending to water his horse, Jiyaji caught sight of the woman as she walked along the path to the riverbank. Struck by her beauty, the king drew close and leered at her. The ensuing exchange would become familiar to generations of Gujaratis:

> He says, Vaniyan, what is the price of your water pots?
>> Forget about it, *Thakor* Jiyaji; let it be, King of Morbi.
>>> I refuse to set prices!
>> Your entire harem will be ruined for these water pots!
> A Vaniyan of Morbi goes to the Machhu's waters.
>
> He says, Vaniyan, what is the price of your bangles?
>> Forget about it, *Thakor* Jiyaji.
>> Your elephants will be ruined for these bangles!
> A Vaniyan of Morbi goes to the Machhu's waters.
>
> Then speak up, Vaniyan—the price of your hair-bun?
>> Your kingdom will be ruined for this hair-bun!
> A Vaniyan of Morbi goes to the Machhu's waters.
>
> Tell me then, Vaniyan—the price of your feet?
>> Your head will be ruined for these feet!
> A Vaniyan of Morbi goes to the Machhu's waters.[4]

In spite of the woman's refusal, Jiyaji remained insistent.

Left with no escape, the Vaniyan threw herself into the Machhu's waters. From the shore, the stunned king heard her cry out, "For your indecency, King Jiyaji, you will pay! Seven gener-

ations from now, neither your lineage nor your city will remain!"
Her curse cast, the woman disappeared under the waters and
drowned.[5]

The nameless Vaniyan's words did not trouble the inhabitants
of Morbi. The city went on to grow and flourish under Jiyaji and
his descendants. Over time, successive generations of the Jadeja
dynasty transformed Morbi into "the Paris of Saurashtra,"
described by administrators throughout India as a "model city."[6]

Nonetheless, the minstrels of Gujarat did not allow the tale of
Morbi's Vaniyan to be forgotten. There would always remain the
remote knowledge, shrouded in layers of legend, that the city of
Morbi bore a curse that originated in the Machhu River.

Chapter 1

On the Banks of the Machhu River

The sun rose above a hazy horizon to reveal that the river remained completely dry.[1] It was late July. The monsoon still had not reached Gujarat, but life in Morbi went on.[2]

A steady stream of traffic swerved, honked, and shouted its way into downtown on the Buffalo Bridge—a grand masonry structure whose arches spanned a quarter of a mile across the empty Machhu riverbed. Two bronze bulls, imported from Italy at great expense by Morbi's king nearly a century before, surveyed the traffic from their pedestals near the center of the bridge.[3] Those who could afford to take their eyes off the road—passengers in auto-rickshaws, schoolboys balancing on the racks of bicycles, wives clutching children while riding behind their husbands on overloaded mopeds—beheld a panorama of grand architecture, the legacy of centuries of prosperous royal rule.

On the Machhu's eastern shore, south of the Buffalo Bridge, a tower rose up from a gleaming, white marble palace, the former residence of Morbi's royal family. Across the dry riverbed, the Machhu's steep western bank tapered into a vertical masonry wall. Dotted with an intricate pattern of balconies and large windows, the wall rose up five stories into the old royal court.

5

Downstream, the ornate towers and turrets of the Mani Mandir complex loomed over traffic entering downtown via the bridge. Built at the turn of the century by King Vaghji Jadeja after the death of his beloved concubine Manibai, the Mani Mandir consisted of a central temple surrounded on all four sides by a majestic, two-story castle. Dazzling carvings adorned every arch, pillar, and banister in the immense, red sandstone structure. Surrounded by lush green trees, the building stood, regal and serene, at the entrance to an otherwise frenetic downtown.[4]

Morbi had expanded greatly in recent decades. Its inhabitants now numbered more than sixty thousand, and its choked avenues could barely accommodate the traffic flowing off the Buffalo Bridge.[5] Long-horned buffalo with humped backs sat in the middle of the road, paying little heed to the pandemonium around them. Schoolgirls in colorful uniforms darted across lanes, giggling and clutching their books. Auto-rickshaw drivers, craving a morning dose of sugar and tobacco, swerved over to stop in front of their favorite *paan* shops. Their idling vehicles puttered as they approached the small storefront windows, exchanged pleasantries with the shopkeepers, and placed their orders.

Paan shops were ubiquitous in Morbi. Though little more than a brightly painted cabin located just north of the main market, Pratapbhai Adroja's paan shop was one of the most popular. The counter at Bhoot Tambool (Ghost Paan) directly faced the street, and on this particular morning, the line outside the window snaked well down the block. The space behind the counter was cramped, leaving just enough room for Adroja's stool. Bags of chips, peanuts, and various Indian snacks lined the walls. A small stack of newspapers sat for sale. Candy and fruit also competed for customers' attention in the limited counter space.

In spite of the variegated offerings, most visitors came to the shop for the paan. Sitting on the counter in front of Adroja, a small set of wooden drawers held a rich assortment of ingredients: betel nut, fennel seeds, fruit preserves, shaved coconut, tobacco, and spices. As each new customer approached the window, Adroja spread a betel leaf on his cutting board and set to work, meticulously laying down pinches of every ingredient requested. When finished, he would fold the leaf just so, securing it with a toothpick and passing it into an eagerly outstretched hand. The customer would tuck the leaf between his gum and his cheek, sucking on the sweet blend of juices that turned saliva bright red. Prosperity as a paan merchant rested on the ability to achieve a perfect balance among diverse ingredients, and Adroja's workmanship always seemed just right.[6]

At the same time, the small man's constant smile, high-spirited banter, and quirky sense of humor did much to endear him to his customers. In Ghost Paan's scant free space, Adroja kept a sizable personal collection of ghost and goblin likenesses. The shop's hand-painted sign sported two ghoulish skeletons, and stylized skulls and bones studded the awning's metal frame. Sometimes, a customer would ask Adroja about his shop's unusual theme. The response, delivered in a nasal squeak, never varied: "I love ghosts!" When his interlocutors seemed dissatisfied with the explanation, Adroja simply laughed.

Ghost Paan demanded long hours, but the lively rhythm of business made the time pass quickly. Selling paan entailed a constant stream of social chatter coupled with careful attention to craft and ingredients. Many might find the work exasperating, but Adroja always seemed at peace amid the hubbub.

Adroja was in good spirits when he closed the shop that evening, pulling the metal grate down over the narrow entrance and securing the lock. It was only a short walk to his house in Mahendrapara (the Mahendra Quarter), where his son, his wife, and a hearty meal of lentils, rice, vegetables, and buttered flatbread awaited. Adroja strode jauntily down Morbi's wide commercial avenues. The shops on either side offered a dazzling array of goods. Every night, Adroja passed storefronts displaying pots and pans, electric water pumps, school supplies, jewelry, colorfully patterned cloth, sacks of grain, radios, and spreads of berries and guava. Other shopkeepers would wave at Adroja as they, too, closed up for the night.

Walking through the immaculately swept streets, which stood in sharp contrast to refuse-strewn public roads all over India, Adroja could clearly see why administrators and citizens alike had long regarded Morbi as a "model city." There were, of course, the grand monuments of the Jadeja dynasty, to which the city owed its moniker—"The Paris of Saurashtra." More important, Morbi possessed a physical and social infrastructure that placed it first among its peers. Power lines supplied houses in even the poorest neighborhoods with reliable electricity. An excellent system of sewers kept waste out of the streets, preventing the water-borne epidemics that plagued many other cities. Since the turn of the century, telephone lines had extended from downtown to even the farthest-flung villages in the area. With time, Morbi had developed an extensive network of free grade schools, an acclaimed high school, and several well-regarded colleges.[7]

Even more important than infrastructure or institutions, however, were the people who populated Morbi. Adroja perceived a distinctive vigor and confident spirit in his customers. Especially of late, he had noticed a discernable optimism in the air. New factories were opening on the city's outskirts at a breathtaking clip, and money was flowing freely.

As Adroja rounded the last bend toward home, he reached up to pat the wad of rupees in his breast pocket, the product of a long day's work. It was a good time to be a shopkeeper in Morbi.[8]

≋≋≋≋≋

A sprawling mansion, marked by the subtle signs of slow decline, overlooked a wide avenue in southern Morbi.[9] On the bungalow's first story, a pretty woman swept dust across the kitchen floor. She was dressed in a tunic and baggy trousers. A scarf covered her hair, as per the custom of Muslim women of her high social standing.

Khatijaben Valera belonged to one of Morbi's most illustrious families. Over decades of royal rule, the men of the Valera clan had served the Jadeja kings as official court singers. Their musical wizardry had earned them considerable riches and public esteem. Even three decades after Indian independence, the Valeras remained an intensely proud holdover of the feudal era. After marrying into the family, Khatijaben had come to embrace its heritage as her own.[10]

Khatijaben was a woman of great presence, strong in body and personality. Though not yet thirty, she had already given birth to five children, whom she guarded fiercely. She carried herself with a confidence and boldness that set her apart from other married women of her age. At the same time, as a good wife, she readily obeyed her mother-in-law's directives in domestic matters.

While Khatijaben and her younger sister-in-law scurried about the kitchen, a heartrending melody floated down from the floor above. Everyone said that Shaukatbhai, the youngest of the four Valera brothers, possessed a prodigious talent. From his youngest years, his smooth, strong voice had held audiences' rapt attention. In a family that had built its reputation on singing ability, he had always appeared poised to become his generation's standard-bearer.

As Shaukatbhai's song soared, a raspy quality overcame its gentle tones. Of late, Khatijaben had heard the unwelcome twinge often. Though Shaukatbhai's voice remained perfectly pitched, it had lost its purity to an abrasive edge.

Khatijaben knew the rumors. People around Morbi whispered that someone had poured vermilion in her brother-in-law's drink, permanently searing his vocal chords. No one knew for certain who had done it. Some ventured that a jealous family member might have ruined Shaukatbhai's voice. Valera family pride had proven too strong to permit discussion of the matter, and it remained a subject of speculation for outsiders.

Those who knew Khatijaben's clan realized that the poisoning of its youngest voice might have been more than a vindictive act of envy. It might also have been a shrewd business decision in a rapidly growing household still adjusting to a life unsupported by the beneficence of Morbi's royalty.

A look around the Valera compound told much of the story. The multistory concrete bungalow, whose windows and terraces surrounded a central courtyard, had begun to show the first signs of disrepair. The royal family had built the mansion to house Khatijaben's father-in-law, his older brother, and their children; now, though, the children had begotten children of their own, and nearly seventy people inhabited the increasingly cramped compound. The royal family had left Morbi, erasing the steady stream of money, gifts, and prestige that had sustained the Valeras for generations. Since Indian independence, the family's men had survived by offering music lessons to the children of Morbi's emerging modern gentry. But all the Valera men were singers, and each faced stiff competition from within the walls of the family compound. It seemed eminently possible that someone, troubled by the exigencies of the postroyal years, might poison a rival family member in order to secure better economic prospects.

Khatijaben enjoyed greater economic security than most of the Valeras. Some years earlier, the clan patriarchs, sensing that drastic changes loomed, had established a trucking company as an alternate source of income; now, Khatijaben's husband Bashirbhai, the oldest of four brothers, played a leading role in Valera Transport. Managing an impressive fleet of vehicles, he ensured that his wife and children would not go hungry. While the Valeras' ways remained rooted in tradition, Khatijaben was reaping the rewards of modernizing change.

In truth, much had changed in and around the clan's bungalow. Gaudy signs advertising vocal lessons by different Valera men hung all around the formerly stately compound, competing for the attention of passers-by, who paid little heed. An exodus of laborers filed past the mansion in the early morning as the poor residents of the surrounding neighborhoods, formerly subsistence farmers and service workers in a traditional economy, commuted to the new factories on the city's outskirts. Although the royal family and its wealth had departed, many in Morbi were becoming quite well-off; more than a few cars now competed for space with the goatherds, bicycles, mopeds, and auto-rickshaws on the street in front of the bungalow. The area's shops, previously limited to groceries, had begun to carry small modern luxuries. Morbi seemed to be growing more vigorous with each passing day. From Khatijaben's vantage point, the bungalow seemed like a decaying nineteenth-century vestige amid a twentieth-century city.

Though she had joined the Valera clan only recently, Khati-jaben had heard countless tales of its former glories—private audiences with the Jadeja kings, compliments from high-ranking British administrators, jaunts around western India aboard the royal plane, and the adulation of Morbi's public during crown-sponsored concerts. Her husband's relatives had recounted the stories so many times that she could vividly picture the night of a major function at the royal palace. . . .

Guards in trim uniforms greeted guests as they passed through the gates and began a thousand-foot walk past towering fountains to the palace entrance. The melodic voices of Valera men drifted through the vast interior courtyards, where assorted dignitaries chattered ceaselessly. King Lakhdhirji Jadeja, Morbi's ruler from 1922 until Indian independence, wandered about, shaking hands and exchanging pleasantries with the guests.[11]

Lakhdhirji was the eleventh of the illustrious Jadeja kings.[12] He traced his lineage back to Jiyaji—the man who had wronged the Vaniyan of Morbi—and even further back to Kayaji—the dynasty's founder.

Kayaji did not found Morbi; a chieftain named Mayurdhvaj ("The Peacock Flag") had established it almost two millennia before him. The founder had dubbed his city Mayurdhvajpuri, or "City of the Peacock Flag." Over the centuries, the name had become shortened to "Morbi."[13]

The city had existed for over seventeen centuries before Kayaji Jadeja took the throne, but he and his descendants would determine Morbi's lasting shape. In 1698, Kayaji lost a struggle for the throne of Kutch, a northern Gujarati kingdom. Seizing Morbi, which belonged to the Kutchi crown, he declared independence. Within a few years, his kingdom stretched from Morbi to the Gulf of Kutch, encompassing the city and more than one hundred surrounding villages on the peninsula known as Saurashtra—"The Good Country." Kayaji and his descendants would rule over Morbi for exactly two hundred fifty years, eventually building it into the envy of other princely states.[14]

Although the city became part of a unified India in 1947, the Jadejas had woven themselves into the physical fabric of the city to such an extent that Khatijaben Valera still could not move through the Paris of Saurashtra without thinking of the royals. The royal court, the Mani Mandir complex, the Buffalo Bridge, the Lakhdhirji Engineering College, and the grand clock tower gate at the entrance to the main market—renamed "Nehru Gate" in a postindependence paroxysm of republican spirit—all bore the Jadeja imprimatur. The artifacts of royal beneficence reminded Khatijaben that the kings had acted as loving fathers to Morbi and its people.[15]

By 1979, however, the Jadejas themselves were gone. In 1957, Lakhdhirji, Morbi's last sovereign king, had passed away. That same year, Lakhdhirji's son Mahendrasinh had moved to England with his family. And just eleven months earlier, in August 1978, Mahendrasinh's son Mayurdhvaj—the thirteenth Jadeja of Morbi—had been killed in a bar fight in Europe, leaving no male heirs to the throne. The death of the prince, who shared a name with Morbi's founder, had marked the end of the dynasty that had ruled the City of the Peacock Flag for centuries.[16] His memorial ceremony, one of the finest displays Morbi had ever seen, had drawn thousands of mourners to the royal palace.[17] It was a fitting end to a glorious era.

Khatijaben had paid her respects at the royal palace. A year after the end of the Jadeja lineage, Morbi rushed onward outside the Valera family's bungalow. Inside, time remained slow, the clan of court musicians preserved as a relic of the past. As Shaukatbhai's mournful song drifted down from the upper floor, Khatijaben finished sweeping the kitchen floor.

≋≋≋

Bhagvanji Patel walked with a slightly impatient gait down the dusty road, occasionally glancing at the browning fields that stretched for miles on either side.[18] The crops—peanut, millet, wheat, castor, assorted vegetables—were not faring well. The drought had laid siege to farming in the village of Lilapar, leaving the monsoon harvest in jeopardy.

Despite this situation, Bhagvanji did not worry much. Having recently established a small tile factory, he possessed an alternate source of income. More important, he was a Patel. Struggle with the earth, and the fortitude built therein, were specialties of his people.

Bhagvanji had built up considerable strength during a youth spent tending fields in the manner of his forefathers. His slight frame belied hard muscles, toughened by years of working the land with the aid of only rudimentary tools. He was not young anymore, but he was not quite middle-aged, either. His gaunt face and sharp grin complemented a firm, forthright manner that impressed friends and intimidated employees.

"Patel" was not merely Bhagvanji's surname. It summarized his occupational position, his social station, and his way of life: his *jati* identity. The notion of jati represented the practical articulation of what might be referred to as "caste." Belonging to a Hindu jati—or its Muslim equivalent, a *quom*—meant much more than belonging to a particular occupational tradition and an inescapable social status, as the term *caste* might imply. It suggested participation in a broader community. Jatis and quoms formed occupationally based strata, but they were also social circles. Members of a community tended to live on the same streets, frequent the same places of worship, and socialize nearly exclusively with one another. The community formed an intermediate structure of social kinship between the extended family and the broader village society. Moreover, it usually transcended the village level; members of a jati or quom tended to identify strongly with their brethren in other villages. Even among groups with lower social status, the shared identities of jati or quom membership were sources of great pride.[19]

Bhagvanji was immensely proud of his jati. As he saw it, Patels served as Gujarat's social backbone. Farmers by tradition, they were known for their intrepid and persevering character. Generations of working the land had made many Patel families quite prosperous. For about a century, Patels had also been launching industrial and commercial enterprises, entering professional life, and building up a proud tradition of leadership in politics, as exemplified by Mahatma Gandhi's most trusted deputy, Sardar Vallabhbhai Patel. Nonetheless, most Patels remained farmers. They stood at the forefront of agriculture in the Machhu River Valley, where they constituted a substantial fraction of the population.[20]

Various other jatis filled out the social tapestry of mainstream village life. Satwaras and Kolis, of lower social standing and more meager means than Patels, were also traditional farmers; of late, they increasingly offered their labor to rich landowners and industrialists. Several pastoralist jatis typically dedicated themselves to herding cows, buffalo, goats, and sheep, though villagers of many different backgrounds kept at least some animals. Vaniyas, belonging to the same community as the woman who had cursed Morbi, traditionally engaged in trade, while Brahmins served as priests and teachers. A variety of other jatis, from Kandois (sweet makers) to Sonis (jewelers) to Luhars (ironsmiths), played integral roles in village life. In most villages, members of these "respectable" groups farmed the land to a certain extent.[21]

Jatis at the bottom of the village social structure fulfilled service roles within the agricultural economy, toiling at occupations

traditionally deemed unclean on account of their necessary proximity to filth or dead animals. A village's diverse "Untouch-
ables"—Hajaams (barbers), Chamars (leatherworkers), Bhangis
(sweepers), Mochis (cobblers), and various others—were often
described with the collective label "Harijans," which had been
popularized by Mahatma Gandhi as a politically correct substi-
tution for various derogatory terms.[22]

While Harijans also maintained fierce pride in their community identities, jati divisions constituted a clear hierarchy. Members of high-status jatis viewed their low-status counterparts as
not only dim-witted and dirty but also morally tainted. A clear
distinction existed between "good folk" and "backward
people"—perpetuated, as one might expect, by the self-identified
members of the former category.[23] Bhagvanji, for one, often complained about the vulgar ways of the Harijans who worked in his
factory and swept his streets.

Bhagvanji's village, like most in the region, reflected jati divisions in its basic layout. Lilapar's nucleus consisted of a few
streets lined by the village council office, temples, shops, schools,
and other public places. High-jati citizens who played lesser roles
in agriculture, such as Brahmins and Vaniyas, resided there. Some
Patels and other farmers chose to live in the central area as well,
trekking out each morning to the fields surrounding the village;
others stayed in huts scattered throughout the farmland.

The Harijans lived in the Harijan Quarter, a cluster of houses
at just the right distance from the center of Lilapar to maintain
separation while ensuring ready provision of labor. They wor-
shiped at their own temple and congregated in their own plaza.
They virtually possessed a village of their own, albeit one bereft
of many amenities. As in the city of Morbi and most other
Machhu River Valley communities, the Harijan Quarter in
Lilapar lay on the most undesirable land in the village.[24]

Bhagvanji did not see the cramped, uneven streets of the Harijan Quarter. He lived in the village center, surrounded by other
comfortable and upstanding citizens. His daily circuits—to his

factory and to his fields—carried him past the houses of other "good folk."

Bhagvanji took great pride in his village. Although it was afflicted by the drought, it remained unbowed. Like many residents of Lilapar, Bhagvanji considered his village first among the more than one hundred in the old kingdom of Morbi—not in the date of its founding, but certainly in the integrity, courage, and goodwill of its people. Lilapar was a model village at the leading edge of prosperity in the Machhu River Valley.

In recent years, it had become one of the first villages in the area to embrace the next step in development: mechanization. Most wealthy Patels in the Morbi region had begun to employ machinery in their farming. But some Patels in Lilapar, including Bhagvanji, were progressing even further—they were starting factories.

For centuries, farming had formed the backbone of society along the Machhu River. The kings of Morbi had relied heavily upon revenues from agriculture to fill their royal coffers. In turn, they had worked to ensure continued prosperity for farmers through infrastructural developments, institutional reforms, and favorable policies.[25]

Nonetheless, even while working to strengthen agriculture in villages from Lilapar to the Gulf of Kutch, the last few kings of Morbi had devoted some attention to industrial development. Near the turn of the century, decades before Bhagvanji's birth, King Vaghji Jadeja—the erector of the great sandstone Mani Mandir—had commissioned studies of his kingdom's mineral resources, hoping to uncover possible launching points for industrialization. The surveys revealed that the region's red clay would prove ideal for manufacturing ceramic products.

In 1928, the first ceramics enterprise—Parshuram Potteries—began using donkeys to transport red clay from nearby villages to an abandoned building in Morbi. Laborers mixed the clay with water and black soil and then molded the resulting slurry into tiles, pottery, and other ceramic products. The pieces baked in long outdoor trenches sandwiched between the blazing India sun and a slow charcoal roast. Both crucial factors of production—labor and clay—proved cheap, and Parshuram Potteries grew rapidly.

By 1933, Morbi's first industrial plant employed four hundred workers and produced more than 20 million pounds of pottery annually. Soon, it supplied pottery and tiles throughout India, its wares going to market in far-off Delhi and Bombay. Ceramics became a major component of the local economy and a substantial source of local income.[26]

Over the subsequent decades, an inexorable expansion transformed Morbi into an industrial city. New factories dedicated to the production of flooring tiles, roofing tiles, and pottery sprang up around the city's outskirts. Morbi's tile-manufacturing sector grew into the largest in western India.

During this period of development, clocks joined and then surpassed ceramics as the city's most famous export. By the late 1970s, less than thirty years after the establishment of the first clock factory in Morbi, the city produced sixty percent of India's timepieces. Fourteen major companies put out the finished products, relying on small partners for specialized parts and processes; as a result, accessory industries dedicated to boxes, cabinets, leather straps, watch hands, electroplating, and engraving thrived. Many members of the middle class became capitalists by starting small-scale ventures.[27]

Morbi's industrial prowess in the late 1970s rested squarely on the efforts of individual entrepreneurs who had broken out of the traditional agrarian mold; the Patels were the most notable among these. One expert on industry in Morbi—himself a Brahmin—would explain the Patel jati's role in development by saying:

> Brahmins, Vaniyas, backwards jatis—we are not suited to industry. We run our businesses according to fixed plans, within fixed boundaries. But industry requires something else. Industry is a risk. Industry requires courage. And it requires effort. . . . We are not accustomed to having to put in long days of hard effort. We are not accustomed to tilling soils all day under the

hot sun. We are not accustomed to working hard for little return. We do not strike out on our own to create new things for ourselves. We remain where we feel comfortable. Industrial progress cannot possibly be carried forward by such people. A very different type of person is required for industrial progress.

That type consists of the Patels. They are uneducated and rustic, but they are also prosperous. And their prosperity is a result of courage and effort. A tradition of farming has built up their constitutions. They are hardy people, not afraid of uncertainties or hard work. These people have the courage and the determination to take their hard-earned money and use it to set out on an unmarked trail.

To start out in industry is to till soil for the first time. Would Brahmins, Vaniyas, backwards people do this? Certainly not. Where we would falter, they push right ahead.[28]

The Patel ethos, with its emphasis on persistence and industriousness, equipped the jati to drive forward Morbi's economic development. Patel entrepreneurs also benefitted from their traditional engagement with farming, which enabled them to lay down large tracts of land as collateral for capital, and from their jati community, which provided connections to individuals in various positions of authority.[29]

Bhagvanji had founded Sri Lilapar Potteries two years ago. The factory, which crafted roofing tiles out of the Machhu River Valley's red soil, lay roughly halfway between Morbi and Lilapar.

Production had halted for the monsoon season, but Bhagvanji occasionally tended to administrative matters in the factory complex. He turned in through the gate on Lilapar Road, kicking up dust as he entered. Massive mounds of red soil dotted the complex. To one side, a furnace, which had come to replace the baking trenches of the early days, sat idle. After the monsoon had passed, the furnace would once again burn coal from Kutch, releasing fumes through the chimney and filling the complex with an acrid, unsettling smell.[30]

Bhagvanji entered the one-room office. He switched on the

fan, which provided much-needed relief after the scorching walk from Lilapar. Sitting down behind a simple desk, he set to work. Given the drought, he could have continued to produce bricks for almost two months after the initial rains prompted him to halt. Normally, regular downpours made it impossible to dry ceramics during the monsoon, but this year, his decision to send the laborers home had cost him many weeks of productive time.

The low-jati men and women who worked at Sri Lilapar Potteries would flock in from nearby villages after the monsoon. Bhagvanji provided them with lodging in his "laborer colonies"—long, narrow, wooden buildings divided into small rooms, each of which held a family. Most of the rooms sat vacant at the moment, their tenants passing the unexpected drought in their home villages.

With little work to do, Bhagvanji soon emerged from the office. Walking past the makeshift sign posted near the entrance, he turned right onto Lilapar Road and began his trek home. Though the sun had descended a bit, the heat remained oppressive.

After Bhagvanji had walked some distance, he could see the long earthen walls of a colossal structure that rose above the horizon. Bhagvanji knew that the imposing façade deceived; a void lay behind the mighty dam. The rains had not arrived, and the reservoir remained empty.

Kanubhai Kubavat's sandals kicked up cloudlets of dust as he walked to the temple.[31] Between his ankles, the trailing edge of his *dhoti*—a rectangular piece of cloth elaborately folded so as to produce two legs—hung just above the cracked dirt of the Tiger Quarter's main road. Even as the sun moved rapidly to the west, a searing heat seemed to envelop him. It did not feel like the holy month of Shravan, usually full of rain, had arrived.

Kubavat was tall, with a sinewy build and imposing features. A thick wad of paan rested in his cheek. His sleek hair, parted from one side, glistened in the dying light. The Brahmin ambled more than he walked, his swaggering gait appearing to widen his body with every step.

During the day, Kubavat taught Principles and Elements of Education at a teachers' college just north of Morbi's main market. But when he returned to southern Morbi's Vaghpara (the Tiger Quarter), he traded his pants for a dhoti and took up his second job.

For thirty-one years, Kubavat's family had officiated at the small temple near his house. Alongside his father, and like his grandfather before him, he faithfully discharged his priestly duties, leading daily evening prayers and marking the myriad holidays of the Hindu calendar.

Unlike the solar calendar that structured Kubavat's day job, the Hindu calendar tracked the progression of a month by the phase of the moon. Each month began on the day after a new moon and comprised two fortnights, waxing and waning.[32]

Of all twelve months, Shravan held a special importance for Gujarat's people. It was the holiest of months, when Kubavat and other Brahmins were at their busiest. Moreover, in direct contradiction to the drought besetting the Machhu River Valley, Shravan exemplified the monsoon in the Gujarati imagination; its mere name conjured images of heavy clouds and constant rain.[33]

The month's holiness dated back to a Shravan day near the beginning of time, when Shiva the Destroyer had swallowed a vat of poison that threatened to annihilate the world. Suspending the poison in his throat for eternity, the god had fulfilled his role as a member—along with Brahma the Creator and Vishnu the Preserver—of the holy trinity that balanced the Hindu cosmos.[34] In commemoration of Shiva's monumental act of destruction, Hindus honored Shravan as the most spiritual of months, marking it with special austerities aimed at destroying the poisonous feelings of desire, anger, greed, attachment, pride, and envy.[35]

The fourth day of Shravan's waning fortnight—August 11 in 1979—began a week of continuous holidays. Kubavat's wife, and other women blessed with a male child, would spend Bol Chauth (Dipping Fourth) fasting to celebrate their good fortune. Then, on Naag Panchami (Cobra Fifth), Morbi's Hindus would honor a plethora of divine serpents, from Shesh—the thousand-headed ruler of the underworld who served as Vishnu's throne—to the cobra that always hung around Shiva's neck. Kubavat's wife and the other women of the Tiger Quarter would spend the next day, Randhan Chhat (Cooking Sixth), toiling in the kitchen to prepare fried delicacies, heavy milk-fat sweets, and an array of snacks. The women would store the foods away, for cooking was forbidden on Shitala Saatam (Smallpox Seventh); the lighting of fires would anger Shitalaa Maa (Mother Smallpox), a mysterious deity who visited sickness upon impious families.[36]

The midnight after Smallpox Seventh ushered in Janmaashtami (Birth Eighth). This Hindu Noel marked the birth of Lord Krishna, an *avatar* (incarnation) of Vishnu who enjoyed wild popularity in Gujarat, having spent his later years ruling over the western tip of the Saurashtra Peninsula. Birth Eighth was the month's most joyous occasion, a climactic paroxysm of religious fervor.[37] Moreover, the legend of Krishna's first moments on earth, commemorated on that eighth day of the waning fortnight, epitomized the sublimity of Shravan's rains.

Many millennia ago, a princess named Devki married a prince named Vasudev. Shortly after the wedding, Devki's brother, the demon king Kams, received a prophecy that he would die at the hands of his sister's child. Enraged, Kams imprisoned the couple. Over the subsequent years, he watched his sister and brother-in-law carefully, visiting their cell to kill the newborn baby whenever Devki gave birth. When she became pregnant for the eighth time—with Lord Krishna—she began dreading the day when her brother would once again do his deadly work.

On the waning seventh of Shravan, while Devki endured the pains of labor, Vasudev peered out at a violently stormy night. Wind shook the trees. Rain battered the dungeon walls. Wet, chilly air filtered in through the cell's barred windows.

At midnight, the child was born. The cell filled with the overpowering brilliance of the Lord. The voice of Vishnu explained to Vasudev that he would be able to carry the baby to safety across the Yamuna River.

As Vasudev picked up the child, a deep sleep overcame the prison guards. One by one, the locked doors opened of their own volition. Vasudev soon found himself out in the storm, the newborn boy in his arms.

He walked toward the Yamuna River but despaired upon reaching its shore. Dark, thrashing waters lay as far ahead as the eye could see through the driving rain. To Vasudev's surprise, the waters suddenly parted to give him passage.

As he began crossing, the Yamuna, eager to obtain the Lord's blessing, reached up to touch the infant's feet. The roiling river crept upward, rising to Vasudev's chest. When he hoisted Krishna onto his head, the waters rose even further, submerging his neck and face. Just as the river seemed poised to drown Vasudev, the baby kicked his heel into the water, and the flooding subsided.

On the opposite shore, Vasudev hauled himself and the infant onto the slippery bank. There, he left Krishna with the local king and queen, who would nurture the child as he grew into the most beloved figure in Hindu mythology.[38]

Birth Eighth—the anniversary of Krishna's entry to the world—was the most important and evocative day of Shravan. In 1979, the holiday happened to fall on August 15—Independence Day; on that date, all of India would enjoy a double celebration. Kubavat would remain home from the teachers' college, stuffing his cheek with an extra paan or two. In the evening, he would officiate as the Tiger Quarter temple filled with revelers who would sing hymns and push an ornate swing bearing an image of Lord Krishna.

Kubavat served a congregation that flocked from the various side streets of the Tiger Quarter. The neighborhood housed a diverse array of Hindu jatis and Muslim quoms. Satwaras formed the biggest group. An agricultural jati, the Satwaras were generally not as affluent as the Patels, but they enjoyed more social mobility than Harijans and members of other low-status communities. (Morbi's representative in Gujarat's legislature, for example, was a Satwara.) Many of the jati's men worked the fields surrounding the city. A number were beginning to transition to manufacturing labor. In many ways, the Tiger Quarter, full of moderate incomes, typified Morbi's growing middle-class character, which had risen out of hard work in farms, small shops, and factories.[39]

As Kubavat reached the temple's threshold, he removed his sandals. A layer of dust from the main road coated them. Kubavat hoped that the monsoon rains would arrive soon and provide the appropriate Shravan atmosphere. Six thousand years after Krishna began life amid torrential rains and a flooding river, it would be the greatest of ironies to celebrate Birth Eighth in the scorching heat of a monsoon drought.

Mayor Ratilal Desai furrowed his brow as he looked at the documents on the desk.[40] He tended to narrow his eyes most of the time, even when engaged in mundane tasks. This habit gave people the impression—not unjustified—that he was constantly thinking, constantly evaluating, constantly searching for flaws to fix.

As on most days, Desai had walked to his city hall office from his house near Morbi's main market. He wore a white, short-sleeved collared shirt; wide, gray bellbottoms; and leather thong sandals. His mustache, little more than a strip of fuzz above a thin mouth, might have looked comical on a boy twenty years his junior, but Desai carried it with panache. He slicked back his wavy hair and wore large, boxy glasses. Overall, his facial appearance made him seem cold and calculating; although he was not quite either, he could be remarkably determined and efficient in matters of municipal business.

At the moment, Desai was handling paperwork related to the

upcoming Smallpox Seventh carnival. On August 14—the seventh day of the waning fortnight of Shravan 2035—Morbi's populace would observe a holiday in deference to Mother Smallpox. Children would gorge on milk-fat sweets prepared the previous day by their mothers and sisters. Women would take a rest from cooking, decking themselves out in their finest saris and heaviest jewelry in anticipation of the midnight celebration of Krishna's birth. Worshippers would fill the city's temples, slowly building the excitement toward Birth Eighth. And a carnival would draw nearly forty-five thousand people to the crematorium.[41]

Morbi's crematorium, which lay just north of the Mani Mandir on the Machhu River's western bank, contained an open field that often housed large events. The space sat far enough from the crematory furnaces that most visitors could ignore its morbid associations. Fancy, slightly decrepit mausoleums—survivors from the days of royal rule—surrounded the field on all sides.

The crematorium's field would serve as the site for Morbi's Smallpox Seventh carnival. Performers, merchants, and ride operators from the farthest corners of Gujarat and beyond would entertain the city's populace. Dozens had applied to the city for space at the carnival, and ultimate responsibility for approval fell to the mayor.

Desai had arrived at the position of mayor reluctantly. When he stopped to think about it, he sometimes felt as if he had become Morbi's first citizen almost by accident. Of course, it had all begun with the paint factory.

A Vaniya by jati, Desai had grown up the son of a cloth vendor in downtown Morbi. Upon coming of age, he had struck out on his own by establishing the city's second paint factory. Since 1968, Nilesh Paint, located amid the poor residential neighborhoods of southern Morbi, had produced oil paint for distribution to merchants throughout the city and beyond. Unlike Bhagvanji Patel's Sri Lilapar Potteries, Desai's factory consisted of little more than a pair of sheds. Three employees and a few machines provided all the work necessary to produce paint. In many ways, Nilesh Paint exemplified Morbi's trend of middle-class industrialization, in which capitalists of modest means established small-scale factories.[42]

For several years after its founding, the factory provided Desai with a steady, unspectacular income. His stable earnings supported a young wife and two sons. He did not aspire to more.

In 1972, however, friends encouraged Desai to run for election to the city council. He initially rebuffed them; he did not desire to enter public life. But his friends persisted, noting that he would benefit from the support of the influential Muslim paint merchants who lived in his ward.

Eventually, under considerable pressure, he contested the election and became a member of the city council. Seven years later, in June 1979, the council chose him as the next mayor. By the time he sat at his desk reviewing the carnival paperwork, he had assumed ultimate responsibility for smooth administration in Morbi.

At a time when many municipal governments suffered from corruption and inefficiency, Morbi's government continued to maintain the city's position as a "model city." Utilities functioned marvelously, at least by Indian standards. The city's streets were among the cleanest in the country. Bureaucrats handled finances with remarkable rectitude.

Although Desai had initially entered public service with some reluctance, he felt compelled to devote his full energies to fulfilling his duties as mayor. He approached his role with neither humility nor pride, but with supreme pragmatism and a sense of civic obligation. He bore Morbi a quiet, abiding love, a love that manifested itself not in spectacular shows of patriotism, but in a thousand small acts of mundane kindness and service.

His concern for the public interest tolerated few improprieties. Small vexations easily agitated Desai; even the most minor hiccups in public administration could summon his ire. His speech was exceedingly blunt. His voice, which vacillated between hoarseness and squeakiness, could sound harsh even when quiet. Desai showed no compunction about speaking out when he found fault with a government officer, whether the offender was a subordinate or a superior.

The mayor reserved a special contempt for the nepotism, favoritism, corruption, and divisive politicking that he felt had infected the state government in Gujarat, Mahatma Gandhi's homeland.[43] In Desai's view, partisan bickering and flagrant abuses of power had begun to hamper the state's administration. In sharp contrast to Morbi, where civic pride suffused the spirit of the city council, leaders in Gujarat's capital, Gandhinagar, focused unduly on personal gain. The political profiteering disturbed something deep within Desai. If he had been more romantic, he might have identified the wounded emotion as patriotism or dedication to public service; in actuality, he framed his complaints in more prosaic, practical terms, noting that government shortcomings diminished general welfare. He would often cut out relevant newspaper articles and underline particularly profound or egregious sentences, preparing himself to rant about them to anyone who was willing to listen.[44]

Although the mayor's vexation ran deep, he would not allow it to distract from municipal affairs. His overriding duty was to Morbi's people; he could not afford to waste time in frustration over outside matters. His fellow citizens had entrusted him with the city's upkeep, and he intended to discharge his duty to the fullest.

Sipping chai from the four-ounce glass an assistant had placed on his desk, he began poring over the documents before him. The carnival demanded his full attention.

A short distance from Mayor Ratilal Desai's office in city hall, a killer sat idly in the afternoon heat. He raised his gaze toward the barred window that sat at the top of his cell wall and glanced out at southern Morbi's Police Line, a quarter-mile complex containing prisons, police stations, and barracks. A subterranean recess in the subdistrict prison offered few comforts, but the man did not regret the murder he had committed a year earlier. There had been no choice.[45]

Gangaram Tapu hailed from the poor neighborhood of Kabir Tekri (Kabir Hill), where his wife remained with their children. Before he found himself behind bars, Tapu had raised goats, tended an orchard located near Lilapar, and carried out various shady, disreputable side jobs. He was short and stocky in build, and his shoulders and arms rippled with muscle. A jet-black mustache filled the middle of his wide, chiseled face. Although his stare could wither, Tapu was known for his hearty, convulsive laugh, which lit up his dark brown eyes and often echoed down the prison's bare corridors.

Years later, Tapu proudly regaled listeners with the story of the fateful encounter that led to his incarceration. His eyes would narrow as he recalled:

> The Muslims had all of Morbi in their grip! You know . . . the main square in front of Nehru Gate? If anybody went near there, they would jump on him and beat him up! And nobody did anything about it.
>
> One day, five Miyanas were out to get me at the railway station. One of them slashed at me with a sickle that he must have picked up from around there.
>
> So I took my knife and stabbed him in the stomach. He was done. Then I went home. The others took his body and ran away.[46]

Tapu saw little reason to regret his crime. The men he had tussled with were Miyanas, members of a Muslim quom that provoked wild disdain among many of the region's Hindus. The Miyanas had gained notoriety for being "notorious outlaws and marauders,"[47] and according to the accounts of British historians, they were "pre-eminent for their depredations and their contempt of authority."[48] To hear Tapu tell it, he had killed the Miyana as an act of vigilante justice against a feral tribe.

While Tapu was not necessarily the stoic hero he portrayed himself to be, his altercation fell into a long tradition of Hindu confrontations with the Miyanas. The historical particulars of the conflict might have eluded him, but as a Hindu of Morbi, Tapu bore a centuries-old animosity toward the citizens of a town twenty miles to the north called Maliya.

Upon his ascent to the throne in 1734, Morbi's second Jadeja king, seeking to avoid internecine struggles, granted small clusters of villages to his six younger brothers, who would rule as his vassals. The arrangement satisfied all save one brother—the man who had received Maliya and three other villages near the site where the Machhu River entered the salt flats of Kutch. Seeking to break away from the kingdom of Morbi, the first king of Maliya turned to the Miyanas, "a most criminal and turbulent tribe"[49] of Muslims with a reputation for violence and thievery. He encouraged the ruffians to settle in his kingdom, drawing them away from their ancestral home north of Kutch by offering land and impunity.[50]

Upon arriving in Maliya, the Miyanas set to work harassing the villages north of Morbi with periodic raids and annexing small tracts of land to their patron's fledgling kingdom. Their armed presence delivered a clear message: Maliya's king had declared his independence.[51]

Although the kings of Morbi repeatedly endeavored to subjugate their unruly northern cousins, every attempt at reconquest merely widened the chasm between the two kingdoms. The third Jadeja king spent his twenty-four year reign (1740–1764) trying to win back Maliya. As soon as he took the crown, the fourth king launched a campaign against the rogue kingdom; according to one historian, "the Miyana people ran away and disappeared into the desert every time, so that the fight never moved forward." In the 1770s, the fifth Jadeja king hired mercenaries and sacked Maliya. Nonetheless, on account of the barren area's low relevance and the difficulty of subduing its fierce population, the Jadejas did not reestablish firm control over it.[52]

In the first years of the nineteenth century, King Jiyaji, who would eventually attain infamy through the Vaniyan's curse, undertook the boldest attempt to subdue Maliya. When he formed an army to attack neighboring kingdoms, he encouraged the Miyanas to join the force. On the return route from a successful raid, Jiyaji invited the Muslim tribesmen to dine in his tent. There, the ready soldiers of Morbi systematically slaughtered them and took the king of Maliya captive.

Upon receiving news of the massacre, Maliya's people flew into a rage. Vicious attacks beset the villages of Morbi until the king of Maliya was returned safely to his lands. While Jiyaji's plot generated a great uproar and bred long-lasting ill will, it failed to upset the prevailing political order. At the end of his reign, a clear division prevailed along the banks of the Machhu.[53]

The division still remained clear a century and a half later, when Tapu committed his crime. Morbi was a prosperous, stable city blessed with fertile soil and widespread admiration; Maliya was a kingdom on infertile land and branded with the shameful marks of rebellion and criminality.

Though the Miyanas had stopped conducting open piracy in the Machhu River Valley, they remained, in the eyes of many, a threat to Morbi. Tapu strongly believed that he had struck a blow for justice by committing his crime. In killing his assailant, who happened to be the nephew of a major Miyana gang leader, he had sent a message to the unruly Muslims: Hindu Morbi would not tolerate intimidation.

From what Tapu imagined, he had already become something of a folk hero among young men in his jati and beyond. People on the streets spoke of his deed in hushed tones, simultaneously scandalized and enthralled. At the young age of twenty-four, Tapu had achieved celebrity throughout Morbi.

He rose from his cot. It was nearly 3:00 p.m., the time for exercise in the prison compound's small courtyard. Of late, the afternoon sun had beaten down on the inmates with unrelenting intensity. Tapu yearned for the monsoon to come, with its rush of cold air and its torrents of life-restoring water—water that would fill the streets of Kabir Hill, nourish his riverside orchard, and drip into his underground cell.

Each passing week seemed to hold promise, but so far, no rains had come. Dust continued to blow through the bars of Tapu's window as a guard unlocked the heavy door behind him.

A Miyana man sat inside his house, shielded from the baking midday sun.[54] He was enduring the hunger pangs of Ramadan's first days; like Khatijaben Valera in Morbi, he would spend the next month fasting from sunrise until sunset, denying himself even a sip of water to combat the dryness of the Maliya air.[55] Nonetheless, he felt at peace, untroubled by the drought that had parched the surrounding land.

Abdulbhai Mor was a small man, but he carried himself with an indomitable air. He was handsome, with angular features and a crooked, genuine smile. He asserted himself freely, particularly through his quick, acerbic wit. His pugnacious personality had ripened over the course of decades lived as a member of a dreaded and disparaged community.

More than two centuries after their ancestors first settled on the Saurashtra Peninsula, the Miyanas of Maliya still bore a reputation for savagery and depredation. Until Morbi's Jadeja dynasty consolidated its alliance with the British Empire in the early nineteenth century, Miyana bands had gained substantial income from raids on villages and commercial enterprises in the Machhu River Valley. Subsequently, however, they had been forced to turn to agriculture and herding in order to support their families.[56]

Historians of the royal era disparaged the Miyanas' efforts at farming, describing them as "bad husbandmen."[57] These harsh evaluations, which likely reflected the quom's blemished reputation more than objective fact, failed to consider the difficulties of cultivating the land near Maliya. The area's exceptionally rough soil resisted tilling. For most of the year, the harsh sun and arid air baked the fields. The Machhu River disappeared before reaching Maliya. Wells ran dry; with the Gulf of Kutch just beyond the town, those that remained in operation yielded only brackish water. When the monsoon finally arrived after months of desiccation, chaos ensued as the Machhu spilled out of its narrow, shallow riverbed near Maliya to flood the town and its surrounding farmland. But for the most part—and particularly during the frequent periods of drought, as in July 1979—Maliya's fields existed as vast expanses of dust, and farmers struggled against the earth for their sustenance.[58]

A few miles from Mor's house, Jashabhai Samani felt sweat build up under his oversized white turban. An acquaintance of Mor, Samani farmed the dry, dusty scrubland surrounding Maliya. His fields lay before him, flat and browning, transected at periodic intervals by gnarled trees and unkempt bushes. A suffocating humidity filled the air, but there was not a cloud in sight.

Loose white garments covered Samani's wiry but muscular frame. His piercing blue eyes offset sun-darkened features and a thick black mustache. He was a gruff man who spoke only when spoken to. Even his friends knew little about his thoughts. He lived with nearly a dozen family members in an earthen hut amid the ten acres of infertile farmland where he raised cotton, millet, and peanut plants.

Unlike Mor, Samani worried a great deal about the dry heat that had strangled Maliya for two months. He growled a quiet stream of profanities as he thought about the continuing effects of the drought. Drought meant uncertain crop yields. Given that he, like most local farmers, could afford little machinery, drought meant more labor for him and his oxen.

The marginal survival of farmers like Samani reflected the broader conditions of Maliya's existence. It was a harsh land full of stark beauty, quotidian filth, and difficult living. Anyone with the resources to bring prosperity to Maliya had long since used those resources to flee. The king, a descendant of the rebel vassal who had split off from Morbi two centuries earlier, led a modern, metropolitan life in faraway Bombay. The royal palace sat in disrepair at one end of the walled town, its courtyard overrun by stray dogs and cats. Civil servants came when appointed, but they left after suffering through the minimum duration of their assignments; some left earlier.

Maliya was an infernal wasteland, a place that few visited and most ignored. Too large to be a village and too small to be a city, it served as Morbi's negative double to the north, stagnant and pessimistic.[59]

Despite its difficulties, Maliya attracted little outside sympathy. Although the town housed a diverse group of citizens, including Hindus of many jatis and Muslims of several quoms, outsiders continued to identify it with the Miyanas' criminal past. Mor would explain:

> This town's reputation is great. When a government official or important guy comes by here, he turns right around and leaves. He does not even stay to observe our circumstances. We are not people of any importance. Whether we live or die does not much matter. They see us as bad people, as a quom of bandits. You go to the bank, and they take your money. An officer comes into town and pulls some scam. The out-of-towners, those damn Patels, they get everything. We are left with nothing. What result can we expect?[60]

The lack of possibilities outside of the tenuous agrarian realm contributed to the general malaise and hopelessness of life in Maliya. The few nonagricultural options that existed hardly provided an escape. Like farming, they required grueling labor and fell prey to the fickle whims of weather and changing prices.

The salt trade was one alternative to agriculture. Mor remained indifferent to the drought because he earned his living as a salt manufacturer. While Samani labored in the fields, Mor enjoyed his off-season, waiting until the day in September when he would recommence production.

The salt industry represented the modern world's only significant incursion on daily economic life in Maliya. Mor would explain, "In this town, there is nothing but salt. There are no industries, and no one seeks to start industries. Salt. That is it."[61]

Risk pervaded the salt business. Profits were high when they came, but so were losses. Compared to Morbi's industries, the rough-hewn enterprise lacked niceties, such as factories and offices. Except for the very last stages of production, salt manufacturing was a tense collaboration between man and the elements: water, air, and sun. The industrialist invested little capital, but he subjected himself to the vicissitudes of nature. In many ways, salt production—coarse, simple, toilsome, and dangerous—suited Maliya's character. The proximity of vast, chronically flooded salt flats rendered the town marginally relevant to a society that remained otherwise indifferent to its existence.

The various salt ventures that dotted the shore north of Maliya had begun appearing in the years following Indian independence. Most of the early plants had belonged to outside industrialists who saw an opportunity and pounced on it. Recently, after years of watching others reap profits, a few local citizens had finally begun to transition into salt production.

By establishing India Salt Works, Mor had become one of Maliya's first homegrown salt entrepreneurs. With the help of twenty laborers—mostly out-of-season fishermen—he managed a brine-evaporating complex on one hundred acres of land. The complex comprised a vast, desolate grid of levees dotted with shacks and machines. Gas-driven motors pumped brine from the Gulf of Kutch into initial evaporating ponds, each of which would dwarf the average house in Maliya. From there, the brine moved to ponds of increasing salinity, until the salt crystallized in terminal evaporating ponds. Then, the salt was iodized, packaged, and shipped to the farthest reaches of India and even beyond, to Bhutan and Nepal.

At the moment, Mor's plant sat idle. Since the evaporating process required the brine to reach a temperature of twenty-four degrees Celsius, the Indian summer, from March to June, represented the ideal season for salt production. If Mor heated the brine, he could also wrest some yields during the winter, which ran from November to February. But the monsoon's intermittent rains and flooding precluded any salt production. Mor enjoyed the rainy season, which offered a respite from the struggle of succeeding as a Miyana entrepreneur in the face of mistrust and deprecation.[62]

As Mor relaxed at home, the smell of seafood from the nearby fish market reminded him that one of his childhood friends was working harder than ever. Somewhere in the shallow waters of the Gulf of Kutch, Husainbhai Manek floated along in a ramshackle, rudderless boat, hoping to happen upon a solid catch. Fish, shrimp—anything would do, as long as it fetched a decent price. As he scoured the gulf, Manek was carrying on the tradition of the Miyanas' forefathers, who had trolled the sea centuries earlier from coastal villages.[63]

At thirty-five years old, Manek was a man of slight build and chilling demeanor. His thin black mustache sat on a face that had darkened from weeks of unrelenting sun. His light brown eyes seemed to survey everything around him with extreme scrutiny, and his words were frequently enigmatic and unsettling.

As per the custom of the Miyana fishermen, he had begun fishing a few days earlier, even though the rains had not yet come. He intended to continue until November. While he hoped for rain, he expected little, given the cloudless sky and the luck of his people.

Manek had begun working as a fisherman in the days of his youth. Like many before him, his father had "worked, worked, and died,"[64] and Manek had become the man of the household. In the off-season, he would remain in town and offer his services as a laborer to farms and salt plants. For a few months every year, however, while the monsoon rains filled the Gulf of Kutch with water and water creatures, he would pursue the occupation of his ancestors. Along with two hundred other fishermen, he moved from his house in town to a shack on the seashore. He launched his boat from the shack every morning and returned there every evening, going into Maliya only to sell his catches.

Unlike Gujarat's storied fishermen who prowled the Arabian Sea and brought back ships laden with food, Manek did not enjoy rich hauls. His catches extended just far enough beyond subsistence to earn a few rupees in the fish market. The shallow waters of the gulf—which was, in truth, little more than a flooded salt plain—did not harbor the bounty of the open sea.[65]

This year, the waters north of Maliya contained less than ever before. The Gulf of Kutch remained unusually shallow, running completely dry at the mouth of the Machhu River. There, amid a parched estuary of dying reeds and rushes, the sea found that its tributary had disappeared. From Morbi to Maliya, and into the gulf where Manek skimmed along in search of a catch, the drought had strangled the Machhu until only a few isolated puddles remained.

Chapter 2

"The Government Decides, and the Government Builds"

On April 12, 1948, Jawaharlal Nehru, the prime minister of a newly independent and unified India, attended the ceremonial laying of the first stone for what would become the Hirakud Dam. Spanning the Mahanadi River in the eastern state of Orissa, the project would generate power and provide irrigation for a vast region. Once completed, it would rank as the longest dam in the world, with earthen embankments spanning sixteen miles across a wide river valley. The Hirakud Dam also presaged the future of public works in postindependence India; it was the first of several enormous dams the central government would build across the rivers of eastern India as part of a nationwide push to harness water resources, widely referred to as *jal-sampatti*—"water-wealth."[1]

Nehru swelled with pride and exhilaration as he rose to speak. India was embarking on a new path. Having finally cast off the yoke of imperialism the previous year, the nation's people were moving forward with bold initiatives. The future seemed to hold limitless potential. Nehru began his address by exalting the promise of public engineering:

No invitation to me is more agreeable than this, to come to Orissa and to take part in this auspicious ceremony of building the Hirakud Dam. In Delhi I am overwhelmed with all manner of problems. These problems are of far less importance than the great river valley schemes we have in India. For our political and other problems will find some solution, good or bad, and will probably be forgotten after some years. But these constructive feats will not only change the face of India and bring prosperity to millions but will make that prosperity endure for a thousand years.[2]

The Hirakud project embodied the large-scale, state-sponsored development that Nehru believed would ensure India's prosperity. Under the prime minister's leadership, the central government had begun heavily promoting industrialization and infrastructure improvements. Hydro-engineering projects held a special place in Nehru's vision for a modern nation; as he proclaimed in his address at the Hirakud ceremony, dams would form "the foundation of all future development in India," providing consistent irrigation to farmers and abundant power to nascent industries.[3]

Few believed that India's progress would come painlessly. Development projects serving the greater good required personal sacrifices. The filling of the Hirakud reservoir would displace many residents of the upstream area, forcing them to settle elsewhere and begin their lives anew. In Nehru's view, this was a regrettable but necessary cost for the betterment of the nation's welfare; when called upon to make such sacrifices, citizens ought not to cause problems or question the government's wisdom. The prime minister remarked to the dignitaries assembled around the Hirakud Dam's first stone:

People should cooperate wholeheartedly with their national government. Although the primary responsibility of carrying on the work lies with the government, it cannot succeed without help and cooperation from the people themselves. . . . We should view these projects with a broad outlook and see whether the schemes benefit the people of the country in general or not.[4]

In 1957, Prime Minister Nehru returned to Orissa for the Hirakud Dam's official commissioning. Gathering runoff from a drainage area twice the size of Sri Lanka, the dam would generate electricity, protect downstream areas from flooding, and irrigate thousands of square miles of crops. The formation of its thirty-four-mile-long reservoir—the largest artificial lake in Asia—had displaced twenty-two thousand families.[5]

Although nine years had passed since the laying of the first stone, Nehru had lost none of his enthusiasm for dam construction. The prime minister inaugurated the Hirakud Dam with the lofty rhetoric he so frequently deployed at engineering conferences and project openings, dubbing the colossal structure "a modern temple of India."[6]

Since Nehru's 1948 speech, the nation had made great progress toward taming its water-wealth. All across the subcontinent, dozens of projects were under way. One, still in the early planning stages, sought to harness the waters of a river that meandered lazily across drought-prone plains in western India.[7]

The Machhu River begins its hundred-mile journey amid low hills that rise above the central plains of the Saurashtra Peninsula.[8] From these hills, innumerable creeks run westward through sparse forestland, where spotted deer roam among nightshades and fig trees. Joining together, the creeks spill onto a vast patchwork of farmland. Passing under the occasional banyan tree, the growing rivulets trace lush green lines across the open landscape of fields.

Eventually, one of the larger streams—the Machhu—gathers the others and directs itself northwest. A wide, rocky channel develops. The river occasionally passes close to a small village, but open farmland lines most of its course. Clusters of Indian jujube trees, heavy with small, green- and red-mottled fruit, dot the banks where sandy-coated wolves and panthers formerly stalked their prey. Fifty miles from its headwaters, still acquiring tributaries, the river passes just to the east of Wankaner, the capital of one of Saurashtra's old principalities.

Twenty miles downstream of Wankaner, the Machhu River arrives at Morbi. The western bank becomes a steep ridge lined with the houses of shop owners and craftsmen. On the eastern bank, marsh plants gradually give way to *peepal* (sacred fig) and *aasopaalav* (Indian fir) trees as the land slopes gently upward from the river.

The riverbed measures roughly a quarter of a mile across at Morbi. For much of the year, the Machhu is only a trickle flowing through the mud and rocks of a vast gash that bisects the city. In the dry months, hardy weeds and tufts of elephant grass punctuate the cracked brown earth of the riverbed; lotuses and water lilies choke the stagnant water of isolated puddles. During the monsoon, however, the channel fills with rich, muddy water, and the Machhu River bridges its own banks.

Beyond Morbi, the landscape surrounding the Machhu becomes increasingly flat and barren. Sandy soil and small bushes line the river's banks, yielding to the occasional village on one side or the other. As the river continues on its northward course, the groundwater becomes more saline and the land less arable, and farms grow infrequent.

Twenty-two miles north of Morbi, the now brackish Machhu River passes half a mile to the east of Maliya. From the river to the stunted trees at the edge of town, the land lies completely open, save for the withered crops of a few struggling farmers. Just downriver of Maliya, flamingoes cover brine ponds in pink, while hawks and eagles soar overhead. The grayish-brown earth stretches out in every direction as far as the eye can see.

A few miles north of Maliya, the Machhu River meets the

Gulf of Kutch, a vast salt plain that consumes the river. During the monsoon, the gulf fills with water and becomes an extension of the Arabian Sea; pomfrets, anchovies, eels, prawns, and shrimp flood into the area near the Machhu's mouth. During the dry months, however, the water recedes, and the gulf's salt-encrusted mud slowly bakes to hardness. This landscape sucks the Machhu River dry. The river fragments and meanders aimlessly into the dry expanse, diminishing until it ceases to exist somewhere amid the great salt flats.

≋≋≋

Bhagvanji Patel, the fledgling factory owner from Lilapar, felt the thirsty earth crack beneath his sandals as he stood amid his browning crops.[9] The month of Shravan had already begun. August was drawing near. And still the rains of 1979 had not arrived. Week after week, Bhagvanji and the other farmers of the Machhu River Valley had watched the horizon in eager anticipation. They awaited the sight of dark clouds—clouds grown fat over the Indian Ocean—whose moist cargo would color the valley green again.

Bhagvanji had witnessed the advent of dozens of monsoons. The experience was so joyous, so visceral, that the thought could sweep him away from the dry reality surrounding him. . . .

A slow patter of heavy raindrops began to wet the earth. The cadence increased, a cool gust blew, and then the rain fell in sheets, pouring itself out over the land. Children laughed and screamed, running through fields that quickly turned to mud. The air chilled noticeably, and the gleeful revelers soon began to shiver. Back home, wringing out their sopping clothes, they smiled at the dull roar on their rooftops. Minutes of rain turned into hours, perhaps days. Muddy torrents gushed down streets, and fields became shallow ponds. The Machhu's riverbed, dry after the scorching summer, filled with life.[10]

The rainy season's splendor, so dear to Bhagvanji and his

fellow Gujaratis, remained elusive this year. After six promising days at the end of June, when the heavens had opened up to deliver six inches of rain, the monsoon had abruptly paused. In all of July—usually the month of the heaviest rainfalls—not a single drop had fallen.[11]

A relentless, dusty heat enveloped the landscape around Bhagvanji. A humid haze blanketed the horizon and tinted the sky yellow. Although Lilapar and its surrounding farmland sat in a wide, open valley, the haze rendered distant objects indiscernible. Reality shrank to perhaps half a mile in every direction; anything beyond took on the quality of a mirage.

Of course, Bhagvanji knew that even if the monsoon rains did come, temporarily battering down the haze, the vistas near Lilapar could never return to their former grandeur. The north–south axis on which the Machhu River charted its course had once afforded distant views, but a wall of earth and concrete now spanned the shallow river valley from rim to rim, obscuring the southern horizon.

Completed by the state government six years earlier, the barrier was known as the Machhu Dam-II. (A similar structure called the Machhu Dam-I had been erected upstream, near Wankaner, decades earlier. The presiding engineers had evidently not felt particularly inspired when naming either dam.) The Machhu Dam-II was not tall—Bhagvanji could scramble up the earthen embankment in a few seconds—but it measured two and a half miles from end to end.[12]

The dam's reservoir had swallowed swaths of Bhagvanji's farmland. The government had provided him some compensation, but not enough. Then again, as work on the dam drew to a close, the government had also displaced entire villages that were inconveniently located in the proposed reservoir basin; in comparison, Bhagvanji supposed, he had been fortunate.

Though a farmer, Bhagvanji felt no gratitude for the Machhu Dam-II. In a cruel irony, the dam's water did not reach the relocated villagers, who now lived and farmed along the reservoir's edges. The irrigation canal extended northwest from the dam site and served downstream villages, ceasing its deliveries just short of Jashabhai Samani and the other farmers of Maliya. Like every villager who had lost his land to the reservoir, Bhagvanji continued to rely on the precipitation falling over his fields.[13]

Yet as he stood on his replacement land, praying that August might bring rains, Bhagvanji harbored no resentment toward the Machhu Dam-II. He had suffered substantial losses and gained nothing, but many others were benefitting. He felt neither grateful nor bitter. This, he understood, was the nature of sacrifice for the greater good.

〰〰〰

By July 1979, when Bhagvanji Patel surveyed the drought-stricken landscape around Lilapar, the artifacts of the Machhu Dam-II's design and construction sat neglected on grimy shelves. Memoranda, maps, budgets, and reports had been loosely organized, stacked a foot high, and bound together in sheets of burlap. Wrinkled by the humidity of several monsoons, the yellowing documents recorded—albeit incompletely and imperfectly—the tedious chain of bureaucratic events that had transformed a region.

If Bhagvanji and his fellow citizens had enjoyed access to the paperwork produced by the state government, they would have found evidence of a long, iterative process. Toiling away in paan-stained offices, engineers performed calculations and drew up plans for a dam that would guarantee the area around Morbi an ample, consistent water supply. At intervals, the engineers corresponded with the Central Water and Power Commission (CWPC) in New Delhi, which oversaw and approved all water infrastructure projects in India. Over the course of nearly two decades, they outlined and executed an ambitious scheme to tame the Machhu River.[14]

In 1955, unbeknownst to the Machhu River Valley's inhabitants, state engineers sent the CWPC a proposal for a dam five miles upstream of Morbi. The document included hydrological analyses of the Machhu River basin, a tentative design, detailed information about the anticipated construction site, a preliminary budget, and a rosy cost-benefit analysis.[15]

The motivation for the project seemed straightforward: the Machhu River represented an underexploited resource in a dry corner of India. On average, the northern portion of the Saurashtra Peninsula received little precipitation. Moreover, it frequently suffered severe droughts, during which the monsoon brought almost no rain at all. Weak, unpredictable monsoons led to weak, unpredictable harvests. A dam across the river would prevent invaluable water-wealth from going to waste in the Gulf of Kutch and ensure long-suffering downstream farmers a steady trickle of irrigation for their fields.[16]

When the state government submitted its proposal, the idea of constructing a dam near Morbi had existed for several decades. In the 1920s, when the men of the Valera clan still sang in the royal court, King Lakhdhirji Jadeja considered damming the Machhu River upstream of his capital. He reasoned that a large reservoir would provide his kingdom's farmers, long dependent on the fickle monsoons rains, with a bountiful, reliable source of water. The king undertook preliminary investigations for the project, even inviting Sir M. Visvesvaraya—arguably the most eminent engineer in Indian history—to personally consult on the matter.[17]

Despite his initial enthusiasm, Lakhdhirji soon abandoned the dream of damming the Machhu. According to official accounts, logistical constraints doomed the scheme. Early studies showed that the reservoir of any dam built upstream of Morbi would flood lands belonging to the neighboring kingdom of Wankaner. Years later, in their planning documents for the Machhu Dam-II, state engineers would report that the complexities of territorial sovereignty had led Lakhdhirji to drop the project.[18]

But some citizens of Morbi, such as Mayor Desai, would cite

a different reason for the king's decision. They would claim that the engineer Visvesvaraya warned Lakhdhirji that the topology of the Machhu River Valley was such that the reservoir's waters would decimate Morbi in the event of a dam failure; the structure would be "like a cannon trained on Morbi." According to this version of history, it was Visvesvaraya's advice that caused the king to abort all plans for dam construction.[19]

Upon the creation of the Indian republic in 1947, while the rest of Gujarat joined the Marathi-speaking lands to the south as part of the new Bombay State, the Saurashtra Peninsula's 222 principalities united to form a state of their own. Two years later, the government of Saurashtra began construction on a dam across the Machhu River thirty-three miles upstream of Morbi, near the city of Wankaner. The structure would ultimately measure well over a mile and a half in length, and water falling on 270 square miles of land—the "catchment area"—would feed into its reservoir. The Machhu Dam, as the project came to be known, would provide much-needed irrigation to farmers around Wankaner.[20]

Nonetheless, the need for a dam near Morbi persisted. The Machhu Dam's catchment area represented only a fraction of the river's drainage basin, and the water collected from it would not reach the farms downstream of Morbi. A great deal of the Machhu River's flow remained untapped, and the region's agriculture was suffering as a consequence. In addition, silt had begun to fill the old reservoir from which Morbi drew its municipal water supply; absent a dredging of the entire lake, the city itself would soon require a new source of water for its fast-growing population and factories.[21]

In its 1955 submission to the CWPC, the government of Saurashtra presented the Machhu Dam-II as a tool for capturing much of the water-wealth still being lost to the Gulf of Kutch. With a catchment area that encompassed 463 square miles downstream of the original Machhu Dam, the new project would collect rainfall from almost twice as much land as its upstream cousin. The Machhu Dam-II would extend two and a half miles—twice the length of the Machhu Dam-I—across the imperceptibly sloped river valley upstream of Morbi. It would rise only twenty-nine feet above the riverbed, retaining a shallow but wide reservoir with more than three billion cubic feet of storage capacity.

Because a two-and-a-half-mile-long concrete structure would prove prohibitively expensive, the state engineers proposed a hybrid dam, with both concrete and earthen sections. A central concrete "spillway"—so called because it allowed water to spill into the riverbed downstream—would provide a means of regulating flow from the reservoir. The remainder of the dam would rise out of a free, abundantly available resource: the soil of the Machhu River Valley. The hulking concrete spillway, flanked on both sides by long earthen embankments, would become the Machhu River's gatekeeper.[22]

The project outlined in the state government's 1955 proposal was ambitious, but it was just one of many. Under Nehru's leadership, India had plunged wholeheartedly into the work of taming its rivers, and far larger dams were under construction all over the country. As a moderately sized dam on a minor river with little hydroelectric potential, the Machhu Dam-II likely struck engineers at the CWPC as relatively mundane.[23]

〰〰〰〰

Despite its relatively unexceptional position within the totality of India's hydro-engineering projects, the Machhu Dam-II demanded extreme diligence from the men who planned and executed its construction. Any dam entails a great deal of risk. Water in a riverbed wants very badly to flow downhill; the more water humans impound, the more difficult it becomes to hold the water back. Amassed water pressure can cause a dam to fail in many different ways, and dam failures near large population centers can lead to catastrophic destruction.[24]

From the earliest stages of planning for the Machhu Dam-II, the government of Saurashtra bore responsibility for safe-guarding the structure against four types of failure that could endanger the downstream population: spillway collapse, internal erosion, slope failure, and overtopping. In order to avoid collapse of the central concrete spillway, state engineers would have to construct it from strong concrete and anchor it on a layer of solid bedrock. Just as important, in order to avoid breaches in the earthen flanks, the engineers would have to confront the three enemies that could endanger any earthen dam. If the inner core of the earthen embankments showed any weakness, high-pressure water would quickly bore through, creating gaping holes in a process known as "internal erosion." Similarly, a lack of cohesion within the outer shell of the earthen embankments could generate "slope failure"; as in a landslide, portions of the angled wall would slough off, leading to the dam's precipitous demise. Finally, if the reservoir ever spilled over the earthen embankments—a phenomenon known as "overtopping"—water would rapidly wash away the dirt ridges from above. Like spillway collapse, any of these three occurrences—internal ero-sion, slope failure, or overtopping—could fatally breach the Machhu Dam-II, emptying the reservoir onto the downstream area and wreaking untold havoc in Morbi.[25]

Fortunately, the proposed dam site offered several advantages with regard to three of the four major risks. For the spillway, bor-ings made along the Machhu's riverbed had revealed a layer of basalt that would serve as an ideal foundation, and the sand and lime that filled the bottom of the river's channel would produce excellent concrete. Similarly, the soil that fed into the area's pot-teries provided the optimal raw material for crafting earthen walls that would remain impermeable inside and cohesive outside. Molded into a structure of the proper shape and size, the Machhu River Valley's mineral resources would help to ensure that the downstream populace would never suffer the devastating effects of spillway collapse, internal erosion, or slope failure.[26]

By contrast, the prevention of overtopping required more than just strong materials and sound construction. Even the most solid earthwork would fail if the reservoir reached its crest. Overtopping water would erode the earthen wall, cutting deep channels through which even more water could rush. Rapid disintegration would inevitably result. In order to avoid such a fate for the Machhu Dam-II's flanks, government engineers had to design the structure such that the reservoir would never threaten the tops of the earthen segments.[27]

Straddling the riverbed, the dam's spillway would provide the all-important means of releasing excess water from the reservoir. Floodgates—adjustable openings in the spillway—would allow fine control of the outflow rate at any given instant. In order to prevent overtopping, the gates would have to be capable of releasing water at a rate equal to the highest rate at which water could conceivably flow *into* the reservoir. In the absence of sufficient discharge capacity, a heavy rainstorm would transform the Machhu Dam-II into a bathtub with a partially clogged drain: water from the faucet would pour into the tub faster than it could empty, and the tub would eventually overflow. In order to ensure that the dam's reservoir would always remain at a safe level, the government of Saurashtra needed to design the dam to withstand and pass the worst flood that could possibly occur in the Machhu River basin. Upon calculating the influx of water into the reservoir from this hypothetical "design flood," the state engineers would be able to design the spillway with an adequate discharge capacity.[28]

Although the concept of a design flood might seem relatively simple, determining the maximum conceivable inflow into the Machhu Dam-II's reservoir proved, at best, an inexact science. Surface hydrology—the discipline devoted to determining how rainfall in an area might translate into runoff and river flow—provided few definitive answers in the 1950s and 1960s. Variations in precipitation patterns and in the composition of the river basin's soil, vegetation, and geographical layout could mean the difference between a nearly dry channel, a gradually increasing

flow, and a flash flood. To make matters more difficult, calculation of the upper limit for rainfall in the Machhu River's basin—
the "design storm" leading to the design flood—entailed significant estimation and conjecture, given that regional rainfall data
stretched back only a few years.[29]

Designing a spillway with enough capacity to prevent overtopping therefore presented a conundrum for the men who drew
up the plans for the Machhu Dam-II. In ensuring that the structure would never suffer from spillway collapse, internal erosion,
or slope failure, the government engineers could rely on solid
earth, concrete, and bedrock; but in ensuring that the reservoir
would never overtop the earthen embankments, the engineers
would have to rely on incomplete data, uncertain projections,
and inexact calculations. A former government engineer, himself
a veteran of dozens of dam projects, summed up the predicament facing the men who prepared the proposal for the Machhu
Dam-II:

> Hydrology is not a field where there are final answers. You use
> all the data you have with you to come up with an estimate.
> Then, new data comes along, and you revise your estimate.
> Sometimes, the answers are clarified not by deeper analysis, but
> by greater experience.[30]

In order to calculate a safe outflow capacity for the Machhu
Dam-II's spillway, engineers would have to undertake years of
study, incorporate surrogate figures, and make many guesses.

In its 1955 submission to the CWPC, the government of
Saurashtra compensated for a dearth of hydrological data with
estimates and empirical formulas derived from observations
made elsewhere in the world. State engineers determined the
design flood on the basis of rainfall data collected over nineteen
years at fourteen rain gauge stations in and around Morbi. Few
severe storms had taken place during the monitored span, but the
engineers trusted their calculations to compensate. On the basis

of the available data, they approximated the maximum precipitation that could fall in the Machhu Dam-II's catchment area. After making estimates about how the rainfall would translate into river flow, the engineers utilized three empirical formulas to determine the dam's design flood. The formulas yielded slightly different values, the largest of which stood at 160,000 cubic feet per second (cusecs).[31]

From the calculation of the Machhu Dam-II's design flood, the project's physical layout took shape. The state government's 1955 proposal called for a concrete spillway with several adjustable gates that would permit the discharge of up to 160,000 cusecs of water during periods of heavy inflow. Curved earthen embankments, their crests well above the water, would line the front and sides of the reservoir. Soundly constructed from solid raw materials and capable of releasing a massive torrent to keep its earthworks safe, the Machhu Dam-II envisioned by the government of Saurashtra would safely provide much-needed irrigation water to downstream farmers.[32]

The gears of bureaucracy sometimes turn slowly. After submitting the Machhu Dam-II project proposal to the CWPC in 1955, the state government waited more than a year for a reply. When the CWPC's comments finally arrived in 1957, they proved sobering. From the comfort of their New Delhi offices, the central government's engineers had found fault with much of the proposal.[33]

The CWPC's response contained several major criticisms. First, it noted that the state engineers had made a fundamental error in determining an adequate outflow capacity for the Machhu Dam-II's spillway: they had computed the design flood without anticipating the additional water that would enter the river from the Machhu Dam-I's reservoir in a major rainstorm. By neglecting to account for outflow from the upstream dam, they had drastically underestimated the largest conceivable inflow that the Machhu Dam-II could encounter. As might be expected, the CWPC demanded that the state government incorporate the Machhu Dam-I's discharge into revised design flood calculations.[34]

The New Delhi engineers also expressed concern that the basic methods employed in deriving the design flood would prove inadequate. The commission recommended that state engineers promptly begin taking careful measurements of the Machhu River's water level over time. These measurements would help to lay the groundwork for a more robust calculation of the design flood through a cutting-edge method known as "unit hydrograph." A unit hydrograph approach would ensure that the state accurately estimated the largest possible flood the Machhu Dam-II might face.[35]

Finally, the CWPC's engineers expressed doubt about the optimality of the location chosen for the project. A dam at the proposed site would submerge three villages, forcing the relocation of nearly two thousand people. King Lakhdhirji Jadeja's 1924 plans for a Machhu dam had envisioned a location half a mile upstream from the point proposed by the state government; it appeared that this original site would, at the very least, lead to less human displacement. In its comments, the commission called for a careful comparison of the two sites.[36]

The CWPC's 1957 communication critiqued the Machhu Dam-II as envisioned by the government of Saurashtra, but a different entity would bear responsibility for compliance with the central government's instructions for modification. In 1956, the state of Saurashtra had merged into Bombay State. Four years later, Bombay split along linguistic lines, and the state of Gujarat came into being. The government of Gujarat adopted all ongoing government obligations and projects in Saurashtra, including the Machhu Dam-II. Over the subsequent years, the new state's engineers would drive the dam toward completion.[37]

Under the government of Gujarat, the CWPC-mandated revision of the Machhu Dam-II's design flood progressed unevenly. In light of the glaring omission of the Machhu Dam-I's outflow in previous calculations, state engineers quickly performed new hydrological analyses and adjusted the design flood upward, from 160,000 cusecs to 191,000 cusecs. But in defiance of the central government's demand for a unit hydrograph approach, the state continued to utilize old empirical formulas; the engineers did not incorporate flow data from the Machhu River into their computations.[38]

The failure to implement the unit hydrograph method earned the government of Gujarat a written rebuke from the CWPC. In a 1961 message, the commission wrote:

> In our previous comments, it had been specially suggested that observations should have been made. . . . After five years, no attempt has been made to prepare the project based on discharge observations. The project is still based on empirical relationships. The state government may therefore carry out discharge observations and check the validity of the empirical relationships used for the calculations.[39]

Despite the New Delhi engineers' insistence, the government of Gujarat did not undertake the necessary studies. Entering the mid-1960s, state engineers had yet to definitively determine the largest possible influx of water that the Machhu Dam-II would have to pass in order to avoid overtopping.[40]

Although the dam's ultimate discharge capacity remained unknown, the government of Gujarat forged ahead with planning for the spillway. Based on the provisional design flood of 191,000 cusecs, the state engineers designed a concrete spillway with eighteen large, adjustable gates. Curved steel sheets would swivel up and down to control the flow of water through the immense openings, which would measure thirty feet in length and twenty feet in height. Resembling sections cut from the surface of a cylindrical can, the radial gates (also known as Tainter gates after their inventor, a Wisconsin structural engineer) would provide precise and reliable regulation of reservoir outflow. While ignoring the CWPC's instructions regarding determination of the spillway's discharge capacity, state engineers designed and refined an impressive concrete centerpiece for the Machhu Dam-II.[41]

As in the matter of unit hydrograph calculations, the government of Gujarat essentially disregarded the New Delhi engineers' comments on the project's proposed location. The state never seriously considered shifting the dam site. While acknowledging that a move upstream would avoid submerging two of the three villages located in the anticipated reservoir, the Gujarati engineers asserted that an upstream reservoir would submerge several stretches of extant railroad tracks. Without submitting any comparative studies to support their claims, they maintained that the cost of relocating the railroad tracks would exceed the cost of relocating the two villages.

In 1963, under pressure from the CWPC, the state government finally carried out a cost-benefit analysis of the two proposed dam sites. Conveniently enough, the study found that locating the dam farther upstream would actually displace two other villages, rendering a shift futile. The dam would rise at the downstream site, and the three villages in the proposed reservoir bed would have to undergo relocation.[42]

In the early 1960s, the residents of Jodhpar, Adepar, and Lakhdhirnagar remained unaware that their future was being quietly weighed in government offices as part of a complex calculus of costs and benefits.[43] Despite living and working near the proposed dam site, they knew nothing of the project that would soon submerge their fields and ancestral homes. Preliminary surveys of the area had begun in 1955 and grown more frequent with time, but many upstream villagers did not learn of them until nearly a decade later.

For most, news of the dam came as a shock. Government surveyors, dressed in fancy western clothes and laden with bulky equipment, appeared in the fields surrounding the villages. They moved deliberately across the farmland and into the residential neighborhoods, taking careful measurements and recording their findings. One man from Lakhdhirnagar would later recall, "They went through all of these procedures. They came. They measured the town. They took surveys. So of course we knew that something was going to happen."[44] When asked, the surveyors informed the people that a dam had been planned, and that the government would relocate their villages within a few years.

The submergence of Jodhpar, Lakhdhirnagar, and Adepar would displace nearly two thousand people. A fourth village—Lilapar—would lose much of its farmland. The residents of all four communities depended on agriculture, cultivating the flat expanses of land that stretched out in either direction from the Machhu River; most would therefore lose not only their homes but also their livelihoods.[45]

The affected villagers would have to depend on the government's beneficence, trusting it to offer fair compensation for their losses. They would also need to find new farmland for purchase—no small task, given the large number of buyers entering the market all at once. As accounts of the government surveyors spread, and as villagers learned of the dam that would follow in their wake, many began to look to the future with anxiety.

≋≋≋

With a herd of students in tow, Executive Engineer B. J. Vasoya strolled between ample mounds of dirt and rock.[46] In every direction, the landscape reflected three years of hard work. As he walked, Vasoya explained the details of the now-finished earthen embankments, impressing the wide-eyed young men with his knowledge of the Machhu Dam-II's design and construction.

Even as Vasoya expounded upon the project's technical specifications, he knew that the students could not grasp the full extent of his job. The challenge of building a dam did not lie solely in layering sediments and mixing concrete; it also lay in managing people. The group was walking along an earthen wall that had emerged from an arduous process, an ordeal colored by an uncooperative contractor, hostile villagers, drought-prone farmers, and a stubborn ascetic.

As the executive engineer in charge of the Machhu Dam-II, Vasoya supervised a vast construction apparatus. But he also served as the public face of the project. He represented the government of Gujarat and the Machhu Dam-II to visiting dignitaries, townspeople in Morbi, downstream beneficiaries of increased irrigation, and—most formidably—upstream villagers who would soon lose their homes and ancestral land. As he lectured the visiting students on the minutiae of the nascent structure, he gently omitted details of the daily interactions that composed much of his job. Lakhdhirji Engineering College, located just a few miles downstream on the Machhu River's eastern bank, trained the young men as engineers, not as politicians.

For their part, the students looked upon Vasoya with a sense of vague awe. Though he belonged to their specialized world, twenty years and several degrees of hierarchy set him apart. Marching through the work site with him, they felt keenly aware that they were accompanying the man singularly responsible for the Machhu Dam-II's construction. From his office in Morbi, Vasoya monitored the work of several deputy engineers who oversaw individual aspects of the project; these engineers, in turn, supervised junior engineers who bore responsibility for the execution of individual construction tasks. Vasoya carried with ease a rank that the students could hope to attain only after decades of hard work.[47]

The students' visit formed a part of Vasoya's public relations campaign, which he had initiated in order to soften resistance to the dam's construction. From the very beginning of his time in the Machhu River Valley, the executive engineer had sensed hostility

in the local populace. Dam projects inevitably embittered the villagers they displaced, but in this case, citizens of Morbi had also
seemed highly suspicious—even frightened—of the reservoir that
would soon gather just out of sight, upstream, to the south.

To counter the public's misgivings, Vasoya had issued open
invitations for the local people to visit the dam site, hoping that
transparency would help assuage the generalized antipathy
toward the project. Every other Sunday, he brought groups from
Morbi and the surrounding villages to observe the construction,
sometimes serving them chai on site. Gesturing in a manner both
expansive and precise, he explained the project with simple language, mixing in just enough jargon to impress the captivated
audience.

Public visits to the construction site had proven a brilliant
innovation. Negative feelings toward the dam decreased as the
local people came to understand that the government of Gujarat
was undertaking a safe, effective project. In one instance, just as
the project's deepest excavations were taking place, Vasoya had
brought a prominent regional politician to visit the site. Making
their way down a precariously placed ladder, the two men had
reached the bottom of a deep pit, sixty or seventy feet below the
ground. A short time later, the politician had hauled himself out
of the hole, his hand clenched around a fistful of gravel. He had
shown it to the press the next day, pledging that local officials
were carefully monitoring the quality of the materials and work
that were shaping the dam.

Vasoya welcomed any gesture that might inspire greater diligence in the contractor. Although state engineers supervised every
aspect of the project, a private corporation executed the actual
construction. The government of Gujarat had awarded the contract for the Machhu Dam-II to Manibhai & Brothers Construction, a company that specialized in large public works projects,
such as dams and bridges. In later years, some citizens of Morbi
would claim that Manibhai & Brothers had won the job because
of jati connections to Gujarat's public works minister, longtime

public servant Babubhai Patel. Regardless of whether Vasoya harbored any suspicions about favoritism, he felt obvious contempt toward the contractor and repeatedly lodged formal complaints; in June 1972, as the dam was reaching completion, he would write, "In general, it was really a difficult task to extract the work from the contractors Messrs. Manibhai and Brothers due to his dubious behaviour."[48]

In spite of the friction between the government engineer and the private contractor, the dam had risen. As Vasoya looked out over the landscape of half-finished construction, he marveled at how drastically the view had changed in the course of just a few short years.

Beginning in November 1967, tractors and bulldozers had rolled across a two-and-a-half-mile-long stretch, clearing trees, digging up roots, removing rocks, and leveling the land on which the dam would stand.[49] Then, in early 1968, the earthen flanks had begun their gradual, inexorable rise. Laborers had excavated soil from meticulously scouted areas on either side of the river. In a special on-site laboratory, geologists from the government of Gujarat had tested the soil's density and internal cohesion. Work crews had laid thin layers of dirt, ranging in composition from gravel to clay, over the length of the embankments. Tractors and rollers had compacted each layer, producing the foundation for the next. Vasoya's geologists had tested the compressed soil again to confirm that it would hold back the reservoir's waters; by the end of construction, they would conduct 8,899 individual assays on the soil in the earthworks. Immense, tightly packed walls— 8,000 feet long on the western flank and 4,600 feet on the eastern flank—had gradually taken form.[50]

Meanwhile, not far from the work site, Vasoya had pursued the most delicate aspect of his job: dialogue with upstream villagers who would lose their homes and fields to the dam's reservoir. A special deputy engineer administered the resettlement process for soon-to-be-displaced villagers; his duties included everything from supervising the construction of resettlement villages around the reservoir to administering compensation for lost land. Nonetheless, as the head of the project, Vasoya felt a personal responsibility toward the people who lived and worked in the projected reservoir bed.

Time and again, the executive engineer had traveled out along dusty roads from his Morbi office to visit the affected villages. In meetings with leaders and ordinary citizens alike, he had taken pains to explain the rationale for the dam, so that the villagers might understand the import of the sacrifice they were being asked to make. Dressed in sharp western clothes, down to his polished leather shoes, Vasoya had sat side-by-side for hours with barefooted and sandal-clad villagers. He had listened patiently as they listed their grievances. He had answered question after question, striving to provide what small consolation he could through information.

Between countless sips of milky chai, he had described the immense difficulties faced by downstream villagers. In the northern part of the river basin, near the salt flats of the Gulf of Kutch, the salinity of groundwater reached such high levels that farmers could not water their crops with well water. Agricultural wells everywhere ran dry in times of drought. Entire villages went hungry when the rains did not come. The Machhu Dam-II, Vasoya explained, would ensure a reliable supply of water for downstream farms. With a guaranteed irrigation source, the region's production of grain and other crops would increase and become more consistent. In addition, the dam would guarantee a dependable supply of drinking water for thousands. Overall, Vasoya had stressed to the villagers that their sacrifice would do a great deal of good for many people in the area.

The villagers had not embraced the engineer's message, but they had not adopted a combative stance either. They understood the rhetoric of sacrifice for the greater good, and they were largely resigned to bearing the costs of the project. Years later, farmer and industrialist Bhagvanji Patel of Lilapar, who lost many of his fields to the reservoir, would reflect upon his own stoic outlook at the time of construction:

We knew that we were not benefiting, but we also knew that other people were benefiting. And why should we complain, if it was doing someone else good? Sometimes, with projects like this, that happens. And those people really needed the water, otherwise they would not have been able to carry on their farming. The groundwater by them was too saline. So they really needed it. We had to pay the price, but why should we complain if it was really doing them good?[51]

Perhaps Patel accepted his fate more readily than villagers from Lakhdhirnagar, Jodhpar, and Adepar; after all, he did not lose his home. Still, no concerted protests had taken place within the villages designated for relocation. One citizen of Lakhdhirnagar would later explain the prevailing local mind-set at the time: "The government decides, and the government builds. What would we have to say in these matters?"[52]

Because most citizens had adopted a passive attitude toward their relocation, the one man who refused to go gently had quickly become well known. Just a short distance upstream of the dam site, a small hummock—in truth, little more than a large mound of dirt—punctuated the flat plain that extended to the east from the Machhu River. For years, a bald, white-bearded ascetic had made his home in a tiny hermitage on the hill. The man and the physical feature had become synonymous, such that the hill was sometimes known as Jog Bapu's Hummock, and the man sometimes as Jog Hummock's Bapu. People had come from miles around to seek his blessings and advice on matters financial, medical, spiritual, familial, and existential.

The old man had been shocked, then, to discover that the government intended to unceremoniously inundate his living space, submerging his sacred hermitage all the way up to the triangular flag that capped its dome. He had seethed for months, his thick eyebrows furrowing and his mouth scowling somewhere behind an overgrown beard. When finally forced to relocate, he had allegedly vowed, "This dam will break. *Morbi* will break."[53]

Vasoya had virtually ignored Jog Bapu. Most citizens had

cooperated—albeit halfheartedly—with their government. Loading their last possessions onto donkeys, oxen, or their own backs, the villagers of Lakhdhirnagar, Jodhpar, and Adepar had abandoned their ancestral homes to the Machhu's waters and trudged to new locations just outside the bounds of the imminent reservoir. The government had provided each family with a plot of wasteland and two thousand to three thousand rupees for construction of a new house. The new plots were clustered together by village so that old social structures remained intact.[54]

During the relocation process, many villagers had felt slighted by the government's meager compensation for lost farmland. For some, merely subsisting became a yearly struggle from that point onward. A farmer from Lakhdhirnagar would explain, "We did not even purchase new land. How could we, when there was no money? We plant the land we have left and say our prayers."[55]

A few savvy villagers had sued the government for better compensation, but most had simply accepted their lot. While many might have desired to personally lobby the government for fair treatment, they found its bureaucracy too daunting. Bhagvanji Patel of Lilapar would later recall, "Sure, people complained. But who would listen? People did not even know where the relevant office was."[56]

Having come to know the villagers intimately through his many excursions as executive engineer, Vasoya had lamented their maltreatment. He had argued vociferously with his superiors for more generous compensation on their behalf. But the money was not forthcoming.

Despite the quiet disaffection and occasional flare-ups in the reservoir bed, work at the dam site had continued moving forward. With the earthen embankments nearing completion, the contractor had excavated the portion of the river gorge that would serve as the foundation for the concrete spillway. Work crews had prepared concrete, mixing cement with sand and lime excavated from the riverbed.

As Vasoya led the engineering students on their tour, he described the process by which the concrete grew, day by day, into a massive spillway. He explained the quality-control protocol: for every 2,500 cubic feet of mortar laid down, supervisors subjected a sample cube to strenuous compression tests. (By the end of the project, they would test 942 mortar cubes.)

Though the 676-foot spillway was only half-finished, its hard edges and monumental dimensions captured the students' attention. With large openings and moving metallic parts, it would act as the face of a dam that consisted almost entirely of unremarkable earth, rock, and greenery. The spillway framed eighteen cavernous floodgates through which the entire Machhu River would one day pass. Eighteen large motors would soon crown the concrete spillway, providing the force necessary to rotate the curved metal sheets that covered the gate openings. Topped off with a smooth concrete path and a small workroom, the spillway would serve as the locus of control for the reservoir's waters.[57]

Discussion of the spillway served as a satisfying capstone to the students' visit. The entire experience had been engaging enough for them to temporarily forget the laborious studying that awaited them upon their return to Morbi. As the young men departed, Vasoya felt satisfied at having shown yet another group the good work being done on the Machhu Dam-II.

Even as Executive Engineer Vasoya drove the Machhu Dam-II toward completion, one critical issue remained unresolved. More than two years after the start of construction, the government of Gujarat had not yet settled upon a final calculation for the dam's design flood.[58]

More than a decade earlier, state engineers had derived the preliminary design flood on the basis of empirical formulas, which estimated the Machhu River's maximum flow using available rainfall data. While granting tentative authorization for the project in 1961, the CWPC had demanded that the state perform new calculations with the cutting-edge unit hydrograph technique.[59]

Unlike earlier methods, which estimated the relationship between precipitation and flow using observations from other river basins, the unit hydrograph method would compare flow data from the Machhu River and rainfall data from the Machhu River's basin. The unit hydrograph approach would also ensure more accurate modeling of the "largest conceivable" storm that could strike the basin, through incorporation of hourly rainfall data from a large storm in the Saurashtra region. By combining local precipitation data with a refined understanding of the relationship between rainfall and river flow, a unit hydrograph study of the Machhu River basin would yield a more accurate design flood, thereby ensuring that the Machhu Dam-II's spillway possessed an outflow capacity sufficient to safeguard against overtopping.[60]

While the government of Gujarat enthusiastically embraced the CWPC's 1961 approval for the project, it did not comply with the commission's directive regarding the design flood calculation. At first, the problem lay in faulty monitoring equipment. State engineers had installed a flow gauge near the proposed dam site in 1959, but standing water impeded accurate readings, rendering three years of data collection fruitless. Eventually, a more reliable gauge was established, and sound data emerged. Nonetheless, the government of Gujarat continued to rely on empirical estimates, willfully disregarding the CWPC's instructions.[61]

When the state requested permission to begin construction of the Machhu Dam-II in 1967, the structure's design flood remained the empirically calculated figure of 191,000 cusecs. The CWPC, displeased with the noncompliance but unwilling to hold back progress, allowed building to proceed on the condition that "project authorities . . . check up the figures by unit hydrograph studies, as promised."[62]

The New Delhi engineers' call went unheeded until 1970, when the government of Gujarat finally undertook a unit hydrograph study of the Machhu River basin. By that time, the dam's construction had reached an advanced stage. If the unit hydrograph–derived design flood differed substantially from the previous empirical estimates, costly reconstructions of portions of the structure would become necessary.[63]

In order to determine the relationship between precipitation and flow on the Machhu River, the state engineers utilized data from rain gauges in the river basin and from the corrected flow gauge installed near the dam site. But the storms that had occurred during the monitored period were all relatively small, and the engineers had to look elsewhere for data to model the "largest conceivable" storm that could occur in the basin. They settled upon a heavy bout of monsoon rain that had fallen on Porbandar—a coastal city ninety miles southwest of Morbi, and Mahatma Gandhi's birthplace—in August 1968.[64]

With the runoff data from the Machhu River basin and the rainfall data from the Porbandar storm, project hydrologists constructed a model of flow on the Machhu River in the event of a very large storm. Factoring in discharge from the Machhu Dam-I, the Machhu Dam-II's design flood came to 218,000 cusecs, or 27,000 cusecs more than the previous "maximum" flood used to design the dam's spillway.[65]

The slight discrepancy between the original figure and the unit hydrograph revision did not particularly concern state engineers. Although the dam could release no more than 191,000 cusecs, its reservoir could tolerate a somewhat higher influx because, as an additional precaution against overtopping, the earthen embankments of every hybrid dam rose several feet above the highest anticipated water level. The distance between the maximum reservoir height and the crests of the earthworks— the "freeboard"—ensured that the dam would withstand even large waves and flash floods. Project hydrologists estimated that with rainfall like that of the 1968 Porbandar storm, the Machhu Dam-II's reservoir would rise less than five feet; against this, the dam possessed nine feet of freeboard. Even under conditions of heavy precipitation, the reservoir would remain well below the tops of the earthen embankments.[66]

In later years, critics would allege that the government of

Gujarat had produced a "tailor-made" unit hydrograph. They claimed that, with the earthen flanks largely complete, the state had not wished to contend with results that would significantly alter design requirements; it had therefore employed data and assumptions that would ensure that the findings of the unit hydrograph study—ostensibly a prerequisite for dam design—supported the construction already under way. According to some critics, an accurate study would have yielded a design flood closer to 500,000 cusecs.[67]

At any rate, the state settled upon the figure of 218,000 cusecs. Without changing the design of the Machhu Dam-II, the unit hydrograph study of 1970 met the CWPC's demands.[68]

The earthen embankments reached completion in July 1971. The concrete spillway followed in August 1972, and construction of the Machhu Dam-II was finished.[69]

Sitting in his house near the main market, Mayor Desai contemplated the Sunday headlines.[70] The Machhu Dam-II was far from his thoughts. Completed six years earlier, the structure had become a fixture of the landscape—like the Buffalo Bridge or the Mani Mandir or the Machhu River itself, except perpetually out of sight. Desai vaguely knew that, as mayor, he would receive notice from the dam if the crew planned to open the floodgates, since the sudden torrent issuing forth might inundate the city's lower-lying neighborhoods.

At the moment, a release of water from the Machhu Dam-II seemed like the remotest of possibilities. A few significant discharges had taken place in 1975, 1976, and 1977; on those occasions, Desai had chuckled at the reactions of poorly educated residents in Morbi's vulnerable areas, who had marveled at the fact that engineers could predict when and by how much the streets would flood. Of late, however, the gates had remained still. In 1978, a drought year, reservoir levels had remained so low that not a single drop had passed through the dam's spillway.[71]

As the newspapers made clear, the 1979 monsoon—Desai's first in office—was also passing without any sign of rain. Nothing had followed the promising showers of late June. With the end of July only two days away, much of Saurashtra faced the dangerous possibility of a rainy season without rain. Public officials made gloomy pronouncements and farmers waited nervously.

Nonetheless, Desai's attention gravitated toward a story with wider implications: the formation of a new central government. For more than two decades after Indian independence, the Congress Party—the successor to Mahatma Gandhi's Indian National Congress freedom movement and former Prime Minister Nehru's party—had dominated Indian politics. After coalescing from fragmented opposition groups in the early part of the 1970s, the Janata Party—Desai's party—had quickly ascended to power. Until recently, Janata leader Morarji Desai, a prominent freedom fighter and longtime statesman, had presided over the first non–Congress Party government in the country's history. But two weeks ago, the eighty-three-year-old Gujarati—unrelated to Ratilal—had resigned as prime minister after Charan Singh, a prominent politician from his own party, withdrew his support. On Saturday, July 28, Charan Singh had become prime minister with the support of certain Janata factions and a Congress Party led by Nehru's daughter, Indira Gandhi. For Mayor Desai, the rise of the day-old central government reeked of pettiness and betrayal.[72]

Of course, the state of Gujarat did not lack for partisan machinations. In Gandhinagar, the capital city, Chief Minister Babubhai Patel's Janata government found itself at constant war with Congress leader Madhavsinh Solanki, whose criticisms of the ruling party appeared almost daily in the press. Babubhai had arrived at the post of chief minister after a long career of service as a freedom fighter, legislator, and state cabinet minister; though he boasted considerable stature, extensive experience, and deep civic commitment, he found his government beset by crippling attacks.[73]

If Desai stopped to think about it, he might recall that the Machhu Dam-II reflected some of the very political maneuvering that he detested. According to Desai's understanding, Gokaldas Parmar—the local representative in Gujarat's legislative assembly —had played a crucial role in securing the dam's construction. As a member of the Satwara agricultural jati and the representative for various downstream villages, Parmar rose from a farming-centered constituency. Desai felt certain that Parmar had influenced deliberations on the dam during his many years in the legislative assembly. After the completion of the dam—even into the drought 1979—the Machhu-II irrigation canal had carried life-giving water to the farmers for and among whom Parmar campaigned.[74]

Of course, if Desai stopped to think about it, he might recall that political power had manifested not only in the benefits from the project but also in the choice of who would build it. He suspected that Manibhai & Brothers Construction had won the contract for construction of the Machhu Dam-II on account of family connections to the former public works minister—current Chief Minister Babubhai Patel. Babubhai would never engage in bribery, but favoritism did not seem unthinkable. The contractor's work did not appear entirely trustworthy, given that a 1975 cyclone had produced large cracks in the three-year-old dam—cracks that Desai had gone to observe himself as a concerned member of the city council. But the government of Gujarat had fully repaired the cracks before the following year's monsoon, assuring the local people that the Manibhai & Brothers–built dam remained completely sound.[75]

Despite his suspicions of favoritism, Desai deeply admired Babubhai, whom he considered a friend. The chief minister often visited Morbi on his trips to the Saurashtra Peninsula. Years ago, during his tenure as public works minister, Babubhai had closely followed the Machhu Dam-II's construction.

Indeed, like Jawaharlal Nehru, the chief minister was captivated by irrigation projects. In recent years, he had heavily advocated for a massive dam—one of the largest in history—on the Narmada River in eastern Gujarat. Named after Sardar Vallabhbhai Patel—Mahatma Gandhi's closest deputy—the Sardar

Sarovar project would stand as a monument to the state's past and future prowess. While displacing thousands of people—most of them in two neighboring states—the dam would provide perpetually drought-prone Gujarat with ample drinking and irrigation water. The project had spawned interstate disputes lasting over decade, but a special central government tribunal was moving toward permitting construction to proceed. During his term as chief minister, Babubhai had vigorously set about marshaling the necessary resources to carry out the massive undertaking.[76]

At the end of the 1970s, the fast-advancing Sardar Sarovar project bore several important connections to the modest Machhu Dam-II. In discussions with World Bank assessors evaluating the feasibility of Sardar Sarovar, Babubhai's government had allegedly highlighted the Machhu Dam-II as a small but sparkling example of the state's engineering capabilities. J. F. Mistry, one of the engineers instrumental in the Machhu Dam-II's design, had recently become Gujarat's chief engineer for irrigation projects, taking command of all new dam construction in the state. And in a few short months, Vasoya—the charismatic executive engineer who had supervised the rise of the dam near Morbi—would become the chief engineer of the Sardar Sarovar project, the head of an entire department created with the sole purpose of driving the monumental dam forward. Despite its seemingly humble position, the Machhu Dam-II was closely tied to some of Gujarat's most important engineering figures and projects.[77]

At the moment, however, the Machhu Dam-II, temporarily rendered purposeless by the drought of 1979, remained far from Mayor Desai's mind. The concern hung heavy on his brow as he passed over the weather-related articles in the newspaper and read about the political turmoil in New Delhi. A drought would influence the agricultural fortunes of one region or another for some brief period. But the shape of the government would determine the response to thousands of such challenges.

Sporting thick, black sunglasses, H. K. Khan emerged from his official car.[78] He strode purposefully across the tarmac at the airport in Ahmedabad, Gujarat's largest city. Though Khan was far from tall, his posture and vigor lent him an aura of authority that matched his stature within the government of Gujarat. As agriculture secretary, he was one of the state's highest-ranking civil servants. Normally, he sat inside an imposing Gandhinagar office, administering what he described as his "large, omnibus department." But on this day, August 1, 1979, drought was raging across the Saurashtra Peninsula, and duty drew him afield.

Khan belonged to the exclusive fellowship of the Indian Administrative Service (IAS). Arguably the world's most elite corps of government administrators, the IAS dated back to the British colonial era. It had survived in an independent India because of its reputation for solid competence and relentless efficiency. Every year, more than one hundred thousand Indians took the rigorous civil service exam; a few hundred would enter training for the service. Elected politicians passed new laws, but the IAS officers bore the burden of ensuring that the government smoothly discharged its myriad responsibilities, from crafting budgets and forging policy to enforcing the rule of law and responding to crises. Even low-ranking members of the service routinely received assignments of remarkable magnitude. Veterans, like Khan, administered entire state-level departments.[79]

Today, the work of the Agriculture Department called Khan to Saurashtra. On the runway, a Dakota—a twin-engine World War II–era transport plane[80]—awaited. Khan's department rented the plane during droughts, using it for a procedure known as "cloud seeding": when clouds appeared over affected areas, the Dakota flew over them, and its crew released silver iodide flares. The silver iodide particles promoted condensation within the clouds, increasing the chances of rain.[81]

With all of July having passed without a single drop of rain, the Dakota would circle over the parched Saurashtra Peninsula in an effort to bring relief to its farmers and villagers. Meanwhile,

Khan would engage in more prosaic drought relief work. He had scheduled a series of meetings in Rajkot, forty miles south of Morbi, to discuss water shipments and other relief measures for rural villages whose wells were running dry. The Dakota would deposit him in Rajkot, proceed with its cloud seeding mission, and pick him up for the return trip at day's end.

Khan watched as men carried crates of silver iodide flares into the plane's rear hatch. Then, he and the crew boarded, the hatch closed, and the Dakota lumbered slowly down the runway before lifting lazily into the humid yellow sky. As the plane continued to climb, the city below gave way to tan, flat countryside obscured by a gentle, brown-gray sheet of haze.

Just over an hour later, the Dakota left Khan in Rajkot and continued with its mission. For the rest of the day, the crew circled the plane above promising clumps of clouds, releasing flares at regular intervals. After a full day's work, the cloud seeding had not triggered any substantial storms. Dark clouds, however, loomed on the southern horizon. Relief, as always, remained just out of reach. The crew returned to Rajkot, picked up Khan, and pointed the plane toward Ahmedabad.

The drone of the engines and the fatigue of a long day's work lulled the men as the plane climbed. They hardly noticed the patter of raindrops that appeared on the Dakota's windows. Then, the bottom seemed to drop out from under the plane. "Suddenly," Khan would recount decades later, "we were caught in such a terrible storm."[82]

The turbulence tossed the men about in the cabin, and sheets of rain poured over the plane's fuselage. "Only a Dakota could have weathered that storm and brought us safely back to Ahmedabad," Khan would recall with a smile. "A modern plane would have been lost."[83]

The monsoon of 1979 had begun in earnest.

Chapter 3
"This Monsoon Descends"

The drought of 1979 quickly became a distant memory. During the first three days of August, the Machhu River basin collected more rain than would typically fall in the entire month. By August 4, the heaviest day of precipitation yet, the river valley's dusty patchwork of fields had become an expanse of shallow lakes.[1]

The Shravan rains had laid siege to the entire Saurashtra Peninsula. From the Gulf of Kutch to the Arabian Sea, people bided their time indoors, waiting for the skies to clear and the water to subside. Monsoon downpours rarely lasted more than a few days; the rain-laden clouds would typically blow away, leaving weeks of pleasantly clear and cool weather in their wake.

But the rain only grew heavier. Rather than blowing northward and dissipating the storm, the prevailing winds strengthened and circulated, trapping clouds over Saurashtra.[2]

Each passing day drew more attention to the weather. An article in the August 8 edition of *Phulchhab* declared, "Today, for the ninth straight day, steady, heavy showers continued to drench various parts of Saurashtra. . . . Since the wind is blowing along with the rain, chilliness has descended. Everyone is waiting for the sun's light, which might bring some relief."[3]

By August 8, the pounding rains had given rise to a host of dangers. All across the Saurashtra Peninsula, shoddily constructed buildings collapsed as water soaked through their walls. High winds kicked up violent surf in the Arabian Sea, sending twenty-foot waves crashing ashore and closing most ports. Storms severed telephone connections, including the main trunk lines connecting various cities.[4]

The extraordinary weather sent government officials scrambling. To maintain order and contend with widespread flooding, the government of Gujarat mobilized a civilian reserve force—the Home Guards—in every city and town of more than five thousand residents. Overflowing latrines and sewers threatened to ignite outbreaks of disease. As rivers spilled over their banks and roads continued to wash away, entire villages required evacuation by flat-bottomed police boats, and the need for rescue quickly dwarfed the available supply of boats.[5]

By August 10, rapidly filling reservoirs had joined the mounting concerns. The reservoir behind the Bhadar Dam—the largest in Saurashtra—reached its storage capacity, and the dam's spillway began releasing massive quantities of water; the state government initiated hasty evacuations as downstream areas flooded. Similar scenes took place downstream of the peninsula's smaller dams, many of which had also started to release water to keep pace with the inflow to their reservoirs. Saurashtra's riverbeds, barren just days before, had come alive.[6]

≈≈≈≈≈

Even as the monsoon filled many reservoirs to dangerous levels, the Machhu Dam-II did not provide cause for panic.[7] For Lakshmanbhai Mohan, the mechanic on the dam, August 10 had passed fairly routinely, at least by the preceding week's standards.

It was early evening. Mohan leaned against the metal railing that extended along the dam's catwalk, scanning the misty horizon. He watched as raindrops sent tiny ripples across the reservoir's vast, gray-brown surface. The dam's long earthen arms enveloped the water to his right and left, fading into the clouds miles away. Mohan could just make out the cluster of small buildings on the dam's eastern earthwork, where he and the six other crew members slept and ate.

During the four months of the monsoon, Mohan and his fellow workers lived on the dam full-time. Their job was deceptively simple: to keep the floodgates in working order and to open them when necessary. A gate operations manual, prepared by state government engineers, provided the crew with precise instructions on management of the reservoir under various combinations of water level and inflow expectation.[8]

Even with the manual, however, managing the gates correctly could prove difficult. Mohan and the other crew members received limited rainfall data from the Irrigation Department; the Machhu River's basin contained only two rainfall gauges, and even the information from these reached the Machhu Dam-II after a twenty-four hour delay. Consequently, the dam workers could not forecast flow on the Machhu River and discharge additional water through the gates in anticipation of large influxes. They could only calculate current inflow based on changes in the reservoir's height and adjust outflow accordingly.[9]

The Irrigation Department's reactive strategy for responding to flows on the Machhu River left little room for error. If a sudden, large influx hit the Machhu Dam-II's reservoir, the crew would have to quickly open all the dam's gates in order to keep the water at a safe level.

A more conservative approach—maintaining the reservoir well below its maximum level in order to allow a buffer for unexpected inflows—would violate the terms of the cost-benefit analysis that the state government had originally used to justify the dam's construction to the Central Water and Power Commission (CWPC). As an irrigation project, the Machhu Dam-II bore the obligation of impounding as much water-wealth as possible behind its gates. One Irrigation Department officer would later explain, "The gates must be operated according to the manual, such that the reservoir remains full at the end of the monsoon." Given the Saurashtra Peninsula's fickle rains, the Machhu Dam-II's gate operations manual essentially instructed Mohan and the rest of the dam's crew to fill the reservoir completely and then begin releasing just enough water to keep pace with inflows.[10]

For eight days now, the Machhu Dam-II's reservoir had stood at its maximum level. Each day, Mohan and his companions had bled water out for a few hours at a time. The gates could open to twenty feet, sending torrents down the riverbed toward Morbi and the Gulf of Kutch, but on most days the crew had not needed to open the gates more than a few inches to counter the inflow to the reservoir. At the moment, a quiet rush of water slipped through six-inch cracks beneath the barely opened gates.[11]

Mohan made his way along the slick metal catwalk, passing the line of electric motors and gearboxes that stood high above the steel gates to which they gave life. With a twenty-ton lift capacity, each motor could open its gate fully in less than a minute. The gates themselves were curved steel plates that rotated on long, trussed arms; their circular design enabled them to smoothly narrow or widen their apertures, even under the tremendous pressure of a full reservoir.

The crew operated the gates from the dam's control room, a small concrete structure that protruded from the junction of the concrete spillway and the eastern embankment. Through a tiny window, the men could peer out at the spillway to ensure that the gates were working properly. The control room also afforded easy access to a shed on the eastern earthwork that housed a forty-kilowatt electric generator; though the dam's motors typically drew power from the electric grid, the generator served as an alternative supply in the event of a power failure. In case the generator also failed, the gates possessed cranks that would permit Mohan and the other crew members to open them by hand.[12]

Seven men worked on the Machhu Dam-II. The supervisor—the crew's highest-ranking member—directed maintenance, communications, and gate operations, splitting his time between the dam and an office in Morbi. Mohan (the mechanic) and the electrician worked directly under the supervisor. Four laborers from the village of Jodhpar—one of the villages relocated by the Machhu Dam-II's reservoir—composed the remainder of the crew. One managed paperwork and operated the dam's wireless telegraph unit at the inspection bungalow, a small building near the crew's living quarters on the far edge of the eastern earthwork; the other three worked wherever they were needed.[13]

Deputy Engineer A. C. Mehta—the man responsible for both dams on the Machhu River—would sometimes come to the Machhu Dam-II from his downtown Morbi office in order to personally oversee gate operations. In light of the ongoing rain, Mohan expected that Mehta might appear soon.

Nonetheless, the Machhu Dam-II, unlike many of Saurashtra's dams, was actually experiencing relatively little inflow. For the moment, Mohan and his fellow crew members could manage the outflow quite well even in the absence of supervision.[14]

≈≈≈≈≈

The early evening of August 10 brought a much-welcome respite from the rains that had battered the Saurashtra Peninsula for ten days.[15] For a few hours, the clouds thinned, and the downpour slowed to a drizzle.

Shortly thereafter, the Shravan showers returned, stronger than ever before. Torrential rains—like those that had graced Lord Krishna's birth millennia earlier—drenched fields, battered roofs, and muddied the streets. Although the downpours were proving more formidable than any in living memory, the people of Morbi, Maliya, and the surrounding villages remained relatively nonplussed; the evacuations and turmoil ravaging much of Saurashtra had not affected the region, and common citizens con-

tinued living the humdrum days that followed the initial exuber-
ance of the monsoon. In their houses and neighborhoods, the
townspeople and villagers of the Machhu River Valley passed a
muted Friday evening, using the warmth of family gatherings to
ward off the wind, rain, and chill.[16]

A short distance downstream from the Machhu Dam-II's
spillway, in the village of Lilapar, Sri Lilapar Potteries owner
Bhagvanji Patel idled at home. Numerous small streams had
flooded the route to Bhagvanji's fields and his factory, rendering it
completely impassable. With the monsoon crop finally receiving
adequate water and no more than a few Harijans occupying the
laborers' quarters at the silent pottery factory, there was little need
to venture out. Until the rain relented, Bhagvanji would remain
indoors as much as possible, enjoying the rare respite.

Further north along Lilapar Road, in southern Morbi's Tiger
Quarter, the rain had mildly dampened the Shravan festivities
unfolding around Kanubhai Kubavat on the eve of Dipping
Fourth. As the Brahmin sloshed his way to the temple, the street
teemed with expensive jewelry and clothing. Decked out in colorful saris, Satwara women scampered to return to their parents'
homes, where they would remain until Birth Eighth. Steady
streams of raindrops pattered against the heavy anklets, bracelets,
necklaces, and earrings that festooned the women's bodies. Gathering together the trailing edges of their dhotis to keep them from
the cloudy water afoot, men hurried toward the shelter of the
neighborhood's temples, where Kubavat and others would lead
them in ecstatic worship. Only children lingered unnecessarily in
the muddy streets, splashing about giddily to start a weekend that
would blend seamlessly into the coming holidays.

To the northeast, up and down the streets that surrounded
Pratapbhai Adroja's Ghost Paan, the shops of Morbi's commercial zone stood shuttered. A haze of darkness and downpour
enveloped the neighborhood. Like Adroja, virtually all the city's
merchants had finished their Friday business early in order to
escape the elements. They had dispersed to various middle-class

neighborhoods, where they ate mundane suppers with their wives and children.

North of the main market, at the crematorium, dozens huddled inside the tent city that had sprung up abutting the Machhu's western bank. Vendors, ride operators, and assorted vagrant figures had been pouring into the city from far-flung places for the carnival that would take place on the following Tuesday, Smallpox Seventh. Many preparations remained pending, for the day had offered little opportunity for work outdoors. A layer of muddy water covered the open field where the carnival would take place. Raindrops pelted anyone who dared to venture out.

Much farther to the north, near the Gulf of Kutch, the Miyanas of Maliya quietly broke their Ramadan fasts. As always, the monsoon rains had turned the arid town into one massive puddle—still barren, but waterlogged. With the streets covered in waist-deep water, most of the town's citizens had remained at home for the day. Stray dogs cowered in the sheltered corners of the decaying royal palace's courtyard, and wet goats and sheep bleated in the town's narrow alleys, heralding the fall of night on a desolate Ramadan Friday.

Back in the City of the Peacock Flag, Khatijaben Valera's family passed a quiet evening after enjoying an *iftaar*, the sunset meal used to break the Ramadan fast in Islamic tradition. In decades gone by, Morbi's royal family might have requested the men of the clan to fill monsoon evenings with the notes of *Raga Malhar*, the melodic mode in Indian classical music most intimately associated with an atmosphere of torrential rains. On this evening, the strains of Malhar hung faintly in the damp air of the family's compound, more memory than melody.[17]

Across the river, raindrops beat against the shuttered windows of the royal palace. Seven generations after the Vaniyan's curse—and almost exactly a year after the death of Mayurdhvaj, the last of the Jadeja princes—the household had hollowed to a shell of its former self. Silence shrouded the immaculately maintained gardens that lay behind the main gates. Peacocks wandered among the well-trimmed bushes, crowing boisterously as beads of runoff dripped onto their extravagant tails. Once in a while, their calls pierced through the sheets of rain to reach the ears of those living around the palace, on the eastern periphery of the city the Jadejas had left behind.

Shortly after 8:30 p.m., the principal of Morbi's arts college, T. R. Shukla, walked briskly past the palace compound's northeastern corner with his wife. The Shuklas and their four adult children, reunited for the Shravan holidays, had been dining at the nearby home of a Lakhdhirji Engineering College professor. The partygoers had filled the evening with laughter and song, but the worsening rain—and fear of a leaky roof back home—had drawn the elder Shuklas away.

Shukla, a fifty-something man of considerable height, possessed a proud, ramrod-erect walk that struck fear into misbehaving students. Although his paunch had grown considerably over the past decade, he retained a full head of thick, black hair, with one shock perpetually dangling onto his forehead. A poet who never published, he soaked up inspiration from the Shravan air as he strode homeward.

In fact, the monsoon season had provided the inspiration for one of Shukla's favorite poems, a song that he and his wife might have sung for their hosts if they had not left the party prematurely. "This Monsoon Descends" had come alive exactly twenty-five years earlier, during the rainy season of 1954, but its vividness had not diminished one bit:

This monsoon descends,
And the peacock calls aloud.
With the first tiny drops of water,
The earth's body gives off a sweet fragrance.
This monsoon descends.

The thundering cloud runs around in the sky-cave above.
The flashing lightning covers the Earth with brightness.

Darkness falls, and the wilderness is surrounded.
The wind sings Raga Malhar with perfect beats.
This monsoon descends.

The clouds dance and drizzle in the company of
    dear companions.
Sweet delight spreads through the lakes, rivers, and seas.
The jungle's hem is drenched, as if soaked in liqueur,
And joy fills the beloved of the wet village outskirts.
This monsoon descends.

A sunbeam wished to play in the lap of a lotus on Earth.
On its path through the sky, a wildly adoring cloud
    embraced it.
The embrace was churned up by the light's edge;
    what color spilled forth?
A spirit has leapt across the sky as a garland.
This monsoon descends.

This monsoon descends,
And the peacock calls aloud.
With the first tiny drops of water,
The earth's body gives off a sweet fragrance.
This monsoon descends.

A more prosaic manifestation of the rainy season greeted the Shuklas when they arrived home. Wearing only her blouse and petticoat, their maidservant stood shivering in front of the house. Gesticulating wildly, she explained that a large black cobra had slithered into her quarters. The Shuklas took her into the bungalow, lending her a *sari* and telling her to make herself comfortable.[18]

Shortly thereafter, a solitary car passed through the watery, desolate streets near the Shuklas' house. Inside, Morbi's representative to the state government battled his impatience. Earlier in the day, Gokaldas Parmar had set out from Gandhinagar to return to his home in Shakti Plot, a middle-class neighborhood near the center of downtown Morbi. His driver had spent hours following circuitous routes to bypass flooded areas, only to discover that the waterlogged streets of Morbi's eastern outskirts seemed nearly impossible to traverse.

Eventually, the driver found a clear path near Lakhdhirji Engineering College, and the car reached the Buffalo Bridge. As Parmar crossed, the river crashed against the bridge's tall arches, sending sprays up toward the bronze bulls' lowered noses. At the entrance to downtown, water had pooled in the Mani Mandir's compound, placing a muddy moat around the red sandstone walls of the Taj Mahal of Saurashtra.

It had grown quite late by the time Parmar reached Shakti Plot, where his wife awaited. For a short time, Parmar surveyed the flooding in the streets around his house. Then, after a brief period of meditation and prayer, he retired to bed as the Shravan rains continued to pour down outside.[19]

Upstream of Morbi's drenched inhabitants, mechanic Lakshmanbhai Mohan peered at the Machhu Dam-II's reservoir through the downpour and the darkness. The reservoir was nearly full, holding steady at two feet below its maximum level and ten feet below the crests of the dam's earthworks.[20]

Normally, the dam's crew would work under close supervision during such heavy rains. But on the evening of August 10, Mohan and the electrician had been the highest-ranking men present. The supervisor had left at 1:00 p.m. to complete paperwork in downtown Morbi. He had yet to return. Mohan and the other men had continued adjusting the dam's discharge according to the Irrigation Department's gate operations manual, releasing just enough water to keep the reservoir below its maximum level.[21]

Shortly after 8:00 p.m., the dam's wireless telegraph operator rushed onto the spillway, bearing a message from the deputy engineer, A. C. Mehta. The Machhu Dam-I would soon begin discharging water from its reservoir. Once outflow began at the dam thirty miles upstream, massive quantities of water would hurtle toward the Machhu Dam-II. Mehta made it clear that the dam's floodgates, whose openings stood at a mere six inches, would have to open to at least six feet in order to hold the reservoir steady.

Suddenly, after days of mundane work, the dam's crew sprang into frenzied action. The ongoing storm had knocked out power to the dam, so two of the men hurried toward the shed on the eastern earthwork in order to start the backup diesel generator. As soon as the generator electrified the motors, Mohan began punching buttons on the control room's console. To avoid sending an abrupt wave downriver, the mechanic opened the gates two feet at a time, in batches of three.[22]

By 9:30 p.m., the roar of rushing water filled the crew's ears. Mohan had opened sixteen of the eighteen gates to the required six feet. The remaining two gates, 15 and 17, were proving vexatious. Though the power supply from the generator was functioning, both gates had jammed.

Frustrated, the electrician climbed onto the spillway's slippery metal catwalk. Grabbing the guardrails, he worked his way down the row of electric motors. Arriving at the first of the troubled gates, he opened the hatch to the motor and discovered a broken fuse. With any luck, it would prove a simple repair.

As the electrician worked, the others took regular measurements of the reservoir level. Driving wind and choppy waves prevented a precise reading, but it seemed that the waters behind the dam were now creeping upward. To counter their rise, Mohan and the rest of the crew began opening the gates further, a few feet at a time.

After more than an hour of work, the electrician had made little progress. He had replaced the troublesome fuse on gate 15's electric motor several times; each time, the fuse had failed when he opened the circuit. Gate 17 had behaved similarly, with the added nuisance of a malfunctioning electromagnetic brake coil.

Opening either gate further would require use of the hand cranks.

The electrician retreated from the catwalk. For the moment, further opening of the sixteen working gates could compensate for gates 15 and 17.

But the situation worried the crew. The spillway's discharge was nearing the highest value it had ever reached, and yet the reservoir continued to climb beyond its maximum allowable level. The Machhu Dam-II, spared from the heavy flooding that had plagued Saurashtra's dams for several days, had suddenly fallen into crisis. As Mohan, the electrician, and the remaining crew members opened the gates further, the rain grew heavier.[23]

≋≋≋

Shortly before midnight, a mud-splattered jeep rolled up to the Machhu Dam-II's spillway. Deputy Engineer A. C. Mehta and his driver stepped out into the chilling downpour. In the hours since receiving Mehta's orders, the men on the dam had continued to open the floodgates at increments, trying to keep pace with the immense flux entering the reservoir. Except for the two jammed gates, most had reached openings of ten to twelve feet. The reservoir had dropped by half a foot in the hour after initiation of gate openings, but it had resumed its steady climb thereafter.[24]

The reservoir's continued rise distressed Mehta. Upon his arrival, he "immediately gave orders for all the gates to be opened completely," according to mechanic Lakshmanbhai Mohan's later account.[25] By 1:30 a.m. on August 11, the crew had opened fifteen of the eighteen behemoth gates fully, to twenty feet. Gates 15 and 17 remained jammed, and gate 9's fuse had begun malfunctioning as well.

Once again, the electrician ventured out onto the slick catwalk, enduring the driving rain and the penetrating cold. Mohan soon joined him, and the two men worked to repair the motor for gate 9. The rush of water below had reached such proportions that that they had to shout to hear one another. As soon as they had replaced the fuse, they attempted to open gate 9, and the gearboxes began whirring.

Almost immediately, however, the apparatus faltered again. Exasperated, the crew members began turning the gate's hand crank. Struggling to turn the stiff handle, the seven men managed to coax the gate just a few feet further before it jammed completely. Gate 9's aperture now stood at sixteen feet—just four shy of the maximum—and Mehta decided that the crew's energies would be better spent working on gates 15 and 17.

Mohan and the other men spent the night out on the catwalk, struggling against the troublesome gates. At daybreak, they had managed only a few feet of progress. Mohan would write, "We were all physically wrecked. Owing to the constant rain and wind overnight, we were not in a state to keep working."[26]

Even as Mohan and his fellow crew members labored in vain, a bigger problem loomed. In the eight hours since Deputy Engineer Mehta's arrival, the water in the reservoir had risen another three feet; it now swirled just seven feet below the crests of the earthen flanks. Full opening of the three refractory gates would increase the dam's outflow by several thousand cubic feet per second, but the flood filling the reservoir demanded far more. With the Machhu Dam-II releasing water at a rate just short of its 196,000-cusec capacity, the reservoir continued to climb up the earthen embankments.[27]

Muddy water lapped at Collector A. R. Banerjee's waist as he waded steadily down the boulevard. On most days, he made his way to work in the comfort of a chauffeured government sedan. But today, his car idled behind him, its headlights projecting dim shadows on the buildings that lined the deserted street. Banerjee would have to overcome the floodwaters, which had immobilized his car, on foot.[28]

Like Agriculture Secretary H. K. Khan, with whom he had met just ten days earlier to discuss drought mitigation measures, Banerjee was a member of the elite Indian Administrative Service. His title—district collector—harkened back to the British colonial administration, which had relied on powerful officers called "revenue collectors" to handle taxation in specific regions. The Gujarat Revenue Department, to which he belonged, had retained the British system's top-down structure while acquiring a radically broadened mission. The Revenue Department now served as the state government's conduit for centralized administration in almost every aspect of public life, from taxation to disaster management. As the chief civil servant in one of Gujarat's twenty districts, Collector Banerjee bore responsibility for the well-being of two million citizens. From his office in the city of Rajkot, he oversaw thirteen subdistricts of the northern Saurashtra Peninsula, including those headquartered at Morbi and Maliya.[29]

Squinting with bloodshot eyes, the collector could just make out the imposing walls of the Rajkot collectorate compound through the downpour. He had hardly slept. Beginning at 8:30 p.m. the previous night, he had received telephone reports of emerging crises all over Rajkot District. Municipal drains and earthen huts had begun to fail under the pressure of the intensifying rainfall. The increased flow into the district's irrigation reservoirs was swelling rivers, threatening dams, and flooding entire villages. With the phone ringing almost continuously, Banerjee had given up any hope of sleeping. Before sunrise on August 11, he had summoned his driver and set off for his office to begin a long day of crisis management.[30]

At 6:00 a.m., Banerjee arrived, sopping wet and on foot, to find that the skeleton staff on duty had set up a flood control room in the spacious collectorate, bringing in maps, scratch paper, and additional telephones. As his first order of business, Banerjee ordered telephone calls to wake his workers from their weekend slumber; they would have to report to the office as quickly as possible. Then, he attempted to contact the subdistrict magistrates, his direct subordinates in Rajkot District's thirteen subdivisions. Because the stormy weather had disrupted telephone connections, several—including those in Morbi and Maliya—could not be reached.[31]

At 8:00 a.m., Morbi's subdistrict magistrate stepped onto the Machhu Dam-II. Around midnight, Deputy Engineer A. C. Mehta had sent him a telegraphed warning that the dam's crew would soon increase outflow from the reservoir to high levels, possibly flooding the low-lying areas of Morbi. Then, in the early hours of the morning, a desperate message from the Maliya subdistrict magistrate had arrived: the Machhu River, swollen by the discharge from the reservoir, was threatening to submerge large parts of the downstream town and its surrounding villages. Unable to establish contact with the dam, Maliya's subdistrict magistrate had asked his counterpart in Morbi to inform the crew of the emergency and request that the floodgates be closed. Accompanied by Mayor Ratilal Desai, the Morbi area's chief civil servant had sped off to the south in the municipal ambulance.[32]

A haggard Deputy Engineer Mehta received the two men at the dam. He had spent the entire night supervising the crew's futile attempts to open the malfunctioning gates. Still, the reservoir had risen to twenty-two and a half feet—just six and a half feet below the crests of the earthen flanks.[33]

After listening to the public officials' request to reduce the outflow from the reservoir, Mehta informed them that he could not comply. He would later write:

> I notified them of the heavy inflow, which made it impossible to close the gates under any circumstances. Similarly, it was impossible to reduce their openings. In fact, efforts were under way to open the jammed gates fully, so I informed them that the

flooding could increase further, entering Morbi's low-lying areas.[34]

While insisting that he could not reduce the discharge from the Machhu Dam-II, the deputy engineer did not suggest that the dam might encounter problems even at its current rate of outflow. It is unclear whether Mehta or the other crew members fully recognized the dire danger facing the dam. Perhaps the prospect of the earthen embankments overtopping seemed unthinkable on the morning of August 11; after all, the water would have to rise another seven feet—still quite a long way—before disaster struck. With the gates releasing the largest conceivable flood foreseen by the Irrigation Department's engineers, perhaps it seemed that the inflow could not possibly overwhelm the spillway's outflow capacity. At any rate, even with two officials present who could quickly mobilize widespread downstream evacuations, Mehta did not raise concerns about the Machhu Dam-II failing. The subdistrict magistrate would later write, "The deputy engineer did not give us any indication that the dam would breach."[35]

Instead, Mehta expressed the necessity of contacting his Irrigation Department superiors in Rajkot. With his own jeep's engine waterlogged, the deputy engineer decided to return to Morbi with the mayor and the subdistrict magistrate. At 9:00 a.m., the three men piled into the municipal ambulance and set off along the eastern earthwork.[36]

Around the time Deputy Engineer Mehta left, a man and his motorcycle rode up from one of the dam's earthen embankments. Soaked through to the skin, the supervisor had finally arrived to assume his position at the head of the dam's crew. The night before, desperate to reach the dam on account of the heavy rains, he had tried to ford deep water on a road leading out of the city. His motorcycle's engine had flooded. Only after draining and drying the engine overnight had he been able to reattempt the journey.

Upon his arrival, the supervisor found a dam in chaos. Inflow to the reservoir remained heavy. The water had risen well above its maximum allowable level. Waves were beginning to lap at the crests of the earthen embankments. Despite nearly full gate opening, the reservoir continued to climb. No options remained to further increase outflow from the dam; as the supervisor later wrote, "all procedures for opening the gates listed in the gate manual had been exhausted."[37]

Nonetheless, facing a crisis that had long ago escaped their control, the six men remaining on the dam—the supervisor, the electrician, the mechanic Mohan, and the four laborers from Jodhpar—desperately searched for ways to fully open the three malfunctioning gates. Though the inflow to the reservoir exceeded the outflow by several multiples of the spillway's still-unutilized capacity, the men continued to grasp for measures that remained within their abilities.[38]

≋≋≋

The morning of August 11 was a quiet one in the village of Jodhpar, located on the Machhu Dam-II's eastern flank.[39] Most residents intended to spend the Dipping Fourth holiday indoors, away from the pounding rain. Old men sat inside and smoked hand-rolled cigarettes. Women, having bathed early in the morning, carried on fasts for the health of their sons. Children played restlessly behind closed doors, held in by mothers worried about them catching colds. Upon finishing their morning chores, some young men congregated at the village's school building and marveled at the water rushing violently out of the Machhu Dam-II's spillway.

Around 9:30 a.m., a truck rolled to a halt in Jodhpar's central plaza, interrupting the morning's languor. The driver bore an urgent message from the dam: several of the large floodgates had jammed, and the crew desperately needed help.

The young men of Jodhpar, brawny from years of labor in fields and orchards, stepped out into the rain from the school and the surrounding earthen houses. While later accounts of a hundred souls crammed into a single truck were likely exaggerated, the vehicle was full to the point of overflowing as it sputtered out of the village and up the eastern earthwork.

After disembarking, the men inched along the slippery catwalk to the uncooperative gates. Upon reaching the gearboxes, they heaved to turn the large metal handles. Participants would later describe the scene as one of absolute bedlam. Dozens of boys sometimes clustered around one crank, pushing hard to make it budge. Mere inches separated their feet from water splashing over the top of the concrete dam.

For over an hour, the young men of Jodhpar labored mightily. The dam's crew had led them to believe that they were working to save the dam, but their effort could, in fact, do little to stem the inexorable inflow that was raising the reservoir level; even if they opened the three remaining gates fully, a minimal increase in outflow would result. The water continued to creep up behind them as they pushed in vain.

When spray from the reservoir's waves began tapping the young men's backs, they decided to abandon their effort. They hurried off the dam together, eager to wring out their sopping clothes and anxious about the still-rising reservoir.

Seven men—the dam's crew—remained behind. By that point—around 11:00 a.m.—they, too, had abandoned the idea of opening the remaining gates. Mechanic Lakshmanbhai Mohan would later write, "The water level kept rising, and if we had tried any harder, the cable or chains might have snapped. So we gave up the effort to open the gates further."[40]

Even as the young men from Jodhpar fled and the reservoir continued to climb precipitously, the dam's crew members—perhaps unwilling to confront the looming possibility of a dam failure—did not send a warning to Morbi.

Around midmorning on August 11, a messenger arrived in Lilapar with troubling news: the Machhu Dam-II's reservoir had filled to dangerous levels, and a breach seemed imminent.[41]

In later years, politicians and common citizens alike would decry the fact that no Irrigation Department employee—from the dam's laborers to Deputy Engineer A. C. Mehta to higher-ranking officials—ever warned public officials in Morbi and other downstream areas of impending danger. Somehow, Lilapar received the alarm that eluded the rest of the Machhu River Valley. The source of the warning would eventually fall into oblivion, with some maintaining that the father of a crew member had journeyed to the dam earlier in the day and returned with the message,[42] but the people of Lilapar would never forget the man's fateful words: "There is a lot of water filling up the dam. The dam is going to fail. Make your arrangements."[43]

Upon learning of the danger, villagers went to the dam and quickly confirmed the rumor: waves were lapping at the crests of the earthworks, and several gates had jammed. At 10:00 a.m., as the news spread, an informal assembly convened at the central plaza.

Bhagvanji Patel and the other men of the village reviewed the situation. Lilapar lay half a mile directly downstream from the dam's western earthwork. If the dam burst, the floodwaters would annihilate the village. The people could not remain in Lilapar, but they possessed few choices for evacuation. Heavy flooding blocked every road leading out of the village. The best hope lay in setting out across the fields for Lakhdhirnagar, the small community to the west of the western embankment.

Late in the morning, around the time that the young men of Jodhpar fled from the dam, a caravan of people and cattle began wending its way along the base of the western earthwork from Lilapar. Driving animals in front, trailing children by the hand, and carrying their most precious possessions on their backs, Bhagvanji and his fellow villagers marched across the open fields at the foot of the dam toward safety.

≈≈≈≈

As the people of Lilapar began planning their evacuation to Lakhdhirnagar, the rising waters in southern Morbi's streets struck fear into Khatijaben Valera. Years later, she would recall:

> The atmosphere was very stormy. . . . It was the kind that would make you shiver, make you afraid. My mother-in-law told me, "You all stop gossiping and start cooking!" So my sister-in-law and I got together and made lentil soup. . . .
>
> We finished up cleaning and other chores. . . . Then, when it got to be about 9:00 or 9:30, a lot of water backed up into the area. The water in the creek running by our house stopped—it became stagnant. Whenever that water became stagnant, we knew the flooding was bad, because the creek flowed towards the river, and that water was backing up into the creek. At that point, the water was backing up into the neighborhood.

All around the Valera clan's decaying bungalow just north of Vajepar, the streets had become streambeds.[44]

By midmorning, Khatijaben's anxiety increased further as the people of Morbi undertook their own evacuations. In contrast to the situation in Lilapar, urgency did not grip all citizens; those who lived in higher-lying neighborhoods, such as the main market, hardly worried about floodwaters, which did not approach their houses even in the heaviest rainy seasons.[45] But the residents of many southern areas—from the farming community of Vajepar to the Harijan Quarter to Gangaram Tapu's Kabir Hill—saw their Dipping Fourth transformed in mere minutes.

Some time after 9:00 a.m., Mayor Ratilal Desai and Morbi's subdistrict magistrate had returned from their visit to the Machhu Dam-II. Forewarned by Deputy Engineer A. C. Mehta that the floodgates would remain fully open under any circumstances, they had decided to set up a control room at the Morbi police station to cope with the inevitable flooding in the city's low-lying areas.

They had hastily called together a diverse collection of public servants to coordinate evacuations of the most vulnerable neighborhoods. As Mayor Desai and other public officials would later note, they had initiated evacuations as a "measure of abundant precaution" in light of the heavy outflow from the dam; unlike in Lilapar, no one imagined that the dam might fail.

By 10:00 a.m., an armada of vehicles was setting out to bring residents of low-lying areas—located primarily west of Lilapar Road in southern Morbi—to V. C. High School, Gibson Middle School, and other safe sites north of the main market, as well as to the Police Line. Police officers and citizen volunteers known as Home Guards directed the compliant and coaxed the reluctant, striving to direct as many as possible to safety. The municipal ambulance, which had ferried the mayor and the subdistrict magistrate to the dam just a short time earlier, meandered across the low-lying neighborhoods, blaring megaphone warnings about the rising waters.[46]

The evacuations upturned entire neighborhoods. Linking arms, families waded through waist-deep sludge in Vajepar to reach Lilapar Road, where the State Transport buses idled in order to avoid the water. Satwara women, decked out in fancy saris and jewels for Dipping Fourth, cradled their babies and inched up the Tiger Quarter's slippery main road toward the vehicles parked near the Police Line. Trucks crawled through the Harijan Quarter and Kabir Hill, periodically stopping to pick up men, women, and children.

Cold and drenched, the evacuees crowded onto musty buses and flatbed trucks. A steady stream of vehicles rolled northward, while a small offshoot moved toward the New State Transport Bus Stand, on the city's southwestern outskirts. Dozens of rain-speckled faces peered down at the splashing tires and passing scenery as the vehicles jerked haltingly forward. Tractors, jeeps, and other private vehicles followed in the shadows of the official transportation, their most able-bodied passengers hanging off to one side or the other. Home Guards, police officers, and volunteers rounded out the caravan, leading and following on foot, by bicycle, and by jeep. Occasionally, a goat kid peered out from a window or a truck bed, bleating into the torrential shower.[47]

Despite the evacuations unfolding around them, many citizens of Morbi's low-lying areas chose not to leave. In the Tiger Quarter, Brahmin Kanubhai Kubavat saw little reason to interrupt his quiet Saturday at home. While knee-deep flooding had filled the street, his house stood on a raised foundation. The water would have to rise more than three feet—unthinkable even with continued discharge from the Machhu Dam-II—in order to reach the front steps of the building. Moreover, Kubavat's pride would not allow him to spend his Dipping Fourth as a refugee. Like the residents of higher-elevation neighborhoods throughout Morbi, he and his family would pass the rainy day at home.[48]

Unlike Kubavat, the women of the Valera clan eventually decided to leave their compound as the frenzy of evacuations mounted. Khatijaben Valera would recall:

> It got to be around 10:00, and I said, "Let's get out of here." My husband's uncle said, "No, nothing is going to happen." But the whole area was emptying out. I looked to both sides, and I said, "These people are gone. Those people are gone. I have small children—I am afraid."

Despite her in-laws' reluctance to evacuate, Khatijaben could not remain at the bungalow any longer. She and the other women resolved to set off with the family's young children for a cousin's house, which lay on higher ground.

In order to leave the compound, the women would use an auto-rickshaw that belonged to Valera Transport. Khatijaben would remember, "We got into the rickshaw. My mother-in-law, my sister-in-law—those two were big people. . . ." She would pause to chuckle and then continue, "We got all the children together. I took my oldest son in my lap. In his lap, one of my daughters. In her lap, another daughter. We got them arranged properly, then I took one girl in my arm like this, and one in my arm like this."

Crammed into the small vehicle, eight members of the Valera clan, like thousands of others throughout Morbi's southern neighborhoods, puttered toward safety.[49]

By midmorning, proceedings at the Rajkot collectorate had settled into a frenetic rhythm.[50] Wet footprints crisscrossed the floor, phones rang incessantly, and a din of voices filled the air with a sense of purposeful urgency.

The staffers summoned for emergency weekend duty had populated a now-humming control room. Telephone operators scribbled furiously, taking down reports of stranded villagers, overflowing reservoirs, and collapsed buildings. Meanwhile, other workers coordinated rescue and relief efforts with local and state government bodies, police forces, fire brigades, Home Guard units, dam engineers, and a host of civic and religious groups. Collector A. R. Banerjee orchestrated the efforts, struggling to focus his sleep-deprived mind on the numerous problems facing Rajkot District.[51]

At 9:30 a.m., a new arrival demanded Banerjee's attention. As he wiped the mud from his boots and wrung rainwater from his traditional homespun cotton suit, state Agriculture Minister Keshubhai Patel struck a comical figure. Endowed with a boyish face but a prolifically rotund build and a thick mustache, he dominated the room with his imposing figure. A wad of paan filled his cheek, and his every word carried a rasp.[52]

A native son of Rajkot District, Keshubhai had arrived from Gandhinagar a few days earlier to personally oversee the government's response to the widespread flooding. As Gujarat's agriculture minister, he oversaw a portfolio that included all farming activities in the agrarian state, as well as all Irrigation Department activities and dam management. While the collector and other Revenue Department officers bore immediate responsibility for disaster relief, Keshubhai would remain on hand to receive updates and offer his input wherever he saw fit. As he rose to greet the minister, Banerjee quietly hoped that he would not interfere unduly with the control room's ongoing work.[53]

After the agriculture minister's arrival, the morning passed in a blur. Upon dispatching a fleet of vehicles to coordinate evacuations in the city of Rajkot, the collector turned his attention first to Morbi and Maliya. The lack of contact with officials in the two locales troubled him. The heavy rain in the Machhu River Valley—and the continuous eleven-foot-deep torrent issuing from the Machhu Dam-I—threatened to submerge low-lying areas in the northern subdistricts. Although Banerjee expected that local officials might have begun evacuating vulnerable citizens, he could not be certain. In order to ensure that subdistrict officials were undertaking all necessary measures, he dispatched a subordinate named Bhatt to personally visit Morbi and Maliya.[54]

With that step taken, the collector turned his attention to other matters. As he would later note, outflow from the Machhu dams was "a common phenomenon." Evacuations generally proceeded according to routine, and the situation required little attention from the collectorate.[55]

By contrast, developing crises in other parts of Rajkot District had grown quite alarming. The tremendous outflow from Saurashtra's largest dam, the Bhadar, was overwhelming towns and villages on the southern periphery of Banerjee's jurisdiction. Shortly after 11:00 a.m., the collector received word that the rising floodwaters had stranded forty villagers. "If the water level continued to rise at the same speed," he would later explain, "there was danger to the lives of all those people."[56]

Anxious to avoid a major loss of life in his district, Banerjee began placing desperate telephone calls to request rescue boats. After contacting a local naval base, the state-level flood control room in Ahmedabad, and a nearby air force base, he finally managed to secure two helicopters for the operation.

Taking stock of the mounting crises, the collector decided to alert the state government to the district's plight. Around noon, he dictated a curt wireless telegraph message:

> *UNPRECEDENTED HEAVY RAIN ALL OVER RAJKOT DISTRICT SINCE 10TH EVENING(.) DAMS OF BHADAR, MACHHU-I AND MACHHU-II, NYARI, AJI, MOJ ALL OVERFLOWING MUCH ABOVE DANGER LEVEL(.) RAIN ABOUT THIRTEEN INCHES IN RAJKOT CITY IN LAST TWELVE HOURS(.) SIMILAR RAINS IN OTHER SUBDISTRICTS ALSO(.) FORTY (40) PEOPLE MAROONED AT JETHPUR . . . (.) AIRFORCE HELP SOUGHT TO RESCUE THEM(.) WANKANER SUBDIS-TRICT IN SERIOUS DANGER AND PEOPLE BEING EVACUATED(.) RAJKOT CITY SPECIALLY LOW-LYING AREA BADLY FLOODED AND EVACUATION OPERA-TION GOING ON(.) HELP OF ARMY AND NAVY BOATS ALSO SOUGHT(.) SHRI KESHUBHAI, HON'BLE AGRI-CULTURE MINISTER ALSO PERSONALLY SUPER-VISING EVACUATION OPERATION(.)*[57]

At the subdistrict prison on Lilapar Road, thick raindrops pocked the surface of the shallow lake that had accumulated in the fenced-off courtyard.[58] Just to the north along the Police Line, in a hectic control room, Morbi's highest officials scrambled to coordinate evacuations. To the south and west, hundreds of families navigated through muddy streets to pile into vehicles that would ferry them to safe ground. At the prison, however, the inmates stood sullenly around the wet courtyard.

Most had slept little the previous night, worried by the rains that threatened to fill their underground cells. At 6:00 a.m., before the light of the rising sun had turned the sky gray, they had emerged groggily for exercise. But few of them moved around the courtyard.

Led by Gangaram Tapu, they warned the guards that they would refuse to return to their cells for the regular 12:00–3:00 p.m. lockup. The guards would either transport them to safer quarters in Rajkot or leave their cells unlocked for the remainder of the day. Tapu and his fellows would not tolerate further endangerment.

The guards had come to know Tapu well during his year of incarceration, and they respected him—not only for his fierceness but also for his sense of honor. They made every attempt to reassure him that the cells would be unlocked again at 3:00 p.m., as usual.

Courteous but firm, Tapu persisted. He noted that some of the morning's visitors, who tended fields at the foot of the Machhu Dam-II, had mentioned that the reservoir was full to the brim; heavy outflow from the dam would continue to rush into the river, producing greater flooding along Lilapar Road and potentially transforming the subterranean cells into death-traps.

After several hours of dispute, the guards relented. The cell doors would remain open. Contrary to protocol, Tapu and his fellow prisoners would roam free for the rest of the afternoon.

Tapu exulted in his victory. Shortly thereafter, using one of his well-cultivated covert channels, he smuggled a message out to his wife and daughters in nearby Kabir Hill, instructing them to leave their house for the safety of a school.

<hr />

Across the river from the subdistrict prison, nine sets of eyes peered at a cobra through a gingerly opened doorway.[59] The snake rested atop a large storage barrel, its jet-black body coiled over itself time and again. Its broad hood hovered in the air, casting a pall over the room.

The previous night, after returning to find their maidservant shivering with cold and fright at the snake occupying her quarters, Principal T. R. Shukla and his wife had taken the girl into the main bungalow. Now, midmorning on August 11 found the cobra still firmly ensconced. The Shuklas, their four children, the maid, and her two brothers crowded outside the door to the cabin. They hesitantly crossed and recrossed the threshold, hoping to scare the animal away. It watched them, impassive. One day before Brahmins all over the Machhu River Valley would make offerings for Cobra Fifth, the Brahmin residents of the old bungalow stood, impotent, before a great monsoon serpent.

With the family reunited for the Shravan holidays, Shukla had planned an excursion to watch a noon matinee film at a theater across the river. But until the Shuklas resolved the situation in the maid's cabin, they could not depart for downtown Morbi. Nine flustered minds grasped for a solution.

First, the maid's brothers, putting their faith in the old folk belief that cobras loved milk, slid a saucer of milk into the room. The snake summarily ignored it.

Then, Shukla's wife recalled her father's teaching that cobras could not tolerate the smell of burning butter. After inserting a wick into a large saucer of butter, she lit the makeshift lamp, and one of the maid's brothers placed it on the floor of the cabin.

As the aroma of burning fat filled the air, the snake hissed. Within a few instants, the flame had flickered out. For years afterward, the Shuklas would claim that the animal actually extinguished the flame as a person might, by blowing out of its mouth.

In spite of every effort, the cobra would not move. Every reasonable option exhausted, the Shuklas, the maid, and her brothers retreated to the main bungalow. The clock had already passed eleven, and the opportunity to see the noon matinee film was rapidly evaporating. But until the snake slithered away, the Shuklas could only wait.

By noontime on August 11, a layer of sludge several feet thick covered the streets of Maliya. After months of atypically dry weather, the resurgent monsoon had driven the Machhu River's estuarine terminus into town. The roads, in a notoriously poor state of disrepair, had filled with up to three feet of standing water. The farmland surrounding the town, usually painfully dry, had become an uneven quilt of inundated paddies.

With the river pouring the entire basin's excess water onto Maliya, the flooding had reached truly extraordinary levels, even by the standards of a town that often experienced sudden heavy inundations. On August 11, for the first time in eleven days of constant rain, the Miyanas altered their daily routines. Salt industrialist Abdulbhai Mor decided to evacuate his workers from their residences near his plant; with some difficulty, he traveled to India Salt Works and personally helped shift the twenty employees to higher ground. In light of weather that rendered impossible even the simplest work in the fields, farmer Jashabhai Samani cloistered himself indoors. Fisherman Husainbhai Manek, fearing the brutal rain, lashing wind, and violent waves, returned from the Gulf of Kutch to his house in town.[60]

In low-lying areas, the government initiated evacuation efforts. Under instructions from the subdistrict magistrate, and with the assistance of police officers and other officials, Mor and other residents untied their goats and buffaloes, placed their valuables on high shelves, and slogged to designated evacuation sites.[61]

Around noon, a message flashed over the All-India Radio broadcast from Rajkot:

> With eleven feet of water flowing over the Machhu Dam-I, there is a possibility of the Machhu Dam-II having to release water soon as well. Maliya's subdistrict magistrate is requested to take all necessary steps immediately, and people are requested to shift to higher ground. The Maliya subdistrict magistrate and public officers will receive periodic instructions over the radio.[62]

Communications between Maliya and the rest of the world had largely failed, but the government still managed to send the town bad news.

Unbeknownst to both district officials and citizens of Maliya, the crisis on the Machhu River had already far exceeded the bounds anticipated by the radio message.

It was early afternoon. A beaded curtain of runoff veiled the entrance to the Mehta Machinery shop.[63] From his seat behind the counter, Dhirubhai Mehta glanced out at the Mahendra Quarter, the middle-class neighborhood northwest of Morbi's main market. A gushing stream filled the street, and a damp coolness hung in the air. Although large-scale evacuations were under way in the city's low-lying neighborhoods, life in the Mahendra Quarter continued to follow the routine of a mundane rainy day. Dhirubhai Mehta pored over his business's ledgers.

For the most part, Mehta was an unremarkable man. His bland shirts and pants covered a body that stood average in both height and build. He tended to remain silent, holding his gravelly voice in reserve except when compelled. His dark face rarely betrayed emotion.

Like Mayor Ratilal Desai and the woman who had cursed the city centuries earlier, Mehta belonged to the Vaniya merchant jati. Unlike Desai, he had not achieved widespread distinction. He had spent his life in the Mahendra Quarter, quietly tending his agricultural machinery business and bringing up three daughters. He passed his days haggling with farmers, praying at the local temple, and socializing with fellow members of the Rotary Club.

Recently, however, he had found a new passion in life, something that filled him with satisfaction and a small degree of self-importance. Over the last five years, Mehta's son Vimal—the only boy after a string of three girls—had become the greatest joy in his life. Neither father nor son could bear long separations, and Mehta doted on the boy in every way possible. Years from now, Mehta Machinery, like many shops in Morbi, would pass from father to son, and Vimal would carry on the family legacy.

At the moment, the patrimony remained silent. With the rain pounding the streets, few customers would trudge to the shop. Mehta had come in primarily to complete some pending paperwork. Although fellow Rotarians occasionally stopped by to make social inquiries, the shop was largely deserted. Happy to wring some productivity out of the dull afternoon, Mehta reviewed and completed his ledgers.

Unlike Mehta Machinery, most shops in Morbi were closed. The Dipping Fourth holiday had kept many shop owners at home. Others had simply glanced outside and decided against opening up their shops. The roads had become muddy trenches, and even the shortest walk outside meant getting dirty and drenched.

Most of the intrepid merchants carrying on business in the morning had given up by noontime. At Ghost Paan, Pratapbhai Adroja, who lived only a short distance from Mehta in the Mahendra Quarter, had pulled the shutters down over the small window through which he dispensed his magical leaves. The driving rain had flattened demand for paan and cigarettes. With time on his hands, Adroja had offered to retrieve some food containers for the neighboring merchant, who had filled them with snacks for hungry evacuees and entrusted them to volunteers earlier in the day.[64]

Unlike Adroja and other shop owners, Mehta continued to enjoy the solace of a rainy afternoon at work. Alone in the chill, dank air, surrounded by dozens of steel machines, he labored on. Within an hour or so, he would return home to eat a hot lunch and play with Vimal.

Outside, the rain spilled off the roof and into the street.

By midafternoon, at least 6,400 people had taken trucks and buses from Morbi's most vulnerable neighborhoods to higher ground, primarily at the middle and high schools. Numerous other citizens had made the trip in smaller vehicles. Nonetheless, the government officials coordinating the evacuations in the control room at the Police Line remained preoccupied.[65]

Much of the ongoing activity in the control room stemmed from the fact that some residents of low-lying neighborhoods remained steadfast in their refusal to evacuate, despite the upheaval and the increasing rainfall. Like Kanubhai Kubavat, they remained in their homes due to some combination of sloth, pride, and incredulity. Many also felt loathe to leave their neighborhoods on the Dipping Fourth holiday; in the agricultural community of Vajepar, for example, a large number of Satwaras refused to evacuate to anywhere besides the local temple, which had stood well above the floodwaters of 1959—the highest in living memory.[66]

As the afternoon wore on, the evacuations increasingly became a matter of convincing, cajoling, and imploring. Mayor Ratilal Desai and the subdistrict magistrate set out in a jeep to sweep through some low-lying areas of the city. The municipal ambulance continued its circuitous journey through the streets of Morbi, warning that ongoing outflow from the Machhu Dam-II would raise the floodwaters to even higher levels. Police officers and Home Guards labored to persuade reluctant citizens to leave their homes.[67]

For the areas of the city with large Satwara populations, the government deployed Gokaldas Parmar, Morbi's representative in the state legislative assembly. Parmar stood barely over five feet tall, but his steely eyes, heavy jowls, and stern demeanor lent him an intimidating presence. Having marched alongside Mahatma Gandhi during the independence movement and subsequently served Morbi for many years, he garnered great respect from the public.[68]

As Parmar traversed the city's vulnerable areas in a jeep and knocked at his obstinate constituents' doors, many grudgingly agreed to board the waiting buses and submit to an uncomfortable Dipping Fourth in one of the designated evacuation sites. In the course of his work, the legislator stopped at his daughters' houses in the Tiger Quarter; although his sons-in-law chose to remain at home, he insisted that his daughters and grandchildren move to the safer confines of his residence in Shakti Plot.[69]

Throughout Parmar's journey of persuasion, the Machhu Dam-II hovered in his mind. His thoughts lingered on that morning's conversation with Deputy Engineer A. C. Mehta. After coming to Morbi in the municipal ambulance with the mayor and the subdistrict magistrate early in the day, the engineer had been unable to contact his Irrigation Department superiors in Rajkot, and he had set out to access intact lines of communication. But before he left, Parmar had spoken with him briefly. The legislator would later attest:

> At 10:30 a.m., he called to inform me that the Machhu Dam-II's gates had been opened. I asked him, "Is there a danger of the dam failing?" He said, "There was a danger of the dam failing before. . . . Because of the apparent risk, I threw open the floodgates. Sixteen gates are open; two, we have not been able to open."[70]

The deputy engineer's statements had done little to reassure Parmar. As he rode along on the back of the jeep with several Public Works Department engineers, he continued to ask whether the dam might fail. Irritated, the engineers deflected his queries, and the men continued on their mission to evacuate the areas most prone to flooding.[71]

Back at the Police Line, the subdistrict magistrate, harried after several hours of constant frantic activity, attempted once again to contact the collector in Rajkot. Upon finding all channels of communication still nonfunctional, he prepared a brief message to his superior:

Since the wireless and telephone are not working, I have sent you a personal messenger. The telegram and hotline are not working either.

Maliya is in danger because all of the Machhu-II's gates are completely open, and the gates cannot be closed under any circumstances, because the dam's water is four inches above the maximum allowable level. . . . Thus, you are asked to send immediate aid for Maliya.

People in Morbi city's low-lying areas have been shifted to schools by bus. All necessary safety measures have been taken.

The subdistrict magistrate entrusted the missive to a subordinate and sent him to Rajkot. Then, turning his attention back toward Morbi's immediate needs, he climbed into a jeep with the mayor and returned to the fray of evacuations. The time was 2:00 p.m.[72]

Twenty minutes later, an official by the name of Bhatt, dispatched from Rajkot earlier in the day by Collector A. R. Banerjee to check on the situation in the Machhu River Valley, arrived in the control room. He learned from the local officers that evacuations were under way in the city's vulnerable areas. Upon placing a call to Maliya, he discovered that the situation to the north was rapidly deteriorating. He instructed Maliya's subdistrict magistrate to take precautionary measures and vowed to mobilize a helicopter and a busload of Home Guards to aid in rescue operations. Unable to connect to Rajkot in order to make the necessary arrangements, he entrusted his message to a railroad worker with instructions to contact the collectorate. Then, the officer set off for Maliya, terminating the district government's only contact with Morbi that day.[73]

As the afternoon wore on, the situation facing Collector A. R. Banerjee grew even more dire. All of Rajkot District's dams were discharging immense streams of water, and the flooding was subsuming large swaths of land. Local politicians, concerned about the rising waters, were calling the collectorate to clamor for adjustments in the outflow. Reports of new problems continued to pour into the control room.[74]

Not long after Banerjee had secured two helicopters to rescue forty villagers marooned on rooftops in the southern portion of the district, the control room received word that the floodwaters had stranded fifty people near another town. The collector spent most of an hour coordinating resources for the new rescue, all the while monitoring the crises springing up throughout his jurisdiction.

At 1:45 p.m., the day's worst piece of news arrived by telephone. Of the two helicopters dispatched to rescue the forty stranded villagers, one had been grounded by mechanical problems, and the other had been unable to land due to the driving rain. Floodwaters continued to rise, and the villagers now faced imminent danger. Banerjee began frantically calling military bases all over Saurashtra in search of boats to send to the scene.

Before the collector had made much progress, however, yet another issue presented itself. Agriculture Minister Keshubhai Patel, who had been resting at his lavish guesthouse quarters, returned to the control room with Saurashtra's most senior Irrigation Department engineer in tow. He seemed agitated. He explained that, after hearing the superintending engineer's report of continued flooding on the Machhu River, he would need to drive there to survey the situation himself.[75]

Pushed to the edge of his patience, Banerjee gently attempted to dissuade the powerful politician. He would later explain:

> Since security and safety of a cabinet minister in the district is the collector's responsibility, Mr. Patel was told that since the roads were flooded and everybody else was busy dealing with the floodlike situation in many places, it was not advisable from his safety point of view to proceed. . . .[76]

But Keshubhai would not relent. Banerjee later recounted, "Keshubhai assured [me] that he had proper means of vehicle and staff with him, hence there was no problem of safety, and he even insisted that he would be OK given a high altitude vehicle. And he ultimately proceeded."[77]

Determined to investigate the situation near the Machhu Dam-I for himself, the agriculture minister set off toward the north. He dragged along the superintending engineer; though loathe to leave his Rajkot post, from which he could monitor all of the Saurashtra Peninsula's dams, the Irrigation Department man could not disobey the commands of his ultimate political boss.[78]

Upon Keshubhai's departure from the collectorate, Banerjee threw himself back into the management of Rajkot District's ballooning emergencies. Over the subsequent hours, the situation on the district's southern periphery continued to deteriorate. With immediate intervention growing more imperative by the moment, Banerjee eventually resolved to set out for the endangered area himself. Shortly before 6:00 p.m., as he prepared to depart the collectorate, a messenger arrived bearing a comforting dispatch from Morbi's subdistrict magistrate; although floodwaters had wreaked havoc in the area, evacuations were under way. Banerjee would later write, "Since this message indicated that all necessary precautions have been taken at Morbi, to that extent, my worries about Morbi were lessened."[79]

Confident that his subordinates in the Machhu River Valley were undertaking all necessary safety measures, Banerjee grabbed his raincoat and set off toward the south.[80]

〰〰〰

At 2:30 p.m., the Machhu River rushed under the massive arches of the Buffalo Bridge, carrying driftwood and sundry debris from upstream toward the Gulf of Kutch. Scattered along the length of the bridge, curious citizens, their trousers rolled up to the knees, peered and pointed at the violent flow. Near the center of the brick structure, rainwater poured down the backs of the two bronze bulls, which stood impassive against a dark gray backdrop.[81]

Just to the north, the crematorium grounds remained a pool of tent tops and muddy waters. Huddled indoors, the carnival operators, congregated from far and wide, waited for the clearing that would allow them to finally prepare for Smallpox Seventh.

Across the river, arts college principal T. R. Shukla's family turned in for a nap. After a tense morning standoff, the cobra occupying the maid's quarter had vanished shortly after noon. By then, the Shuklas' chance to watch a matinee film showing had slipped away; with the rain showing no signs of relenting, they had decided to spend a quiet day indoors. A hearty lunch and an indolent card game behind them, they were now settling down for a late afternoon rest.[82]

Immediately below the dam's western earthwork, farmer-industrialist Bhagvanji Patel and his fellow villagers marched in the direction of Lakhdhirnagar. Feet sinking into the pastelike mud with every step, the column of refugees from Lilapar trudged toward safe ground.[83]

Back at the Police Line in Morbi, Gangaram Tapu and his fellow prisoners stood idly about the subdistrict prison grounds, freed from their entrapping cells but beset by the rain. Next door, the flood control room continued its hectic activity. To the west, in the low-lying neighborhoods of southern Morbi, vehicles and volunteers struggled to evacuate vulnerable residents to safe ground.[84]

Thousands crowded into the designated evacuation sites in northern Morbi, sharing their Dipping Fourth and Ramadan holy days with neighbors and strangers. Having recovered his neighbor's food jars from one of the evacuation sites, Ghost Paan proprietor Pratapbhai Adroja set off for his house in the Mahendra Quarter.[85]

All across the city, men who had worked through the rainy day grew hungry. In the Mahendra Quarter, machinery merchant Dhirubhai Mehta closed up his shop and returned home to sup and play with his son. Member of the legislative assembly Gokaldas Parmar, tired after an afternoon of touring with Public Works Department engineers on a rain-soaked jeep, found his way back to Shakti Plot, where his wife, daughters, and grandchildren awaited. Mayor Ratilal Desai ordered his jeep to park in front of his home in the main market area, and he and the subdistrict magistrate ducked in to eat a late lunch. In high-lying neighborhoods like Mehta's, Parmar's, and Desai's, Morbi's middle class passed a quiet monsoon afternoon in mundane inactivity.[86]

Far to the north, the Miyanas of Maliya coped as best they could with the pouring rain and the raging streets. At various evacuation sites, ranging from the local schools to the decrepit royal palace, sullen townspeople sought safety from the pools rapidly submerging the town's lowest-lying areas. Standing on terraces and school roofs, they gaped at an expansive gray sky that seemed bent on shedding every last drop of water over the Machhu River Valley.[87]

Chapter 4

"Something out of the Ordinary"

Around 5:30 p.m. on August 11, 1979, Agriculture Minister Keshubhai Patel's elevated vehicle slowed to a halt in the small town of Sanala, a few miles southwest of downtown Morbi.[1] The minister had departed from the Rajkot collectorate several hours earlier, intent on surveying the outflow from the Machhu Dam-I near Wankaner himself; for good measure, he had insisted that the superintending engineer in Rajkot accompany him on the quest. Together, the government men had endured miles of slow progress along the Saurashtra Peninsula's flooded highways. Despite their vehicle's high clearance, swelling waters had blocked the direct route from Rajkot to Wankaner, forcing a circuitous detour to the north.

Now, Keshubhai and the superintending engineer found their progress halted again just outside of Morbi. A snarl of traffic—elaborately painted trucks, puttering auto-rickshaws, and open oxcarts—clogged the highway. Ignoring the downpour, the men jumped out of the car to investigate the standstill.

They almost immediately encountered one of the superintending engineer's subordinates, the regional executive engineer.

The latter had set out for Morbi earlier in the day upon hearing that the Machhu Dam-II was out of telephone and wireless telegraph contact. As he explained to the new arrivals, he had not been able to reach the dam. Gesturing toward the stationary queue of vehicles, he informed the men from Rajkot that he had been stuck in Sanala for three hours.

Shielding his eyes from the rain, the superintending engineer peered in surprise at the sight before him: a short distance ahead, the road disappeared into a lake that stretched as far as the eye could see. Suddenly curious, he waded into the water, testing its depth. Keshubhai and the executive engineer looked on as tiny waves lapped first at his ankles, then at his knees, then at his waist. The intrepid engineer turned around, shaking his head. Given Sanala's relatively high elevation and the topology of the surrounding land, no amount of rain could have flooded the area so completely. The provenance of the impeding water puzzled the men.

Hoping that the flooding would subside, Keshubhai and the engineers settled in for what proved to be a long wait. The choppy waters remained high. The sky, unleashing still more rain upon the queue of traffic, slowly dimmed.

By 7:00 p.m., Keshubhai had grown impatient. Departing for Rajkot, he left his two companions at Sanala.

Over the coming weeks, years, and decades, the rationale for this arrangement would remain unclear. With the monsoon rains causing serious problems at dams throughout Saurashtra—and with mysterious floodwaters covering Morbi's periphery—the agriculture minister returned to the comfort of the Rajkot guesthouse, leaving two of the peninsula's senior-most dam engineers idling in a small village, cut off from contact with the outside world. The minister would later claim that he had "dispatched" the engineers to investigate the troublesome situation.[2]

The two men would remain in Sanala until well after midnight. The superintending engineer would later write:

We decided . . . to wait to see if the water decreased. Around 10:00 p.m., as the water had decreased a bit, we attempted to enter the city of Morbi, but it was still impossible. A little bit later in the night, we tried again to enter the city, but we made no headway. After that, the executive engineer was able to go a bit further. But with the rain and the darkness, it was not possible to advance. Considering it necessary to inform the collector, we returned to Rajkot some time between 3:30 and 4:00 a.m.[3]

A heavy rain was still falling when a young villager began traversing the open fields west of Madhapar.[4] In light of the foul weather and the upcoming holidays, he wanted to set affairs in order at his small factory in Lati Plot.

He had traveled a short distance along the path toward downtown Morbi when he encountered a turbulent creek. Decades later, he would recall:

There was water flowing in the stream—a lot of water, chest-high. So I could not get across. I took a seat, saying, "It will go down in an hour or two."

After a little bit, the water was still rising, and very fast. There was water all over. I said, "This is too much water. Given the amount of rain, this is too much water." I walked there all the time, so I had an idea as to the limit of rainwater; it could only come so far. But the water just kept coming, and the area I was in began to get covered up. So I turned back.

I knew something was going on. Water never reached my village. Even if the river were overflowing, the water would not reach my village—it was at a very high elevation. Morbi could be sunk and water would not reach my village. So when the water reached me on the road, I knew something out of the ordinary was going on. This was no normal flow.

Then I started looking around, and I saw everything getting dragged by. Big trees, entire roofs, huge stones that must have been parts of structures—all these things were being carried past me by the current.

I had to take a roundabout way back to my village. I had already crossed another stream [on the journey toward Morbi], but on the way back, it was flooded, so I had to go around. When I arrived back at the village, water was slowly entering. It was carrying with it all kinds of household goods. Between our village and Morbi, it was one big sea.[5]

≋≋≋

On the Machhu River's sleepy eastern bank, a cry from the maid-servant roused Principal T. R. Shukla's family.[6]

"Look at how much water there is!"

Having missed the noon matinee film downtown after bat-tling against the entrenched cobra, the Shuklas had been enjoying an afternoon nap; now, they rubbed their eyes and turned over on their mattresses as the girl shouted.

"Look at how much water there is!"

Still drowsy, Principal Shukla's wife admonished, "Well, then turn the faucet off. Can you not see that everyone is sleeping?"

"No, no, not that water! Get up and look outside!"[7]

Deep water covered the cricket field behind the family's bun-galow. The field often flooded during the monsoon, but the Shuklas had never seen so much water there. The open expanse had become a shallow, muddy pond.

The view through the front window elicited even greater sur-prise. Decades later, Mrs. Shukla's eyes would still widen in awe as she recounted the eerie sight: "Railroad cars were being thrown around like toy carts by the water."[8]

Heavy steel boxcars normally sat lazily in the repair yard across from the Shuklas' house. Now, those boxcars, each weighing several tons, were being lifted up and rocked from side to side by a raging current. It suddenly appeared that the flooding might soon reach the house, as it had never before done. The sit-uation mystified the family.

As the Shuklas grappled with the strange sights surrounding them on all sides, loud knocks sounded at the back door. A group of concerned students from the neighboring Lakhdhirji Engineering College stood outside.

"Sir, you do not even have an upper floor, and you are still here? Please, you must leave the house right now!"[9]

Concerned for the safety of the principal and his family, the students insisted on escorting them to a nearby multistory dormitory. The principal's wife hurriedly snatched her jewelry box, which contained the family's most valuable possessions, and the Shuklas, their four children, the maid, and her two brothers prepared to leave.

As they attempted to leave the house, they discovered that the flooding had completely blocked the front walkway. Water had besieged the bungalow on three sides. In a matter of moments, the house would become an island.

Racing to the back door, the refugees and their escorts ran out into the pouring rain. Gathering up their pants, saris, and skirts, they sloshed up the gentle slope toward the towering dormitory. Once there, they settled down in one of the rooms to wait.

Well upstream along the swollen Machhu River, Deputy Engineer A. C. Mehta sat inside a truck that had not moved for hours.[10] One of the Machhu River's minor tributaries was submerging a bridge on the path from Morbi to Wankaner. For the better part of the afternoon, the man in charge of both Machhu dams had waited with his driver in the same place.

Earlier in the day, broken lines, faulty transmitters, and signal-scrambling weather had stifled Mehta's numerous attempts to reach Rajkot by telephone and wireless telegraph from Morbi. In the late morning, the staff driver—fresh from ferrying the young men of Jodhpar to the Machhu Dam-II so that they might try to crank open the jammed gates—had arrived in

Morbi to retrieve the engineer. On attempting to return to the dam, the pair had found the return trip blocked by rushing rapids deep enough to flood their truck's engine. Deciding to seek a working telephone in Wankaner, they had begun a journey that remained suspended at the flooded bridge.

Sitting inside the parked truck, Mehta felt frustrated with the futility of his day's work. Nearly nine hours after leaving the Machhu Dam-II, the deputy engineer had not successfully made contact with his superiors in Rajkot. Nor had he been able to contact the crew on the dam for an update on the situation there. Until the bridge became passable again, he could do little but wait.

Around 4:30 p.m., the waters finally began to recede. The driver coaxed his truck across the still-waterlogged bridge, accelerating confidently when he reached safety on the other side. A short time later, the truck rolled into Wankaner. There, to Mehta's relief, he was able to place a telephone call to Rajkot, informing the staff at the Irrigation Department office of the hours-old situation at the Machhu Dam-II.

After a short respite, Mehta and his driver set off once again for the dam. The truck slipped its way slowly down the road's deep, muddy ruts, but the crossings, despite the still-pouring rain, proved passable. At 9:30 p.m., the two men finally arrived at the tip of the dam's eastern embankment. Though still half a mile from the Machhu Dam-II's concrete spillway, they stood on the reservoir's edge.

Peering westward through the downpour, Mehta squinted, unable to believe his eyes. He beheld a vast, empty plain of mud. The reservoir had completely drained. Gazing through the darkness, the deputy engineer could just make out a void where the western earthwork should have been. The dam's earthworks had washed away.

Decades later, citizens of Jodhpar would recount the engineer's reaction with contempt in their voices: "Mehta came after the dam broke. He staggered up . . . and fainted. . . . He saw it, and he got dizzy, and he fainted."[11]

Chapter 5

"Not a Single Brick
Will Survive"

At 1:00 p.m. on the afternoon of August 11, 1979, seven men remained on the Machhu Dam-II.[1] A. C. Mehta, the deputy engineer responsible for the dam, had left in the morning to contact his superiors in Rajkot. The young men of Jodhpar had hurried away after their unsuccessful attempt to open the three jammed gates. Now, mechanic Lakshmanbhai Mohan and the six other crew members stood on the concrete spillway, impotent in the face of the still-climbing reservoir.

The water level had risen nearly seven feet since 9:00 a.m. It now stood at twenty-nine feet—high enough to lap at the crests of the dam's earthen embankments. Large waves had been slamming against the top of the concrete spillway for hours, but now they began to crash over the earthworks as well. Failure by overtopping seemed inevitable. One of the laborers on the dam later recalled with a rueful laugh, "We knew that the dam was going to fail. We knew around noon or 1:00. The water was simply not controllable. There was just too much water. . . . But the wireless telegraph—everything was dead."[2]

By the time the men atop the Machhu Dam-II knew overtopping was certain, the opportunity to notify Morbi and other downstream communities of the impending failure had slipped away. As the laborer had stated, the dam's telephone and wireless telegraph units had failed. The young men from Jodhpar had left the dam in the morning without instructions to issue a warning. A warning had somehow reached the villagers of Lilapar, but most residents of the downstream area would face an entirely unanticipated catastrophe.

At 1:30 p.m., Mohan and the other crew members, fearing the imminent collapse of the earthworks, decided to attempt an escape to Jodhpar along the dam's eastern embankment. The mechanic would later write:

> We attempted to leave the dam and reach safe ground, but water flowing over the earthen dam had made it soft, and our feet began to sink in as we walked on it. Walking along in this way, we might get stuck in the middle, with no way to reach safety on either side. Since nothing would happen to the concrete dam, and the rain and flooding were continuing, we went back to the concrete dam.[3]

The men turned back toward the concrete spillway after walking just a few hundred feet along the earthwork; the entire surface had become, in the words of one crew member, "soft and slushy."[4]

Seeking to save themselves, the seven men crowded into the tiny control room on the spillway's eastern end. From there, they would witness one of the greatest failures in the history of dam engineering. In his official account of the incident, the supervisor explained:

> Around 2:00, 1.5 to 2 feet of water began to overtop the dam. At 2:15 in the p.m., the left earthwork began to wash away, and water began to enter the downstream portion of the river from the side. Thereafter, we noticed more water coming from the right earthwork, and it seemed like there was a breach in the

right earthwork; more water began flowing into the river from that side. After that, the earth under the generator on the . . . concrete dam's right edge washed away, and the generator room, with generator, came crashing down. From there, the water went flowing downstream.[5]

Decades later, mechanic Mohan would provide a more impressionistic description of the event:

First the Lakhdhirnagar side broke. Then the Jodhpar side broke. It broke slowly. Little zigzags of water. A little bit of water would run over here, and a little bit of water over there. It made little cuts in the dam. We did not even realize that the Jodhpar side was breaking; we were fixated on the other side. We were looking one way, and of course it was washing away on the other. The whole thing just got washed away.[6]

The overtopping reservoir cut and then deepened channels in the massive earthen walls. Progressively larger torrents rushed through. Gradually, portions of the embankments disintegrated and slid into the current. There was never a sudden break—only steady and irreversible erosion. Within a short time, each earthwork had sustained breaches totaling more than two thousand feet in length.[7]

Mohan and the other crew members sat, transfixed by the site of the raging reservoir flowing past. One of the men would later write, "The river's current had split into two parts. We were stuck on the concrete dam. And the river flowed on both sides of us, so we had nowhere to go."[8] Mohan would attest, "In this frightened condition, we sat in the cabin, at God's mercy."[9]

For several hours, a vast, raging river surrounded the spillway. The Machhu Dam-II's entire reservoir emptied swiftly around the tiny control room and hurtled downstream, toward Morbi.

In Jodhpar, the small agricultural community on the dam's eastern flank, the citizenry had congregated at the temple.[10] The roof of the temple, as the highest point in the village, offered a clear view of the Machhu Dam-II. By 1:00 p.m., when the village's young men returned from their attempt to crank open the jammed gates, the dam appeared to be in serious danger.

One of the youths would later recall:

> After getting back from the dam, we ate, and then we all went up to the temple. There was constant rain in the village, and we went to the temple because it was relatively sheltered. . . . We saw water shooting over the dam. It sounded like a bomb blast. Around the same time, the pole holding up the flag on the temple dome snapped. Right around 2:30. There was a big noise. And everyone thought, "That is it—the dam is finished."[11]

Little streamlets started trickling down the face of the western earthwork. The massive wall began to erode. Washing over the top of the embankment, the reservoir's water grew heavy with red soil. By the time floodwaters started rushing forth from the eastern earthwork a few minutes later, a steady torrent was pouring out of the western wall.

Witnessing the mounting destruction, the villagers began invoking the wrath of God. Many gave copious thanks for having been saved. Others, watching the waters wash away the crops, trees, and soil of Jodhpar's low-lying farms and orchards, turned their minds to more practical matters; the president of the village council at the time would recall thinking, "Our land—our bread—is gone."[12]

The enormous outpouring of water left an indelible impression on the mind of one of the young men who had visited the dam earlier in the day. Years later, he would recount:

> There were trees nearby—orchards. There was water passing over those trees. The trees must have been at least thirty feet tall. We could not even see those trees. We all thought, "With water this big, how can Morbi possibly survive?"

The river was full. So the extra water had to go somewhere. When the dam broke, the water went straight toward Lilapar. Water flows along a slope, right? The land is slanted away from our village. So all of the water went straight for Lilapar.[13]

※※※※

At approximately 2:30 p.m., Sri Lilapar Potteries proprietor Bhagvanji Patel stood across the raging Machhu River from Jodhpar.[14] From the high ground of Lakhdhirnagar, the village at the end of the Machhu Dam-II's western earthwork, he and his fellow villagers could see down into the reservoir. The turbulent waters had begun to lap at the top of its embankments.

Earlier in the day, almost everyone had left Lilapar. Only a few dozen citizens—elders too feeble to walk, brash young men willing to disregard the warnings, and sundry others—had remained behind. Like Bhagvanji, most had trekked through the driving rain toward the safety of Lakhdhirnagar, arriving in the early afternoon.

Shortly after 2:00 p.m., the last refugees were still walking along the tail end of the western embankment. They formed a scraggly column that stretched from Lakhdhirnagar along the earthen wall. Twenty Harijans—the last villagers to leave Lilapar —brought up the rear.

The Harijans were nearing the western end of the earthwork when the section near the concrete spillway finally gave way. They turned and watched in awe. A few thousand feet away from where they stood, the reservoir rapidly ate through the embankment. Gathering soil from the earthen flank, the water began an unstoppable roll toward their homes.

In a flash, the floodwaters had traversed the open half mile between the reservoir and Lilapar. As water started entering the village, the fifty or so citizens who had remained behind flew into a panic. Leaving their homes and cattle sheds, they clambered onto the roofs of the community's tallest buildings—the school, the temples, and the homes of the most affluent citizens.

The sheer quantity of water exceeded what anyone had expected. It arrived in three waves, each higher than the one previous. The first wave, three to four feet in height, covered the entire village in a layer of water. The roads disappeared, and the frightened citizens stared down at the turbulent, muddy waters from the precarious safety of their roofs.

Almost immediately thereafter, a fifteen-foot wave swept over Lilapar, nipping at the heels of the stranded villagers. On lower-lying roofs, people felt the current jerk them about. The wave snatched up cows and buffalo and dragged them to the north. Earthen buildings began to disintegrate.

Then, the third wave came. Although its exact height remains unclear, witnesses generally estimated it to be about twenty feet. The water submerged all of Lilapar. The roofs of the tallest buildings in the village—normally two floors above street level— became islands that poked up out of a vast lake. Many houses, including a few on which villagers had taken refuge, collapsed and drifted away. The villagers remaining in Lilapar tightened their grips on the beams and tiles of intact roofs as the current pulled at their ankles, waists, and necks. For the next several hours, a steady flow, nine feet in height, would wash over the streets of Lilapar.

Near the tail end of the western embankment, the Harijan men and women looked on in horror as floodwaters engulfed their village. Overcome by shock, most simply slumped and cried.

A short distance ahead along the evacuation route, Bhagvanji Patel stood on the high ground of Lakdhirnagar and watched, awestruck. From his high vantage point, he saw the failure of the western flank, the failure of the eastern flank, and the destruction of Lilapar. He continued to stare as the water surged northward, soon to engulf his factory and wreak havoc on Morbi. He would later recall, "The whole town was together. And we all thought, 'Our town is gone, destroyed, leveled to the ground. Cattle, possessions, everything—gone. Not a single brick will survive.'"[15]

〰〰〰

From Lilapar, the wall of water rushed north toward the outskirts of Morbi.[16] In the agricultural community of Vajepar, flooding due to the heavy rains and the overflow from the Machhu River had already filled the streets with water. Some of the area's Satwara farmers had evacuated their families to designated sites in northern Morbi, but most had decided to remain in Vajepar for the Dipping Fourth holiday. If the flooding increased further, they had reasoned, they could climb up to a second floor or evacuate to the temple, the highest point in the neighborhood. One Satwara man would later recall:

> When we had another disastrous flood in 1959, the water only came up to the first step of the temple. So everyone thought that the water would come up to there, no higher. . . . That was our mistake: "It came up this high in 1959, so it cannot come up higher." That was our mistake.[17]

When the Machhu Dam-II's water arrived in Vajepar, it left little refuge, even in the confines of the temple. The wave was massive, covering the two-story buildings in the neighborhood's center. People ran for their lives, but the current swept many away. A cacophony of shrieks filled the rainy air as relatives called in vain to one another.

One laborer watched his father die while narrowly escaping with his own family. He recounted:

> When the water started rising, the three children, my wife, and I went into the street across from us. There was a building with a terrace there. . . .
>
> My mother and father went toward the roof of a nearby building. My father stopped to help some small children climb up; then the water came, and he was dragged away. . . . The water came, and he got sucked into it. His dead body was left behind around here. . . .

> We went into the street across from us and climbed onto a terrace. Still, the water came up to our noses! My ten-year-old daughter was pulled away by the water. My older son grabbed her and pulled her back up. As we climbed up, the water was right behind us.[18]

Vajepar's desperate residents did whatever they could to survive in "the time of Shiva," as many survivors would later call it. One woman, paralyzed from the waist down since birth, clung to a large wash bin and rode the rising tide. Eventually, she managed to grab a rooftop and hoist herself to safety.[19]

Many ran to the temple, but the community's supposed ultimate sanctuary soon became a death trap. The refugees huddled inside the building could access its roof only by way of a fragile ladder; as a stampede of panicked people attempted to climb up, the ladder broke, and a mass of humanity became trapped. One survivor, only eleven years old at the time, would remember:

> There were seven of us. With the dam's break, the water started rising. We all climbed up onto the roof, except for my father and my younger brother. The two of them were left behind. . . . In a flash, there was water everywhere. We were up on the roof, and the water was everywhere. We knew right away that my father and brother were gone.

The boy's mother began sobbing uncontrollably. The five surviving family members stood in shock with dozens of others lucky enough to have climbed the ladder before it broke. A sealike expanse had surrounded the temple, rendering its roof a small island of marooned survivors.[20]

Inside the temple, more than one hundred people flailed against a suffocating inflow. The congregation's spiritual leader, a woman named Hemiben Devda, would later recount:

> When the water came, there were lots of people in the temple. So I grabbed onto my mother's hand and moved toward the

altar. I got my hand on the altar, but my mother slipped away. My mother was left behind. The force of the water carried me up onto the shrine. There was nothing to hold onto up there— I was just stuck. . . .

Everyone else was swallowed by the water. Down there, people were flailing around. And from above, I was screaming—"Someone save me! Someone save me!" . . . Up on top of the shrine, I was covered in water up to my neck. . . . Only God knows how I was saved.

The fast-rising waters pressed Devda against the ceiling, leaving just enough space for her to breathe. Surrounded by more than one hundred corpses, the sole survivor inside the Vajepar temple would remain trapped above the altar for several hours.[21]

⚇⚇⚇

By 3:00 p.m. on the afternoon of August 11, most residents of the Harijan Quarter and the surrounding poor neighborhoods had evacuated to designated sites on the high ground of northern Morbi and the Police Line. With the heavy rain–induced flooding, the denizens of the city's lowest-lying region could ill afford to remain at home. Nonetheless, some intrepid souls, like the members of the Valera clan, had decided to evacuate to houses on the higher-lying periphery of the area, where they would fight for their lives against the wave of water.

One young mother stood with her son and mother-in-law at a tall bungalow in the Harijan Quarter, having linked arms and waded through waist-deep water earlier in the day to reach safety. Now, as the reservoir's water filled the neighborhood, she and the women around her scrambled to reach safety. She would later remember:

Once there was a fair amount of water, we took our children and climbed up into the big bungalow. We went to the second floor. The water rose to the second floor, so we went to the third

floor. The water rose to the third floor, so we went to the roof.
We climbed onto a cabin on the roof, and even there, the water
was up to our chests.

The woman, her mother-in-law, and her son clutched one
another tightly as the water raced over them.[22]

Elsewhere, Khatijaben Valera was sitting on the first floor of
a relative's house, where she had sought refuge earlier in the day
along with her brother, mother, sister-in-law, mother-in-law, and
children. The wave took her by surprise. She recounted:

> My brother and my mother were with me. They went out to
> take a look. They came running back. We said, "What is it?
> What is it?" And they said, "There is a huge wave!" It was a
> wave. It looked like a mountain running toward us. They said,
> "The water is coming! The water is coming!" They ran to us
> and told us to climb up further. So we all scrambled to a room
> that was higher up. Once we climbed up, we saw the water
> flowing by.
>   My brother's daughter was left behind. She was left behind!
> In a short time, my brother realized that his daughter was still
> stuck downstairs. He ran down, quickly picked her up, and got
> out. He ran back up.

While Khatijaben's brother rescued his daughter, Khatijaben
focused her attention on her husband and the other men of the
family. A short time earlier, they had decided to return to the clan
bungalow in order to protect their belongings from looters and
rising waters. Now, even with the raging floodwaters forcing
them to reconsider their plans, Khatijaben's husband and a few
others were attempting to tie down the family rickshaw. As the
water level rose, the women's anxiety surged. The Valera family's
strict code of etiquette forbade women from speaking their husband's names, but Khatijaben's concern soon overwhelmed her
restraint.

"Bashir, the water is coming! Bashir, get up here!"

Khatijaben's exclamation—desperate, shrill, and entirely improper—achieved its intended effect. She would remember:

> Then they all came running up. The rickshaw got carried away. We watched from up on the roof. People, trucks, they were all getting swept away. The trucks, cars, rickshaws—all these big things were carried away. Then the animals got lifted up. There were buffalo, other animals, floating by us. I just kept staring.

As the Valeras stood atop the third floor of the house, they could reach down with their hands and touch the swift-flowing water.

As the floodwaters continued to creep upward, the family began anxiously eyeing ways to climb even higher. Khatijaben explained:

> There was no ladder placed where we would have to climb up if the water rose further. But the water carried the neighbor's ladder toward us. It floated up to us, on its own. We grabbed it, and we set it up so that we could climb even farther up.
>
> I made my two daughters climb up. Then I made my sons climb up. . . . But one child slipped, through the ladder. How would I hold him? He slipped out of my hands! . . . I screamed, "My son is still down there!" So one of the men went down, grabbed the boy, and lifted him back up. My father-in-law took him, wrapped him in a blanket, and put him in my lap.

Finally safe on the highest part of the house to which they had evacuated, Khatijaben and the other members of the Valera clan huddled together for warmth as the rain poured down and the floodwater poured past.[23]

Within minutes of engulfing Vajepar, the Harijan Quarter, and the surrounding neighborhoods of southern Morbi, the floodwater began to inundate murderer Gangaram Tapu's neighborhood of Kabir Hill.[24] Despite the day's warnings and evacuations, the area remained woefully unprepared for the wave that struck. Heavy jewelry, donned for the Shravan holidays, weighed many women down as they attempted to escape the current. Water filled the upper stories of buildings, where residents had placed goods and animals to keep them safe from the water.

Only one foot of Tapu's house stuck out above the water. Sitting atop the building, his father, his brother, and his nephew survived by holding onto the central roof beam while the flow buffeted them. Tapu's other brother and nephew lived through the flood only by grabbing the highest limbs of a neem tree and holding on for their lives.

A short distance to the east, Tapu and his fellow prisoners stood together in the subdistrict prison's fenced-in exercise yard, watching as panic-stricken guards and police officers dashed past through the sheets of rain. The wives and children of law enforcement personnel, lodged at the nearby Police Line barracks, ran out into a maelstrom of confusion. Some officers popped up on the flat roof of the police station next to the prison; they began screaming and gesturing for their families to join them on the perch. Most of the shouts proved incomprehensible to the prisoners, but one of the men made out something about a large incoming wave.

Tapu and his companions exchanged wide-eyed glances as everyone outside the prison fence disappeared into the police station and emerged on the roof. Locked in the exercise yard, they lacked a set of stairs or a ladder that might provide a path to higher ground. They would have to improvise a way to safety.

With the help of his fellow inmates, one man took hold of a second-story window and, after some scrambling, managed to haul himself onto the prison's roof. He quickly reached down, pulling one man after another to safety. Gangaram Tapu, among the strongest of the prisoners, remained on the ground, providing boosts to the inmates as they climbed.

The witnesses atop the police station would describe one large wave, twenty to thirty feet in height. It uprooted large trees and carried them forward as it rolled along. It swept people off the roofs of smaller buildings on the Police Line. Even those who had taken refuge on taller buildings, such as the police station, stood mere inches above the rushing water.

By the time the water arrived, nearly all the prisoners had reached safety. Tapu grunted as he lifted the last man toward the waiting arms of his companions.

Suddenly, Tapu's world filled with water. The wave upturned and then righted him, pushing him forward with terrible velocity. He tried to gasp, but he could only choke on the muddy slurry. His vision blurred as a tree trunk, riding on the current's crest, thwacked his head. The men on the prison roof looked on helplessly as their friend and comrade was thrown over the exercise yard fence and swept away.

≋≋≋

Like the Harijan Quarter, the Tiger Quarter had largely emptied before the wall of water arrived shortly after 3:00 p.m.[25] Nonetheless, many residents, such as Gokaldas Parmar's sons-in-law and Brahmin Kanubhai Kubavat, had chosen to remain in the neighborhood, confident that flooding from the heavy rains would not touch their higher-lying houses.

The influx of water from the Machhu Dam-II's reservoir shattered every illusion of security. A ridge at the Tiger Quarter's southern edge deflected direct northward flow of the floodwaters, forcing them to either side of the neighborhood. From the east and the west, however, torrents began running into the quarter's relatively low ground. The water rose just slowly enough to allow residents some chance at escape.

While legislator Parmar had evacuated his daughters and grandchildren to his own house in Shakti Plot, his sons-in-law had not wished to leave the Tiger Quarter. As flooding overwhelmed the neighborhood, they leapt from roof to roof, struggling to stay above the roiling waters.

As the floodwaters rushed into Kubavat's street, they shocked the Brahmin out of his complacency. He would remember:

> Until the water came up to our front steps, I thought the flooding would not reach us. Then, suddenly, it was about to come into the house. As it started coming in, I said, "Oh goodness, the water is coming into the house! Let's get out!"
>
> So my wife threw some clothes, money, and jewelry into a bag. And we set out. She had our four-month-old son in one hand and the bag in the other. I took my aged father on my shoulders. And we went out through the door. There was water rushing down toward us. . . . The water was up to our legs when we left. By the time we got to the temple, it was up to our chests.[26]

As the family waded through the Tiger Quarter's main street, Kubavat's panic intensified. He frantically scanned the area for signs of his two older children, who had been playing outside in the stagnant water but a short time earlier. He could not find them. All around, he saw only flailing arms and contorted faces.

Suddenly, sounds of splashing drew Kubavat's attention back to this side. His wife was stumbling forward, nearly lurching into the water. He could not see through the muddy flow, but he guessed from her jerky gait that, deep below, her sari had become caught between her legs. For a moment, she struggled to right herself without releasing the bag in her hand. Then, as she began to lose her balance and her infant son's head dipped toward the water, she gave up. Releasing the bag to free her arm, she quickly disentangled the sari. Within moments, she had regained her balance. She and her husband gave one glance over their shoulders at the muddy red water racing away from them, knowing that it carried with it their life savings.

Then, the Kubavats turned and looked up the main street. A heavy current raged down toward them from the Police Line. Husband and wife tightened their grips on their loved ones, braced themselves, and began wading forward.

≋≋≋

In Shakti Plot, the middle-class neighborhood west of the Tiger Quarter, Parmar sat eating a quiet lunch.[27] As he dined, Morbi's representative in the state legislature listened to the patter of rain and the happy shouts of his playing grandchildren.

Shortly after 3:00 p.m., a sudden exclamation interrupted Parmar's meal.

"There is water entering our house!"

The cries of Parmar's daughters filled the room. Surprised, the legislator stood up and looked out a window into the street to find a sudden current rushing through the neighborhood. Looking to the water's remarkable velocity and unusually dark color, Parmar would maintain time and again afterward, he "knew that the dam had broken."[28]

In a flash, the legislator began herding his family toward the roof. He would explain:

> I dropped everything, closed the doors, and made everyone—my wife, my daughters—climb up onto the roof. The water came, and water on top of that, and water on top of that. . . . You saw just an entire sea.[29]

Even as Parmar and his family climbed, the sea continued to rise. He would later attest:

> The water kept coming, so we climbed onto a neighbor's roof. . . . To this day, I do not understand how I made it to such a height, how my wife made it to such a height—a height that we could not reach again if we had to today. But at that time, we reached it naturally.
>
> The water entered our house at 3:25 p.m. By 5:10 p.m., there were five and a half feet of water above my roof—in Shakti Plot, which is considered a higher area.[30]

Having spent the afternoon coordinating the evacuations of thousands from the city's low-lying neighborhoods, Parmar now stood on his neighbor's roof, a refugee himself.

From his high vantage point, the statesman watched the annihilation of the city that he had called his home since birth. He would later declare in somber tones:

> At that time, I witnessed with my own eyes destruction that you have heard of, read of, but never seen. Tankers and trucks were sweeping past in the water's powerful flow. Huge animals were being pulled around. I witnessed this with my own eyes. And I can tell you that I am here today on a borrowed life.[31]

≋≋≋≋

As the Machhu Dam-II's reservoir spread to the north and west, it brought unprecedented flooding to the high-lying areas of the City of the Peacock Flag.[32] The highest land in the city—that of the eastern main market, near the Royal Court—remained above the surging floodwaters, but the rolling wave submerged the rest of downtown Morbi.

From the Police Line, the water rushed northeastward, inundating the riverside neighborhoods that lay between the prison and the main market. The area's narrow streets became deep canals, filled with fifteen or more feet of water. The wave careened around corners and crashed against buildings, pulling in many hapless victims. The denizens of one street used a bed as a makeshift ladder to scramble up onto the roof of the highest house. They huddled together there, filled with terror. One survivor would later explain:

> We were terrified for our lives. First, there was the turmoil of the raging water. Second, there was such immense wind. Third, we were all on one small terrace. We were, of course, frightened. It was a fear that can never be forgotten, for the rest of my life.[33]

As the citizens watched from their precarious refuge, the Machhu's waters flowed through the neighborhood and hurtled into the riverbed, careening down the bank where King Jiyaji Jadeja had stood nearly two hundred years earlier while a Vaniyan cursed his dynasty and his city with destruction.

To the north of the main market, the wall of water swept over the Mani Mandir compound, burying the delicate riverside garden and hiding the first floor of the red sandstone structure. At the crematorium, the wave uprooted and carried away the tents of peddlers and ride operators who had congregated on the open field for the Smallpox Seventh carnival.

Farther to the west, the waters attacked Gibson Middle School, V. C. High School, and other evacuation sites. Residents of Morbi's low-lying southern neighborhoods, moved to the high ground because of impending flooding, watched in awe as a muddy surge began climbing up the steps of the schools. They raced to the upper floors and roofs of the schools and gaped as the floodwaters rose to nearly ten feet in height. There, on some of the highest ground in the city, they witnessed scenes that would have seemed unimaginable even in their own neighborhoods just that morning. Decades later, many still could barely verbalize the destruction they witnessed. One woman would simply state, "Cattle were dragged by. People were dragged by. Cars and rickshaws were dragged by. Children were dragged by. Everything was dragged by—everything was dragged by."[34]

The Machhu Dam-II's floodwaters arrived in the main market area just as Mayor Ratilal Desai set out from his home with Morbi's subdistrict magistrate to resume evacuating citizens from low-lying areas of the city.[35] He would recount:

> The two of us had gone to eat at my house. We had eaten flatbread and bananas—just a couple of bananas!

Then we set out in the subdistrict magistrate's jeep. We were driving through the street, and a short distance before Nehru Gate, we saw a child being carried toward us on the water. I was sitting on the edge of the jeep, so I got down. I picked up the child. . . . I thought that somebody would come looking for it soon enough. I had no idea what had happened.[36]

Seeing no signs of life in the child, the mayor cradled the boy in his arms and trudged back to his house. There, he left the body in the care of his wife, explaining the circumstances under which he had found it and providing instructions in case a relative should come in search of the lost child.

Desai would later reflect with a dark laugh, "If I had had any sense of what had happened, what would have been the point of carrying one solitary child's corpse to my house? I had no idea. I thought this was one unfortunate child being dragged along. I had no idea!"[37]

Hiking his pants up, the mayor slogged through the water once again to rejoin the subdistrict magistrate and resume the work of evacuations. The two men had traveled only a short distance toward Nehru Gate when the subdistrict magistrate turned to Desai with a look of fear. He somberly declared, "You stopped to pick up this child, but everything is finished here."

Confused, Desai asked, "What is finished?"

"Everything."[38]

As Desai looked toward Nehru Gate, he noticed mud-red water flowing rapidly uphill toward him. He would recall, "The water was suddenly coming with great force. People were running and screaming in panic. Large poles and pillars had fallen over. There were cattle hanging from the power lines."[39]

As Morbi's two highest civic officials looked on helplessly, Shiva's dance of destruction laid waste to the city's main market.

Given its location near Morbi's northwestern limits, the Mahendra Quarter was one of the last neighborhoods in the city to feel the effects of the Machhu Dam-II's collapse.[40] By the time the reservoir's water arrived there, it was no longer moving as a wall, but rather producing a steady, deadly rise of flooding in the streets.

The floodwaters caught Ghost Paan owner Pratapbhai Adroja on his return trip from southern Morbi, where he had gone to retrieve some food containers for a neighboring shop owner who had donated to the evacuation effort. He would recall:

> I saw the water coming fast, and I knew something was wrong, so I ran. The water was so red! And there was so much of it! So I ran. It was rising steadily. I ran home. There was a lot of water by the time I got home. We all climbed onto my neighbor's terrace.[41]

Heeding the calls of relatives and neighbors, Adroja hauled himself onto the roof of the house next to his. It was one of the few flat-topped buildings in the neighborhood, and many had taken refuge there. He later remembered, "There were forty or fifty of us on the terrace. . . . And we spoke of it as the wrath of the Mother Goddess."[42]

Elsewhere in the Mahendra Quarter, the floodwaters surprised Dhirubhai Mehta as he paid a social visit with his son Vimal. The owner of Mehta Machinery would later recount:

> Shortly after lunch, I had taken my son and gone to my next-door neighbor's house. We were talking there. Then the first flow of water came into my street, like a big wave. So I ran home to save my mother, my wife, and my other children.
>
> There were seven people in my family at the time—my wife and I, our three daughters, our one son, and my mother. As soon as the water came, we tried to close ourselves in the house. But the force of the water was so great that the doors would not close. The water kept rising.

All seven of us backed into one room. As the water kept
rising, we climbed onto the pantry we used to store grains. . . .
The water's flow was so great, we kept climbing. . . . I helped
my wife and children climb up. Then the flow of water
increased even further, and they all started clamoring.

Mattresses from another cabinet fell out and started
floating around in the water. I grabbed onto one of them—I was
not on the pantry. The water increased even further, pushing me
up. I grabbed onto a beam between the roofing tiles. The tiles
had become wet. I punched at the roof, and one of the tiles
broke. Then I knocked out a few more tiles, making a hole to
the outside. Pushing through, I was able to pull myself up.

My son was in my arms, and my daughter in my wife's
arms, on top of the cabinet. Well, the girl slipped out, and I
dropped Vimal. Into the water.[43]

As Mehta watched Vimal thrash about, he desperately attempted
to grab the boy by the hair on his head. But the rising flooding
soon pulled him under.

Mehta's wife threw her head under the water in a futile
attempt to find the three-year-old daughter she had dropped. But
the raging flood had picked up too much soil; the mother could
see nothing through the muddy slurry.

Shrieks filled the rapidly filling room. Shock flowed through
both husband and wife, but they could not afford to pause. The
water was still rising.

Mehta quickly turned his attention back toward the family's
escape. He would relate, "We broke the tiles and climbed out. I
went out first, then I lifted my mother and wife out."[44]

Just as Mehta's wife reached safety atop the roof, the pantry
pitched to the side, throwing off the family's two remaining girls.
One managed to take hold of the room's ceiling fan, but the other
plunged into the mud-reddened water that held her siblings.

Desperate to save their remaining children, Mehta and his
wife screamed instructions down. The girl floundering in the
water grabbed onto her sister's ankle. The two children remained

hanging for what seemed like an eternity, their aching muscles tensed, while the flood roiled around them. Eventually, Mehta managed to reach down and lift them out of the wrecked home.

As the waters continued to rise, the wet tile roof—soggy, slanted, and slippery—became a precarious refuge. The family decided to move to a neighboring building. Mehta explained:

> We went to an old building next door. There was a five-foot gap in between. We put a cement slab across the gap, and neighbors pulled us across. The building was unoccupied, but people from the surrounding buildings had taken refuge there. There was a laborer and some other strong men—they helped us across.[45]

The Mehtas struggled over the makeshift bridge and collapsed on the other side.

Exhausted, the head of the household surveyed the destruction of the Mahendra Quarter in disbelief. The incomprehensible flooding had ruined his house, likely destroyed his business, and taken two of his children. In the span of half an hour, his life had imploded.

〰〰〰

By 3:30 p.m., most of downtown Morbi lay under a vast expanse of rushing water.[46] From the terrace of a Lakhdhirji Engineering College dormitory on the Machhu River's eastern bank, arts college principal T. R. Shukla and his children watched as the muddy flow ravaged the city.

The Shuklas had evacuated some minutes earlier to the safety of the multistory dormitory. Now, the floodwaters had surrounded their small bungalow, which they could just barely make out through the pouring rain. On the other side of the river, dozens were drowning in the theater where the Shuklas might have been watching a matinee film, if not for the fearsome cobra in their maid's quarters. The family looked on in disbelief as water, mud, and debris washed over the entire landscape.

On the eastern bank, the raging flood ripped up seven massive tamarind trees—each about two hundred years old—and lodged them behind the arches of the Buffalo Bridge. Soon, large rafts of mud, driftwood, and other debris had accumulated behind the immense brick structure. Flow under the bridge slowed, and the water level upstream started rising precipitously. The Machhu Dam-II's reservoir began to recoalesce behind the Buffalo Bridge, threatening to inundate the higher-lying eastern bank where the Shuklas lived. One witness attested, "The water came with great force. Waves of water were hitting the bridge. . . . It was like a sea. Just like the large waves of the sea, there were tall waves flying over the bridge. There was water rolling over the bridge!"[47]

As the floodwaters refluxed onto the Machhu's banks upstream of the clogged bridge, riverside residents panicked. Decades later, one woman would shudder as she recounted the scene of desperation:

> I saw then that nothing is as dear to oneself as one's own skin. We praise our children, we love them. But in the end, nothing is as dear to oneself as one's own skin, that became clear. Women with children in their arms were trying to scramble up trees. When they could not grip the trees properly, they dropped the children into the water and saved themselves. The children died, but the women lived. In the end, nothing is as dear to oneself as one's own skin.[48]

With the Machhu Dam-II's waters drowning the banks upstream of the bridge, people did whatever they could to survive.

Some time between 4:30 p.m. and 5:30 p.m., the pressure against the colossal arches of the Buffalo Bridge grew too strong. The Shuklas stared in shock as the massive brick wall cracked and washed away near its eastern terminus, just below the bronze bulls' lowered noses. One witness would recall, "The bridge broke on the eastern side. A cloud of dust flew up in the air, and there was a great sound. An explosion—'Boom!' A path had been cleared for the water, and it slowly passed away. And the flooding began to recede."[49]

Torrents of water rushed in front of the impassive bulls, released for a second time from captivity behind a man-made edifice. The water slowly began to drain from Morbi's flooded neighborhoods, but hours more would pass before it had completely left the city's ruined streets.

≋≋≋≋

In the midst of the inundated main market, Mayor Desai was beginning to comprehend the magnitude of the catastrophe that had overcome Morbi.[50] His stomach tightened as he thought of the thousands of citizens that he and other civic officials had evacuated to the Police Line, Gibson Middle School, V. C. High School, and other ostensibly safe locations. If the floodwaters had covered the front steps of buildings in the city's highest area, evacuees at the various sites might be in immense danger.

Taking stock of the situation, Desai and the subdistrict magistrate quickly resolved to visit the Police Line and check on the safety of Morbi's most vulnerable evacuees. They jumped into the subdistrict magistrate's jeep and raced southward, following the most direct route to the Police Line. Before they had advanced more than a few hundred feet, rising floodwaters rendered the narrow, muddy road impassable. Turning around, they sped toward the Royal Court and turned south, intending to reach the Police Line via the high-lying neighborhoods on the Machhu River's western bank. Once again, the water levels proved prohibitively high.

Determined to reach the evacuees at the Police Line, Morbi's leading government officials decided to outflank the deep flooding by crossing the river, traveling south, and then crossing back into the city farther upstream. They maneuvered the jeep in the direction of the Buffalo Bridge. Passing the Mani Mandir, they were struck by the height of the turbulent sludge that had filled its sunken compound. Undulating red floodwaters covered the first story of the Taj Mahal of Saurashtra, eerily blending with its impassive sandstone walls.

The men halted the jeep at the Buffalo Bridge. Violent waves crashed over the structure, sending thick plumes of spray many feet into the air. The road itself had become flooded and littered with large debris. As Desai and the subdistrict magistrate scanned the scene before them, their eyes fell upon the most shocking sight of all: near the river's eastern bank, an entire section of the bridge, dozens of feet long, was simply missing.

Stymied once again, the mayor and the subdistrict magistrate turned to retrace their path. Their location afforded a wide vista on Morbi. The sky had grown darker in the minutes since their emergence from Desai's house. As they peered through the driving rain, it appeared as if a great darkness had covered the city. Desai later remarked, "It looked just like a cloud—as if there were a great cloud descending."[51]

The mayor turned to the subdistrict magistrate and shouted, "Do you think those are clouds?"

Overhearing the public officials' conversation, a passerby slowed from his run. Catching his breath, he exclaimed, "That is no cloud! The dam has broken, and that is the reservoir's water!" Then the man ran off.[52]

Looking back at the horizon, Desai stared in horror as the dark, rolling sheets of water continued to smother his city. Decades later, his disbelief remained raw: "No one imagined that this could happen. You would not have imagined it if you had been there. We all thought this was a flood—a regular flood. But the water just kept rising. No one could have imagined it."[53]

As the two officials drove southward in the jeep, resuming their desperate attempts to reach the Police Line, they encountered fleeing police officers. Barely slowing as he ran past, one shouted, "The entire Police Line is sunk. It is impossible to go there. Everything is finished!"[54]

≈≈≈≈

At the Police Line, murderer Gangaram Tapu thrust his head out of the turbulent current and coughed up water.[55] The flood had snatched him and another prisoner as they attempted to climb onto the roof of the subdistrict prison. The two men had hurtled forward and flipped over, twisted and submerged by the waters.

Yet both had somehow managed to right themselves in the water. They had grabbed hold of the subdistrict police station, held on, and hoisted themselves up. Tapu would later observe, "The wave was fierce. But if you knew how to swim, you could survive."[56]

Unfortunately, few of Morbi's citizens could swim. Standing on the roof of the police station, Tapu and his fellow prisoner saw dozens of people flailing about in the water. The current flung bodies together with brutish force. Children were snatched from mothers. Along the length of the Police Line, men and women coughed haplessly before sinking below the surface.

Almost immediately, the two prisoners knew what they would do. The other man turned to Tapu and somberly declared, "Alright. We may die doing this. But let's do what we can."[57] Both dove into the floodwaters.

They first encountered a frail old woman floundering amid the heavy flow. Working together, they pulled and pushed her toward the safety of the police station. Lifting her up, they gingerly set her out of harm's way on the roof. Then they threw themselves back into the roiling sea.

Tapu noticed a police officer struggling in the water. Separating from his companion, Tapu swam over to the officer and wrapped his arms around the man. But the torrent yanked the police officer out of the killer's slippery hands. Before Tapu could do anything to save the man, he was gone.

Alone now, Tapu persisted. For the next three hours, he swam through Morbi's flooded streets, saving people who were drowning. The rush of water was powerful, but he periodically took hold of buildings to steady himself. Whenever possible, he swam to the helpless and pulled them to the safety of flat roofs. When swimming seemed too dangerous, he took up debris floating in the floodwaters—ropes, cables, planks of wood—and extended it toward the flailing arms of the drowning; his bulging muscles quivered as he pulled multiple people to safety.

Riding the current northward through the city, Tapu rescued people of every caste, creed, and age. Over the course of his journey, he would save nearly seventy individuals.

The last few rescues eluded the prisoner. Near the main market, Tapu grabbed onto another police officer. But the officer's wife struggled in the nearby water; try as she might, she could not reach Tapu. Seeing the current sweep her away, the officer let go of Tapu in order to give pursuit. Both husband and wife would drown.

Tapu's journey ended as it had begun, with an old woman. By the time he reached her, his limbs were stiff and numb from hours of swimming through the cold, muddy slurry. He could feel his strength fading as he took hold of the woman. An eddy ripped her from his arms. He flailed desperately in pursuit, but he could do no more. He watched helplessly as the woman drifted away in the swift current.

Cold and exhausted, Tapu finally hoisted himself onto a neem tree near the main market, ending his daring swim. Slowly, as sensation returned to his feet, he began noticing a sharp pain. Looking down, he saw that one of his feet was covered in congealed blood from a puncture wound.

As Tapu glanced around the large tree, he recognized approximately fifteen people from various walks of life. A doctor and a lawyer sat some distance away. Next to Tapu huddled another one of the police officers he had come to know during his year of incarceration.

Cold and uncomfortable, the murderer and the police officer settled in next to one another. They could do little but wait for the waters to recede.

Once released from behind the Buffalo Bridge, the Machhu Dam-II's reservoir rolled toward the Gulf of Kutch.[58] The land north of Morbi flattened out into a large floodplain, and the wall of water that had struck the city fanned out into a wide, surging front. While the wave became shallower and more diffuse, it retained much of its deadly potency, quickly raising water levels from the streets to the roofs in the already-inundated communities of the Machhu River Valley.

When the wave front finally reached Maliya around 9:00 p.m., the flooding in the town climbed to overwhelming heights in a matter of minutes. Although the area's residents had grown accustomed to severe monsoon floods, the inflow of water on the night of August 11, 1979, exceeded even their worst expectations. Earthen buildings collapsed under the pressure of the current, and many families broke through windows and walls to escape the torrents rushing into their houses.

Forced out of their homes by the precipitously rising floodwaters, Maliya's citizens scrambled to reach safety. Salt industrialist Abdulbhai Mor and many others joined the official evacuees at the town's schools. Others sought refuge at the dilapidated royal palace or with relatives.

Because the wave had diminished in height by the time it reached Maliya, the residents of the town's central hill, like the residents of Morbi's Royal Court area, remained oblivious to the flooding. Safely situated in their high-lying homes, fisherman Husainbhai Manek and others would not come to know of the disaster until the following morning.

By contrast, families living on the farmland surrounding Maliya experienced destruction as savage as any seen in Morbi. The open fields offered few barriers to the flow of water, and the wave visited its full wrath upon the area's isolated houses and inhabitants.

Farmer Jashabhai Samani was sleeping inside his earthen hut

when the flood struck. Without warning, water began to rush in through the front door and seep through cracks in the walls. Samani quickly herded his family outside. He hoisted his wife and mother up into a tree that stood near their house. Then, with the water rising higher, he took his two-year-old daughter in his arms and climbed up himself. His six other children clambered onto the roof of the hut.

From the tree, the farmer watched as the current annihilated his livelihood. The wave ripped millet, corn, and peanut plants from the ground and swept them away. It lifted up oxen like playthings and carried them toward the Gulf of Kutch. The farm's carts, tools, and soil disappeared in the span of a few moments.

Suddenly, Samani heard anguished cries from the direction of his house. Turning to look, he watched in disbelief as the roof of his hut, weakened by the battering water, collapsed. Six children—all of his offspring except for the daughter in his arms—sank into the house and under the floodwaters. The flow dragged away their bodies, along with the mud that remained from what had, moments earlier, been a home.

Carrying the Samani family's corpses on their muddy crest, the floodwaters rolled toward the salt flats of Kutch. Along the way, they dissolved massive mounds of salt from the plants where they awaited processing or packaging; at India Salt Works, 2,500 tons of Abdulbhai Mor's product melted into the wave. Then, as the current approached the seashore, it snatched up the fishing gear, boats, and huts of Husainbhai Manek and Maliya's other fishermen. Carrying Maliya's salt, fishing, and farming within it, the Machhu Dam-II's water finally spilled into the Gulf of Kutch.

≈≈≈≈≈

Darkness descended upon the Machhu River Valley. The rain softened somewhat, but it continued to fall steadily into the evening. From the Machhu Dam-II to Maliya, people settled in to wait out the night.

The men on the dam were trapped. The overtopping waters had washed away the earthen walls leading up to the concrete spillway on both sides. Mechanic Lakshmanbhai Mohan and the other crew members found themselves on an island in the air. They prepared for a cramped and uncomfortable night in the small control room. Severe hunger pangs descended with the darkness. The men sat quietly, struggling to grasp the enormity of the disaster that had surrounded them just hours earlier. Not one could sleep.[59]

West of the dam, Bhagvanji Patel and the other citizens of Lilapar settled in for a sleepless night in the undamaged village of Lakhdhirnagar. All had lost their houses, and some remained uncertain regarding the survival of relatives who had stayed behind. The families of Lakhdhirnagar, who had lost their own homes to the reservoir's waters less than a decade earlier, showed great generosity, feeding the refugees in spite of the village's short supply of food. Bhagvanji would later comment, "We had all become each other's family at that point."[60]

Farther downstream, on Morbi's southern outskirts, survivors slowly stirred in the ruined remnants of the agricultural community of Vajepar. Hemiben Devda, the woman lifted by the floodwaters onto the high altar in the neighborhood's temple, continued gasping for air as the waters gradually subsided. With electrical connections destroyed, full darkness had filled the temple; Devda could not see her hand in front of her face. As dazed survivors began to descend from the temple's roof, she cried out for help. The first few responders to reach the floor shuddered as their feet sank into the softness of mud and bloated bodies. The bravest stepped delicately between the tangled corpses and helped Devda climb down from the high altar. Gagging on the putrid air, Devda and her benefactors emerged from the temple into a chilling rain.[61]

Just north of Vajepar, Khatijaben Valera and her clan found a surprise inside the house whose roof had served as their refuge. She recalled:

When the water went down around 7:00 or 7:30 p.m., we got down. We looked through one of the windows into the house, and we saw mud and water and all kinds of things filling it. There was a child inside there—we found it. And there was a lady nearby. Well, my father-in-law took the blanket, wrapped it around the child, and gave it to the lady, and they went away. The child was still alive.

Then we stayed up the whole night. The children, hungry and tired, fell asleep. But we sat up. There was no way we could sleep. We spent the entire night without sleeping.[62]

To the northwest, nightfall found legislator Gokaldas Parmar and his family still stranded on a neighbor's roof in Shakti Plot. Occasionally, they heard the lowing of a cow that had been deposited by current on a nearby roof. Parmar's daughters wept for their husbands, who had remained behind in the Tiger Quarter during evacuations and had, by now, almost certainly drowned.[63]

Near the main market, Gangaram Tapu and more than a dozen others climbed down from a neem tree around 1:30 a.m. Because he had sustained a severe foot wound while rescuing people from the floodwaters, other survivors carried Tapu to Gibson Middle School, where his wife and children had sought refuge as evacuees.[64]

Just south of the market, in one of Morbi's old riverside neighborhoods, Brahmin Kanubhai Kubavat staggered to the end of his long journey. Along with his wife, his infant son, and his aged father, he had somehow managed to trudge from the Tiger Quarter to his uncle's house. As the Kubavats knocked on the door, they stared in disbelief at the disarray in one of the city's highest-lying areas. Several houses had collapsed completely. Eighty people were descending from one roof, and one hundred fifty from another. As they settled in for the night with Kubavat's uncle's family, they wept for their daughters; after playing in the street all afternoon, the two girls had disappeared with the floodwaters.[65]

Across the Machhu River, arts college principal T. R. Shukla and his family returned home from the Lakhdhirji Engineering College dormitory where they had taken refuge. The floodwaters had not entered their bungalow, but a layer of mud filled the yard. Lighting a few candles, the family prepared a simple dinner, stunned that a cobra, seemingly menacing, had saved them from near-certain destruction on the eve of Cobra Fifth.[66]

Near the Royal Court, Mayor Ratilal Desai and the subdistrict magistrate stood on top of a roof, wet and shivering underneath the rain and darkness. The next day, the subdistrict magistrate would write:

> Our car could not get anywhere, and we climbed up on the patio of Morbi-Maliya Processing near the Royal Court; even there, the water reached six feet. Seeing people's things getting dragged past by the current, unable to get anywhere, we were powerless to move from there. . . . All the roads were closed, and we had no choice but to spend the night on the patio.[67]

Throughout Morbi and the downstream area, thousands of people sat on roofs, huddling against the cold and rain. In the Mahendra Quarter, merchants Pratapbhai Adroja and Dhirubhai Mehta sat on neighbors' terraces, still in shock at the afternoon's events. On the roofs of Gibson Middle School, V. C. High School, various Police Line buildings, and hundreds of houses, survivors settled in to wait for the break of day.[68]

Some time after midnight, one survivor set out from the Royal Court area. Wading through the mud, he navigated toward Morbi's main hospital, near city hall. His mother had undergone minor surgery in the morning; now, as he walked through streets filled with bloating corpses and rotting debris, he breathed sharply, wondering whether he would ever see his parents again. "It was a terrible sight to see," he would later say of the city, "but I had to go to see if my parents were alive."[69]

Reaching the hospital, the man found the rooms in a state of empty chaos. Medical equipment, beds, and debris littered the darkened wards, but not a single human being could be seen. The survivor raced through the entire hospital. He threw open every door, desperately hoping to find his parents.

Breathless, he reached the hospital's storage closet. And there, in a space designed to house a few mattresses and shelves of medical equipment, his parents stood amid a crowd of nearly seventy people. Patients, nurses, and doctors huddled together in terror. A few of the sickest patients lay on soggy mattresses that had begun to reek. The others stood restively, cold and harrowed.

Crying, the man embraced his parents. Then, he settled in for the night with the denizens of the storage closet.

"That night," he would recall years later, "no one had a tongue to speak."[70]

Chapter 6

"Even the Pests Were Dead"

At 3:30 a.m. on August 12, an official car pulled to a halt in front of the stately government compound of the Rajkot collectorate. A lone figure emerged. His gumboots sloshed through the muddy puddles that covered the grounds. The cold rain had long since slipped under his rubber coat, seeping into the light cotton shirt that lay beneath. Exhaustion had set in hours ago.

Collector A. R. Banerjee, the chief administrative officer in Rajkot District, had been awake for more than twenty-four hours dealing with the effects of the flooding ravaging his jurisdiction. Returning from an ongoing attempt to rescue people stranded in one of the district's southern villages, Banerjee felt physically and emotionally exhausted as he entered the control room at the collectorate. To his relief, he found a relative lull in activity. The banks of telephones that had been ringing constantly earlier in the day now sat mostly silent. Disheveled staffers lay asleep with their heads on desks and tables.[1]

Nonetheless, the wireless telegraph operators, whose service constituted a last-ditch means of communication when stormy weather disabled telephones, remained busy. They scribbled and tapped away, sending and receiving messages from all over the district. Banerjee learned that every subdistrict was reporting by either telephone or wireless telegraph, save for Morbi and Maliya. The lapse in communication with the northern Machhu River Valley seemed most likely the result of a technical glitch, and the collector hardly gave it a second thought.[2]

Collapsing into a chair, Banerjee nodded curtly as an aide brought him a steaming cup of sweetened, milky chai. His hand jittered as he raised the cup to his lips. He had barely finished the first sip when a staffer rushed in, bearing a disturbing message from Agriculture Minister Keshubhai Patel.

Against Banerjee's advice, Keshubhai had spent the previous afternoon trying to reach the city of Wankaner, which lay on the Machhu River thirty-three miles upstream of Morbi. To the collector's knowledge, the minister had given up after finding the Rajkot–Wankaner highway blocked. But now, the staffer informed Banerjee that Keshubhai had made a second attempt to reach Wankaner via a different route. The minister had redirected his driver toward Morbi, intending to cross the Machhu River there and then double back to Wankaner along the river's eastern bank.

His heart beating faster, Banerjee learned that Keshubhai had found the road to Morbi impassable at the village of Sanala, on the city's southwestern outskirts. Arriving at the village some time in the early evening, he had encountered water that threatened to submerge his vehicle. He had turned back, completely stymied in his attempts to reach Wankaner.

Returning to the Rajkot control room at approximately 9:00 p.m., Keshubhai had ordered the staffers to establish wireless telegraph contact with Sanala. When this proved impossible, he had instructed a deputy administrator by the name of Pathak to travel to Morbi and investigate the situation there. Then, without raising any further alarm about the potentially disastrous flooding, the agriculture minister had turned in for the night.

As Banerjee processed the unexpected information, Pathak returned to the control room with a troubling report. He had tried to enter Morbi, but large quantities of debris had blocked his path. He had seen collapsed buildings and anticipated that damage to the city might be widespread.

A few moments later, a haggard worker from the bus depot on Morbi's southwestern outskirts staggered into the control room with disturbing confirmation of the apparent disaster. He stated that a remarkable flood had inundated the city. He had personally seen several corpses near the bus stand. Something terrible had occurred.[3]

The reports shocked Banerjee, who would recall, "Morbi was not at all in the priority of my problems." Startled and sleep-deprived, the collector could hardly process the new information. He struggled to devise an initial response to the catastrophe. He would later write:

A few things were clear to us:

1. If we could enter the city we would find many more dead bodies.
2. In order to enter the city obstacles like twisted railway lines, etc. are to be cleared.
3. Water tankers should be arranged.

These three things struck me at that time.

Banerjee arranged for two bulldozers to rush to Morbi and clear the debris blocking the roads into the city. He called for two water tankers and medical supplies, which would provide emergency relief to beleaguered citizens. Anticipating the need for more manpower in Morbi, he also requested the deployment of reserve police units and army troops from elsewhere on the Saurashtra Peninsula.[4]

The collector then set out to inform his superiors about the developing situation. After rousing the agriculture minister from his slumber with a telephone call at around 4:30 a.m., he drafted an urgent telegram message alerting higher government officials, including the chief minister and his staff, to the situation. He wrote:

> *CIRCLE POLICE INSPECTOR, MORBI MR. HARAIYA INFORMS THIS OFFICE AT 4:15 A.M. TODAY THAT THERE IS HEAVY CASUALTIES IN MORBI CITY(.) WATER ENTERED THE CITY AT ABOUT 4:00 P.M. ON 11TH AND RECEDED AT ABOUT 9:20 P.M. (THREE) DEAD BODIES IN NEW S.T. BUS STATION AND 1 (ONE) DEAD BODY ON THE ROAD SIDE IS SEEN(.) ELECTRIC AND TELEPHONE POLES UPTURNED(.) HEAVY MUD ON THE CITY ROADS(.) . . . IMPOSSIBLE TO ENTER CITY(.) AS REPORTED MALIYA MIYANA CONDITION FEARED TILL WORST(.) COLLECTOR WITH ARMY & OTHER EQUIPMENTS RUSHED TO MORBI.*[5]

Thirteen hours after the failure of the Machhu Dam-II, news of the disaster would finally reach the state government in Gandhinagar.

Having made preliminary arrangements for relief, Collector Banerjee set out for Morbi with his senior staffers at around 5:30 a.m. By that time, others were already well on their way.[6]

≋≋≋≋

The earliest outsiders to reach Morbi on August 12 could not pause to process the scenes of death and destruction that greeted them.[7] Rushing to Morbi in the early morning hours, the police officers and Home Guards from Rajkot thought only of imposing order upon a chaotic postdisaster city.

A file of mud-splattered jeeps raced along the highway between Rajkot and Morbi. District Home Guard Commander Ushakant Mankad sat in one of the leading vehicles, peering out at the gray landscape through thick-rimmed black glasses. With pallid skin and a slight paunch, he appeared less obviously impressive than many of his fellow law enforcement officers. But as the inhabitants of Morbi would soon discover, he wielded an iron will.

Rubble and twisted metal littered Mankad's path into the ruined city. Just after 6:00 a.m., his jeep had navigated through as much of the debris as it could. Mankad disembarked and began trudging into the heart of the city on foot. He would later note with pride that he was "the first person to reach Morbi in an official capacity."[8]

Dawn was breaking as the Home Guards and police officers struck out into downtown Morbi, but the rain and clouds cast a pall of darkness over the city's streets. The men hastened toward the Police Line, hoping to regroup the local police force. When they arrived, however, they found only nine officers, all of them clinging to trees and utility poles. Most of Morbi's constables had fled or been swept away. The men from Rajkot would face the task of single-handedly bringing order to the city.

According to numerous survivors, looters had overrun Morbi on that first terrible morning. In most accounts, the thieves were Miyanas and members of other jatis known for their criminal qualities. Wielding large blades, the shadowy figures purportedly severed fingers, ears, hands, and feet from bloating corpses in order to snatch fine ornaments donned for the Shravan holidays. It appears likely that such macabre looting, though certainly present, was not widespread; a few citizens witnessed it firsthand, but most would simply hear of it afterward. More often, thieves broke into ruined shops and houses to steal commercial and household goods.[9]

Regardless of its form, Home Guard Commander Mankad and his fellow law enforcement officers were determined to stamp out every bit of looting. Over the subsequent days, the police and the Home Guards would establish a strict order in Morbi. At one point, the imposing district superintendent of police would allegedly threaten to drag looters to death with his jeep, telling Mayor Ratilal Desai, "I will handle the punishment. You stand back and remain silent."[10]

The iron rule of law enforcement began in the first hours of August 12, before other outsiders had even arrived in Morbi. Mankad later explained:

> When we arrived, at six in the morning, some antisocial people were breaking into stores. I have seen the looting with my own eyes. They would break open stores and pull out whatever they could. It wasn't very successful, because water had gotten into all of the stores and ruined the goods. . . . But still, people tried. So we hammered them. We hammered them like hell.[11]

≈≈≈≈≈

Shortly after the arrival of the police officers and Home Guards in Morbi, a rain-battered convoy stopped on the city's southwestern outskirts. Inside the vehicles, a variety of government officials, from Rajkot District Collector A. R. Banerjee to state Agriculture Minister Keshubhai Patel, prepared to face the devastation wrought by the Machhu Dam-II's waters.[12]

Banerjee later wrote:

> We saw people coming from Morbi junction. We stopped them and asked them about the situation. The situation, as per their report, was indeed grim. I gathered that half portion of the Morbi [sic] was washed out with complete devastation to the city. The magnitude of the situation was becoming very clear as we were approaching the city.[13]

After disembarking, the government officials began the same laborious trek the law enforcement officers had undertaken a short time earlier. They progressed slowly under the morning's first light. Mud, broken glass, twisted railway ties, and shards of Morbi's renowned ceramics littered the highway. Although the storm had calmed from its peak the previous day, the lashing wind and rain continued. Banerjee reported, "The wind was very strong, at least 75 to 80 [kilometers] per hour, and we were not in a position to even open our umbrellas. It was even difficult to walk."[14]

As the collector and his companions struggled through the debris, they began to encounter more haunted survivors. Before long, one Dr. Jeswani, a former mayor of Morbi, staggered toward them. "Water above, earth below," he croaked, fighting back tears. "Until yesterday, we had everything. We lived in happiness. Now we have nothing. Just the water above, the earth below."[15]

Jeswani told of a pitch-black night spent under the violent rain without food or water, and of countless people and animals that had been carried away to the north. The old man's account elicited animated chatter from the small press corps that had accompanied the government convoy. After gathering the basic facts of the disaster, some reporters returned to Rajkot, determined to inform the world of Morbi's obliteration.[16]

Soon, Banerjee had also seen enough. He turned back toward the idling cars, his pace quickened by a profound sense of urgency. He would have to marshal a massive relief operation as rapidly as possible. With the telephone lines dead, he could do little without returning to his office in Rajkot. The collector's vehicle sped off to the south at 10:30 a.m., just as army troops began to clear debris from the roads leading into Morbi.[17]

Banerjee arrived back in Rajkot around noon. He hastily began establishing the lines of communication he would need to coordinate relief operations in Morbi. He spoke with the state government's chief secretary by telephone, securing assurances that massive relief convoys were mobilizing to bring food, water, supplies, and workers to the flood-stricken area.[18]

The collector then turned his mind to the public health crisis that threatened to further ravage Morbi. If not cleared promptly, the decaying corpses littering the city's streets would begin to spread disease among the flood's survivors. After consulting with the district's chief medical officer, Banerjee drafted a telegraph message to the state government:

LARGE SCALE DEAD BODIES ABOUT 1000 (ONE THOUSAND) CORPSES EXPECTED OUT OF SALVAGE OPERATION FROM MORBI CITY ALONE. MOST OF BODIES DECOMPOSED AND UNIDENTIFIABLE. DANGER OF SPREAD OF EPIDEMIC DISEASES IN VIEW OF LARGE NUMBER OF CORPSES INVOLVED. PRAY PERMISSION FOR DISPOSAL CORPSES BY BURNING WITHOUT WAITING FOR FULL PROCEDURE OF IDEN-TIFICATION ETC. WHEREVER IT IS NOT POSSIBLE.[19]

At the time, Banerjee could not have known that his estimate of the death toll—one thousand—would fall far short of the true figure.

≋≋≋

One hundred fifty miles east of Rajkot, in Gandhinagar, Gujarat Chief Minister Babubhai Patel was immersed in a routine morning meeting when an aide entered the room around noon. The man reported that Agriculture Minister Keshubhai Patel, who was visiting Saurashtra to supervise the flood response there, wished to speak with the chief minister by telephone.[20]

At the age of sixty-eight, Babubhai was two years into his second stint as the head of the state government. Like many politicians of his era, he was a product of India's independence movement. Marching with Mahatma Gandhi, he had endured seven separate imprisonments under British rule. He had subsequently risen to prominence as a legislator and civic leader, holding several cabinet-level positions during the 1950s and 1960s and serving as Gujarat's public works minister during the construction of the Machhu Dam-II.

More than three decades after independence, Babubhai still eschewed Western cloth in favor of the homespun cotton fabric that had come to symbolize Indian self-sufficiency. As a politi-cian, he embodied the peculiar alchemy of asceticism and pop-

ulism inculcated into the members of Gandhi's *satyagraha* movement. He enjoyed taking leisurely strolls in the capital to "meet
the people," bringing no security detail in tow. At the same time,
he cultivated a rigorous self-discipline, beginning each day by
practicing yoga and ending each night by making meticulous
notations of the day's events in his diary.[21]

Recounting the events of midday on August 12, Babubhai
would write, "Keshubhai wishes to speak on the telephone. . . .
Conversation by telephone: there has been widespread loss of life
in Morbi. Machhu-II has broken. Nothing is known about
Maliya."[22]

Upon learning of the catastrophe, Babubhai wasted no time.
After alerting the chief secretary—the state's senior-most bureaucrat—to the situation, he rushed to the All-India Radio station,
which provided the surest means of disseminating information
broadly and rapidly across the state. The station director, who
had also come to know about the disaster, received the chief minister in the broadcast booth.[23]

Interrupting regular programming, Babubhai delivered a
hastily prepared address. Somber and straightforward, he
explained that a great flood had struck Morbi. He pledged to
depart for the city and urged the people of Gujarat to offer whatever aid they could. Before signing off, he declared, "This is not
the problem of Morbi, but the problem of Gujarat. We should
help. It is our duty."[24]

Babubhai would spend the remainder of the day in Gandhinagar and Ahmedabad, coordinating the provision of relief to
Morbi and preparing to leave for the city himself the following
morning.[25]

A short distance away from Chief Minister Babubhai Patel's
offices, Agriculture Secretary H. K. Khan—the chief civil servant
in one of Gujarat's most important government departments—

reclined on a couch in his living room.[26] In the eleven days since his rain-battered return from drought relief meetings in the Rajkot collectorate, the government had grappled with constant crisis-level flooding; Khan had remained perpetually busy, buffeted by demands from every corner of the state. But on this quiet, overcast Sunday, he could simply relax. He read the newspaper and enjoyed a leisurely smoke, watching the rain fall outside his windows.

Khan felt startled in the early afternoon when the chief secretary for the government of Gujarat—the state's highest civil servant—arrived at his door. He knew immediately that something was amiss; the chief secretary had never visited unannounced on a Sunday, and his grave expression as he entered the house suggested a grave problem.

Khan's superior briefed him on the limited information available about a disaster that had just taken place in Rajkot District. A dam had burst near Morbi. Many had died. The chief minister was demanding an unprecedented relief effort and requesting that Khan lead it.

The chief secretary explained that, after consultation with Agriculture Minister Keshubhai Patel, Babubhai had decided to designate Khan as the special secretary for relief. Although the Indian Administrative Service man had never even seen Morbi, he readily accepted the assignment.

Khan called for a car to convey him to Saurashtra, but he realized almost immediately that going alone "would have no meaning." He instructed a high-ranking state police official to assemble a team of several engineers, commandeer a heavy truck, and gather a set of essential supplies. Shortly thereafter, having mustered a small party, the special secretary for relief set off for Morbi.

〰〰〰

As the state government rapidly mobilized to provide relief to the flood-stricken area, parallel activity took place within Gujarat's well-developed civil sector. Nonprofit organizations, temples, mosques, and civic associations prepared to rush workers and supplies to the Machhu River Valley.

In Ahmedabad, the members of the large charity known as Sadvichar Parivar were gathered at a spiritual event when news of the catastrophe arrived. Thirty-five of the organization's boldest members immediately crammed into a car, a jeep, and a truck and struck out for Morbi. Those who remained behind began gathering more funds and volunteers for the monumental task that awaited.[27]

Meanwhile, the Rashtriya Swayamsevak Sangh (RSS), a Hindu nationalist organization, had already mobilized to provide relief to Morbi. Agriculture Minister Keshubhai, originally from Rajkot District himself, enjoyed close ties to the local RSS. He personally informed RSS leaders of the disaster in the morning and asked them to provide assistance. By the time other organizations were receiving information about the flood, RSS volunteers from Rajkot were already racing toward Morbi.[28]

The Rajkot collectorate had also contacted a number of organizations known for their relief work. Among these was the Ramakrishna Ashrama, a large temple that had fed thousands of people displaced by flooding elsewhere in the district during the previous week. When the temple's head monk came to know of the Machhu dam disaster on the morning of August 12, he called for the preparation of seven thousand food packets within two hours. Nearly three hundred volunteers threw themselves into cooking. They worked in three large kitchens to prepare dry snacks, which they then stuffed into plastic bags. Just about two hours after the head monk's initial announcement, several volunteers climbed into two trucks to deliver the food packets to Morbi's survivors.[29]

As the Ramakrishna Ashrama rushed the first food relief to the Machhu River Valley, religious societies throughout the state began mobilizing for the relief effort. On Gujarat's southern coast, members of the Swaminarayan sect gathered relief supplies for Morbi. Farther north, young monks at the Santram Mandir temple started making arrangements to bring a large relief kitchen to the city. All across Gujarat, religious organizations started preparing to respond to what would soon emerge as one of the greatest disasters in the state's history.[30]

≋≋≋

The volunteers and government officials who sought to reach the flood-affected region on August 12 faced tremendous obstacles. In particular, those traveling to Saurashtra from eastern Gujarat encountered a nightmarish passage. Although the 150-mile-long Ahmedabad–Rajkot highway was among the best-maintained roads in the state, the continued downpours had rendered several sections of the highway impassable.

A bridge near the midpoint of the journey posed the greatest challenge. With the flooding at alarming levels, traffic came to a standstill. Travelers could barely discern the crossing, which sat under a layer of rushing water. On the western side of the bridge, a State Transport bus had already become trapped in the mud.

When the members of the Ahmedabad-based Sadvichar Parivar arrived on the scene, they immediately resolved to ford the turbulent crossing. One of the group's leaders grabbed a large wooden staff and began feeling his way across the bridge. Following his lead, nearly a dozen others took staffs and formed a moving chain across the bridge, stringing a rope along to secure themselves and mark the way. The process was painstaking and slow, with a crossing of just a few hundred feet requiring more than an hour of effort, but the men's boldness opened up the bridge to traffic once again. Encouraged by the Sadvichar Parivar volunteers' bravery— and comforted by the poles and rope that now marked the road's presence, travelers began traversing the bridge once again.[31]

Still, when Special Secretary for Relief H. K. Khan arrived at the crossing a short time later, bystanders remarked that reaching the other side remained a risky proposition. As Khan contem-

plated how to proceed, at least one member of his party vociferously objected to continuing toward Rajkot. J. F. Mistry—the
man who had served as the Machhu Dam-II's overseeing design
engineer before rising to the rank of chief engineer in the Irrigation Department—insisted that the crossing was "far too dangerous" and urged Khan to turn the small government convoy
back to the state capital.

Khan disregarded the engineer's imprecations. He ordered
staffers to tether two trucks together with a thick cable to create
a more massive vehicle. With Mistry sitting tensely in the back,
the ad hoc tandem crept across the bridge. Upon reaching the
other side, the police officers in Khan's party quickly decoupled
the vehicles, and the party sped off toward Morbi.[32]

After a cramped and sleepless night spent in the tiny control
room, the morning of August 12 merely confirmed the previous
day's surreal events for the men trapped atop the Machhu Dam-
II. Blinking groggily as they made their way out onto the
walkway that ran across the concrete spillway, mechanic Lakshmanbhai Mohan and the other crew members beheld a silent,
postapocalyptic sight.

The long earthworks on either side of the dam were gone. The
reservoir had completely drained. A flat plain of mud surrounded
the dam, stretching out at least a mile in every direction. Innumerable puddles, rippling from the continuing rain, dotted the
vast wasteland. Nothing moved, save for the slow trickle of water
down the riverbed.

Pacing the length of the concrete spillway, the men pondered
how to climb down to the ground. Their frayed nerves and empty
stomachs left them with little patience, and they bickered as they
contemplated their predicament. A solid remnant of the western
earthwork near the spillway appeared to be their best hope, but
a deep chasm hung between them and the earthen mound.

Around 6:00 p.m., one of the crew members found a long metal pipe while scrounging about. With some experimentation, the men were able to extend the pipe from the spillway to the surviving portion of the western earthwork. Having secured the makeshift bridge, they shimmied down, one by one, and regrouped on the ground. Then they began a six-hour trek across the muddy expanse toward Morbi.[33]

A gruesome scene awaited them in the city. The next day's headlines would call it, without hyperbole, THE GREATEST DESTRUCTION IN THE HISTORY OF SAURASHTRA.[34]

≈≈≈≈≈

At daybreak on August 12, citizens all over Morbi descended from roofs to find their homes utterly ruined. The mud lay thigh-deep. The current had completely leveled earthen houses, and few buildings had escaped the disaster intact. The flooding had carried away or ruined household goods. Grain and other food-stuffs, waterlogged and dirty, had begun to reek.[35]

Many survivors could hardly recognize their neighborhoods. Upon seeing a pile of mud and rubble at the site of his family's Mahendra Quarter home, Ghost Paan owner Pratapbhai Adroja's three-year-old son turned to his father with wide eyes and simply declared, "This is not our house."[36]

For the most part, refugees who had spent the chilly night at evacuation sites did not bother to return to their neighborhoods in the morning. The blanket of mud and corpses covering the streets made the prospect of a walk back to Morbi's low-lying areas daunting. In any case, most evacuees suspected that a trek home would end in disappointment; few possessed houses that could have withstood the Machhu Dam-II's raging waters. Consequently, thousands remained, hungry and thirsty, on the roofs of Morbi's evacuation sites, waiting anxiously for uncertain help to arrive.[37]

A few evacuees did set out for home in the first light of

morning. Gangaram Tapu, who had spent the night with his wife and children at Gibson Middle School, limped back to Kabir Hill and found a muddy wasteland. More than a dozen goat carcasses lay strewn about his yard and his house. Disgusted by the filth, Tapu slowly made his way to a friend's house in the main market area; injured and exhausted, he would convalesce there in the company of his family.[38]

As survivors descended from Morbi's rooftops, they discovered a city filled with death. The sickly sweet stench of decay filled the air. Human corpses and animal carcasses lay everywhere—on the streets, in the houses, in the temples, and on the power lines. Dead goats, buffalo, sheep, cows, and human beings littered the rubble, greeting many as they returned to their homes. Most, soaked by the flooding and rains, were bloating to gruesome proportions.

Mud had encased some of the bodies, and rigor mortis had set in for all. A number of corpses had frozen in ghastly tableaus: a mother and child clutching one another, a young man flailing in vain, an old married couple in their last embrace. In one house, relief workers found the intertwined bodies of eleven people who had drowned while clutching one another.[39]

At many sites, corpses were piled on top of one another in large masses. Eighty filled the municipal preschool, where the water had risen too rapidly to permit the people taking shelter there to flee. Between one hundred and two hundred lay in the Brahmin Dining Hall behind the Police Line; the roof had caved in from the weight of evacuees standing on it, crushing those who had sought refuge inside. Just to the east, near the Machhu River's bank, a layer of mud covered a cluster of fifty-two bodies.[40]

The most poignant story was that of the Vajepar temple, where 116 souls had perished. Hemiben Devda, who had been pushed onto the altar by the rising water, was the sole survivor among those trapped inside. On the morning after the disaster, Devda identified her mother's body among the bloated corpses laid out on the street. Utterly distraught, she would guard it jealously for three days before finally relenting and allowing volunteers to cremate it.[41]

The first responders on August 12 faced the formidable task of collecting the bodies that had begun to rot in every corner of Morbi. By early afternoon, the government of Gujarat had granted Rajkot District Collector A. R. Banerjee's request for permission to expedite removal of corpses, and he issued instructions "to dispose of the dead bodies on an emergency basis." Army, Home Guard, and police units, joined by a few volunteers, began to gather together the thousands of corpses.[42]

Nonetheless, even with government officers working to clear bodies from Morbi, the task of finding and removing corpses often fell to those who had lost their loved ones. Upon climbing down from a neighbor's roof in the Mahendra Quarter, Dhirubhai Mehta entered his house to find the sight he had dreaded all throughout a sleepless night. He would recall, "One girl and my one boy—we found their bodies here in the morning. There was so much dirt in the water that they were just stuck there."[43]

After twenty-four hours without food and water, even the macabre scenes in Morbi's streets could not suppress survivors' hunger. The flood had soaked and ruined the entire city's food supply. Some fortunate citizens received the food packets, potable water, and milk that arrived from Rajkot in the afternoon, but most simply endured the pangs of hunger. Many drank the rainwater that was collecting in pipes and dripping from trees. Others, afraid of waterborne illnesses, went thirsty.[44]

In southern Morbi, Khatijaben Valera and her sisters-in-law contended with the cries of their famished children. She would recall, "The children started saying, 'Mummy, we want to eat. Mummy, we want to eat!' Then, one of my husband's friends came by, and he said, 'Come on, let us find some food.'"[45]

Setting aside their storied family pride, the men of the Valera clan went to a commercial area to scavenge for food. In one shop that had been thrown open—perhaps by its owner, perhaps by looters—they found unspoiled fruits. Loading their precious find into an upturned umbrella, the men returned to the house where they had taken refuge the previous day. There, they fed the hungry children.[46]

Across the Machhu River in eastern Morbi, Principal T. R. Shukla's family, which had escaped the flood without damage to its house or food stores, delivered nourishment to Lakhdhirji Engineering College professors whose riverside houses had been submerged by the flood. Shukla's wife would recall:

Our milkman came at 6:30 a.m. Everything was dry in his village, further west, so he had no idea that the disaster had occurred. He had loaded up his cart and come, as usual. . . . When he came, I told to him, "Parbhu, you will not be able to go into the city today. . . ."

That boy—the milkman—must have been seventeen or eighteen years old. He said to me, "What should I do with all of this milk, ma'am?" I replied, "If you do not mind, I will pay you for all of it. I will give you two big vessels; just leave it with me. In the engineering college lodging, they have not even had chai since yesterday. So I can make chai for them."

There were thirty or forty hungry people, and many of them small children. So I made a big pot of tea. I also made rice cakes. And my children and I took them and gave them to the engineering college faculty.

They had climbed down, after a terrible time, into mud and dirt. And they just cried. I told them, "I have brought you milk, sugar, and tea. And here are some snacks. Eat now; I will make rice and lentil soup for you in the afternoon."

They were all so affected. Tears came to the poor people's eyes. They said to me, "You would do this much for us?" I replied, "I have everything in my house right now—it is the least I can do."[47]

Few survivors enjoyed the fortune of the Shukla family's beneficiaries or the Valera children. For most, Cobra Fifth would be a long day of starvation.

≋≋≋≋≋

Climbing down from his rooftop in the morning, legislator Gokaldas Parmar found his Shakti Plot home in complete disarray. One wall of the building had partially collapsed. The floodwaters had tossed about large pieces of furniture, leaving many of the rooms unrecognizable. Broken glass and shattered pottery studded the layer of mud covering the floor. When Parmar and his family opened the wardrobe to change their rain-soaked clothes, muddy water spilled out onto them. Parmar's grandchildren began shivering as their cold, wet shirts clung to their skin. Their mothers undressed them and warmed them up as best they could.[48]

Shortly thereafter, one of Parmar's granddaughters, tired and hungry, wandered idly into the street in front of the house. A disheveled man was surveying the piles of corpses, his shoulders slumped from exhaustion and despair. Their eyes met. Running toward the girl, the man cried out, "Who is alive?"

Innocently, she replied, "Everyone, Daddy."

"You lie! I cannot believe you!"

"Really, Daddy. Everyone is alive."

Parmar's son-in-law, overcome by emotion, began to weep. After remaining in the Tiger Quarter while his wife and children evacuated to Shakti Plot the previous afternoon, he had expected to find his family dead. Entering the house, the man delivered the welcome news that both he and his brother-in-law had survived the disaster by leaping from roof to roof in the flooded Tiger Quarter.[49]

Parmar soon discovered that his neighbors had not shared his family's good fortune. A friend came to inform the legislator that four corpses lay in the adjoining building. The night before,

Parmar had watched the parents and children struggle to climb out of a window before falling back inside the flooded house. Now, going to investigate, he found their bodies lying in the mud.

Several Shakti Plot men had congregated at the house. They briefly considered attempting to carry the corpses to the crematorium but quickly ruled the idea out. Parmar would explain, "It was impossible to take them to the crematorium—there were trees everywhere, poles everywhere." The men would have to cremate the bodies themselves.

Reaching through the broken wall of a nearby shop, Parmar and his neighbors pulled out containers of vegetable oil. They collected soggy driftwood from the street, doused it with oil, and lit a pyre to perform the last rites for the deceased family.

Sorrow remained in Parmar's voice when he recalled the scene decades later:

> They did not even get a shroud to cover them. Normally, we would have covered them with a shroud. But at that time, the clothing of each and every household was ruined. What could we give them? So, in that situation, the members of a happy family—a prosperous family—could not even get a shroud at their funeral.[50]

East of Shakti Plot, teacher Kanubhai Kubavat descended from the Police Line into the Tiger Quarter with apprehension.[51] Given the force of the floodwaters that had forced him and his family to flee the previous day, he fully expected to find his earthen house collapsed.

Despite his almost certain homelessness, Kubavat felt only a muted despair. Against his every suspicion, he and his wife had been spared the greatest possible loss in the disaster.

The previous afternoon, Kubavat had arrived at his uncle's house on the Machhu River's western bank with his father, his wife, and his infant son. He had not found his two older children during the family's panicked flight from the Tiger Quarter, and he dreaded the news of their demise.

At some point during the night, however, he had come to know that a friend, driving through the neighborhood at around 2:00 p.m., had seen the children playing outside. Concerned by the rising water but unable to reach Kubavat's doorstep, he had brought them back to his house in the Royal Court area, where they remained safe throughout the flood. Kubavat and his wife had sobbed uncontrollably as they reunited with their children.

Now, the Brahmin returned to the Tiger Quarter alone to survey the damage to his home. As he trudged through the mud in the streets, he heard hushed conversations all around. Above all else, Kubavat's neighbors expressed concern for the lives of each other's loved ones. The first query between friends was almost invariably "Everyone *is*, right?" Too often, responders could answer only with tears.

Most seemed to believe that the previous day's flooding had resulted from a breach in the Machhu Dam-II. Speculation as to the cause abounded: the design of the earthworks had been flawed; their construction had been weak; the gates had not been opened in a timely fashion; the Irrigation Department had attempted to hoard too much water; the engineer responsible for the dam had been watching a film in Morbi on the night of August 10.[52]

Some spoke of curses. Devotees recalled the ascetic Jog Bapu's fierce resistance to the construction of the dam, whose reservoir had submerged his hermitage. They invoked his apocryphal words: "This dam will break. Morbi will break."

Others cited the dying words of the Vaniyan of Morbi. Almost two centuries earlier, she had laid a damning curse on Jiyaji, the seventh of the Jadeja kings.

"Seven generations from now, neither your city nor your lineage will remain!"

Jiyaji's dynasty had ended in August 1978 with the murder of

Mayurdhvaj, the thirteenth and last Jadeja king. Almost exactly a year later, Morbi lay in ruins.

The whispers receded as Kubavat approached his street. His heart pounding, he arrived at the site of his house. Only a pile of debris remained.

〰〰〰

Just north of the Tiger Quarter, amid the rotting stench of the vegetable market, Mayor Ratilal Desai began working at city hall.

After passing the whole night on the roof of a factory with the subdistrict magistrate, he had returned to his unaffected home in the main market area around 7:00 a.m. There, his wife had informed him that the small corpse he had carried to the house the previous afternoon, before either of them could grasp the magnitude of the disaster, remained unclaimed.

She also told him, fear in her eyes, that their son Sanjay was missing. The fifteen-year-old boy had traveled to southern Morbi the previous day with one of Desai's friends to help with the evacuation effort. Nearly twenty-four hours later, he had not returned, and no one could attest to his whereabouts. Stunned by the worrisome news, Desai spent some time simply staring at the small body in his sitting room, unsure of whether he would find his son in the same state.

Eventually, growing restless, the mayor waded from his house to city hall, hoping to alleviate his anxiety by throwing himself into work. Upon arriving, he sent two municipal firefighters to Rajkot in a truck, entrusting them with an urgent request for help. Then, he set about surveying the situation in the city and assessing the best course of action. As Desai worked, he continued to worry about Sanjay's fate.[53]

At some point during the day, Gujarat's revenue minister arrived at city hall. As the politician in charge of the Revenue Department, which was tasked with district- and subdistrict-level administration throughout Gujarat, the minister was the state's nominal chief of disaster management. According to most reports, he felt overwhelmed by the situation in Morbi from the moment of his arrival.

Desai, for one, scorned the revenue minister's behavior on August 12. He would later recall indignantly:

> He insisted on drinking water he had specially brought in from outside. I said to him, "This is not going to fly, buddy." He was with his daughter, who was sitting there knitting. Both of them drank water specially brought in from outside. I said to him, "This is not going fly, boss. You are going to have to drink our water."[54]

The inconveniences of the devastated city proved discomfiting for the revenue minister, who was accustomed to the luxury of the state capital.

In the early afternoon, the revenue minister requested to meet with local legislator Gokaldas Parmar, his colleague in the legislative assembly. A short time later, Parmar arrived at city hall unkempt and exhausted. He would remember:

> The clothes I was wearing were the ones from the previous day. I had passed the whole night in them. They had picked up dust and dirt. I had a day's stubble. My sandals—well, one of them had been washed away by the water, so I did not bother to put on the other one. I did not have anything else to wear. So I took a walking stick. I had a walking stick, and my clothes were wet and dirty, and my face was unkempt. When I got to city hall, I had to tell the revenue minister, "I am Gokaldas Parmar, member of the legislative assembly from Morbi."[55]

Having just cremated the bodies of his neighbors, Parmar urged the revenue minister to make immediate arrangements for the disposal of corpses; food and water, he believed, were lower priorities. The revenue minister calmly responded that it was Parmar's place to make suggestions, and that the police and others would carry out any work deemed necessary. Outraged, the normally dignified Parmar hurled a stream of profanities at the revenue minister. He would later confess contritely, "I spoke words to the revenue minister that I cannot repeat."[56]

Although Parmar briefly composed himself and apologized, he remained—like the rest of Morbi's populace—heavily agitated. Shortly after his exchange with the revenue minister, he grew furious when a military officer arrived at city hall and reported that he could not clear corpses from a particular neighborhood because a fallen utility pole was blocking the access path. The legislator thundered, "Are you a government? You have no capacity to remove this one pillar? Why have you come here? Get out!"[57]

Still seething, Parmar was escorted home in a police jeep.[58]

The outbursts from Desai and Parmar shocked the revenue minister enough that he spent the remainder of the day brooding quietly. Over the subsequent weeks, he would maintain low visibility in Morbi despite his all-important position.

By contrast, Agriculture Minister Keshubhai Patel had already thrown himself into the work of relief on the afternoon of August 12. His dedication immediately impressed Mayor Desai, who discussed many important matters with the minister on that first day. Even Rajkot District Collector A. R. Banerjee, who had grown frustrated with Keshubhai's interference the previous day, would quickly come to appreciate his dedication to establishing a well-functioning control room at city hall. Less than twenty-four hours after returning from the brink of the Machhu dam disaster without reporting what he had witnessed, the agriculture minister was leading the effort to bring relief to Morbi. It may have been a guilty man's atonement.[59]

Near the Machhu Dam-II's wasted western embankment, Bhagvanji Patel emerged from his host's house to find another rainy day.

The previous afternoon, he had watched as the reservoir's waters rushed down on Lilapar. Then, along with 1,500 other disconsolate villagers, he had passed a restless night in Lakhdhirnagar.

On the morning of August 12, Bhagvanji and the other men of Lilapar rolled up their pants and plodded erratically through the alternately sucking and slick mud, descending to survey the damage in their village. Because almost all the villagers had evacuated by the time of the flood, few had lost their lives. But the physical structures of the community had almost entirely vanished. According to Bhagvanji, Lilapar had become "an open field." The men could barely discern where their streets and houses had stood. Even the few buildings that had withstood the flood had partially collapsed, with sinking roofs and fallen walls. Bhagvanji despaired as he thought of his factory, which lay just a few miles north along the road to Morbi.

After taking in the desolate landscape, the villagers returned to Lakhdhirnagar. Wary of alarming the women and children, the men dissembled, reporting that Lilapar would return to normal with the clearance of some mud and debris. They instructed their families to stay with relatives in unaffected villages while they cleaned their community and made it livable again.

Once their wives, children, and parents had gone, the men of Lilapar released their emotions. Bhagvanji later explained:

> We all felt for each other. There was a collective grieving. Normally, one man loses something, and we all feel sad for him. Here, I lost everything, you lost everything, the next man lost everything—we all lost everything. So we were all sad together.[60]

Villagers and townspeople from the dam to the Gulf of Kutch shared the grief of Lilapar's villagers. The disaster had swallowed the city of Morbi, the town of Maliya, and a full thirty-two agricultural villages in Morbi and Maliya subdistricts. In all the afflicted communities except Lilapar, the catastrophic flooding had arrived without any warning. Now, with roads clogged by mud and with relief providers overwhelmed by the situation in Morbi, survivors in downstream villages remained stranded, left to speculate about what had just occurred and what would happen next.[61]

Because massive mud deposits had isolated Maliya, little information about the outlaw town would reach the rest of Rajkot District until several days after the flood. On August 12, the outside world could do little but speculate about the fate of the Miyanas. The following day, the front page of one Gujarati newspaper would proclaim, A FEAR THAT THE 10,000 PEOPLE OF MALIYA ARE SUNK.[62]

Everyone was leaving Morbi. By early evening, the roads leading out of the city, cleared of debris by the army, had grown thick with knots of people, cars, trucks, and buses. Patriarchs and matriarchs herded children along, driving them gently forward and leading some by the hand. Young men and women guided wizened elders, pausing every few hundred feet to rest. Haggard men with unshaven, dirty faces and torn pants carried soggy white bundles—repositories of all their remaining possessions—on their stooped backs as their sandals shuffled through the grime. Dozens of survivors hung off the backs of trucks that chugged slowly through the mud. Periodic bursts of discordant honking punctuated the funerary silence of the exodus.[63]

Much of Morbi's population exited the city by the night of August 12. With foodstuffs ruined, homes destroyed, utilities obliterated, and bodies decaying at every street corner, the city had become, as many survivors would recall, "unlivable."[64]

Many refugees slogged to the homes of relatives in unaffected villages. Other displaced residents caught rides to Rajkot and other cities in Saurashtra from kindhearted motorists. Some of the benefactors were natives who were leaving Morbi with free space in their vehicles; others were outsiders who had come to deliver goods or volunteers and had taken pity upon the survivors. A large number of refugees left Morbi on State Transport buses. These buses departed from the New State Transport Bus Stand, which sat on the southwestern edge of town, near Sanala village. Roads leading up to the depot from downtown Morbi remained largely impassable, so a steady stream of refugees trudged there on foot.[65]

Survivors reaching the New State Transport Bus Stand found an utterly chaotic scene. The State Transport Department had resumed bus service from Morbi earlier in the day with an increased number of trips, but even the additional buses proved insufficient to cope with the profusion of refugees. The government was offering citizens free passage to wherever they desired, but the wait to board a vehicle often lasted for hours. As buses arrived, the tightly packed refugees pushed and jostled to secure places. A litany of fearsome rumors—one of which suggested that more floodwater would soon hit Morbi—exacerbated the tension. Shouts, mutters, and sobs filled the air with a cacophony of emotion. The bloating corpses surrounding the bus stand only added to the menacing atmosphere.[66]

Despite the journey's arduousness, most survivors, desperate to escape from the decaying city, chose to undertake it. Machinery merchant Dhirubhai Mehta, still distraught over the drowning of his daughter and only son, left with his wife, his mother, and his two surviving daughters. Khatijaben Valera and her large clan decided to seek shelter with her husband's friend in Rajkot. Paan seller Pratapbhai Adroja took his family to his sister's house, also in the district capital. Kanubhai Kubavat's parents, wife, and children—all deeply disturbed by the previous day's events—evacuated to other parts of Saurashtra.[67]

A few determined souls remained in Morbi. Many who had taken shelter at evacuation sites chose to pass the night there, at the very least sure of some shelter. Much to the chagrin of his family, Gokaldas Parmar, member of the legislative assembly, insisted on staying in Shakti Plot, arguing that Morbi's representative to the state government could not simply abandon the city in such dire times. Gangaram Tapu flatly refused to leave, scoffing, "We have our forefathers' house—it is all set!" Having sent his family off, Kubavat stayed in Morbi to clear the debris from his plot in the Tiger Quarter. Principal T. R. Shukla, left relatively unscathed by the disaster, decided to remain in eastern Morbi until he could give a downtown administrator the keys to the arts college.[68]

Like Shukla, Mayor Ratilal Desai found himself anchored to Morbi by a practical obligation. Despite his deep dedication to Morbi, he, like most of the city's people, had grown desperate to escape. But the little body he had lifted out of the floodwaters the previous afternoon still lay in his house, unclaimed; he strongly felt that, until someone came by to collect it, he could not leave the city.[69]

As the mayor kept vigil over the dead child, he cried without bounds. His son Sanjay was gone.

Decades later, tears would return to Desai's eyes as he retold the narrative he had received with shock on the afternoon of August 12, 1979:

> Sanjay had been immersed in the work of evacuating people from low-lying areas. He and my friend Jadavji were returning home. They parted ways near city hall.
>
> He had just passed through a gate that led from the Tiger Quarter to the riverside neighborhoods when the water came. . . . There was a urinal there, near city hall and the Police Line. He climbed up the wall of the urinal. The water was coming, so he climbed up. There were a number of people on taller buildings nearby, and they shouted to him to climb up further.
>
> But the water kept rising. It came in a big wave, and he was gone.[70]

As Desai watched over the body of a stranger's child, he wept profusely, knowing that his missing son would never return.

As refugees poured out of a flood-wrecked Morbi, relief trucks arrived to aid those who had remained in the city. By the evening of August 12, Rajkot District Collector A. R. Banerjee was directing the distribution of relief traffic. After spending the afternoon dispatching police units, briefing politicians, and soliciting assistance from private organizations and the state government, the collector had returned to supervise work in Morbi.

Banerjee and other senior officials stood up to their knees in mud, coordinating the relief effort by relaying messages to and from drivers. With tens of thousands of wet, starving people growing increasingly desperate for aid, the officials barked out hoarse orders tinged with a pleading sense of urgency. Banerjee would write:

> We were in fact racing against time and each department had to take its own initiative to tackle the immediate problems first. Even movement of people was restricted due to bad conditions of roads, lack of vehicles, and once an officer was on the field he got stuck up there. . . . Even I had to physically rush around to requisition trucks on the street and hand over them to the required people and direct operations as per the situation standing on the street.[71]

While substantial, the incoming relief was insufficient to meet the needs of Morbi's cold and traumatized populace. The collectorate simply could not access enough cleaning personnel, food, lighting implements, and vehicles to fix an obliterated city. Morbi would need an extensive, well-organized relief apparatus during the subsequent weeks. Banerjee and his staff could make only tentative provisions until more government aid arrived from Gandhinagar.[72]

Special Secretary for Relief H. K. Khan—one of the first officials to leave the state capital—would reach the outskirts of Morbi late at night, accompanied by a party of sixty policemen, several dozen municipal employees, a number of Rajkot volunteers, and a few state government engineers. Despite more than twelve hours of work on the part of government officers, the city remained a place of disorder and discomfort. Hundreds of discontented and dejected refugees continued to wait at the New State Transport Bus Stand, periodically charging incoming buses in hopes of securing a seat. All around the seething crowds, Khan saw mud and "dead bodies strewn all over the place." It was, according to his later recollection, "just a scene of total chaos."

Leaving a small group to maintain order at the bus stand, Khan continued on into the city. With its electric lighting facilities destroyed and its candles and gas lamps washed away or ruined, Morbi lay under a cloak of darkness. Khan and his party found themselves relying on the limited illumination offered by old-fashioned lanterns and their car's headlights. Everywhere they fell, the lights revealed dirt and death. Eventually, the mud and corpses in the street became such a hindrance that the government officers disembarked and proceeded into Morbi on foot. Wading through the sludge in knee-high gumboots, the men sought out those who would spend another terrifying night in the city.

Before anything else, the relief personnel sought to simply situate refugees, guaranteeing them places to sleep and clean water to drink. For the most part, the officers led survivors to the schools and other large buildings to which the Rajkot collectorate had sent water tankers, food packets, and bedding supplies.

As the men from Gandhinagar chaperoned shivering refugees toward the ad hoc shelters, they knew that they—like Banerjee and his officers—could offer only limited comfort to Morbi's beleaguered citizenry at the moment. With the break of day on August 13, Special Secretary for Relief Khan and his staff would have to begin a herculean relief effort.[73]

On the night of Cobra Fifth, within a prevailing environment of agitation, discomfort, and mass exodus, survivors performed hundreds of small acts of kindness, doing what they could to soothe aching bodies and disturbed minds.

On the Machhu River's eastern bank, Principal T. R. Shukla's family delivered a simple meal of rice and lentil soup to several dozen Lakhdhirji Engineering College faculty and staff families whose riverside houses had sustained severe damage the previous day. Elsewhere in eastern Morbi, Parshuram Potteries—the city's first industrial enterprise—served a simple dinner of lentil rice and vegetables to over five hundred survivors. Throughout the city, individuals and businesses with intact food stocks fed their starving neighbors. At Gibson Middle School, V. C. High School, and the Police Line, volunteers from Rajkot offered meager meals to grateful evacuees.[74]

Nevertheless, all the kindness in Morbi could do only so much to soften the terror of that dark night. With the city's lighting and electrical infrastructure destroyed, nightfall on August 12 poured pitchlike blackness over the city. The limited flashlights, lanterns, and candles in Morbi merely served only to cast an eerie glow on collapsed buildings, dazed survivors, and bloated corpses. The smell of rot hung heavy in the air, covering the city with an inescapable blanket of death.[75]

The Paris of Saurashtra had descended into a total silence, one undisturbed by even the tiniest signs of life. Not terse, mumbled conversations between morose survivors. Not the howling of street dogs or the lowing of cows. Not the quiet buzzing of a monsoon-bred mosquito in a weary, sleeping ear. As one observer from Rajkot later said, "Even the pests were dead."[76]

Chapter 7
"They Would Work and Cry, Cry and Work"

By daybreak on August 13, 1979, the Machhu dam disaster had become worldwide news, plastered across the front pages of newspapers across the globe. New Yorkers woke up to the headline HUNDREDS DIE IN INDIA AS DAM BREAK FREES 20-FOOT WATER WALL. Pakistan's *Karachi Dawn* exclaimed, 1,000 FEARED DEAD IN INDIAN DAM BURST. The *London Telegraph* ventured, INDIA DAM TOLL MAY BE 25,000.[1]

Evening news programs in the United States carried the story as well. CBS's Dan Morton gravely intoned, "Too much rain is the cause of disaster in western India. After two weeks of monsoons, a dam burst today, burying the city of Morbi under twenty feet of water. At least a thousand persons died, and one official says the final toll could be 5,000." ABC's Sam Donaldson and NBC's evening anchor also mentioned the flood, describing a wall of water fourteen feet high and citing a death toll of more than one thousand. In subsequent days, many Gujaratis would allege that American television, keyed in by a spy satellite, had broken news of the disaster before the government of Gujarat even knew it had occurred; years later, this belief would persist among a large number of flood survivors.[2]

In England and Mumbai, BBC radio reports of the flood sent expatriate Gujaratis into a panic. Terrified by the news that Morbi had been wiped out, they frantically attempted to contact loved ones who lived in the area.[3]

In Gujarat, the disaster dominated the front page of every daily. The newspapers spared no superlative in breaking the story: IN A DISASTER UNLIKE ANY SAURASHTRA HAS SEEN IN A THOUSAND YEARS, 1,000 DIE AS THE MACHHU DAM BURSTS NEAR MORBI: 250 CORPSES FOUND; THE GREATEST DESTRUCTION IN THE HISTORY OF SAURASHTRA; IN MORBI, THE DEATH OF FOUR THOUSAND BY WATER-ANNIHILATION: UPON THE BREAKING OF THE MACHHU DAM, THE BIGGEST HUMAN DISASTER SEEN IN GUJARAT IN CENTURIES.[4]

Based on the eyewitness accounts of harried survivors and on the reports of the journalists who had travelled in Collector A. R. Banerjee's dawn convoy on August 12, the newspapers spun stories that shocked the people of Gujarat. The correspondent for *Phulchhab*, the most popular daily in Rajkot, began:

> A flood catastrophe of a kind never before seen in the history of Saurashtra came to be yesterday when the Machhu Dam-II, located near Morbi, ripped open. Two to three thousand people have died in Morbi, Maliya, and the villages on the banks of the Machhu. The city of Morbi has been turned into a graveyard. Damage worth millions of rupees has occurred, and, at this writing, there are still no reports of Maliya or Lilapar. . . .
>
> As I write this upon making a quick survey of Morbi and coming back to Rajkot, my hand trembles with rage at this abomination of nature. Streams of tears flow from my eyes. Death has gone wild, and Mother Machhu has destroyed the people living on her banks. Noble, beautiful Morbi has been turned into a graveyard.[5]

A headline in *Sandesh*, another Rajkot newspaper, declared, EVEN PEOPLE WHO CLIMBED UP ONTO ROOFS AND TREES WERE DRAGGED AWAY BY THE RAGING FLOOD; THE POLICE AND MILITARY HAVE STARTED RESCUE EFFORTS; MORE BODIES EXPECTED TO EMERGE

FROM THE DEBRIS. *Phulchhab* lamented THE TEARFUL SIGHTS OF MORBI'S EARTH, reporting that Mayor Ratilal Desai had lost his son and that member of the legislative assembly Gokaldas Parmar had survived with only the clothes on his body.[6]

The articles painted a portrait of a broken city. Bodies hung from power lines. Sixty percent of buildings were wrecked. Household goods, dead cattle, and human corpses littered streets, and dogs milled about in their midst. Survivors wept alone, having lost their entire families. The people of Morbi found themselves unable to speak, unable to cry. One little boy asked repeatedly, "Will the water come again? Will the water come again today?"[7]

The coverage would grow even more frenzied over the subsequent week, as the magnitude of human suffering became clear. Couples had lost daughters brought home for the Shravan holidays. One family's beloved son, on the threshold of making a new life for himself in the United States, had perished in the floodwaters. A man and woman had been washed away on their engagement day. One Home Guard had drowned after evacuating more than two hundred people from the Harijan Quarter. The muddy floodwaters had hurled Kishorebhai Daftari—the young lawyer who was broadcasting warnings to low-lying neighborhoods via the megaphone on the municipal ambulance—against a wall, killing him. (A photograph of Daftari, frozen in death, would become one of the iconic images of the flood's aftermath.) Eventually, the newspapers would also highlight some hopeful stories—two women had delivered healthy babies amid the carnage, for instance, and a convicted murderer had saved dozens of drowning people over the course of several hours. On August 13 and for weeks thereafter, however, most articles told tales of woe.[8]

The disaster would remain in the national and international news for almost a full week, appearing on ABC's nightly telecast in the United States through August 17. Four days after the disaster, as footage of the afflicted area became available, a somber correspondent narrated a brief feature story for American audiences:

The city, once a royal capital built by a Maharaja, is destroyed. Buildings on the fringes still stand, but much of the center of Morbi is buried in up to twenty feet of mud. There is still no reliable death toll. About a thousand bodies have been recovered, but more are buried in the mud. Unofficial estimates of how many more go as high as 25,000. No one will know until the mud recedes. Between fifteen and twenty thousand survivors are being evacuated, carrying all they now own. Some survivors say there were last-minute loudspeaker warnings that the dam, completed just last year about five miles upstream, was about to break, but that most residents ignored them.

The video showed an aerial view of the concrete spillway surrounded by a mud flat, clips of the ongoing drops of food packets from helicopters, and shots of the vast wreckage that filled the city of Morbi.[9] Ironically, in an era in which a limited number of Indian households possessed televisions, only a few domestic viewers would ever see footage of one of the country's greatest calamities.

Wisps of smoke curled up from the tip of H. K. Khan's cigarette.[10] He brought it to his lips and took a long draw. Surveying his domain, the special secretary for relief beheld a scene of barely constrained chaos. Soldiers and staffers scurried about the hastily cleaned offices of Morbi's official control room, established the previous night at the waterlogged city hall. The stench of rotting produce drifted in from the surrounding vegetable market. It was early on the morning of Monday, August 13, and the largest relief effort in Gujarat's history had just begun.

Holding his breath as the smoke seared his lungs, Khan closed his eyes. Ever since his brief dawn survey of the destruction, unsettling images had swirled in his mind. He remembered the raw, bleeding hands of an old woman who had survived by hanging for four hours from a dead electrical cable just above the raging waters. The image collided with that of two stiff corpses in rocking chairs—an elderly couple that had been relaxing on the porch when the waters came. Khan took another puff on his cigarette, reminding himself to stay grounded in the present. The magnitude of the task was too enormous to dwell upon.

The previous night, in a meeting with the revenue minister and Agriculture Minister Keshubhai Patel, District Collector A. R. Banerjee had delegated relief responsibilities to the officers under his command. The jobs included disposing of carcasses and corpses; carrying out salvage operations; undertaking health measures; providing vehicles, water tankers, and other transport; restoring electricity; promoting public health; deploying the police force and maintaining law and order; and supplying kerosene, petrol, wood, food packets, clothes, and other critical items.[11]

In light of the overwhelming circumstances, however, it soon became evident that a more immediate, on-the-ground organization was needed. Hoping to bring some order to the situation, Khan split his government officers and volunteers into four parties. One group was charged with disposing of the corpses and carcasses that lay strewn about the city. A second group would clear the mud and debris that threatened to hamper every conceivable relief effort. The third team would feed and shelter survivors who remained in the city. Wary of the water-borne diseases that lurked after disasters, Khan instructed the final party to spearhead cholera vaccinations and other public health measures.

With the initial work under way, Khan left Morbi to report to his superiors. Communication with the outside world was otherwise impossible. Collector Banerjee later lamented in a report to the government, "No message could be conveyed to Rajkot or vice versa. Hence for any small requirement, persons had to be sent with special message to and from Morbi. . . . Thus four hours on an average were being lost for sending messages."[12]

The difficulty of coordinating disparate efforts with minimal communication made the first days of the relief effort excruciatingly difficult. Banerjee later wrote:

From [the twelfth] to about a week thereafter it was not possible to channalize and direct the operations by sitting only in
the control room because everything had to be tackled immediately and there was no system of knowing who is doing what.
This was precisely because there was no telephone system at
Morbi and all the local offices had come to a stand-still. . . . In
these circumstances, it was not possible for all concerned
departments to keep the control room informed or to get necessary direction from the control room at all times. . . . Under
the circumstances, it was more necessary for the officers to
organize things suddenly on the field than to expect the control
room to function in [a] smooth and systematic way.[13]

Adding to the difficulties, the government had to haul in even
the most basic supplies—such as matchboxes, kerosene, and
drinking water—from Rajkot. Debris and "huge layers of mud"
filled "most of the places in the city," and corpses and carcasses
littered the streets, hindering the movement of relief workers.
Factoring in the "element of emotional upsurge of the local
people" and the fact that work would have to stop at twilight due
to the lack of lighting supplies, the relief bureaucrats knew that
August 13 held only hard work.[14]

When Khan arrived in Rajkot after his brief stint in Morbi, he
placed a telephone call to Chief Minister Babubhai Patel.
Knowing now what he faced, Khan issued sweeping demands.
According to his own account, he bluntly asked for "all of the
powers of the state government."[15] In the financial realm, he
requested the authorization to bypass all the levels of clearance
necessary for expenditures. He also demanded the right to command any officer of the state to do anything, further insisting that
he be the sole officer with that right; only administration by fiat
could bring order to the relief process.

Babubhai agreed to all of Khan's conditions without hesita-
tion. A few hours later, after completing essential tasks in Rajkot,
Khan returned to Morbi. For the newly crowned special secretary
for relief, August 13 would be a long and arduous day, one in

which he would not stop to eat even once. Reflecting on the ordeal in later years, he would recall subsisting on "countless cups of tea and innumerable cigarettes."[16]

In the first days of relief, the government's top priority was disposal of the rotting bodies that filled Morbi's streets. One volunteer would later recall:

> With the water gone, wherever you looked, in all directions, there were dead bodies. Your foot would fall on somebody's foot, on somebody's hand. Dead bodies in all directions. Humans, cattle, goats. You would find yourself touching somebody's hand, somebody's head. Dead bodies in all directions.[17]

Soaked by the floodwaters and the constant rain, corpses and animal carcasses lay bloated and decomposing all over the city. Under instructions from District Collector A. R. Banerjee, Home Guards, police officers, army troops, and volunteers began clearing the putrid bodies.[18]

The work was revolting and heartbreaking. Decades later, District Home Guard Commander Ushakant Mankad's voice still trembled as he cried out:

> Inhuman, I say! But the enormous work that we had to do—if we had stopped to see humanity in those dead bodies, we would have failed in our bigger task, which was to save those who were still living. If we had not gotten those bodies out of there, there would have been an outbreak of disease.[19]

Some of the parties charged with the gruesome work did not fulfill their duties. A number of army and police personnel shied away from handling the corpses, likely motivated by a combination of health concerns, psychological aversion, and a tendency to view the disposal of bodies and carcasses as the purview of lower jatis. Within two days, the government had summoned three hundred low-jati street sweepers from all over Gujarat to assist in the clearance. But by that time, much of the grueling labor was already complete.[20]

By all accounts, the Home Guards and members of voluntary organizations—above all the Hindu nationalist Rashtriya Swayamsevak Sangh (RSS)—undertook the bulk of the most difficult removal. Donning gloves and facemasks, they threw themselves into the macabre task with grim determination.

Clearing bodies was a physical horror. Corpses lay all over the city, piled up and waterlogged. To pick them up was to split them apart. In the Brahmin Dining Hall, where the body count exceeded one hundred, Home Guards had to use poles to lift the oozing corpses; still, many disintegrated.[21] Arms or legs frequently fell off as volunteers took hold. One RSS leader would recall with disgust:

> The corpses were in such bad shape. Soaking in the water, they had become bloated. Volunteers would go to grab a hand . . . but a stream of liquid would squirt out, and the grip would go straight through to the bone. Liquid would ooze out, and the hands would go straight through to the bone, and flesh and all kinds of things would pour out from inside. In twenty-four hours, the corpses had become utterly bizarre.[22]

Special Secretary for Relief H. K. Khan later described the work of moving the deformed bodies as "the most gruesome job imaginable."[23] Volunteers would recall the process as being fraught with shock, anguish, and fear. Many law enforcement officers broke down while working. Home Guard Commander Mankad remembered:

> There was a great mental effect. You had to talk to them every two hours. Collect them together, give them a cup of chai, and talk to them. Make them a bit bolder. Because men become afraid when they see dead bodies. . . . We had to give them periodic

A view from the eastern end of the Machhu Dam-II's old concrete spillway. The reservoir is to the left, and the riverbed is to the right. The small cabin in the foreground is the control room where six workers survived the disaster. In the background, the western earthen embankment stretches to the horizon. *(Photograph by Tom Wooten.)*

The view from above one of the Machhu Dam-II's original spillway gates, which survived the flood. *(Photograph by Tom Wooten.)*

The Mani Mandir, also known as the "Taj Mahal of Saurashtra," was Morbi's most distinctive landmark. It served as a highly visible reminder of the city's glittering royal past. *(Photograph courtesy of the Morbi Royal Family.)*

The main market was the heart of Morbi's commercial and civil life. Marked at its ends by Nehru Gate and the Royal Court, and at its midpoint by the Green Chowk tower (pictured in the background), it housed a vibrant blend of rickshaws and oxcarts, merchants and customers, houses and shops. *(Photograph courtesy of the Morbi Royal Family.)*

An aerial photograph of the Machhu Dam-II after the disaster. The concrete dam remained intact, but the earthen embankments had washed away, and the reservoir was empty. *(Photograph courtesy of Gunvantbhai Sedani.)*

The Buffalo Bridge withstood the floodwaters' force for several hours before giving way. *(Photograph courtesy of Gunvantbhai Sedani.)*

Left, after the disaster, objects and animals hung from power lines. *Right,* Kishorebhai Daftari, a young lawyer, was trying to save others in the main market area when the floodwaters pressed him up against a building. This photograph of his corpse soon became an iconic image of the disaster. *(Photographs courtesy of Gunvantbhai Sedani.)*

Left, Morbi's once-vibrant neighborhoods became scenes of profound destruction. *Right,* as Morbi's citizenry staged an exodus from the broken city, cars streamed in to offer relief. *(Photographs courtesy of Gunvantbhai Sedani.)*

Left, hundreds of relief workers rolled into Morbi from Rajkot. *Right,* Chief Minister Babubhai Jashbhai Patel (third from right) and Agriculture Minister Keshubhai Patel (far right) surveyed the damage in Morbi. *(Photographs courtesy of Gunvantbhai Sedani.)*

Flood victims' bodies, bloated and disfigured after soaking in the floodwaters, had to be taken to the crematorium in large trucks. *(Photograph courtesy of Gunvantbhai Sedani.)*

Morbi's mayor, Ratilal Desai (far left), speaks while member of the legislative assembly Gokaldas Parmar (third from left) and Chief Minister Babubhai Jashbhai Patel (far right) look on. *(Photograph courtesy of Gunvantbhai Sedani.)*

Clearing the mud and wreckage from Morbi proved a monumental task, requiring weeks of work from government officials, volunteers, and private citizens. *(Photograph courtesy of Gunvantbhai Sedani.)*

Left, Ghost Paan shop, managed by Pratapbhai Adroja and his brothers, reopened a scant five days after the disaster. Many government officials, including Agriculture Minister Keshubhai Patel, were known to frequent the establishment. It became a symbol of Morbi's recovery. *Right,* their homes and livelihoods destroyed, many of Morbi's citizens felt broken for a long time after the flood. Most would say it took over a year for any semblance of normalcy to return. *(Photographs courtesy of Gunvantbhai Sedani.)*

A few months after the disaster, thousands of mourners attended an interfaith memorial ceremony in the main market. Since 1980, the city of Morbi has held a memorial every year on the anniversary of the disaster. *(Photograph courtesy of Gunvantbhai Sedani.)*

"injections"—that is to say, lectures. "This is the time for us to stand by the people." They would work and cry, cry and work.[24]

Adding to the psychological toll was the fact that the volunteers and relief workers, many of whom had never even touched a dead animal or human being, were often asked to burn bodies on the spot during those first terrible days. With animal carcasses, there was no other choice; they were simply too large to transport elsewhere. Volunteers would clear a pit around a dead goat or buffalo, flip the carcass over with a stick to expose the wet side, and then immolate it with ample kerosene or diesel.[25]

There was a general consensus that human bodies, unlike those of animals, would only be burned at the crematorium. During the desperate early days of relief, however, even this rule was often bypassed, as in the vegetable oil–fueled last rites of Gokaldas Parmar's neighbors. Mayor Ratilal Desai would later recall, "So many bodies were in such a state that there was no choice but to burn them on the spot. Spray on some kerosene, spray on some petroleum. Then burn them. What else was there to do?"[26]

In the most poignant instances, Home Guards and volunteers labored under the tearful gazes of distraught mourners. Years later, Commander Mankad would quietly recall:

> In one house, they told us, "Be careful. Make sure she does not get hurt." They would tell us to be careful with a dead body— "Be careful now, that is my darling"—knowing full well that it was a dead body. "She is very dear to me." There were a lot of stories like that. If I went to tell you them, both you and I would be here forever.[27]

At the large, open-air crematorium on the Machhu River's western bank, joy and anticipation should have filled the morning of Cooking Sixth. The field would have been abuzz with last-minute preparations as food vendors, craftsmen, and performers readied their colorful tents for the Smallpox Seventh carnival.

Instead, on the second morning after the flood, imposing mounds of grotesque corpses had begun to accumulate in the space. Using gurneys and carts, volunteers had wheeled the bodies, one or two or five at a time, from narrow, mud-filled alleys into the city's open spaces, such as the Nehru Gate plaza. From there, government trucks carried them the rest of the way.[28]

The bodies piled up in the crematorium's central field, entangled and mixed—Hindu and Muslim, low-jati and high-jati, woman and man, child and adult. Over the subsequent weeks, the masses of rotting humanity would come to symbolize the magnitude of the August 11 tragedy.[29]

Initially, the heaps of corpses overwhelmed volunteers' capacity to dispose of them. Bodies began arriving at the crematorium on the night of August 12, but a dearth of flammable materials hampered efforts to burn them the next day. The state government made arrangements to rush wood to Morbi from forests all over Gujarat by August 14, but the need for liquid fuel remained unmet.

Some volunteers from the RSS and the Ahmedabad-based Sadvichar Parivar decided to take matters into their own hands. Twenty-seven years later, one Sadvichar Parivar man would recount the events of the afternoon of August 13 with a chuckle:

> We decided that we had to get a diesel or petrol tanker by nightfall. So we thought, there are all these trucks passing on the highway thirty or forty kilometers away. We decided to go there, stop the first tanker we saw, and hijack it.
>
> The tanker driver tried to stop us. We said, "Do you want money, buddy? Then we will give you money. Either way, we are going to take your tanker." Right there, on the highway! We trapped him, as if we were performing highway robbery. . . . We told him, "If you want money, if you want to save your life, do as we tell you."

Fearing for his life, the driver acquiesced and guided the diesel tanker through driving rain to Morbi. There, a cadre of volunteers jealously guarded the fuel until day broke on August 14.[30]

Three days after the disaster, on Smallpox Seventh, the work of cremating the deceased began in earnest. Drawing on wood from Gujarat's four corners, diesel from the hijacked tanker, and their own internal mettle, Sadvichar Parivar and RSS volunteers burned hundreds of bodies at a time. One participant explained, "We made pyres of wood first. We lifted the corpses and put them on top. Fifty or sixty at a time—no one had the strength to count. We would swing the dead bodies between us and fling them onto the pyres. The bodies oozed onto our hands, those rotting bodies." With the corpses piled high, the volunteers threw slashed tires and several gallons of diesel on top and set the pyres ablaze.[31]

From the morning of August 14, the grisly work proceeded for weeks without pause. The volunteers, eventually hardened to the sights of death and carnage, found themselves most haunted by images of the living. Every day, distraught family members arrived at the crematorium searching for still-missing relatives. Weeping as they gagged on the stench, they walked among the corpses, trying to decipher the features of innumerable disfigured faces. The bodies were almost always bloated beyond recognition, and the families left without paying their last respects.[32]

As the cremations proceeded, the corpses themselves became a blur, little more than inanimate objects to be reduced to ash as quickly as possible. One woman who lived near the crematorium recalled with a shudder, "There was no counting the corpses—no counting them." Often, the volume of bodies would carry the work well into the night.[33]

Years later, in spite of never having witnessed the cremations directly, a matriarch who lived south of the Mani Mandir would relate how the gruesome process had seared itself into her memory. During the weeks before the restoration of electricity in Morbi, the woman and her children would turn in for the night amid utter darkness; the only light visible in the entire city was an eerie orange glow on the northern horizon—the mighty blaze of the funerary pyres.[34]

Babubhai Patel glanced down at the waterlogged landscape of the Saurashtra Peninsula. After spending the previous day coordinating initial relief arrangements in Gandhinagar, the chief minister had climbed into a plane and set off westward at 7:00 a.m. on August 13.[35]

Flying through the rain, Babubhai pondered the magnitude of the Machhu dam disaster. Before the creation of Gujarat, in the days of the old Bombay State, he had held top positions in the Public Works and Irrigation Departments; heavy flooding had stricken two Gujarati cities during this period, and he had stayed in each for several days to coordinate relief efforts. He knew that the situation now facing him would require a great deal more leadership.[36]

After an hour-long ride, the plane deposited its passengers in Rajkot. The revenue minister and Agriculture Minister Keshubhai Patel received the chief minister, and together they travelled to Morbi by jeep.

Upon arriving at 11:15 a.m., Babubhai donned knee-high boots and set out immediately for the city's devastated neighborhoods. The chief minister and his entourage encountered immense hostility as they toured from house to mud-filled house. The suffering citizens who had remained in Morbi lashed out at the government for perceived lapses in responsibility. Many called upon Babubhai to bring the culpable parties to justice.[37]

For the chief minister, the harsh reception was nearly as sobering as the carnage on Morbi's streets. Only one resident, it seemed, felt heartened by his presence. As Babubhai passed under Nehru Gate, a harried Mayor Ratilal Desai grabbed his hand. Fatigue and grief had filled Desai's eyes with red, and his countenance conveyed a desperation that commanded undivided attention. His message was simple: *We need you here. Do not leave.*[38]

Decades later, Desai would confess that he did not truly expect the chief minister to heed his request. What happened next, then, came as a surprise. Babubhai did what member of the legislative assembly Gokaldas Parmar called "an astounding thing, a brave thing." That evening, after returning to Rajkot, the chief minister began placing telephone calls. Making arrangements to personally remain in Morbi during relief operations, he insisted that the ministers of his cabinet join him there. For the coming weeks, the city would receive the state government's full support.[39]

On the second day after the flood, Morbi's desolate streets began to bustle with the footsteps of outsiders. Government officers, spurred by Chief Minister Babubhai Patel's determination, established bases of operation in the city. Volunteers streamed in from Rajkot, Ahmedabad, and many other Gujarati cities. Journalists descended upon the rubble, surveying the damage and interviewing dazed survivors. Gunvantbhai Sedani, one of Rajkot's best-known photographers, began snapping the photographs that would become emblematic of the Machhu dam disaster: corpses on power lines, carcasses splayed out in the street, and stricken families slumping in front of their wrecked homes. (Sedani would liberally grant rights to the photographs to the media outlets and nonprofit organizations that sought them, professing a sense of social duty to bear witness to the flood's horrific toll.)[40]

While some visitors arrived to provide relief or document the devastation, others seemed bent upon meddling and gawking. Volunteers delivering relief supplies often insisted on distributing them personally, rather than handing them over to government authorities and clearing out of the city. Even worse, as Collector A. R. Banerjee later complained, "thousands of people started for Morbi . . . to see the situation themselves . . . and even out of curiosity." The prostrate city had suddenly become the destination for a macabre brand of tourism.[41]

Decades later, a senior journalist would recount his sight-seeing experience as a fifteen-year-old boy from Rajkot. On holiday from school due to the heavy rains, he had been excited when his father, who was delivering some relief supplies to Morbi, asked if he wanted to go along and see what had become of the famed Paris of Saurashtra. Somehow squeezing onto a single scooter, father, son, and two other men set off northward.

At a distance of about three miles from Morbi, the boy began to notice a rotten smell. As the four travelers reached the city's outskirts, they were forced to dismount and receive cholera injections at a government checkpoint. Upon reaching Morbi, they delivered the supplies to representatives of a voluntary organization. They then proceeded to take in the sights of the ruined city.

Waterlogged shops, their massive hoards of grain ruined, gave off an unbearable stench; nauseated, the boy and his father had to tie kerchiefs over their faces. In many areas, the group encountered utter desolation. Elsewhere, an indelible chaos impressed itself upon the boy's mind: "I still remember the sights. Stores broken down, wares in the streets; everything had to be wiped out. They took bulldozers to everything. Dogs, cats, cows in the street. And up at twenty or thirty feet, a waterline."

As an adult, the tourist would recall that, by the end of his visit, he had felt discomfited by the gratuitousness of his presence in Morbi. Shortly after his return, Collector Banerjee appealed to the people of Rajkot to refrain from visiting the city to indulge a morbid curiosity.[42]

Many visitors also arrived in Morbi seeking family. They came, as Collector Banerjee described it, to "meet their near and dear," hoping to find their loved ones among the survivors.[43]

In Mumbai, arts college principal T. R. Shukla's family had received news of the disaster from the United States, where Shukla's brother had seen coverage of it on television. Three of the principal's nephews had set out immediately for Saurashtra. Upon reaching Rajkot on the evening of August 12, they had visited each of the makeshift camps set up to accommodate the influx of evacuees from Morbi. Despite searching all night, they could not find their uncle, aunt, and four cousins.

On the morning of August 13, the three men faced the dreaded possibility that their relatives had perished. Nonetheless, one of them insisted on taking a taxi to Morbi in order to indulge their hopes one last time. The taxi driver, like many at the time, levied a hefty premium on their desperation; the Rajkot–Morbi fare, normally fifty or sixty rupees, became four hundred. Given the damage to the roads and the congestion of relief vehicles and evacuees on the highway, the trip proceeded at a crawl, but the men eventually reached the city.

Armed with only a vague knowledge of where their uncle lived, they began scouring the Machhu River's eastern bank. They had wandered for some time when they heard a sudden cry.

"Son!"

The boys looked up to find Mrs. Shukla waving wildly. They went running to their aunt and embraced her, sobbing. The first words out of their mouths were simply "Everyone *is*, right?"

Mrs. Shukla nodded, indicating that her husband and four children were also safe. Reunited, aunt and nephews wept with joy.

Three days later, the Shuklas departed for their home village in southern Gujarat, uncertain of whether they would ever return to Morbi.[44]

〰〰〰〰

During the week after the flood, a great diaspora spread across Gujarat. Relieved but anxious, exhausted but restless, survivors slowly coped with a harsh and bewildering new reality. A number settled in with friends on higher ground in Morbi, just a short distance from their flooded homes. Many took refuge in Sanala, Wankaner, Rajkot, and other villages and cities of Saurashtra. Some travelled even farther, to Ahmedabad and other places outside the peninsula.

Many refugees availed themselves of familial succor in villages and towns near Morbi. They left the city by foot, private vehicle, or free government bus; some, journeying to villages on the Machhu River's eastern bank, crossed over the shattered Buffalo Bridge and inched their way down a long metal ladder that the government had placed at the break in the brickwork. People of every background, from Harijans to Brahmins to Muslims, crowded in with sympathetic relatives. Huddled inside small huts, too shocked and poor to even contemplate rebuilding, they spent days waiting in the cloudy countryside of the Saurashtra Peninsula.[45]

About 14,400 survivors evacuated to Rajkot. The final stopping point for some and the first way station for others, the district capital became the emblematic destination for the exodus from Morbi. Some refugees flocked to Rajkot's school buildings, where volunteers offered them clean clothing, hot meals, and medical care. Others, such as Khatijaben Valera and Dhirubhai Mehta, settled in with friends and relatives.[46]

Mayor Ratilal Desai would not reach Rajkot until three or four days after the disaster struck. His relatives had expected him to evacuate almost immediately, but he found himself unable to leave Morbi; the little body he had picked up during the flood remained unclaimed. Eventually, growing weary of watching over a stranger's dead son, he asked the RSS to take the corpse away and departed for his sister's house in Rajkot. Desai would return to Morbi early every morning to fulfill his duties as mayor, but the city had become, in his view, "unlivable." His voice quivered with disgust as he recalled the situation years later: "The whole town emptied out. It was stinking. There was no clean drinking water, dead bodies everywhere."[47]

Like Desai, Ghost Paan proprietor Pratapbhai Adroja took refuge with his sister in Rajkot. Crammed into a small house with his wife, son, and siblings, he began to grow restless. Although only three days had passed since the flood, he felt anxious to return to Morbi and clean out his shop. He doubted whether he would ever live or work in the city again; he merely longed for the peace of mind that clearing out the wreckage of Ghost Paan might bring.[48]

Unlike Khatijaben, Mehta, Desai, and Adroja, a minority of Morbi's inhabitants chose to remain in the city throughout the disaster's aftermath. Some, their entire social networks confined to Morbi, could not imagine going anywhere else. Pride drove others to remain in their homes. For others still, a sense of duty reigned supreme.

After sending his wife, children, and aged father off to other parts of Saurashtra on August 12, Brahmin Kanubhai Kubavat spent his days clearing the debris from his plot in the Tiger Quarter. At night, he slept in the lobby of a local cinema. He did not obtain a clean set of clothes until four or five days after the flood, when he visited a friend in Rajkot.[49]

Convict Gangaram Tapu, his foot severely wounded from the disaster, stayed in the main market for almost a week with his wife and children. While he received traditional treatment from a local holy man, people he referred to as "my men" cleaned out his house and distributed food to survivors in Kabir Hill. After six days, Tapu turned himself in at the police station. He was sent to Rajkot, along with the other former denizens of the subdistrict prison. All had returned of their own volition.[50]

Legislator Gokaldas Parmar stayed in Morbi out of a sense of obligation. He would attest, "My son came from Rajkot on the 16th and said, 'Father, please come to Rajkot now. What will you do here?' I said, 'I cannot leave Morbi, son. Bring food and water from Rajkot. I will remain hungry until then.'" Dissatisfied but dutiful, Parmar's wife and unmarried daughter grudgingly remained behind with him.[51]

Although they sent their families to stay with relatives in neighboring villages, the high-jati men of Lilapar did not evacuate. Fledgling ceramic manufacturer Bhagvanji Patel and his fellow farmers stayed in Lakhdhirnagar for two days, until they had utterly depleted their hosts' limited food stocks. Then, they returned with their families to the ruins of Lilapar. A few houses still stood, and the main well continued to yield fresh water. Laying down tarps in the mud and crowding into the more intact buildings, the high-jati people of Lilapar settled in together. During the coming weeks, they would eat and sleep as a single unit, depending on relief food to survive. By contrast, Lilapar low-jati inhabitants sought shelter with family members in nearby villages, with the men walking to the ruined village every morning for salvage and cleanup.[52]

Despite the devastation surrounding them, Lilapar's leaders showed little doubt that they would eventually resurrect the finest village in the Morbi subdistrict. Others, faced with the magnitude of the flood's destruction, ached with uncertainty. When Adroja returned to Morbi for the first time on August 15—India's Independence Day and Birth Eighth—the city seemed a hollow shell of its former self. Mud had buried Ghost Paan's façade; the floodwaters had soaked and scattered the store's supplies. Adroja knew that it would be futile to reinvest in a dead shop, on a dead street, in a dead city. He would gut the small space, lock the shop for the last time, and leave Morbi behind.

Adroja's thoughts turned to a friend who operated a restaurant in Rajkot. Perhaps, with his connection, he might find a job there.[53]

〰〰〰

During his first days in Morbi, Special Secretary for Relief H. K. Khan worried that the rubble-strewn city would become a prominent stage for political theater. India's nascent democracy, slowly transitioning away from single-party rule by the Congress Party, was embroiled in a period of tremendously contentious politics. The Janata Party—the first non-Congress party to rule India—had recently fractured, with Prime Minister Morarji Desai finding himself ousted by former ally Charan Singh. In Gujarat, Chief Minister Babubhai Patel's Janata government found itself beset by problems large and small. Across India, Congress politicians waited in the wings for their chance at a return to power; former prime minister Indira Gandhi, still ensconced at the helm of Congress, eagerly eyed the upcoming national elections, and Gujarat Congress Party leader Madhavsinh Solanki exchanged frequent barbs with Babubhai.[54]

As a nonpartisan civil servant, Khan wanted to prevent the turmoil from seeping into Morbi. If he did not proceed carefully, the city's muddy streets might play host to a distracting political circus. Congress politicians would exploit the images of destruction to paint a picture of Janata incompetence and neglect, and Janata leaders would use every cash dole and relief camp to trumpet their party's solidarity with the people.[55]

Within three days of the disaster, accusations were already filling the air. In a scathing press conference on August 14, Solanki accused the government of overlooking complaints about the dam's weakness and failing to warn downstream residents of the imminent flood. He leveled personal criticisms against Agriculture Minister Keshubhai Patel, declaring:

> The surprising matter is that the agriculture minister went up to Sanala, a few kilometers away from Morbi. The dam had burst, the destruction of Morbi had started—and yet the agriculture minister knew nothing about it. The administration knew nothing about it. He turned back from Sanala, but neither he nor the administration knew anything about it. . . . This proves the administration's failure.[56]

Calls for Keshubhai's resignation filled the pages of Gujarat's newspapers. The minister's civil service subordinates also came under attack, with one politician claiming that Irrigation Department engineers had dismissed concerns about the Machhu Dam-II's underdesign two years earlier.[57]

The Janata government, for its part, maintained that its officers had taken every reasonable precaution. The spillway's floodgates had been opened, and the deputy engineer responsible for the dam had called for low-lying areas to receive warnings of impending flooding; the structure had simply faced an unforeseeable inflow. Keshubhai pointed out that a dam worker had gone to Lilapar himself and evacuated the village's citizens. One high-ranking Irrigation Department engineer, diving into the fray on behalf of bureaucrats, noted that Morbi had received "adequate" warning, since the municipal ambulance had been broadcasting megaphone announcements of high water levels all day on August 11.[58]

The Janata government's response to the disaster also came under intense scrutiny. After visiting Morbi, Solanki complained:

> Based on the sights I have seen in Morbi's streets and the smells I have experienced, the clearance of human and animal corpses has not been arranged with sufficient speed. How many people were swept away in the flood or crushed under the debris? How many are missing? No arrangements have been made for inquiring into these questions. . . . There is no water. There is no electricity. . . . There is no wood for burning corpses at the crematorium. . . . There is a lack of coordination here. The chief minister must be told that there is a lack of coordination. What other proof of the administration's indolence can there be?[59]

Even the number of deaths became a point of public dispute. Babubhai and other Janata officials maintained that no more than one thousand individuals had perished. Relief workers estimated that four to five thousand deaths might have occurred. Congress leaders and some others suggested figures of twenty thousand or higher.[60]

The boldest salvo in the political battles came amid Solanki's withering postvisit critiques, when he proposed a radical mechanism for accountability. Distrustful of the Janata Party, he demanded an independent judicial investigation of the dam collapse and the subsequent government response. Hearing the reports, Secretary Khan began dreading a rash of divisive recriminations that would distract from the still-dire situation on the ground.[61]

But the chief minister embraced the idea of a judicial investigation. At an impromptu press conference three days after the flood, Babubhai announced that he had asked the chief justice of Gujarat's High Court to appoint a commission of inquiry for the Machhu flood. He took pains to clarify that the idea of an inquiry was his own; the next morning's newspapers would report, "The chief minister also made it known that this commission has not been formed on account of anyone's request or order."[62] (The contents of Babubhai's exhaustive but laconic diary would lend credence to his claim. In his account of a frantic August 12, amid copious notations about his activities upon learning of the disaster, he had scrawled, "Discussion regarding an inquiry commission.")[63] To highlight the commission's political independence, the chief minister "made it known that if the inquiry should find the government responsible, then the government will have to accept responsibility too."[64]

Babubhai's announcement greatly relieved Khan, as it seemed likely to prevent the disaster from becoming fodder for political bickering at the state level; national politics, however, were another matter entirely. Khan remained worried that prominent central government politicians would overrun Morbi, seeking villains to blame and moments to photograph.

Access to Morbi was already tightly controlled; at Khan's urging, Babubhai readily agreed to limit access for politicians as well. Leaders of all parties would receive the same treatment: they would be permitted to visit, but only on Khan's terms. They would not exploit Morbi's suffering populace for political gain.[65]

Indira Gandhi's much-anticipated visit to the city on August 16 proved the effectiveness of Khan's policy. Accompanied by a fifteen-car motorcade, the Congress Party chief surveyed the destruction from an open jeep.[66] Like Babubhai, Gandhi initially encountered hostility. Mayor Ratilal Desai would later remember with fierce pride, "I stopped Indiraji's car. She was passing through town, and I made them stop. I said to her, 'What is there to see here?' I wanted to know whether she had any help to offer or whether she was just there to look."[67] According to Kanubhai Kubavat's recollection, he also exchanged words with Gandhi as she passed by the spot where he was cleaning his house in the Tiger Quarter; when she offered him grain, he pointed out that he did not possess a vessel to accept it in, impressing upon the leader that Morbi's people lacked even the most basic necessities.[68]

Stopping in the Nehru Gate plaza, Gandhi delivered a brief speech to congregated citizens:

> Today, the clouds of sadness have erupted on Morbi. It is not appropriate to lay blame for that with anyone. Today, it is necessary to take steps to deliver aid to people and get Morbi back on its feet. . . . Today is not the occasion for speeches. On behalf of myself and the Congress Party, I have come to offer my condolences.[69]

Meeting with Khan in his office, Gandhi earnestly stated that the state government seemed to be doing everything in its power to help the people. Having lent her moral support, she quietly departed.[70]

Over the week after the disaster, numerous other national politicians took unremarkable trips to Morbi. Toppled prime minister Morarji Desai and his sitting successor, Charan Singh, paid uneventful visits to the city. Several central ministers came and went, making aerial surveys of the flood-affected area without drawing too much attention.[71]

Around the same time, Morbi's Queen Mother, whose son Mayurdhvaj had been the last of the Jadejas, made an appearance in the City of the Peacock Flag. Moved to tears by the destruction and by the outpouring of relief from all over Gujarat, the expatriate vowed to ruin herself financially in order to restore her kingdom to its former grandeur. Pledging that the necessary support could be arranged if people would only return to the city, she declared tremulously, "My everything belongs to Morbi's people."[72]

Under Special Secretary for Relief H. K. Khan's leadership, the week after the flood proved both frenzied and transformative. Hundreds of bodies fed the flames at the crematorium. Tons of mud and debris were steadily carted out of the main streets. Gallons of pesticide blanketed the city's soggy earth. Volunteers fed, clothed, sheltered, and supplied the survivors who remained behind. The four priorities Khan had laid out on August 13—supporting residents, enacting public health measures, clearing waste, and disposing of bodies—lurched forward through the efforts of state government workers and volunteers.[73]

After the cremation of corpses and carcasses, cleaning Morbi's streets and buildings proved the dirtiest task. At best, it entailed heavy lifting, foul odors, and revolting sludge; at worst, it required the extraction of numerous rotting bodies. Wooden beams, twisted metal, and chunks of rubble littered much of the city. Besides endangering the health and safety of those still in Morbi, the mud and debris complicated the execution of other relief activities.[74]

In the first three days of relief work, one hundred fifty trucks rolled into Morbi to help with the work of cleaning. Bulldozers, loaders, and other equipment also arrived in large numbers, and military troops, police officers, Home Guards, volunteers, and citizens all threw themselves into the effort. Health Minister Hemaben Acharya, a woman known for her zeal, allegedly tied off the trailing edge of her sari and began shoveling mud. By the end of relief operations, work crews would remove more than 115,000 tons of mud from Morbi's streets.[75]

As one of Khan's designated parties worked at clearing waste from Morbi, another addressed sanitation problems. Wherever water tankers had not yet arrived, the government distributed chlorine tablets for disinfection. Workers sprayed every corner of the city with DDT. Medical teams set up a makeshift clinic in the maternity hospital, as well as booths along main roads. Fifty-seven thousand survivors and volunteers received cholera injections.[76]

Meanwhile, scores of water tankers finally established a reliable supply of potable water. Tens of thousands of food packets arrived from Rajkot every day, and voluntary organizations started producing meals locally. Relief workers began distributing essential goods, such as lighters, candles, matchsticks, and milk, to flood-affected households.[77]

Material donations flowed in from families, service organizations, and businesses in Rajkot. Hundreds of pounds of wheat, millet, lentils, potatoes, and onions piled up in the district capital's storehouses. Tankers laden with thousands of gallons of milk set out from the city. Following a common postdisaster pattern, Rajkot's populace donated 14,200 used garments, even though clothing was not among the items solicited by the government. Donations flowed so profusely that one newspaper was moved to write, RAJKOT HAS BECOME THE KERCHIEF TO WIPE MORBI'S TEARS.[78]

Khan was pleased with the outpouring of relief and with the early signs of recovery that accompanied it. On August 14, much to his delight, the government restored the Morbi–Rajkot telephone line. Shortly thereafter, the special secretary for relief gained a telephone connection to Ahmedabad as well. Within a few days of arriving in Morbi, he shifted his relief control room to the stately offices of the city's most emblematic landmark, the Mani Mandir.[79]

Khan quickly earned the adulation of Morbi's populace. His somber, efficient style left an enduring impression. One flood survivor later commented, "No one could match him in the public eye. He was fair—strict, but fair."[80] Mayor Ratilal Desai would simply attest, "He did everything we asked."[81]

〰〰〰〰

Long after relief workers began clearing the streets of Morbi, Maliya's fate remained a mystery to outsiders. The raging floodwaters had destroyed all communications and roads to and from the town. On August 13—the first full day of press reports on the disaster—most newspapers mentioned Maliya only in passing, noting that no reports of the town's condition were available.[82]

Government helicopters began relief sorties over the blighted area two days after the flood, dropping food packets to the starving, rain-soaked refugees; based on what they saw through still-ongoing downpours, the helicopter pilots reported that buildings appeared intact but that little could be ascertained about the state of the people.[83] Later on the same day, a solitary survivor from Maliya arrived in Morbi and told eager journalists that, while the water had covered much of the town and dragged around a few people and goods, no one had died. Establishing wireless telegraph contact with Maliya in the evening, Agriculture Minister Keshubhai Patel learned that there had been no deaths in the town, although a dozen or so individuals might have perished in the surrounding farmland.[84] For the next two days, based on the emerging information, the newspapers printed reassuring accounts of the situation to the north. It seemed that the floodwaters, spreading out laterally to the east and west on their journey toward the Gulf of Kutch, had spared Maliya the wrath visited upon Morbi.[85]

By August 17, however, a more sinister portrait was emerging. The Rajkot daily *Phulchhab* revised its previous report of no deaths, exclaiming, MALIYA-MIYANA WAS NOT SAVED EITHER: 190 CORPSES FOUND: 90% OF BUILDINGS DESTROYED; MORE DETAILS COMING OUT: NEED FOR FOOD, MEDICINE. The newspaper explained that, contrary to earlier accounts, Maliya had suffered tremendous damage:

> According to our correspondents, the reports of Maliya having escaped from the destruction are false. The crops in the farmland on the edge of the town are completely destroyed. Houses are destroyed. The boats and household goods of the area's fishermen are destroyed. . . . The supply of necessary goods in the Maliya-Miyana area has been destroyed.[86]

Seventy-four corpses had been discovered in the area, and estimates of the death toll ran as high as three hundred. One leading citizen claimed to have assisted with seventy-five burials himself.[87]

The reports of death and destruction in Maliya met with considerable skepticism from common citizens and government officials in Morbi, Rajkot, and Gandhinagar. Because public officers had not certified the deaths, many suspected that the Miyanas were inflating the death toll to garner more sympathy and relief. District Collector A. R. Banerjee would write:

> Initially on the basis of on the spot review . . . we had reported that though loss of property and house collapses, etc. were substantial at Maliya, loss of life would be around 10 to 15. But, subsequently, local people of Maliya viz. the Miyanas claimed more than 150 persons dead in their areas. . . . The validity of the statement made by the local people could not be ascertained. As per the statement of the local people the dead bodies have already been disposed of before any responsible officer from the police or revenue or even from the town council could be made a witness. . . .[88]

Over the subsequent weeks, months, and years, the people of Maliya would face great difficulties in convincing the rest of the world that they, too, had suffered losses from the Machhu dam disaster.[89]

During the week after the flood, while the rest of Gujarat ignored and then questioned their losses, the Miyanas struggled simply to cope with the consequences of catastrophe. Maliya's roads—usually little more than uneven, dusty trails—had been wiped into oblivion. Phones, trains, trucks—every connection to the outside world had ceased to operate. Foodstuffs and household goods had been washed away or ruined.

Salt industrialist Abdulbhai Mor spent four or five days in the spot to which he had evacuated, near the subdistrict school; he scrounged together food for himself and his family, jockeying for the relief packets dropped from passing helicopters. Having spent the night of the disaster sleeping soundly in his high-lying house, fisherman Husainbhai Manek emerged the next morning to find that the flood had leveled buildings all over Maliya; he knew that his fishing equipment, left on the shore of the Gulf of Kutch the previous day, was gone forever.

After passing a sleepless night in the tree where he had taken refuge, farmer Jashabhai Samani climbed down around 8:00 a.m. on August 12. His wife, his mother, and his two-year-old daughter had survived alongside him; they had watched their house collapse and listened to the anguished cries of the family's other six children as the floodwaters swept them over the open farmland and out toward the sea. Clinging to one another, the four survivors staggered to a higher part of Maliya's agricultural environs, where relatives took them in for three days. On the fourth day, Samani came to the town to stay with his brothers, whose house was still intact.

He did not know what to expect. He did not even know how he would live from month to month. But he knew that he would go to the Gulf of Kutch—and beyond, if needed—to find the bodies of his dead children.[90]

The line stretched from the window, down the sidewalk, past the truck-sized sinkhole in the still muddy street, and out of sight around the corner.[91] RSS volunteers, Home Guards, soldiers, and returning householders all mingled easily. Some smiled for the first time in days. Each customer eagerly awaited his turn at the head of the line, where deft hands sprinkled tobacco, fruit, and fennel seeds onto juicy betel leaves, folding them rapidly in a valiant but vain effort to keep pace with demand.

Ghost Paan was open for business, and Pratapbhai Adroja brimmed with glee. The shop's resurrection a mere five days after the flood seemed utterly miraculous.

Upon arriving in Morbi on August 15—Indian Independence

Day and Birth Eighth—Adroja found Ghost Paan filled with mud and debris. Despondent at the shop's flood-ravaged state, he resolved to abandon Morbi and seek his fortune in Rajkot. He was sifting through the vestiges of his former livelihood, contemplating what he could salvage, when a gaggle of student volunteers approached him. Full of voluntary zeal, they insisted on shoveling out the shop, restoring shelves to their proper places, and disposing of stale merchandise. Watching the students restore the small space, Adroja began to emerge from his despair. Suddenly, recovery did not seem impossible.

The vigorous activity at Adroja's solitary storefront did not escape notice. The local police chief, a paan lover himself, was overjoyed upon learning of the restoration under way. Eager to see the business reopen, he reached into his pocket and handed Adroja fifty-one rupees with instructions to purchase supplies as quickly as possible. Flabbergasted at the official's kindness, Adroja could barely stammer his thanks.

For the rest of the day, a wave of generosity overwhelmed Adroja. Everyone he encountered on August 15 seemed intent on seeing Ghost Paan reopen the very next morning. A fellow paan merchant, not yet ready to restart his own business, encouraged Adroja to use his stock of ingredients, which had remained above the floodwaters. A utility company sent a crew with the singular mission of restoring electricity to Ghost Paan. The student volunteers, their enthusiasm reinforced by the excitement building around the shop, scrubbed the walls and polished the newly unearthed floor. While the rest of Gujarat celebrated Indian independence and the birth of Vishnu the Preserver as Lord Krishna, all of Morbi seemed focused on rehabilitating Ghost Paan.

At 5:00 a.m. on August 16, Adroja lifted the corrugated tin shade from his small window, offering paan to Morbi once again. Word of the opening spread quickly among the city's nicotine-starved relief workers. By 7:00 a.m., the line of customers became long, and it only continued growing. Agriculture Minister Keshubhai Patel bided his time in the queue, happily trading a few coins for a small pouch of sweetened tobacco when his turn with Adroja finally arrived.

As the day wore on, Adroja greeted an impressive array of politicians, bureaucrats, and soldiers. Many seemed eager to take his renascent business under their wings. Government small-business loans, they assured the shop owner, would be easy to obtain. One well-placed source encouraged Adroja to apply for a license to keep the shop open until 1:00 a.m.; most businesses in Morbi would have to adhere to a curfew, he explained, but law enforcement officials would be happy to make an exception for Ghost Paan.

By most accounts, Ghost Paan was the very first shop to reopen in Morbi's ruined commercial zone. Where Adroja led, other merchants would follow, slowly reviving the city's shops over the ensuing weeks and months.

Decades later, many of the soldiers and volunteers who served in Morbi would delight in telling the story of Ghost Paan—one of the few memories from the time that they could cherish. Emerging from the horrific recollections of bloated corpses and broken families, they would grin as they recalled the friendly little man and his curiously themed tobacco shop.

Chapter 8

"Everyone Was a Beggar"

Every morning, before the sun's first rays pierced the hazy eastern horizon, Chief Minister Babubhai Patel roused himself from a brief slumber.[1] Since his arrival in Morbi two days after the flood, he had settled into a familiar routine. Donning his thick, black-rimmed glasses, he readied himself for the day in the confines of a modest guesthouse room on the Machhu River's eastern bank. He bathed, made his bed, and performed his daily yoga exercises. Then, with a vigor that belied his sixty-eight years, he set off on foot down the rutted, muddy road toward Morbi.

Most flood survivors, already surprised that their chief minister was staying in the ruined city, were further amazed that he had opted for such simple accommodations. Their incredulous reactions elicited a quiet, knowing smile from Babubhai. As a member of the Indian independence movement, he had spent several months of his youth in British-administered prisons; any other lodging seemed luxurious by contrast.

As the chief minister strode vigorously through mud and puddles, it never took long for a small throng to fall in line behind him. The attention left him unfazed; in Gandhinagar, he often left

207

his office on impromptu bicycle forays, chatting with street vendors and accumulating hangers-on along the route. Some in Morbi's early morning crowds wished to air specific grievances—delays in clearing rubble-strewn streets, insufficient food aid, lack of assistance in locating still-missing relatives. Others, more timid or perhaps simply curious, filed along behind Babubhai in silence.

As Babubhai approached the Machhu River, Morbi announced itself with a stench. The sickening smell of rot and decay, wafting out of downtown on a gentle breeze, sometimes prompted those around the chief minister to gag. Babubhai, however, did not flinch, barreling down the riverbank. He would pause briefly, passing his critical eye over the government's work on a temporary earthen causeway for trucks and buses. Then, climbing up a long metal ladder onto the surviving stretch of the Buffalo Bridge, he would continue on toward the regal Mani Mandir.

Underneath the arches of the bridge, the Machhu River was, once again, a mere trickle.

〰〰〰

Immortally carved into the rich red stone, a pair of guards, flanked by tiny elephants, guarded the entrance to the Mani Mandir's inner sanctum.[2] Inside, underneath the dazzlingly painted dome, a pantheon of Hindu deities nestled unnoticed in private alcoves. Outside, government employees crisscrossed the dusty courtyard delivering papers that had curled up in the moist monsoon heat. At all four edges of the complex, the ornate sandstone arcades, untouched by the floodwaters that had ravaged the rest of Morbi, echoed with activity. Sheltered inside the temple, the deities would listen impassively as mortals debated the fate of the City of the Peacock Flag.

Every morning at 9:00, a multitude of government officials assembled at the temporary relief offices located in the Mani Mandir. On most days, Chief Minister Babubhai Patel had already spent several hours surveying Morbi's streets by the time he arrived for the conference. The chief minister appeared non-descript as he filed through the Mani Mandir's grand, thirty-foot-tall entrance, but he always drew notice from soldiers and staffers. He quietly acknowledged their respectful nods as he passed by.

Upon entering the large meeting room, Babubhai would settle in at a small table in an obscure corner. His position emblematized the role he had chosen to play. Believing that his value to the relief effort lay largely in the symbolism of his presence, he "kept almost totally in the background," in the words of one observer.[3]

Special Secretary for Relief H. K. Khan—the man charged with coordinating the government's various relief activities—had quickly won the chief minister's confidence. The secretary's large desk occupied a prominent position in the meeting room; when queried, Babubhai would often direct staffers to Khan. "Look, I am not in charge here," he told them. "I am the chief minister, but I have come as a volunteer."[4]

As the morning conference commenced, it was Khan who led the discussion. The secretary had quickly forged close working relationships with each of the men in regular attendance. Agriculture Minister Keshubhai Patel, who had been a vigorous and stalwart presence in the provision of relief, regularly took a prominent seat at the conference table. The district's Home Guard commander and its superintendent of police, who had been the first government officers to arrive in the flood-stricken city, contributed their stern presence to the daily meetings. Member of the legislative assembly Gokaldas Parmar and District Collector A. R. Banerjee also attended almost every day.[5]

Then there was the man everyone had come to affectionately know as "the government's son-in-law" for his tenacious advocacy—Mayor Ratilal Desai. In the days after the flood, mourning the loss of his son and despairing at Morbi's broken condition, he had harbored thoughts of permanently relocating; he had even begun to look for a house in Rajkot. But a sense of obligation had pulled him back. "I was the mayor," he would later muse. "If I had not stayed, who would have looked out for this city?" Returning to fulfill his duty, he had grown increasingly impressed with Morbi's transformation under Khan's leadership and Babubhai's watchful gaze.[6]

Sitting at the Mani Mandir conference table, Desai marveled at how Khan took firm hold of the morning meetings, laying out an agenda for the day's work and distributing tasks with curt efficiency. Babubhai would observe quietly, letting Khan handle the work of organization while lending his gravitas to the proceedings. As the meeting progressed, Desai would chime in, highlighting unmet needs in the town and suggesting ways to address them. Though only a city official, he had become Morbi's chief advocate, respected by law enforcement officers, bureaucrats, and cabinet ministers alike for his intimate local knowledge and his indomitable will. Desai's higher-ranking peers put their agencies and departments at his disposal, seeking to carry out his requests in any way possible.

Desai mirrored the state officers' respect, admiring the boundless energy that the men—foreigners to Morbi's soil—brought to the relief efforts. He described it as "God's blessing" that Babubhai was chief minister at the time. Similarly, he would remark breathlessly of Banerjee, "I have never seen a man like him in my life." His affection for Khan ran so deep that he would invite the secretary to his daughter's wedding ten years later.[7]

After the morning conference, military officers, volunteers, and citizens would pull Desai to different neighborhoods, proudly exhibiting advances and sharply criticizing delays. Determined to see Morbi return to its former glory, the mayor displayed limitless energy and stony resolve as he toured the slowly reviving city.

Nonetheless, the turmoil of the disaster had not subsided in his mind. He would recall the period as one in which he was "very upset, very disappointed, very despairing." He later confessed that, upon returning to his sister's house in Rajkot every evening, he would "cry for three or four hours," disconsolate over the loss that no government could rectify.[8]

≋≋≋≋≋

Kanubhai Kubavat watched as a truck unleashed chaos upon a Tiger Quarter intersection.[9] A mob of clamoring men and women, all elbows, scrambled for position, struggling to reach the back of the vehicle. Discordant shouts flew up toward the men tossing down sacks of grain—cursing them, thanking them, pleading with them. The overwhelmed distributors kept their distance from the desperate survivors, scowling and hastening to finish as quickly as possible.

Turning away, Kubavat shook his head. He would not—he could not—participate in the madness. But deep down, a part of him longed to accept the succor the big trucks and the stony-faced men offered.

During the month after flood, relief goods became a mainstay of daily life in Morbi. At first, in the absence of a central inventory or coordinating entity, the distribution proceeded haphazardly. The district collectorate in Rajkot sent truckloads of donated goods to the flood-affected areas, but it seemed that every organization, association, jati, and village in Gujarat was also dispatching its own distributors. Occasionally, donors would deliver goods to prominent citizens of a particular neighborhood, asking them to ensure that every resident received a fair portion. More often, they would simply roll to a stop somewhere and begin handing down their cargo to whomever asked for it. Survivors, hearing that relief workers were distributing some good or another, would rush in from the surrounding areas and jostle for a share. The first to arrive would receive deliveries of pots, grains, clothes, shoes, mattresses, pillows, sheets, and lighting supplies. One survivor recalled, "The people would come to distribute. Everyone would run. You got whatever little you could get. Of course, there was a lot of ruckus and pushing. . . . The people would distribute, and then they would go away."[10] Survivor contact with the distributors remained minimal; overwhelmed by the belligerence and still-raw grief of their beneficiaries, many relief providers left hurriedly after delivering their cargos.

Eventually, seeking to stem the disorder that prevailed in the provision of relief goods, Special Secretary for Relief H. K. Khan and the leaders of thirty-four nonprofit organizations struck a deal to systematize distribution. Parceling out Morbi and its surroundings, the new scheme assigned a particular community to each organization. The Red Cross, for instance, adopted the agricultural neighborhood of Madhapar, while the Ahmedabad-based Sadvichar Parivar took on the northern Leatherworker Quarter. The organizations would issue cards to their beneficiaries, and these cards would then serve as the basis for a regulated distribution in the area.[11]

Perhaps predictably, the results were mixed. Some organizations served their areas better than others. Families in the Harijan Quarter found themselves overwhelmed with relief supplies, for instance, while residents of the Leatherworker Quarter received little assistance.[12]

No relief workers even went to the Muslim neighborhood adjoining the crematorium. The residents had resolved not to seek out relief, since a community leader had persuaded the local cotton mill to provide some necessary supplies, and they would later hold forth as a matter of pride the fact that they had not accepted any "charity." But they never failed to recall that no relief workers had ever come to them.[13]

Against the patchwork backdrop of the systematized but still uneven provision of goods, outside groups continued to deliver sporadic donations. In many cases, the donations arrived in the form of kits targeted at specific populations, such as school supplies for families with children, tool sets for artisans, and replacement carts for itinerant food vendors. Often, however, the additional goods were simply basic supplies whose delivery was not coordinated with the government.

The "flood of generosity," as many would come to call the influx of goods and capital to the flood-affected areas, originated in a flurry of donations from Rajkot District, the state of Gujarat, and beyond. Schools, student groups, banks, charities, cities, villages, civic associations, industrial companies, merchants, entire jatis, private citizens, and organizations of Hindus, Muslims, Jains, and Christians committed funds for the relief effort. Millions of rupees flowed into the Chief Minister's Relief Fund, the official government collection receptor for donations. Millions more arrived in Morbi and the surrounding villages independently. Various institutions of the Janata government promised financial aid to the flood-stricken, pledging that the government would not abandon the people; Congress Party officials promised their own aid, pledging that they would not allow the government's negligence to harm the people.

The Machhu dam disaster became a cause célèbre nationally and internationally. Some of India's biggest film stars held a September benefit event in Ahmedabad. London witnessed a charity Indian dance program whose proceeds went to survivors. The Missionaries of Charity sent a group to establish new health and education facilities, and Mother Theresa herself visited Morbi at one point. Donations poured in from numerous countries, including Japan, Australia, England, and the United States.[14]

By the end of August, rumors were circulating to the effect that the government might provide monetary assistance to survivors. It seemed that homeowners, businessmen, and industrialists would receive substantial interest-free loans. There were also rumblings about relatives of the deceased receiving cash doles— cash doles that were intended to ease the suffering, and possibly to soften the government's culpability. Nonetheless, to most survivors who were still emerging from the daze of the disaster, the government's intentions for financial aid and monetary compensation remained remote, inaccessible, and unclear.

As money and supplies inundated Morbi, accusations of corruption began swirling throughout the city. Newspaper stories and street tales spoke of relief administrators and influential citizens who had redirected cash and valuable goods for personal profit. The chief minister, surprisingly unconcerned by such matters, tempered the public anxiety. "For now," he said, "let us make sure that at least forty rupees from every one hundred . . . are reaching the people who need them. Let the other sixty get eaten up. We will reckon with that later. Right now, the people who need money should get it."[15]

While government officials, donors, and common citizens harbored worries about high-level corruption, many distributors felt irritated by what one would call "double trouble"—the hoarding of goods by survivors. One volunteer heavily involved with the provision of relief supplies would lament, "The dam broke because of the heavy rains. But people's morals also broke because of the flood of relief."[16] Another volunteer would comment, "They grabbed anything that came their way. They had no control left."[17] Legislator Gokaldas Parmar told the story of a woman who stored away at least half a dozen stoves in addition to the one she needed.[18] In later years, some flood survivors would openly admit to having lied about the sizes of their families or the goods they had previously received in order to maximize their yield; in their view, the more influential people were destined to get more things anyway.[19] When Principal T. R. Shukla arrived back in Morbi in September, an acquaintance ruefully commented to him, "People have become so greedy that if somebody said that malaria was being distributed, they would go and grab it."[20]

Yet, even as some survivors of the flood hoarded excess goods, a large number found themselves unable to accept even the most basic supplies. Many who considered themselves members of high-status jatis and higher social classes, like Kubavat, could not bear the shame of standing in line and extending their hands for charity. Whereas most—though certainly not all—Harijans, low-status Muslims, and other "backward" people readily sought out necessary supplies, members of "good households" often would not yield. Kubavat recalled, "Those who could scramble around, wait in line, jockey for position—they would take. We had to think about our status, right? We could not push around."[21]

The suffering of the proud did not remain unaddressed. While Khan occupied himself with ensuring that "people of the weaker sections" received relief goods, various organizations, from Vaniya jati associations to the Home Guards, prepared kits for families that would not seek aid.[22] Going from house to house, they offered the flood-ravaged members of the upper classes the supplies they would not accept in the open street. Although some, like Kubavat, never received visits from the itinerant relief providers, the efforts were widespread. In the end, volunteers convinced many proud householders to accept the help they so desperately needed.

In Lilapar, Bhagvanji Patel had no choice but to embrace charity in spite of his pride in his village, his jati, and his status. With their homes utterly destroyed, Lilapar's citizens depended on relief supplies for their survival. A diamond merchant association had first brought relief to the village within a few days after the disaster, struggling to a point half a mile away from the ruins and summoning the survivors to pick up grain, clothes, and bedding. The association began regularly distributing in the area, but other organizations, moved by the plight of Lilapar—the little community at the foot of the dam—provided copious supplementary goods. Eventually, with Khan's systematization of the relief effort, the Rajkot branch of the Ramakrishna Ashrama temple, which had been delivering ready-made food to the village from the very beginning, assumed official responsibility for Bhagvanji and his fellow citizens.

No one refused the food, clothing, or other supplies that poured into Lilapar. Bhagvanji's brother would explain, "Poor and rich were the same. Everybody was needy. . . . We took whatever we could get, because we needed whatever we could get."[23]

The sentiment was shared all over the Machhu River Valley. In the face of catastrophe, few could avoid humbling themselves before one form of aid or another. As Mayor Ratilal Desai put it, "Everyone was a beggar."[24]

Babubhai Patel wasted no time after each morning's conference at the Mani Mandir.[25] As staffers and officials returned to their desks, the chief minister would stride out into Morbi's gray streets to walk among the people.

Harkening back to his days in the independence movement, Babubhai believed firmly that political leaders needed to show solidarity with their constituents. At his insistence, many cabinet ministers were staying in Morbi. (One night, when Babubhai learned that his finance minister was actually sleeping at a government rest house in Rajkot, he telephoned the man at 1:00 a.m., informing him that he would be spending his nights in Morbi from then on.)[26]

During his morning tours, the chief minister stopped to greet clusters of men leaning against their shovels and struck up conversations with young women sifting through what remained of their families' possessions. Survivors sometimes responded coolly or even belligerently. As citizens slowly came to grips with the enormity of the disaster, shock often gave way to anger. Commenting on the populace's agitated emotional state, District Collector A. R. Banerjee would lament:

> We were not allowed to be left alone to carry on the relief operations and we had first to face and pacify the jittery and excited local population by patiently hearing their grievances. As such, in the initial stages the handful of government officers and personnel including revenue, police, and army employed in relief and rehabilitation work were very often surrounded by a mass of people shouting and talking at the same time, each trying to draw the attention to his own problem, and, if possible, virtually drag the officers physically to their houses or areas for immediate solution of their problem. . . . There was no respite from the continuous flow of people who thronged the control room with their grievances. . . .[27]

As the embodiment of the government of Gujarat, the chief minister bore the brunt of the citizenry's discontentment. He endured many condemnations from furious survivors, particularly in the immediate aftermath of the flood.

Despite the overt hostility of many disgruntled citizens, Babubhai never wavered. Projecting an almost serene compassion, he listened carefully and patiently to opinions on his government's provision of relief. Often, survivors' reports directly contradicted updates provided during the morning conference—the streets of a particular neighborhood had not in fact been cleared of mud, for example, or a particular relief kitchen ran short on food every day. In such cases, Babubhai vowed to follow up.

When citizens blamed their plight on the government and its dam, however, the chief minister gently deflected their rage. The flood had been a natural disaster, he would say. The government had arrived to help the people, and he was determined to assist Morbi however he could.

Babubhai's denial of government culpability struck survivors as dubious, but his presence evoked nearly universal admiration. As the weeks passed and the chief minister maintained his mobile vigil on Morbi's streets, hostility slowly yielded to gratitude. Years later, one citizen of Morbi explained:

> I got no government help. . . . But our chief minister was unparalleled. His work was excellent. He brought his entire secretariat here and did tremendous coordination work—there is no denying that. Gujarat will never find another chief minister like Babubhai Jashbhai Patel.[28]

≈≈≈≈≈

While the people and government of Gujarat devoted their attention to Morbi, the citizens of Maliya quietly took stock of their losses.[29] Because the wall of water had become shallower as it approached the town, the wounds it inflicted there varied more widely than in Morbi. Some residents had emerged virtually unscathed. Others had lost everything.

Because fisherman Husainbhai Manek lived on high ground in the middle of the town, the flood had left his house and possessions untouched. Apart from a lack of food supplies, which had run short in the market, he experienced little need for outside help. He knew, however, that the waters had washed his livelihood into the Gulf of Kutch, and he looked toward the uncertain future with anxiety.[30]

Abdulbhai Mor had suffered more extensive losses than Manek. Although he had not yet inspected the damages at India Salt Works, his house was a disheartening sight. Like many of Maliya's buildings, it had emerged from the disaster intact but gutted. Mor remembered:

> All of my possessions were carried away or ruined. They were covered in dirt, covered in mud up to two feet. We grabbed our kids and went to safe ground. We did not stop to take any of our things. Some of my possessions were left, but the grains were rotten, the clothes were ruined—everything was covered in two feet of mud. . . . Nothing was saved.[31]

Slowly, Mor cleaned his muddy house with the help of outside volunteers, who had finally begun to arrive in Maliya.

Relief did not reach the desolate northern town as rapidly as it had reached Morbi. For almost a week, food packets dropped from helicopters constituted the only aid to beleaguered survivors. Eventually, trucks from charitable organizations—Muslim, Hindu, and secular—began arriving, laden with food and relief goods. As in Morbi and the area's flood-affected villages, relief organizations offered foodstuffs, lighting supplies, bedding, and clothing. Given Maliya's large Muslim population, some benefactors delivered coffins.

In some cases, volunteers delivered supplies to individual houses. Some survivors would even recall ordered distribution schemes based on government-issued ration cards. Most often, however, the provision of relief goods replicated the scenes of chaos that dotted Morbi's streets. Mor explained, "It was like throwing scraps to dogs. If you got a sack in your hand, you took it. If it landed on your head, you took it. If it landed on my head, I would take it. There was tremendous pushing and shoving."[32]

With all their possessions ruined, many survivors grabbed whatever came with a sense of desperation. "We did not pay attention to what organization was giving," Mor would later chuckle. "Whether they were from Bhavnagar or America, it was all the same. We did not ask questions."[33]

Like service organizations, government agencies were slow to come to Maliya's aid. While Morbi received the attention of an entire relief cabinet, its neighbor to the north languished. On September 1, long after the government had repaired the roads leading to Morbi, significant work continued on the major highway near Maliya. After flying over the town on August 14, Chief Minister Babubhai Patel had stressed the importance of timely relief provision, but his subordinates made few visits to the area in the weeks after the disaster.[34]

On September 22, well over a month after the flood, District Collector A. R. Banerjee and a team of officers toured Maliya and discussed with leading citizens how best to provide food and basic necessities. According to Banerjee's official correspondence, the residents were still in dire need of oil, kerosene, matches, candles, potatoes, onions, tea, sugar, and vegetable oil at the time of the visit. Since the town's inhabitants could not produce any corpses, the collector and his companions came away doubting the Miyanas' claims of lives lost.[35]

A fortnight after Banerjee's tour, the governor of Gujarat—the ceremonial head of the state—surveyed the damage in Maliya, focusing on the town's low-jati Hindu neighborhoods. In spite of the widespread skepticism about the number of deaths in the town, the state government announced around the time of the governor's visit that it would provide cash doles to those who had lost family members in the flood.[36]

The promise of cash doles offered little solace to farmer Jashabhai Samani, who was struggling to cope with the disaster's aftermath. Save for his wife, mother, and two-year-old daughter, he had lost everything. He would later recall, "The building fell. The carts were carried away. The oxen were carried away. The people were carried away. Nothing that belonged to me was left behind."[37]

Samani found the corpse of one of his children a short distance away from the ruins of his earthen hut in the farmland surrounding Maliya. For the other five, he had to journey farther. He would explain:

> One of my people was here, about half a kilometer away. The rest were by a salt factory on the other side of the sea—in Kutch, on the other side of the bridge. I came to know after a month that there were bodies there. I went to look, and based on the clothes, I recognized them.

Bringing the bodies back to town, Samani buried them. "I was in shock," he would later confess. "I had no idea what was going on."[38]

≈≈≈≈≈

As the weeks wore on, and the acute shock of the days immediately following the flood wore off, Morbi's scattered citizens began processing their experiences.[39] Most would require six months, a year, or even more to feel that everything had returned to normal, but the first adjustments—tentative and unsatisfying though they may have been—took place in late August and early September 1979.

For Principal T. R. Shukla and his wife, every day held reminders of how narrowly they had escaped destruction in a crowded downtown movie theater. On their eastward journey, the Shuklas found that rickshaw drivers and porters refused their money, averring that it was a humanitarian duty to aid survivors of such a terrible disaster. A newspaper printed near their home village in southern Gujarat carried an article entitled A FEARSOME COBRA SAVED THE LIVES OF AN ENTIRE FAMILY IN THE MORBI FLOOD DISASTER, and the story of the miraculous chain of events quickly spread. Principal Shukla's conversations with friends, which frequently evolved into monologues on the horrors of August 11, yielded thousands of rupees in relief pledges.

It gradually became clear to the Shuklas that they would return to Morbi. Heartening reports of the city's imminent recovery began reaching them. The city's colleges, they soon learned, were preparing to reopen. It seemed to the Shuklas that Morbi was slowly recovering normalcy.[40]

To many survivors who had remained in Morbi or Rajkot, the future seemed more uncertain. Khatijaben Valera and her relatives, long tied to Morbi and its kings, felt unsure for the first time about where they belonged. Many members of the clan were experiencing nightmares about the Paris of Saurashtra. (These would continue for many years afterward.) After two of the family's senior singers—Khatijaben's husband's father and uncle—gave a lucrative concert in Mumbai, the men began contemplating a move out of Morbi. With their musical gifts, they could reap rich rewards in Mumbai, Ahmedabad, or Rajkot.

The plans stalled when the Valeras' spiritual leader, with whom they had begun staying after their first days in the district capital, came to know of their ideas. He scolded them roundly, asking, "How can you just pick up and leave?"

Khatijaben and her family knew that they could not act against their spiritual adviser's wishes. They would resurrect their broken lives in the City of the Peacock Flag. As a first step, the patriarchs offered their concert earnings for the purchase of new household supplies. By one month after the disaster, Khatijaben and the other women and children had moved from the spiritual leader's lodging to Rajkot's old tuberculosis sanatorium; the men, angered by reports of looting, had returned to southern Morbi to keep vigil over their decaying bungalow.[41]

Unlike the Valeras, Bhagvanji Patel had gone home just days after the disaster. But he and the other residents of Lilapar faced no less uncertainty. Sleeping in the few intact buildings, surviving by the hands of relief organizations, and slowly clearing the detritus of a village destroyed, they spent long days wondering how they would return to normalcy. State government bulldozers leveled the ground, but it remained a wasteland.

As they took stock of the destruction, Lilapar's citizens sought the bodies of their cattle, hoping to gain closure on their former lives and move toward a new future. Walking and hitchhiking all the way to the Gulf of Kutch, they searched in vain. Bhagvanji would recall ruefully, "I lost fourteen cattle—three goats, four oxen, four buffalo, three cows. All of them were washed away. I spent three days searching for them. I did not find a single one. . . . I went all the way to Maliya. I did not find a single one."[42]

For many of Morbi's citizens, the losses and trauma remained too raw. Although the initial shock of the flood had passed, many could not escape its terror. Like Ratilal Desai, some cried for hours every night over the loss of loved ones. One woman blindfolded herself for days on end, simply unwilling to look at anything else. Sleepless nights were a norm; one survivor would report seeing water every time she closed her eyes. Some had determined never to return to the Machhu River's banks, and a good number would follow through on that resolve.[43]

Kanubhai Kubavat's wife, staying with her brother in southern Saurashtra, was suffering a mental breakdown. After lying awake at night, she would wail and brood all day, reliving the trauma of the terrible afternoon in the Tiger Quarter. Kubavat's brother-in-law, unable to manage his sister's psychic distress, eventually had her admitted to a hospital.[44]

Dhirubhai Mehta's wife had also lost all semblance of mental composure; she cried, shouted, and retreated, completely undone by the loss of her daughter and only son. Her husband, though mentally stable, was utterly disconsolate. Some time later, Mehta's legal counsel would write:

On account of this unwarned and unpredictably voluminous surge of the waters of the evacuating reservoir, the people of Morbi in general and my client in particular had been left with no time to devise ways and means to save lives and property that accounted for their, and his, reasonably happy and unanguished existence. . . .

The shock, agony, and mental setback which my client and his wife suffered on account of this tragic and untimely loss of their children in the flash flood have left permanent scars on their minds and bodies. My client's wife had undergone a tubectomy operation before the disaster, and now she cannot give birth to a child. Nor can she have the benefit of a tuboplasty operation because of her ill health and greatly weakened heart— with which she has become afflicted because of the shock of losing her children. As the son lost was the only son, and also as the wife is no longer in a position to give another child, much less a son, my client has had further cause of mental torture, which continues even today and affects his efficiency to manage his business and conduct ordinary affairs of life.[45]

For weeks after the flood, Mehta and his wife lived in a daze, paralyzed by a sorrow that seemed resistant to all mollification.

Exactly one month after the flood, on September 11, Mehta read in the newspaper that the government of Gujarat had appointed a one-man judicial inquiry to investigate the causes of the Machhu dam disaster. Assisted by the retired chairman of the Central Water and Power Commission and the emeritus chancellor of Ahmedabad's prestigious Indian Institute of Management, the justice would deliver his findings in six months. The newspaper explained:

The commission's mandate is . . . (1) To investigate the reasons for the failure of the Machhu-II on 11 August 1979, and particularly the dam's conception, construction, design, and maintenance as they relate to this disaster. (2) To investigate the appropriateness of the steps taken by various government officers to prevent the disaster before it hit affected areas and to mitigate the effects arising from it. (3) To offer recommendations for future guidance in this context.[46]

The news meant little to Mehta. Simply put, he "did not believe that there would be justice." He would recall thinking, "Who gives a damn? Everything happens inside offices. They do their inquiry their way."[47]

Like Mehta, most flood survivors found little reason for optimism in the weeks following the disaster. For a lucky few, however, the flood had become a source of hope. Ten days after turning himself in—and less than three weeks after saving dozens in Morbi's flooded streets—murderer Gangaram Tapu received a pardon. Citing Tapu's five daughters and his heroism during the disaster, a judge released him from serving the remainder of his sentence. A free man, Tapu returned home to his wife and children in Kabir Hill.[48]

〰〰〰〰

As the burning sun reached its apex, Chief Minister Babubhai Patel would make his way to one of Morbi's myriad relief kitchens, which operated out of tents and buildings scattered across the city.[49] The aroma of crackling *vaghaar*—a distinctive mixture of vegetable oil and spices—mingled with the ever-present stench of rot to announce the lunch hour. Lines formed outside the kitchens, growing longer with each passing day as survivors returned to Morbi's gutted remains.

At each relief kitchen, diners sat cross-legged in long lines on the cool earth. Broad, dried leaves called *patrala* lay before them, serving as disposable dishes. Volunteers moved up and down the parallel rows, ladling hot food onto the leaves from large pots. Servers often teased diners, pressuring them in the typical manner of Saurashtrian hospitality to eat more. Babubhai frequently insisted on serving the survivors and workers himself, sitting down to eat in the last batch. Regardless of their religious affiliations, the kitchens happily fed survivors and workers of all backgrounds, sometimes offering special meals for the ongoing holy months of Shravan and Ramadan.

The cooks, many of whom had honed their art while cooking for thousands at Gujarat's sacred pilgrimage sites, labored with a practiced and purposeful rhythm. They chopped vegetables, rolled flatbread, and stirred immense pots of lentil soup with a speed and grace that belied the work's difficulty.

The operation of a relief kitchen demanded immense effort from volunteers. At one religious organization's tent, for instance, the day started at 5:00 a.m. with meditation and prayer. Shortly thereafter, preparations began for breakfast, which commenced promptly at 7:00 a.m. Pots of savory lentil rice and vegetable stew were already boiling by the time breakfast ended, and lunch ran from 10:00 a.m. to 1:00 p.m. Many survivors and volunteers stopped by for afternoon chai and returned once more for dinner, which was served from 5:00 p.m. to 9:00 p.m. Assisted by fifteen dishwashers, ten full-time cooks allowed the kitchen to serve an estimated ten thousand meals per day. Another fifty of the organization's volunteers roamed the city, bringing food and supplies to survivors who were unable to venture out or too embarrassed to seek help.[50]

Years later, volunteers from various relief kitchens would maintain that the chief minister always ate with them. One volunteer from a religious organization insisted that Babubhai ate at his tent at "least two times a day";[51] similarly, a man who helped to operate the Home Guard relief kitchen at V. C. High School bragged that the chief minister took "every meal" there.[52] In fact, Babubhai purposefully rotated among the kitchens in order to meet diners and ensure that they were being properly fed. But like survivors, volunteers had grown to profoundly admire the chief minister, and their affection would revise their memories over the subsequent decades, transforming the man from a wide-ranging leader into an omnipresent legend.

Member of the legislative assembly Gokaldas Parmar was a stubborn man.[53] In the flood's immediate aftermath, his son had pleaded with him to evacuate to Rajkot, but the legislator would not relent. An inveterate wearer of homespun cotton clothing since his youth as a freedom fighter, he had grudgingly donned his son's synthetic clothes for a few days as a stopgap measure. He had gone almost a week after the flood without bathing; thereafter, he had lugged water from almost a half a mile away on his aging frame. But he would not leave Morbi.

Parmar's wife and daughter suffered the discomforts of the flood-ravaged city with him. For almost a fortnight, they lived in a tiny cabin on the roof, their house occupied by mud and broken glass. Each evening, sitting together in silence, they ate lovingly packed meals sent by their relatives in Rajkot.

Setting out at daybreak to attend to civic matters, Parmar would leave the two women alone in the middle of a desolate Shakti Plot. His wife later lamented:

> He would depart early in the morning and come back at night. We were saddened. We said, "It would have been better if the water had taken us away. You leave us, mother and daughter, all alone here. We get scared." There would be nothing, not even a dog, around. . . . Hungry, thirsty, we remained up in that cabin all day. You could not see anything. Not even a little dog.[54]

When relief workers occasionally arrived bearing questions for the member of the legislative assembly, punctuating the solitude of the women's eerie wasteland, the pair "could only shiver" in response.[55]

Parmar, meanwhile, spent long days listening to the woes of common people and volunteers. Though the work of relief had begun "on a war-footing," in the words of the newspapers, many worrisome stories caught the old statesman's ear during his daily perambulations. Those who had lost their homes did not know how they would rebuild. In the manufacture of clocks and ceramics and tiles, industrialists large and small languished without any avenues for restarting their enterprises. The registration of deaths was crawling forward, with little clarity as to the mechanism by which the government would provide compensation. In every arena of life, the state government's aid was not arriving soon enough for Morbi.

Parmar devoted all his energies to heeding his constituents' concerns. He operated as if in constant crisis, often disregarding even his own appearance. His wife recalled, "You would not even recognize him. You know how those shepherds look, running around behind their animals? That was how he looked—one sandal on, one sandal off, a walking stick carelessly grabbed."[56]

When Morbi's haggard legislator arrived home late in the evening, his wife and daughter took pains to avoid troubling him with their own difficulties, instead offering what little solace they could. "We would have that much pity on him, wouldn't we?" his wife explained. "He had a hard job."[57]

Through the end of August and into the beginning of September, Chief Minister Babubhai Patel pressed forward with an indomitable determination to see Morbi rise up from the rubble of the Machhu dam disaster.[58] Under his watchful eye—and with the expert coordination of Special Secretary for Relief H. K. Khan and District Collector A. R. Banerjee—the city's infrastructure slowly began stirring to life. Freshly leveled roads supported caravans of relief trucks. Electricity coursed through newly strung power lines. A pump on the banks of the Machhu River delivered ample water to central collection points, and the work of laying new pipes and gutters was undertaken with vigor. Banks reopened branches in the city, and schools and colleges started planning for the resumption of their students' disrupted educations. By August 29—eighteen days after the flood—all Morbi's local government offices had resumed operation.[59]

Babubhai surveyed the nascent recovery with a fierce vigilance. Whenever he was not making rounds through Morbi's neighborhoods, he was checking in on government projects. Whether he was inquiring about the repaving of a road or the restoration of a water main, the chief minister's arrival at the work site caused many an engineer to grow anxious; moreover, Babubhai always followed up. Government officers quickly learned that if they promised to complete a project in a week, the chief minister would reliably stride back onto the work site seven days later.

The prospect of disappointing the chief minister terrified officials. If work was not proceeding favorably, Babubhai's calm demeanor would crack. Tales of his displeasure—perhaps embellished through the decades—would become legendary in the paan-stained hallways of government offices around Gujarat.

Once, Babubhai inquired about progress on the construction of a temporary earthen causeway across the Machhu River, next to the damaged bridge. A government engineer confidently reported that he had sent a messenger to Gandhinagar with detailed construction plans, and that work was expected to begin soon.

The chief minister was not pleased. His voice gradually rose as he rebuked the officer:

> Well, in Gandhinagar, the man will go to the chief engineer. The chief engineer will go through the undersecretary, the deputy secretary, and the secretary. The secretary will go to the minister. And then maybe something will get done. How many days will that take? I said this was urgent—treat it as such!
>
> The work should start at eight o'clock tomorrow morning. This is my instruction as chief minister. I am your financial advisor. I am your chief engineer. I am your secretary. I am giving you the approval in all of these capacities. Do you need anything else? I am doing this in my capacity as chief minister. Now take care of it!

Work on the causeway commenced the next morning.[60]

A similar story came to be told about Babubhai's determination to light up Morbi's dark nights. One day, during a dinner meeting with several officers, the chief minister discussed plans for installing new streetlights in the city. Later the same evening, he asked the presiding engineer for an update. The officer replied that he had called another city to request necessary supplies.

The chief minister responded coldly: "Sit down and watch." He contacted all of Gujarat's districts, one by one, and instructed them to remove working streetlights and send them—in their own trucks and with their own workers—for installation. "It is fine if the rest of Gujarat is only half lit," people overheard him say. "Morbi ought to be lit one hundred percent." Then, he turned calmly to the engineer. "At 5:00 p.m. tomorrow," he said, "I expect to flip a switch and see Morbi fully lit. Your job is on the line."

According to the story, at 5:00 the following evening, Babubhai smiled as streetlights across the city flickered to life.[61]

≈≈≈≈≈

Although Special Secretary for Relief H. K. Khan had successfully prevented Morbi's streets from degenerating into a political circus in the week after the flood, controversy swirled around the city during the subsequent month.

The roots of the turbulence lay in the national and state governments. On August 20, the newspapers reported a seemingly foregone conclusion: AT LAST, THE RESIGNATION OF THE CHARAN SINGH GOVERNMENT. With Congress Party chief Indira Gandhi withdrawing support from the Janata Party leader, his coalition had collapsed. Voting for a new parliament would have to take place in early 1980. Within a few weeks, Chief Minister Babubhai Patel declared his intention to hold Gujarat's legislative assembly elections simultaneously with the national elections. A protracted Congress–Janata confrontation would engulf India over the coming months, and Gujarat seemed poised to serve as one of the foci of greatest conflict.[62]

State politicians wasted no time drawing Morbi into the fray. Congress leaders excoriated the government for its estimation of no more than one thousand deaths in the massive disaster. The media quickly snatched upon the debate over the death toll. Editorials skewered the government's claims, with one newspaper asking, "When countless citizens estimate that thousands have died, why are administrators reluctant to accept this bitter and cruel reality?"[63]

Some Congress politicians leveled bolder allegations, accusing the Janata government and its crony organizations of actively covering up the magnitude of the disaster and providing ineffective relief. On September 13, one newspaper reported:

> Gujarat Congress Chief Madhavsinh Solanki today alleged that the Gujarat government had sought to suppress the actual death toll and loss of property caused by the dam burst at Morbi. . . . Mr. Solanki alleged the Rashtriya Swayamsevak Sangh (RSS) workers had thrown several corpses into the river or had burnt them to distort the actual count. According to him, at least 20,000 persons had died during the first three hours after the dam burst.[64]

Congress leaders also charged that the government had failed to deliver effective relief to the flood-stricken. In his September press conference, Solanki maintained that "inept handling of situations by the authority at various states had added to human miseries" and that "the relief and other measures undertaken fell far short of requirement."[65] Another Congress legislator denounced the RSS—widely seen as partial to the Janata Party—for "obstructing the relief works by not allowing others to work," "looting the property of flood-hit people," and "cornering food grains and other articles sent by the people from other parts of the state."[66]

Outcry over perceived lapses of responsibility reached a fever pitch with the leak of a report authored by Rajkot District Collector A. R. Banerjee. Blurred by layers of paraphrase and vagueness, the contents of the controversial documents would quickly find their way into the ongoing battle between the state government and its opposition.

On August 22, the *Hindustan Times* began an article, "How the bureaucracy reacts to an emergency can be known from the Rajkot collector's lengthy confidential report about the Morbi tragedy, sent to the state government, in which he says the Machhu dam engineer had at no stage warned him of the danger to the dam." The remainder of the story summarized much of the so-called Banerjee Report, focusing on the fact that Irrigation Department engineers had never warned the collector of possible danger to the Machhu Dam-II. The piece closed with a troubling allegation: "With the judicial inquiry under way, officials are suppressing, distorting, covering up, and even destroying vital evidence to save their skins. Each is blaming the other. Any delay in seizing the evidence would end the purpose of the inquiry."[67]

Controversy over the contents of the Banerjee Report only grew as the weeks passed. On September 9, an article entitled RAJKOT COLLECTOR COLLARS IRRIGATION ENGINEERS presented large excerpts from the report verbatim. Collector Banerjee's grievances, phrased in technical but pointed language, lay on the page for all of India to read: despite multiple opportunities, engineers had failed to warn authorities of the mounting crisis at the Machhu Dam-II. While the authenticity of the mysterious document remained suspect, the press stories were sufficient to raise a public uproar about negligence on the part of Irrigation Department officers.[68]

Interestingly, the newspapers failed to present the Banerjee Report's most damning finding. In a matter-of-fact paragraph nestled amid the extensive account of his own work on August 11, Collector Banerjee noted that Agriculture Minister Keshubhai Patel had turned back from Morbi due to the high water level; despite witnessing signs of an ongoing disaster, Keshubhai had failed to inform authorities, instead turning in to sleep after issuing standard orders for establishment of contact with the flood-affected area. Dwarfed by the extensive denunciations of engineering irresponsibility, the modest mention of Keshubhai's blunder escaped capture by journalists' typewriters. Nonetheless, it would go on to play a major role in the way the Machhu dam disaster was remembered for decades afterward.[69]

Despite his advanced age and brittle health, Chief Minister Babubhai Patel pushed himself to the limits of his ability in Morbi.[70] After dawn-to-dusk work in the humid monsoon heat and a hearty dinner at one of the city's relief kitchens, the chief minister and his ad hoc relief cabinet reconvened at the Mani Mandir for an evening meeting. The men around the table fought off exhaustion, eyelids fluttering and shoulders slumping. Somehow, Babubhai always seemed alert, peering out perspicaciously through his thick-rimmed glasses.

Whereas the morning meeting was primarily a time to allocate tasks, the evening's conference was about accountability. Special Secretary H. K. Khan's energetic and businesslike demeanor kept the meetings efficient. Officers reported on progress they had made toward their goals and shared advice with one another about how to speed their work along. They had quickly learned that standards were high, and no one wanted to disappoint the chief minister. The men usually dispersed shortly after 9:00 p.m., ready to fall into a deep slumber on their cots.

For Babubhai, however, hours of work lay ahead. When he arrived at the guesthouse after the long, muddy walk to eastern Morbi, a mountain of paperwork usually awaited him. Much could be accomplished in Gandhinagar without the chief minister, but important files required his signature. Of course, given his methodicalness, Babubhai would not sign a single file without reading it. Long after the other government officials in Morbi had turned in to sleep, the chief minister would light candles and settle in for a night of work.

Babubhai pored over files on a diverse array of subjects ranging from monsoon flood relief for other parts of Gujarat to the price of peanut oil in the state. As the night wore on, the pile of papers would grow shorter. The chief minister labored until the last document had been cleared—usually around 1:00 a.m. Only then would he collapse into bed, content with the day's work and knowing full well that he would rise again before the sun.

Chapter 9
"But Courage and Strength Remain"

After almost a month of constant effort on behalf of the disaster-stricken communities of the Machhu River Valley, Chief Minister Babubhai Patel returned to Gandhinagar on September 9, 1979. The next day, he began preparing for a fierce political battle.[1]

On September 17, the Gujarat legislative assembly would commence its monsoon session; in light of the prevailing political currents, Babubhai knew that the session could easily become the most contentious of his long career. With the collapse of the central government's ruling coalition toward the end of August, nationwide elections had become inevitable. In Gujarat, as in the rest of India, the Congress and Janata Parties were sharpening their swords for a political bloodbath.[2]

As the first item on the legislative docket, the Machhu dam disaster would serve as the front line in the confrontation between Babubhai's Janata government and its Congress opponents. After weeks of basking in Morbi's gratitude, the chief minister and his cabinet would face pointed questions and criticisms about the flood from state Congress Party chief Madhavsinh Solanki and other opposing politicians.

Discussion of the disaster began in earnest on Tuesday, September 18, the second day of official proceedings. That morning, 182 men and women climbed up the wide, white steps leading to the legislative assembly building, a hulking box of concrete that was impressive in size but banal in style. Taking their seats, they braced themselves for a bitter fight.

Bedlam soon ensued. Over the course of three days, Gujarat's legislators attacked and counterattacked from every angle imaginable, manipulating the Machhu dam disaster for maximal political gain. Solanki and his fellow Congress leaders chastised Babubhai's government for allowing the flood to occur and for failing to respond appropriately. Meanwhile, Janata politicians sought to avoid questions of blame, shifting the focus onto the ample relief their government had provided over the previous month.[3]

The warring legislators in fact spent much of the discussion arguing over what they would debate. Janata leaders insisted that the chamber could not legally take up questions of responsibility for the disaster, since they fell *sub judice*—under the purview of the incipient judicial inquiry. Congress politicians dismissed their opponents' arguments as mere sophistry, contending that the government was merely attempting to suppress public criticism of its failings. Solanki and others demanded explanations on behalf of the flood's victims, and their Janata counterparts repeatedly sidestepped the issue, insisting on the illegality of delving into questions of culpability. On dozens of occasions during the three days of debate, the discussion would devolve into a quarrel over the terms of debate.[4]

As the session proceeded, Congress leaders portrayed the Machhu dam disaster as the exemplification of Janata incompetence. Many described the catastrophe as "man-made." One legislator thundered:

If a human error has been made, or a human is responsible for this, then it is our duty to say that an unforgivable massacre has been perpetrated on Morbi and Maliya's soil. . . . The heart-cries emerging from the ruined rubble, the voices coming out of the destroyed monuments—these voices cannot forgive the government of Gujarat.[5]

Another Congress leader attacked the Janata administration's relief and recovery operations, lamenting, "This government is incapable of doing anything. . . . This government of Gujarat can dump the blame on whomever it wishes, but it cannot escape from its own failures."[6]

While his deputies delivered theatrical denunciations, Solanki focused on specific questions of lapsed responsibility. He criticized the government's tardiness in reaching Morbi after the disaster and lambasted the insufficient arrangements for evacuation of refugees from the city. He also stressed that the Machhu Dam-II had been constructed under an administration led by the precursor to the Janata Party.[7]

Congress Party member Gokaldas Parmar delivered a complex, ambivalent speech on Morbi's behalf. He presented a harrowing firsthand account of living through the flood and witnessing the government's efforts in the aftermath; when his allotted time expired, his colleagues voted to double it in order to hear his full statement. Parmar lauded the chief minister for his dedication but stated that, in his absence, relief and recovery work had begun to lag miserably. In the end, he too held the government responsible for the suffering of his constituents. "I will not say that this calamity was a natural calamity," he declared. "The responsibility is the government's, and the government cannot escape from it."[8]

Agriculture Minister Keshubhai Patel, who had turned back from the edge of disaster on August 11, became the object of ever-sharper criticisms as the debate wore on. One Congress politician explicitly called for the minister's resignation, accusing him of "killing time in Rajkot with journalists while the flood-stricken people of Morbi were at Death's feet."[9] Some members of Keshubhai's own party also railed against him, hoping to avoid widespread disgrace by conceding and condemning his failure. One blustered, "If it is true that the [agriculture] minister is at fault here, that Irrigation Department officers or workers are at fault, then all of those people should be hanged. . . ."[10]

The most pointed criticism—the one that finally prompted a response from Keshubhai himself—came from Parmar:

[Parmar:] The honorable minister has informed us that he turned back from Sanala at 5:30 on the 11th, and that the water was all over there at that time. Did he not then think of how bad Morbi's situation must have been, with water up to that point? At that point, Morbi had become a graveyard.

[Keshubhai:] When I reached there at 5:30, I dispatched two superintending engineers and two executive engineers. . . . Think of the situation not with today's hindsight, but from the perspective of that time, when it was impossible to advance even four hundred feet. My superintending engineer came and told me, "Sir, there is water everywhere, and it is impossible to go forward." Furthermore, there was a line of trucks and buses stopped there; not one person from that traffic jam told me that such a situation had arisen there.[11]

The agriculture minister maintained that, by "sending" engineers to investigate the situation while he returned to Rajkot, he had acted with due diligence. The argument did little to quiet his critics.

At a few points during the debate, members of the ruling party took up the offensive, accusing Congress politicians of trolling for votes while Janata leaders and Janata-friendly organizations, such as the Rashtriya Swayamsevak Sangh (RSS), handled the hard work of relief and recovery. The fiery representative from Rajkot, whose brother was the RSS's chief relief executive in Morbi, denounced the Congress Party for "baking political bread on Morbi's corpses."[12] For the most part, however, Babubhai and the Janata Party tried to lay claim to some semblance of moral high ground, highlighting the efficiency of their government's response, lamenting the human tragedy of the disaster, and strenuously avoiding discussion of culpability.

The chief minister himself closed the debate with a rather prosaic tally of facts and figures from government's relief efforts. Toward the end of his speech, to reemphasize the gravity of the problems still facing the flood-affected area, he declared, "This is not a small disaster. This is not an ordinary disaster. This is an extraordinary disaster."[13]

≋≋≋≋≋

For the people of Gujarat, October 21 and 22 would be among 1979's most important days. On October 21, Gujaratis would celebrate Diwali, the Festival of Lights. The windowsills, porches, and thresholds of every home would teem with lamps, set out to attract the mother goddess in her embodiment as prosperity and happiness. Revelers would don new clothes and set off fireworks in the streets. Children would receive gifts and wolf down rich foods. Sitting together, families would pray for wealth and financial security.

Then, the day after Diwali would mark the beginning of a new year in the Hindu calendar. The holiday would be an occasion for taking stock and looking toward the future, an occasion for renewal and cleansing. Taken together with the Festival of Lights, it would constitute the most important celebration of the year for Gujarati Hindus.[14]

Consequently, it came as a shock to many when Chief Minister Babubhai Patel announced, a scant five days before Diwali, that he and his family would not partake in any kind of festivities. Newspapers reported that Rajkot District Home Guard Commander Ushakant Mankad—a native of Morbi and one of the main leaders of the ongoing relief work—had written to Babubhai to suggest that the government observe the holidays soberly in view of flood survivors' ongoing despair. According to Mankad's later recollection, he said, "Diwali is coming. My brothers and I have decided that we will not celebrate Diwali this year. Instead, we will stay in Morbi and continue to do the work. When Morbi's people are grief-stricken, this will be our Diwali celebration." The letter greatly affected Babubhai. He cancelled all his Diwali programs and vowed to spend the holiday in Morbi.[15]

Unsurprisingly, the chief minister encountered a cacophony of demands upon his return to the Machhu River Valley. The head of Morbi's citizen-run Flood Relief Coordination Committee urged the chief minister to address the issues of household electrical supply, household water supply, gutter drainage, pavement of roads, reconstruction of houses, industrial recovery, and mercantile loans. Villagers in Lilapar requested government provision of land, long-term loans for home construction, and the myriad equipment and supplies they would need to restart their farms. Morbi's clock industrialists begged the chief minister to save their industry. Every turn seemed to hold a new demand for the man who had spent the better part of a month addressing citizens' concerns without pause. But the very nature of the requests suggested that the work in Morbi was progressing from relief to recovery.[16]

On October 21, Babubhai observed the Festival of Lights in Lilapar, where he distributed sweets to Bhagvanji Patel and his fellow villagers. With District Collector A. R. Banerjee and member of the legislative assembly Parmar accompanying him, the chief minister surveyed the damage to the farming community and listened to presentations from the village council president and other leading citizens. Although the flood had virtually annihilated Lilapar, the chief minister perceived a blossoming excitement about rehabilitation. The head of the Rajkot-based Ramakrishna Ashrama temple, which had adopted Lilapar under Special Secretary for Relief H. K. Khan's sector-based relief scheme, announced a plan to build new homes for the village's families. Even though Lilapar remained completely dependent on donated goods, recovery was beginning to seem possible.[17]

The next morning, a chilling rain spattered Babubhai as he walked through Morbi's streets under the clouded light of the new year's first day. Entering city hall, he took his seat, cross-legged, on the stage next to Parmar and Mayor Ratilal Desai. Rows of solemn faces looked up at the luminaries. Every man and woman in the audience was wearing white—the color of mourning, but also the color of renewal and purity.

The chief minister, dressed in a stiff white tunic and dhoti, smiled as he approached the microphone. He looked out at the gathered crowd, which eagerly awaited his words.

He began his speech with bad news. In response to his request for 2.35 billion rupees of aid, the national government had agreed to grant 430 million rupees. Moreover, it remained unclear what portion of the promised sum would actually reach Morbi. "But," the chief minister quickly declared, "the government and people of Gujarat will meet the challenge of this war-like work."

He narrated the story of how Germany and Japan, ruined after World War II, had transformed themselves into global powers through the "constant effort of one generation." Morbi, too, would rise from the aftermath of catastrophe to shine again. Babubhai assured his listeners:

> Morbi's industrialists and populace undertook this type of massive work before to make Morbi Gujarat's pride. Nature threw a wrench in the works and sent this great disaster. Material wealth was swept away. But courage and strength remain. . . . Let us all resolve to make Morbi even more beautiful. I will not hesitate to do that which falls to me in that regard. If we work quickly, God will help us too. I pray to God that Morbi's populace forget this nightmare and that we see Morbi glimmering in the light of the new year.

Thunderous applause filled city hall as the chief minister returned to his seat.[18]

≋≋≋

The stately corridors of the Gujarat High Court echoed with the brisk clip of solitary footsteps.[19] Dipankar Basu, a confident man whose eyes frequently shone with enthusiasm and amusement, was off to see his new boss.

Accustomed to the commotion of government offices in Gandhinagar and the chaotic honking and haggling of street life in Ahmedabad, Basu found his time in the High Court refreshing. The court's justices carried themselves with a calm, considered air. It seemed to Basu that they belonged to an increasingly rare breed—men enamored above all with the pursuit of ideals. "Justice," they would sometimes remind their audiences, quoting British parliamentarian Benjamin Disraeli, "is truth in action."

For nearly two months, Basu had been laboring at a herculean task. He was the secretary for the state government's new Machhu Dam-II Inquiry Commission; like secretaries everywhere, he did most of the work. Each of the commission's requests for information, solicited by the body's lawyers and consultants, emerged from the strokes of Basu's pen. Each of the thousands of records, affidavits, and technical documents thus requested ultimately arrived on his desk. He oversaw a staff of half a dozen stenographers and clerks, who had set up shop in two of the courthouse's empty chambers.

Shortly after the Machhu dam disaster, Chief Minister Babubhai Patel had asked the High Court's chief justice to appoint a judge to oversee an investigation into the flood. The chief had quickly selected the second-ranking justice on the High Court bench, a well-respected jurist named B. K. Mehta. Another month would pass before the commission's staff and technical advisers fell into place. On September 10, a formal notice brought the commission into official existence. Justice Mehta's inquiry commission would possess the powers of a civil court, including the ability to summon witnesses, subpoena documents, and demand access to any part of the public record.[20]

Technically, Justice Mehta *was* the commission. All official power to solicit documents and affidavits from the government rested solely with him, and the investigation's final report would bear his name. However, Mehta had neither the time nor the expertise to undertake the inquiry single-handedly. He needed to maintain his regular caseload at the Gujarat High Court, and he possessed no background in engineering, hydrology, or administrative affairs. So it fell upon Basu to coordinate the assembled team of lawyers and experts as they carried out the commission's work.

On this particular day in late October, the harried secretary had a few matters to bring to Justice Mehta's attention, though not as many as he might have hoped. The commission had issued a call for documents and testimony weeks earlier; with the November 11 deadline fast approaching, information was crossing Basu's desk at a sluggish pace.

Still, November 11 held promise as a date for the commission to begin its work in earnest; on that day, the state government's advocate general would submit a comprehensive "statement of facts and opinions"—in essence, a document laying out the government's official stance on what had gone wrong before the flood. With this document at its disposal, the commission could begin sorting through evidence, cross-examining witnesses, and drawing its own conclusions.[21]

Even with the bulk of evidence outstanding, Mehta, Basu, and the other members of the commission felt optimistic about the outcomes their work could produce. One of the lawyers for the commission would later recall the prevailing attitude among Mehta's staffers at the outset of their endeavor: "Whatever our investigation discovered, though it might be unpleasant, would bring the truth into the public light."[22]

By the time the communities of the Machhu River Valley began the slow slog of recovery, a more precise understanding of the disaster's toll was emerging. Over 7,000 houses had completely collapsed in Morbi and the surrounding rural areas; 6,000 others had suffered substantial damage. Roughly 173,000 acres of farmland had been affected, with farmers losing 77 million rupees worth of land, crops, and animals. Local industries had sustained 188.9 million rupees of damage; clock factories, roofing-tile units like Bhagvanji Patel's, and salt plants like Abdulbhai Mor's each accounted for about a quarter of the total. The flood had thoroughly ravaged the area's infrastructure, with roads alone enduring 81 million rupees of damage. More than 10,000 animal carcasses had been recovered, and thousands more remained missing. As September and October rolled into November and the monsoon yielded to the mild Indian winter, estimates of the overall destruction covered the pages of Gujarati newspapers and government memoranda.[23]

Yet, the number that most poignantly captured the flood's cost remained a topic of heated debate. By August 31, 1979—the first day that not a single new corpse surfaced in Morbi—1,233 human bodies had been found in the city alone. Even then, twenty days after the flood, many corpses remained at large. The floodwaters had swept a number out to the Gulf of Kutch or other remote locales. Some of the bodies burned by survivors and relief workers on an ad hoc basis in the desperate days immediately following the disaster did not appear in the official tallies. In cases where entire families had perished, it often occurred that no one ever looked to recover the bodies. Furthermore, many survivors, such as the Miyanas of Maliya, claimed deaths for which no corpses could be produced. Even as the number of bodies found dwindled to a few per day in early September, the total death toll remained a mystery.[24]

Amid Gujarat's increasingly acrimonious political climate, the number of people drowned, crushed, or buried by the floodwaters and their wreckage became a focus of intractable dispute. Janata Party politicians, including Chief Minister Babubhai Patel, steadfastly clung to an upper limit of two thousand. The administration's opponents, accusing it of minimizing the human cost of its negligence, quoted figures of ten thousand or higher; they further argued that the chief minister's slavish devotion to a low number had influenced the central government's decision to grant less than a quarter of the aid requested by the state.[25]

Legislator Gokaldas Parmar, with his intimate knowledge of Morbi and his environs, would tell the Gujarat legislative assembly that at least three thousand had died. According to his estimate, the southern farming community of Vajepar alone had lost almost one thousand lives—roughly a third of its population. If this latter figure—corroborated by many of Vajepar's Satwara residents in later years—is accurate, the death toll in Morbi, Maliya, and the surrounding villages may have easily exceeded five thousand.[26]

Ultimately, the government of Gujarat settled on a death tabulation system that ensured the veracity of registered deaths while virtually guaranteeing an undercount. The official toll of the disaster would be determined from the number of death certificates issued by Morbi's city hall, Maliya's town council, and the various village councils of the flood-affected area. Local authorities, being acquainted with the deceased, would be charged with ascertaining the authenticity of relatives' claims. Survivors would receive two thousand rupees of compensation for each death in the family, up to a total of six thousand rupees.[27]

Morbi would register 1,829 deaths by the time a clerk drew the final line at the bottom of the municipal ledger in July 1980. Numerous individuals reported seven or eight deceased relations. One man submitted for eleven people, including his uncle, aunt, niece, nephew, paternal grandfather, and father-in-law.[28]

At the same time, many deaths went unrecorded. Some survivors—particularly the uneducated and those who had left Morbi for prolonged periods of time—remained largely unaware of the scheme for registering the dead. Others—particularly those who considered themselves members of higher classes and jatis—refused to shame themselves by accepting the cash that accompanied a death certificate. Entire families were lost to the official tally when no one remained behind to register their demise. And, in one of the flood's great injustices, many individuals were denied registration of their loved ones' deaths when they could not produce sufficient proof of their identities and losses.[29]

For survivors still reeling from the loss of children, spouses, parents, and siblings, the death registration procedure often felt nearly unbearable. When shopkeeper Dhirubhai Mehta and his brother-in-law arrived at city hall to register the deaths of Mehta's son and daughter, they found out-of-town officers overseeing the process in lieu of Morbi's local authorities, who were still struggling to recover from their own losses. A civil servant from another region of Saurashtra looked up at the two men from behind a wide desk. As Mehta's brother-in-law explained the circumstances of his niece and nephew's demise, the bureaucrat curtly requested proof of their deaths. The grieving uncle shot back, "Should we take out a photograph of the corpses?" The officer remained insistent—could the two men even produce proof of their own identities? He demanded a reference who could verify their claims.

Mehta's brother-in-law grew outraged. He bellowed, "I know Ratilal Desai! You have come from outside. Whom do *you* know? Put up a list! What value does verification have for the person who has the distress of a family death? Why don't you put out a list of all the people you know in Morbi?"

Tempers flared, and the uncle and the administrator seemed on the verge of violence before the latter finally relented, yielding the death certificates and cash. The anger of that moment would never dissipate completely. Decades later, Mehta's brother-in-law would declare bitterly, "Those outsiders—instead of behaving as human beings and giving support, they behaved as officers. With rigidity."[30]

For Jashabhai Samani, the entire process proved easier. He had registered his deaths with the town council in the days after the flood, with little formality. Later, when the government began offering cash for each death, he was summoned to the subdistrict office, handed six thousand rupees, and sent away. With that, he had been compensated for the loss of his children.[31]

≋≋≋≋

A little more than a month after the flood, Kanubhai Kubavat shaped a tiny hovel of mud, corrugated tin sheets, and burlap sacks on his plot in the Tiger Quarter. Laying paper down on the earth, the Brahmin slept under his own roof—uncomfortable and alone, but relieved—for the first time since August 10. Thousands of similar makeshift dwellings were springing up on Morbi's dusty streets. Though modest, they represented a great hope: people were making the city livable once again.[32]

Voluntary organizations and the government had begun to distribute tin sheets and other temporary building materials shortly after the flood in an effort to encourage residents to return to the disaster-stricken area.[33] Now, in partnership with service organizations and banks, government institutions began offering cash subsidies, construction supplies, and loans to home-owners who wished to rebuild their houses. Tons of cement, wood, and tiles rolled into the city on the newly reconstructed railway. Private and semigovernmental banks announced low-interest loan schemes for the flood-affected. Individual house-holders received thousands of rupees in cash assistance for the purchase of supplies, labor, and household goods.[34]

Unlike many homeowners with damaged or destroyed houses, Kubavat did not obtain aid for reconstruction. The government's housing recovery plan included many different provisions and pro-cedures, and citizens often felt unsure of what they could request, and how. Kubavat started an application for a reconstruction loan but grew frustrated with the complexity of the forms and threw them away. He resolved, like many at the time, to build a new house gradually, with his own hard-earned money.[35]

Other citizens were simply too proud to accept any help. Khatijaben Valera and the women of her clan came back to

Morbi three months after the disaster. They found that the men of the family, who had returned almost two months earlier in order to guard their home against looters, were still living outside. The Valeras' two-story bungalow, completely submerged in the flood, had become unstable. Although supplies and financing for repairs were available in the city, the clan's storied pride would not allow the men to take charity. They would rebuild the house properly, with their own labor and supplies. The family would live in the courtyard for days, cooking in improvised brick ovens. The men began their repairs by reinforcing the kitchen, and Khatijaben and her sisters-in-law eventually began cooking inside. Over the course of weeks, the whole bungalow became inhabitable again.[36]

As residents slowly repopulated their communities, other signs of revival gradually surfaced. By December, numerous shops, buoyed by government loans, had reopened around Pratapbhai Adroja's Ghost Paan. Though still distraught over the loss of his son, Dhirubhai Mehta slowly resumed business at Mehta Machinery. Movie theaters prepared to show films once again. Principal T. R. Shukla, settled back on the eastern bank of the river, oversaw the operations of the arts college, which had restarted in late October. And Kubavat walked from his small hut to the temple down the street, where he once again led prayer ceremonies—simple and subdued, but hopeful nonetheless.[37]

≋≋≋

Hanging up the telephone at his desk in the Gujarat High Court, Dipankar Basu shook his head.[38] He wondered how anyone expected the Machhu Dam-II Inquiry Commission to complete its work in six months when the government could not even meet its own deadlines. Two weeks had passed since the November 11 cut-off for submitting affidavits in the case. Of the thirty statements requested by the commission, only two had arrived. The state engineers, it appeared, were reluctant to speak.[39]

Irrigation Department machinations had begun almost immediately after the commission's formation. The superintending
engineer in Rajkot—one of the men who had tried in vain to reach
the Machhu Dam-II on the day of the flood—had sent an urgent
memorandum to his superior in Gandhinagar. Fearful that his
subordinates would provide contradictory or incriminating testimony, he had asked for help. The message read, "The entire
number of persons connected with this affair should be given legal
advice to draft out the affidavit, and accordingly, a legal adviser
may please be appointed to help us in the matter immediately."[40]

Justice B. K. Mehta's inquiry had fallen into a quagmire. As
Basu later explained, those being questioned in the case believed
that the commission was "a means to find the culprit and pillory
him." As a result, "everyone [went] on the defensive." The work
of extracting answers from the government's recalcitrant
bureaucracy became laborious, leading to the delays that left
Basu drained at the end of each day. The stonewalling severely
debilitated the commission, which had been established, in
Basu's words, on "the presumption . . . that everyone [was] for
the truth, in order to avoid a similar disaster from taking place
in the future."[41]

To be fair, it was difficult to conform to the spirit of the commission's founding with so many lawyers involved. The office of
the advocate general mediated the commission's interactions with
the government of Gujarat. Though it was ostensibly tasked with
merely collecting the affidavits and documents that the commission's staff requested, the advocate general's office quickly came
to see itself as the government's defender. According to Basu's
recollection, the entity assigned to help the commission complete
its work was soon doing so "only in theory."[42]

As the secretary struggled to collect affidavits and documents,
he knew that the government's delays were hampering the work
of the commission's other members. The commission's numerous
lawyers remained at least somewhat occupied, given the legal
intricacies that attended any judicial inquiry, but the lack of evi-

dence had completely stalled the analysis of the two living legends who would lend Justice Mehta their technical expertise.

Y. K. Murthy, the commission's engineering consultant, was among the foremost hydrological engineers India had ever produced. A man of modest stature and thinning hair, he was easy to miss as he sat behind a desk, peering at documents through large, wire-rimmed glasses. He possessed a disciplined concentration and a voracious appetite for his work—qualities that had served him well throughout his thirty-five-year career. During his youth, Murthy had spent two years studying at Harvard University as part of an elite cadre of civil engineers selected at Indian independence to pursue advanced degrees in the United States. Upon his return, he had risen quickly through the ranks of India's engineering bureaucracy. He had retired in 1978 as chairman of the Central Water and Power Commission.

Murthy, who had spent the first year of his retirement consulting for the World Bank, would provide the commission with technical analysis of the dam collapse. He took the work seriously and personally; after his time as India's chief dam engineer, the failure of any one of his structures felt like a personal loss. Whenever he received the information requested from the government of Gujarat, he would begin the painstaking process of determining whether the dam had failed due to faulty materials, shoddy construction, poor maintenance, human error, or a fundamentally flawed design.[43]

For questions of government administration, Ravi Matthai, a celebrated professor at Ahmedabad's Indian Institute of Management, would serve as Murthy's counterpart. Revered by colleagues, held in awe by students, and deeply respected by Gujarat's politicians, Matthai ranked as one of India's greatest experts on management. In his view, the thousands of deaths of the Machhu dam disaster had resulted not from a single catastrophic flaw, but from hundreds of problems and events that had culminated in a tremendous disaster. Once the state government delivered the necessary information, he would delve into questions of administrative failings—why no one had warned the downstream area of an impending collapse, why reigning design and operation standards had failed to prevent the flood, and how the government could change its communications and oversight standards in order to prevent similar occurrences in the future.[44]

Unfortunately, neither technical consultant could exert his considerable talents until the affidavits and evidence arrived. As he waited, Matthai could not help but notice an administrative paradox in the constitution of the commission: the people whose help and cooperation were most necessary for the smooth functioning of the inquiry were the same individuals whose work, actions, and decisions would come under intense scrutiny.[45]

The people of Gujarat watched as major transformations reshaped the political landscape over the first half of 1980. January national elections carried the Congress Party to power in New Delhi. While Congress leaders secured 366 of the 529 seats in parliament, the quarreling factions of the Janata Party—haunted by the successive collapses of Morarji Desai and Charan Singh's governments the previous year—managed to win only 72. Of the 26 parliamentary constituencies in Gujarat, 25 elected Congress candidates.[46]

In Gujarati politics, the drubbing of the Janata Party followed a more protracted course. Campaigning occupied the better part of a year, from September 1979 until May 1980. During that period, Chief Minister Babubhai Patel's government slowly lost its internal strength and public support. The prices of peanut oil and other major agricultural products spiraled out of control. Agriculture Minister Keshubhai Patel came under fire for shortages of crude oil and other essential farming inputs. The chief minister's diabetes flared up, forcing him to spend time at home convalescing. Battered by increasingly compelling criticisms from Congress leaders, the Janata government weakened until it could no longer function. In February, Babubhai dissolved the legislative assembly and initiated a period of presidential rule that would last until new elections could take place.[47]

Statewide voting in the last week of May ushered in a drastically altered legislature. The Congress Party won 141 of the 182 seats; the various fragments of the Janata Party secured only 31 places. Babubhai lost his seat to a Congress challenger. Keshubhai, who received 56 percent of the votes in his constituency despite the well-publicized controversies surrounding him, was among the few Janata politicians to hang on. After coasting into the legislative assembly with the support of 76 percent of his constituency, erstwhile opposition leader Madhavsinh Solanki returned to his old position as chief minister on June 7. With a commanding Congress majority in the legislature, he would now form an administration to replace the one that he and his allies had criticized as incapable and unforgivable during the debate over the Machhu dam disaster.[48]

Gokaldas Parmar did not participate in the Congress Party's victorious campaign. Despite his fifteen years of service as Morbi's representative, he did not receive the party's nomination. Parmar's long legislative career, which had begun in 1957 in the old Bombay State, came to a sudden end in the 1980 elections. He would never hold public office again.[49]

Although less noticed, a separate change had pulled away another of Morbi's most dedicated public servants. In the closing days of Babubhai's Janata government, Collector A. R. Banerjee had been transferred to the collectorate in Valsad, a district of southern Gujarat. Such moves were common for members of the Indian Administrative Service (IAS), who were groomed to leave one task for another with quiet equanimity.

Nonetheless, the shift smarted. Morbi had become, as Banerjee would later reminisce, "close to my heart." Moreover, the collector harbored a suspicion that something beyond mere administrative expediency had prompted his transfer. As he moved from one collectorate to another, he wondered whether the publicly mysterious contents of the Banerjee Report had unsettled some men of considerable importance.[50]

BEFORE THE MACHHU DAM-II INQUIRY COMMISSION

The Statement of facts and opinions relating to the matters specified in the Notification No. COI/MD-2/1/79 of the Government of Gujarat.

MAY IT PLEASE THE HONOURABLE COMMISSION . . .[51]

So began the Gujarat advocate general's 181-page statement, which arrived at Justice B. K. Mehta's High Court chambers on March 31, 1980, in two hardbound volumes. After months of delays, the state government had finally submitted its official answers to the questions under the Machhu Dam Inquiry Commission's purview. Justice Mehta and his staff would spend weeks poring over the information.[52]

Engineering consultant Y. K. Murthy began by scrutinizing the government's statements regarding the causes and preventability of the dam's failure.[53] Ever meticulous and skeptical, Murthy narrowed his eyes as he read the assertions contained within the document's opening pages. The advocate general's office had declared, in no uncertain terms, that the government did not bear responsibility for the flood:

> The failure of the Machhu Dam-II was entirely on account of natural calamity beyond any human control and not on account of any defect in the conception, design, construction, or maintenance of the dam by the government or any governmental or human agency.[54]

With a clear sense of the government's overall argument, Murthy prepared himself to dissect the statement. Over dozens of dense pages, the document reviewed the dam's design and construction, emphasizing throughout that the government had executed every step in accordance with prevailing norms. According to the government, the failure of the earthen embankments could be attributed entirely to the intense monsoon rainfall, which had caused a wholly unprecedented flow into the reservoir; the influx had exceeded the spillway's outflow capacity, and overtopping of the earthworks had resulted. While acknowledging that several of the dam's gates had jammed, the statement argued that the heavy precipitation would have caused overtopping under any circumstances.[55]

The government's denial of culpability rested upon the calculations of Irrigation Department hydrologists. Using outflow data from the storm and available estimates of rainfall in the Machhu River catchment area, the hydrologists estimated that the Machhu Dam-II's reservoir had received between 640,000 and 940,000 cubic feet of water per second (cusecs) on the afternoon of August 11, 1979. The spillway's eighteen gates could pass only 200,000 cusecs, which had been considered the maximum conceivable inflow at the time of the dam's design. In light of the unforeseeable flood, the government argued, overtopping and collapse were inevitable.[56]

The admission that the dam had overtopped because of insufficient outflow capacity raised questions about the adequacy of the spillway's design. But a flood three or four times heavier than the largest anticipated one seemed completely outside the bounds of probability and reason. By the government's reckoning, such a flood might occur "not even once in a thousand years."[57] If accurate, the government's figures would render retrospection about the spillway's outflow capacity almost meaningless; even with twice as many gates, the dam would likely have succumbed to the extraordinary inflow. Overall, the government sought to treat the dam failure as a wholly aberrant occurrence, so unlikely to recur elsewhere in Gujarat that no review or redesign of earthen dams in the state was necessary.

Murthy did not feel persuaded by the statement. He was skeptical of the government's high flood estimates, which seemed both shoddily constructed and overwrought. Moreover, regardless of the flood's size, the mere fact that waters had overwhelmed the Machhu Dam-II's spillway suggested problems with the government's process for calculating design floods.[58]

Murthy hoped to press his points with government hydrologists during sworn testimony, but at the current rate of progress, such an opportunity seemed very distant. Although the advocate general's office had submitted the "Statement of Facts and Opinions," dozens of affidavits remained outstanding. Without the supporting evidence, the commission could not proceed with hearings.[59]

As Murthy mulled over the engineering aspects of the Machhu Dam-II's failure, management expert Ravi Matthai considered the adequacy of state officers' attempts to warn vulnerable residents, coordinate evacuations, and generally mitigate the consequences of a potential disaster during the period prior to the dam's failure. Unsurprisingly, the government statement resolutely maintained that officials had done everything within their power to avert the coming catastrophe and to provide warnings to downstream residents.[60]

It seemed, however, that the government was attempting to hide some readily apparent shortcomings. Despite a brief mention of the dam's broken telephone, which had gone without maintenance for four days prior to the disaster, the statement avoided discussing the profound implications of the dam crew's inability to communicate with the outside world. Similarly, the document detailed Deputy Engineer A. C. Mehta's frantic and ultimately futile efforts to contact his superiors on August 11 but failed to address the thorny question of why Mehta had made no mention of danger to the dam when conferring with officials in Morbi on the morning of the disaster.[61]

For every question it answered, the statement seemed to raise many more. Only further investigation—and thorough examination of witnesses—could put the multiplying questions to rest. Until the government submitted its affidavits, the commission could only wait.

≋≋≋≋≋

The blazing sun of summer's last days heated the back of Abdulbhai Mor's neck. His squinting eyes surveyed the simple, barren grid of ponds that stretched out to the right and left. Brine languished in the flat evaporating trays, inching imperceptibly toward the crystallizing pond. Almost one year after the Machhu dam disaster, India Salt Works had resumed production.[62]

Maliya and Morbi's industrial sector, a point of considerable pride, had suffered greatly in the flood and its aftermath. By one estimate, 569 factories and plants had ceased production due to the disaster. Eighty salt works like Mor's had shut down. One hundred twenty-four roofing-tile factories like Bhagvanji Patel's, 153 mosaic-tile factories, and 100 clock factories had done the same. Even with the start of general recovery efforts, industrial rehabilitation had proceeded slowly. Accorded lesser importance than houses, food supply, and other "daily necessities," factories—a major driver of the area's prosperity—had idled in anticipation of aid. At the end of 1979, the process of cleaning out, repairing, and re-electrifying factories was still ongoing, and many industries lacked for their basic raw materials.[63]

Help eventually arrived, and in striking fashion. The state government offered industrialists interest-free loans of up to twenty-five thousand rupees; factory owners could also request expedited, low-interest loans for up to ten times that amount. Artisans with "cottage industries," such as tailors, received loans and donations of work instruments. In June 1980, when Mor stood amid his evaporating ponds, the Machhu River Valley's productive capacity was nearing full restoration.[64]

Mayor Ratilal Desai was among the beneficiaries of the industrial rehabilitation effort. His paint factory in southern Morbi—

the business that had inadvertently birthed his political career— had been wiped away by the floodwaters. Taking out a low-interest loan, he had supervised its reconstruction during his scant moments of freedom from serving as "the government's son-in-law." By the beginning of 1980, Nilesh Paint had resumed normal operations, with one significant difference: in the absence of Desai's fifteen-year-old son, Sanjay, who had done much to lighten the workload for the factory's three employees, selling paint beyond Morbi's borders had simply become too difficult. Desai would never resume his out-of-town business.[65]

On Lilapar Road, Bhagvanji Patel's Sri Lilapar Potteries had sustained minimal structural damage during the flood. Mud had filled the factory complex, but the buildings remained sound. With time, roads opened up, coal began flowing in, and the waterlogged dirt dried out. Six months after the disaster, Bhag-vanji's Harijan workers were producing tiles just as in the previous summer.[66]

Bhagvanji faced greater obstacles in resuming his other vocation—agriculture. The floodwaters had swept all his equip-ment, most of his livestock, and some of his topsoil into the Gulf of Kutch. Thousands of villagers in the Machhu River Valley had suffered similar losses. From Jodhpar and Lakhdhirnagar on the dam's flanks to Maliya on the edge of the Gulf of Kutch, farmers entered 1980 wondering how they would ever regain their livelihoods.[67]

Public and private aid kindled the process of reconstituting agriculture on the Machhu River's banks. The state government gave farmers compensation for lost livestock—150 rupees for sheep and goats, 1,000 rupees for oxen, and 250 rupees with a 100,000 rupee loan for dairy cattle. Civic, service, and political organizations from Gujarat and Mumbai sent cows, oxen, agri-cultural machinery, and seeds for cotton, millet, and wheat. Government bulldozers leveled the ruined farmland in dozens of villages, preparing it for monsoon planting.[68]

Nonetheless, agriculture did not receive the same level of

attention as industry, and Patel farmers would maintain, even years later, that the government had overlooked them. Many, lacking knowledge or understanding of the recovery scheme, failed to apply for compensation. Even when communities received the maximal aid, it simply was not sufficient to restart production by itself, as industrial loans often were. Farmers found themselves forced to purchase new equipment, replant their ravaged fields, and struggle once again with the earth.[69]

The farms of Lakhdhirnagar—the village on the dam's western flank that sheltered Lilapar's refugees—had endured the wrath of the floodwaters at their most powerful. The community's Patels would recall the subsequent lack of aid with bitterness:

> The government of Gujarat did not provide any relief for the damage that was done to our land, if the truth is to be told. Our land was right next to the dam, right up against its earthen flank. And it was washed away. . . . Everyone did what he could. It fell on our heads. They came and they ran the tractors over, but they did it haphazardly. And the rest fell to us.[70]

The farmers of Jodhpar, whose losses on the eastern bank mirrored Lakhdhirnagar's, bore a similar burden. For nearly a year, they sold their labor in Morbi's reviving economy to sustain their families.[71]

Farther downstream, in Maliya, Jashabhai Samani and his fellow farmers faced an even more daunting struggle. They had lost their oxen, carts, and machinery, along with the mediocre topsoil that barely covered their fields. The farmland surrounding Maliya had come to resemble the rest of the infernal landscape. Overwhelmed by the prospect of restarting agriculture under such inhospitable circumstances, Samani, like many other farmers, turned to salt labor in the year after the disaster to feed his surviving family members. He would never till the soil again.[72]

What Samani left behind, Husainbhai Manek took up. The government of Gujarat did not provide tools or loans to fishermen; consequently, with his boat and other equipment washed into oblivion, Manek saw little possibility for continuing his forefathers' trade. Clearing ancestral lands that had sat fallow for years, he began planting peanut, cotton, sesame, and millet.[73]

Unlike Manek and Samani, Mor resumed his previous occupation, albeit with considerable struggle. His plant's buildings had completely collapsed in the disaster, and the current had swept several tons of his salt back into the sea, virtually erasing his 1979 production. Mor rebuilt his business slowly, relying on loans from private financiers who imposed onerous conditions; in later years, he would shake his head and recall, "They could not be called merchants. They were butchers."[74]

Despite the difficulties, Mor persisted. Like his ancestors, he navigated uncertainty and hardship until, one day, amid the June heat, he could watch the sun turn the sea into salt.

There were few surprises when the advocate general's office submitted the dam workers' affidavits to the Machhu Dam-II Inquiry Commission. The crew members all told the same story. Their sworn statements about the hours preceding the flood—likely coached by government lawyers—were nearly identical.[75]

The men wrote that they had started opening the dam's spillway gates on the night of August 10, 1979, as per the deputy engineer's instructions. Although three of the gates had suffered technical malfunctions, the other fifteen had been completely opened by the morning of the disaster.[76]

The dam itself corroborated the crewmembers' account. On the massive concrete spillway, which had sat untouched in the months since the flood, fifteen gates were fully open and the remaining three were partially so. All official indicators seemed to point to the same conclusion: the crew had done everything possible to save the dam, to no avail.[77]

There was just one problem: no one else who had been near

the dam on the morning of August 11 seemed to tell the same story. As commission lawyers collected statements from villagers in Jodhpar and Lilapar, they were surprised by the consistency of a narrative that ran completely counter to the dam workers' version of events. The townspeople insisted that most of the dam's gates had been closed.[78]

The young men from Jodhpar were particularly adamant. They had stood atop the dam that morning, straining in vain to open jammed gates. One of them would later recall the view from the spillway's catwalk: "Two or three of the gates were completely open. The others were open just a few feet." Virtually all the Jodhpar men maintained that only a few of the gates were fully open.[79] The testimony of villagers from Lilapar, who had evacuated past the dam just hours before its collapse, went even further; they maintained that most of the dam's gates had been closed.[80]

Engineering consultant Y. K. Murthy felt taken aback by the villagers' assertions. "They were very emphatic on this," he later recalled. "It was a very big story."[81]

Despite the witnesses' insistence, Murthy found himself unconvinced. The physical evidence simply did not corroborate their version. The Machhu River had been overflowing its banks downstream of the dam prior to the disaster, which could not have occurred if most of the gates had been jammed shut. Moreover, the bonds of professional trust compelled Murthy to doubt the villagers. "We engineers—there is an engineering fraternity," he would explain years later, grasping for words to describe the confidence he held in the practitioners of his vocation. "What engineers tell is what I should take."[82]

The contradictory accounts of gate openings necessitated that commission staffers seek answers outside the sworn testimony they had collected. They soon hit upon the idea of traveling to the dam and testing the electric motors in order to unravel the mystery. If the motors were found to be broken, the villagers' accounts would become more believable; perhaps the crew had not been able to automatically raise the gates and had been able only to crank them by hand once the water pressure behind them diminished—after the collapse. On the other hand, if fifteen of the motors functioned perfectly, there would be little reason to doubt the workers' story. Determined to uncover the truth, the commission made arrangements to test the Machhu Dam-II's motors.[83]

Murthy also desired independent analysis of the government's claim that the Machhu Dam-II had succumbed to a once-in-a-thousand-years flood. He turned to a pair of hydrology professors at the University of Roorkee, a renowned technical academy; the scientists agreed to pore over available rainfall and river gauge data, seeking their own best estimate of flood levels.[84]

To cover every possibility, the commission's staffers also delved into the design and construction of the dam's massive embankments. While eyewitness accounts suggested that the walls had given way after water came pouring over their crests— a circumstance that would lead even the best earthworks to fail— commissioners wanted to verify that shoddy construction had not hastened their demise. While University of Roorkee hydrologists analyzed the available flood data, commission secretary Dipankar Basu enlisted the help of the university's civil engineering department for an investigation of the earthen walls. Two professors visited the dam site with Basu to draw soil samples from the remaining portions of earthwork. They shipped the samples back to Roorkee for tests that would shed light on the soil's composition and compaction. If the results came back normal, the commission would have little reason to suspect a fault in the earthworks.[85]

Although the commission's staffers enjoyed the thrill of extra-mural investigative work, they viewed it as merely a preamble to their ultimate task. Theirs was a *judicial* inquiry, and the most important work would take place in court. There, with all the evidence assembled, they would be able to sort through the information and cross-examine witnesses in fully public hearings.

Unfortunately, just as in its submission of affidavits, the advocate general's office seemed bent upon introducing as many delays as possible to the process of testimony. Originally scheduled to begin in June 1980, the hearings had been postponed indefinitely, with the government citing logistical difficulties and bureaucratic delays as it demanded more time. Justice B. K. Mehta had little choice but to grant the government's requests, since the commission could not succeed without its cooperation. In the end, only full public hearings—and the subsequent written report—could provide some semblance of public resolution for the Machhu dam disaster.[86]

As 1980 wore on, a handsome village slowly took shape on previously undeveloped land less than half a mile downstream of the dam. New Lilapar boasted large plots and wide boulevards. Smooth, white concrete facades proliferated as dignified houses rose from carefully squared foundations. The Machhu River Valley's distinctive red clay tiles crowned completed buildings, with each new roof celebrated as a sign of progress.

Bhagvanji Patel swelled with pride in his village. Shortly after the flood, the Rajkot-based Ramakrishna Ashrama temple had offered to build two-room houses for the entire community at virtually no cost to its residents. Bhagvanji and his neighbors had quickly rejected the proposition, as the mission's proposed houses were simply too small. Many villagers wanted separate rooms for women and the elderly; others required space for storing goods and keeping cattle.

Instead of accepting the Ramakrishna Ashrama's largesse, the villagers had opted to use their own labor, their own designs, and their own money to rebuild Lilapar. They had chosen higher ground for the reconstruction of their community, partly because they feared another disaster and partly because the land had proven cheaper there than near the river. Despite the relative inexpensiveness of their new plots, Bhagvanji and his fellow citizens had expended small fortunes to rebuild. Scraping together savings, asking relatives for help, and taking out loans, most had spent more than one hundred thousand rupees.

Bhagvanji would later recall with a smile, "When all the buildings in the village were done, we called the Ramakrishna Ashrama people in. They were overjoyed. They said, 'We could not have built for you what you have built for yourselves.'"[87]

Simultaneously, a smaller, haphazard settlement took shape just north of New Lilapar's neatly rectilinear street grid. Because they lacked the wealth or social connections to pay for their own plots, Lilapar's Harijans were building their houses on patches of uneven terrain just outside the village entrance. "Next to the village site," Bhagvanji would later recall, "there was government wasteland. We let the backward people—the Harijans, the goatherds, that type of people—take the wasteland for free. We gave them the wasteland, and we bought our own plots."[88]

Once the village's higher jatis rejected the Ramakrishna Ashrama's reconstruction offer, low-jati residents who did not share their neighbors' vast resources were left to rebuild on their own. Donations and low-interest loans helped them cover construction costs, but frustration filled their minds as they began to tame the rocky earth at the edge of New Lilapar.[89]

Indeed, all along the banks of the Machhu River, those who most needed help putting roofs over their heads found assistance most wanting. Social biases, scant resources, and uneven provision of relief often exacerbated inequalities that had festered before the disaster.

The restoration of housing proved particularly difficult for renters. Thousands of displaced tenants found themselves beholden to their landlords' whims, uncertain when their dwellings would become inhabitable once again. Residents of one riverside apartment building in downtown Morbi grew tired of waiting for their landlord, who lived in the United States, to make necessary repairs. They funded the building's renovation themselves, all the while continuing to pay their rent. Because they did not own the building, they qualified for very little housing relief.[90]

In other cases, poor homeowners simply found the available resources insufficient to meet their needs. Under H. K. Khan's sector-based relief scheme, in which various nonprofit organizations adopted small areas, some of Morbi's neighborhoods found themselves in better hands than others. Significant divergences in organizations' generosity and flexibility led to markedly different reconstruction experiences for householders in different parts of the city.

During the initial distribution of neighborhoods, Sadvichar Parivar—the Ahmedabad-based charity that had proven instrumental in the cremation of corpses and the early provision of relief—had adopted the Leatherworker Quarter. When thoughts turned to reconstruction, the organization laid out plans to build square houses that measured ten feet to a side. Because their old homes had extended to fifteen feet in length and breadth, the Leatherworker Quarter families asked Sadvichar Parivar to modify the scheme to allow for larger buildings. The organization's leaders refused.

Because Sadvichar Parivar had already claimed the neighborhood, no other organization could intercede on behalf of its low-jati inhabitants. In the end, the organization and the state government each donated 1,500 rupees per house, and homeowners took out 3,000-rupee interest-bearing loans. Using their own labor, the inhabitants of the Leatherworker Quarter built earthen houses over the year and a half after the flood. They would spend decades repaying the loans.[91]

As the Machhu River Valley's poorest residents struggled to secure housing in the disaster's aftermath, an array of public and private organizations began developing long-term solutions to the shortage. Using government land on the Machhu River's eastern bank and on the southern outskirts of downtown, these groups set out to erect entire neighborhoods for Morbi's homeless former homeowners and renters.[92]

Arts college principal T. R. Shukla, now the president of Morbi's Rotary Club, led one such effort. With the help of his fellow Rotarians, he wrote letters to Rotary chapters all over the world, from America to Africa to Australia. Using his poetic gifts to craft a moving account of the disaster and its aftermath, Shukla issued a poignant plea for donations. With each letter, he enclosed prints of Gunvant Sedani's iconic photographs of the destruction in Morbi. Within a short time, money began pouring in from all over the globe.[93]

By the middle of 1980—less than a year after the flood—organizations like the Rotary Club had secured enough public and private donations to fund the construction of thousands of new homes. The rattle of bricks and the pounding of hammers filled the Machhu River Valley.

As the work progressed, it remained unclear who would reap the harvest of generosity. Allotment of plots in a few neighborhoods had already begun, but most houses were still destined for unknown recipients. Thousands from the city's poor and middle classes had filled out applications, and the government was beginning to distribute lists of potential beneficiaries to the various institutions undertaking construction. Years would pass before some of the neighborhoods filled up completely.[94]

Dipankar Basu, secretary for the Machhu Dam-II Inquiry Commission, could barely believe his eyes when he opened the official notification from the state government's legal department.[95] It was August 27, 1980, and the commission had been in operation for nearly a year. Basu had grown accustomed to the government throwing up obstacles and causing delays at every available opportunity.[96]

Nevertheless, the state's latest salvo left him nearly speechless. Composed in the terse legalese he had adapted to reading, the message requested that the commission complete a partial report on its findings as quickly as possible. The Irrigation Department, eager to rebuild the Machhu Dam-II, hoped to initiate redesign of the dam without further delay.[97]

Striding down the hallway to Justice B. K. Mehta's chambers, Basu pondered the letter's contents. How could the government expect a partial report when the commission had not yet held its first hearing? Proceedings had been slated for June; the government had pushed them back to July, and then again to August.[98]

Basu shook his head as he reflected on the wasted time. The government of Gujarat had proven anything but a willing partner in the search for the truth.

Earlier in 1980, for example, the state had issued an executive privilege claim in an attempt to prevent Justice Mehta from considering a key piece of evidence. Former Rajkot District Collector A. R. Banerjee's postflood report purportedly gave an unflattering account of Irrigation Department engineers, assailing them for not sounding warnings that the Machhu Dam-II might fail. If the document also detailed, as some alleged, Agriculture Minister Keshubhai Patel's nonchalant return to Rajkot after encountering tremendous flooding near Morbi, it held the potential to embarrass one of Gujarat's leading politicians.

Although the commission already possessed a copy of the Banerjee Report, the advocate general's office had taken great pains to have the evidence disqualified. The state had essentially argued that the document qualified as confidential correspondence of a sort whose disclosure might prove deleterious but whose suppression would not injure the pursuit of justice.[99]

The commission's staffers had found the state's contention specious. At one point, as a government lawyer vehemently insisted that the commission could not consider the Banerjee Report as evidence, Justice Mehta had found himself chuckling and shaking his head. "I have the document from the government of Gujarat, and have read it myself," he had interrupted, bringing the matter to an abrupt close. "How can you ask me to disregard it?"[100]

To Basu, the government's adversarial stance—for all the troubles it entailed—seemed less problematic than the notion that the Irrigation Department could rebuild the Machhu Dam-II so quickly, with so little reflection. The commission had not yet determined why the earthworks had collapsed, and it could only do so after completing its investigations and hearings. Moreover, the government had not yet apprised the public of the facts and given it a chance to weigh in on the dam's reconstruction. Charging ahead with rebuilding the Machhu Dam-II seemed reckless to Basu; he doubted that Justice Mehta would enable such a move by releasing an immature "partial report."[101]

Indeed, when Basu informed Mehta of the government's request, the judge was resolute. The commission would compromise its work for no one, he said. He would issue no partial report.

Mehta instructed Basu to arrange a meeting with lawyers from the advocate general's office to explain his decision. The justice was determined to see the commission finish its work on its own terms. Until he heard testimony from the public servants who had continued to avoid public scrutiny, he would not form any conclusions.[102]

On August 11, 1980, a sea of white filled the plaza in front of Nehru Gate.[103] When the square could hold no more, rivulets of white spilled out into the streets and alleys emanating from it. Morbi's citizens, dressed in the color of mourning, had gathered to remember.

Most communities in the flood-affected area had planned memorial ceremonies for the disaster's first anniversary. Naturally, Morbi's would be the largest. Mayor Ratilal Desai and other municipal officers had been preparing for weeks, drawing inspiration from the ceremonies carried out every year by the people of Hiroshima, Japan. All of Morbi—schools, offices, shops, factories—would shut down for the day. After an interfaith prayer ceremony in the Nehru Gate plaza, citizens would set out on a solemn parade to the Mani Mandir. There, in the garden that stood before the Taj Mahal of Saurashtra, along the banks of the Machhu River, the city would unveil a statue dedicated to those who had lost their lives. Mourners would pay their respects. At 3:30 p.m., to mark the dark hour when the flood-waters were unleashed upon Morbi, city hall would sound twenty-one sirens.

As the ceremony commenced, various civic and religious leaders crowded under a makeshift canopy at one end of the plaza, facing the throng. Hindu holy men, dressed in stiff, cotton wraparound robes, sat alongside Muslim clerics sporting beards and turbans. Jain monks, their mouths covered with flaps of cloth to prevent the accidental inhalation (and killing) of flies, shared space with Christian nuns in white habits and black veils. One by one, they stepped up to the standing microphones and offered hymns, prayers, homilies, and words of comfort.

The people of Morbi listened to the distorted sound projected through the rudimentary public announcement system. Men clenched their teeth, holding back tears. Children too young to remember the flood fidgeted in the laps of gently weeping mothers. Gray clouds filled the sky, casting a pall over the ceremony.

At the conclusion of the interfaith program, the mourners rose up together. Two thin men in crisp white suits moved to the front of the now-mobile mass. Raising *shehnais*—Indian oboes—to their lips, they began piping a loud, doleful tune. The parade set off toward the Mani Mandir.

In retrospect, many survivors would identify that day as a key milestone in the return to normalcy. In a year, the city had pulled itself up from ruin to renewal. Morbi's populace enjoyed sturdy shelter and steady employment, both built upon immense struggle. Neighborhoods had recoalesced, and some semblance of social levity was beginning to emerge. For many, the one-year mark would come to represent not a turning point, but a quiet slide from life's extraordinary battles into its ordinary ones.[104]

Nonetheless, nothing seemed ordinary on August 11, 1980, particularly to those who had lost loved ones. In a grand spectacle, thousands of mourners marched through the shuttered city, following the shrill sounds of woe. Bystanders on the upper stories of surrounding buildings watched a white mass of humanity fill up every space the eye could see. At every point along the parade route, the mass of mourners arrived, expanded, and slowly left, carrying on in its inexorable journey toward the Machhu River.

The clouds had thickened by the time the parade reached its destination. People poured into the garden of the Mani Mandir, which abutted the river. The Mani Mandir's thirty-foot gates towered over the mourners as they gathered in front of a small area at the center of the garden. Mayor Desai and retired legislator Gokaldas Parmar stood at the front of the group; leading citizens, such as Rotary Club President T. R. Shukla, stood just off to the side. Hundreds of mourners like Dhirubhai Mehta crowded around, peering to catch a glimpse of the solemn actions at the center.

With the help of a few other men, Desai pulled a thick white sheet off a three-foot rock slab. Shaped like a tombstone, it featured a roughly chiseled image of an outstretched hand, a symbol of offerings to the dead. In bold, slightly uneven letters, someone had engraved across the bottom, "Memorial to the Victims of the August 11, 1979, Machhu Flood Disaster." With great gravitas, the mayor and several other citizens fixed the memorial in its place at the center of the garden.

Then, one by one, the men of Morbi laid garlands of flowers on the stone. Mayor Desai, the corners of his mouth trembling under his thin mustache, placed the first. Dozens of others followed.

By the end of the program at the Mani Mandir, a hard rain had begun to fall. Most of the mourners dispersed to their homes directly from the memorial site.

Some followed Parmar on his march back into downtown. With scores of black umbrellas raised above their heads, the stragglers resembled a disordered, plodding phalanx as they walked along the newly paved road back into the heart of the city. The rain kept falling, and they, too, went home.

At 3:30 p.m., twenty-one sirens rang out.

Chapter 10
"Justice Was Not Done"

By March 1981, the Machhu Dam-II Inquiry Commission, whose work had been projected to last no more than six months, was over a year and a half old. Protracted government delays in supplying witnesses, submitting affidavits, and scheduling proceedings had turned the commission's work into a seemingly interminable struggle with bureaucracy.[1]

Public interest groups and the press had begun to take up the commission's cause. In early March, a small Ahmedabad-based nonprofit organization known as the Consumer Education and Research Centre (CERC) published a report lambasting the government's handling of the commission. The document, which systematically catalogued the state's delays and requests for extensions, concluded, "The government of Gujarat is the only culprit for the delays in the proceedings of Machhu Dam Inquiry Commission." As newspapers took notice of the report, pressure mounted on Chief Minister Madhavsinh Solanki's government to expedite the commission's work.[2]

The commission had slated state Irrigation Department engineers to provide sworn testimony a few days after the release of the CERC report. The first to testify would be none other than Chief Engineer J. F. Mistry, the man who had overseen much of the Machhu Dam-II's design work before rising to the top of the state's irrigation bureaucracy. Now, as on the day after the disaster, when he had protested Special Secretary for Relief H. K. Khan's daring attempt to cross a flooded bridge, Mistry seemed worried.

A short time earlier, the commission had sent a questionnaire to the engineers scheduled to testify, including Mistry; the questionnaire asked, among other things, about the government's calculations for the Machhu Dam-II's original design flood. Terrified at the prospect of being found culpable for the dam's failure, many engineers had appealed to their superiors to have their testimony blocked. With his subordinates in a panic, Mistry looked toward the hearings with anxiety for his department's reputation—and for his own.

As the date of his testimony approached, Mistry announced that he would be unable to testify on account of heart trouble. He attributed his ailment to stress over his impending appearance in court. Once again, the commission's work had hit a snag.[3]

A few days after Mistry's announcement, the chief minister invited the commission's engineering consultant, Dr. Y. K. Murthy, to a private audience. As Murthy later recalled, Solanki made his intentions clear. "If we continue this judicial inquiry," the chief minister reportedly said, "more engineers associated with planning, designing, and construction of the dam may also develop heart trouble. Therefore, the government has decided to terminate the judicial inquiry commission with immediate effect." Nineteen months after first demanding an inquiry into the Machhu dam disaster, Solanki was eliminating it.

The chief minister apparently stressed his desire to protect the engineers who had contributed to the project. In order to assess the Machhu Dam-II's failure without subjecting the Irrigation Department to embarrassing scrutiny, he would appoint Murthy to carry out a one-man technical investigation.

Murthy listened impassively; perhaps more than most civil servants, he had long ago absorbed the conviction that technocrats were duty-bound to carry out the wills of elected officials. Reflecting on the commission's termination decades after the fact, Murthy remarked, "It is up to the government to do what it wants. I have no say in the matter, nor does the judge have any say in the matter. If the government decides to withdraw the judicial inquiry . . . nobody can stop it."[4]

〰〰〰

From behind his wide, black desk, the deputy collector gazed at more than a dozen stern faces. Gokaldas Parmar sat directly across from him, characteristically dressed in a homespun cotton tunic, a rough vest, and a starched Gandhi cap. Sitting just to Parmar's right, Mayor Ratilal Desai stared at the bureaucrat with tightly pursed lips. Several rows of men and women, their gazes full of anticipation, had crowded in behind the two leaders. The small Mani Mandir office felt like a furnace in the sweltering summer heat.

The deputy collector, his elbows planted on the edge of the desk, tensed under his crisp, white shirt as Morbi's representatives began to speak. He was the latest target in the Machhu Dam-II Inquiry Commission Action Committee's quest for justice.[5]

Flood survivors, enraged by the government's decision to disband the Machhu Dam-II Inquiry Commission, had decided to agitate for redress. The action committee had grown out of a spirited meeting that had taken place at Morbi's city hall shortly after the announcement of the windup. Comprised of prominent men and women from various walks of life, the committee had resolved to wage a Gandhian battle against the government of Mahatma Gandhi's birthplace. If Gujarat's leaders tried to ignore Morbi's suffering, the people would shame them into acknowledging it.[6]

Now, on April 9, 1981, the action committee had orchestrated a citywide strike to protest the government's decision. As
one newspaper later reported:

> The shutdown was a total success, with all shops and estab-
> lishments, hotels, restaurants, theatres, and small cabins
> remaining closed. People from all over the town thronged the
> town hall and later went in a procession to present a memo-
> randum to the deputy collector demanding continuance of the
> Machhu-II inquiry commission. . . . Mr. Ratilal Desai . . . and
> other local leaders called on the administrative authorities to
> convey their displeasure.

Sweating in the cramped Mani Mandir office, Desai, Parmar, and
the other members of the action committee demanded redress for
their grievances.[7]

Though sympathetic to the survivors' outrage, the deputy collector for Morbi and Maliya could do nothing. If they desired
true resolution, he explained, they would have to travel to Gandhinagar. For the members of the action committee, the day of the
citywide shutdown ended with the difficult realization that, in
order to gain victory, they would have to present their case to the
state government's highest-ranking officials.[8]

A few days later, Desai, Parmar, and a number of other dele-
gates from the action committee traveled to Gandhinagar.
Demanding a meeting with Chief Minister Madhavsinh Solanki
and other top leaders, they attempted to lay out their arguments
for continuation of the commission's work. According to one
report, "The delegation got the impression that the government
had closed its mind on the subject and was not prepared to have
any rethinking in the matter."[9]

One representative would write, "When I went to Gandhinagar with the other action committee members and met with
Irrigation Minister Amarsinh Chaudhary, he told us that the government's decision was right."[10]

The committee's pleas, like those of flood survivors throughout the Machhu River Valley, fell on deaf ears.

≈≈≈≈≈

The people of the Machhu River Valley did not stand alone in their opposition to the disbandment of the Machhu Dam-II Inquiry Commission. In fact, the government's stiffest challenge came not from Morbi or Maliya but from Ahmedabad. Taking up the cause of the flood's victims, CERC—the young consumer advocacy organization that had previously reported on the commission's delays—had filed a formal petition to Gujarat's High Court, requesting that the windup be overturned.[11]

CERC had closely followed the commission's work from the very beginning. The organization's mission was to advocate for public health and well-being; consequently, it took interest in a wide range of issues, from environmental degradation to the safety of consumer goods. The commission's dedication to uncovering the causes of the Machhu Dam-II's failure resonated with the center's director and trustees, who had eagerly pledged to aid the often-harried commission.[12]

At various points during the eighteen months after the disaster, CERC had acted as a thorn in the government's side. For example, when the commission lacked the expertise and resources to test spillway motors in order to resolve questions about floodgate openings, CERC had interceded. The government had refused to provide the organization with electrical power for the tests, claiming that it would have to establish a special electric line at a cost of hundreds of thousands of rupees; undaunted, CERC had decided to conduct the tests with a five-horsepower portable generator. The tests had eventually taken place in late 1980, with the government's grudging approval.[13]

Around the time of the gate tests, CERC had started drafting a dam safety bill for Gujarat's legislative assembly. Hoping to make use of the commission's growing cache of information, the organization had requested access to a number of documents, including the infamous Banerjee Report. Just as it had done with the commission, the government had attempted to block CERC's access to the report with a claim of executive privilege. The subsequent round of appeals and counterappeals in Gujarat's High Court had dragged the government into a humiliatingly public controversy.[14]

On March 17, 1981, CERC fired its boldest shot yet. Upon somehow discovering that the government intended to dissolve the commission later that day, the center filed a petition in the Gujarat High Court to prevent the windup, contending that the administration was acting in bad faith.[15]

The grounds for CERC's appeal were tenuous at best. The law governing commissions of inquiry in India clearly stated that a commission must "cease to exist when so notified," and that the government could disband a commission if it were "of the opinion that the continued existence of the commission is unnecessary."[16] Moreover, no legal precedent existed in India for a public interest body to take legal action on behalf of the people as a whole; it was consequently unclear whether the organization even possessed *locus standi*—the right to bring action—in the case.

In fact, the High Court proved receptive to the petition. A temporary stay halted the commission's dissolution, and the case found its way onto the court's docket for the summer. The justices would hear arguments from both sides and then determine whether the government had acted legally in quashing the Machhu Dam-II Inquiry Commission.[17]

≋≋≋≋

Behind the counter at Mehta Machinery in the Mahendra Quarter, Dhirubhai Mehta tended to a growing pile of newspaper clippings and correspondence.[18] Still distraught over the death of his son, Vimal, he refused to accept that the Machhu Dam-II Inquiry Commission could simply cease to exist. Amid the controversy following Chief Minister Madhavsinh Solanki's announcement of the windup, Mehta had begun to collect documents pertaining to the activities of the local citizen action committee, the Ahmedabad-based CERC, and various other champions of the commission. Quietly, he had also begun writing his own letters to protest the injustice.

For eighteen months, Mehta had avidly followed the commission's work, his spirit sustained by the possibility of an ultimate explanation for his losses. While the government of Gujarat had been delaying its submission of required affidavits, he had even sent the commission a voluntary statement regarding his experiences during the flood.

He had felt shocked, then, when the government disbanded the inquiry without even informing individuals who had contributed, however modestly, to its investigation. Years later, he would recall bitterly, "I found out about the dissolution of the commission when I read about it in the paper." He would laugh ruefully, his voice filled with disbelief and sorrow, before adding, "Justice was not done."[19]

On April 30, after several weeks of watching others agitate to no effect, Mehta composed and mailed a one-page letter of protest to ten newspapers and thirty-four prominent politicians, including Prime Minister Indira Gandhi, several former prime ministers, the speaker of parliament, more than two dozen members of parliament, a number of state-level politicians. Then, the unassuming machinery merchant settled in to wait.[20]

He was still waiting for responses from most addressees a month later, when an article in the daily *Sandesh* caught his attention. On the eve of the Gujarat Engineering Association's twenty-first annual conference, a few dam engineers had spoken anonymously to reporters. They had accused the state of employing insufficient rain, flood, and storm data in its design of the Machhu Dam-II, pointing out that a bridge over the Machhu near Wankaner, outlined during the same period, possessed a design flood twice as large as the dam's.[21]

The story confirmed Mehta's suspicion that the government had wound up the commission in order to avoid embarrassing revelations. If the nameless engineers were to be believed, the state had demonstrated gross negligence in its planning for the Machhu Dam-II.

Mehta's anger at the government's irresponsibility and subsequent evasiveness exploded two days later, on June 1, when he read about the proceedings of the engineering conference. In addressing the gathering, the Gujarat Engineering Association president—Chief Engineer J. F. Mistry—had spoken words that drew out all the grief and rage Mehta had accumulated over eighteen months of mourning.

Mistry—the man who had helped design the Machhu Dam-II, become Gujarat's top engineer for dams, and come down with heart trouble just before his scheduled testimony—had begun by decrying the fundamental premise of the commission whose potential had sustained Mehta through such trying times:

> Ten to fifteen dams have collapsed in India. Among these, Gujarat's Machhu Dam is infamous. No sooner do these collapses occur than the government names a judicial inquiry. Against this, it is our request that these questions first be entrusted to a technical committee.

Then, in response to a reporter's question about the implications of eliminating broader investigations, Mistry had shot back, "The Machhu Dam-II Inquiry Commission had requested information from engineers. If such an inquiry finds fault with any engineer, Gujarat's fifteen thousand engineers will rise up, and no one will accept responsibility for any dam."[22]

The chief engineer's words, unambiguously recorded in clear black letters, disgusted Mehta, who interpreted them as a brazen threat. With vigorous strokes of his pen, Mehta crafted a rebuttal to Mistry's remarks and sent it to the editor of *Sandesh*, who would print it the next day:

To make this type of statement is a mockery of human rights and justice. If a thorough inquiry is made into a disaster in which thousands of innocents have died, the information emerging will make engineers more vigilant and cause state governments throughout India to build and maintain dams with greater care. The people of Morbi believe that the Machhu-II Dam disaster was man-made. In this disaster, my daughter and my one and only son slipped away before my own eyes. If Mr. J. F. Mistry were placed in a horrendous position like mine, he too would vociferously request that the Machhu [Dam]-II Inquiry Commission continue; he would not attempt to make spurious defenses of engineers. Morbi's city hall has delivered a message to the government of Gujarat requesting the continuation of the Machhu [Dam]-II Inquiry Commission. Consequently, in order to give the people of Morbi justice, the government of Gujarat should keep the inquiry alive. And whoever is found guilty should be punished.[23]

On June 23, 1981, following nearly three months of anticipation, the Gujarat High Court delivered a staggering ruling on the legality of the state government's decision to dissolve the Machhu Dam-II Inquiry Commission.[24]

Lawyers from the advocate general's office had objected to CERC's petition on numerous grounds. First, they had argued that the commission simply lacked enough time to complete a report before its official deadline, such that any order countermanding the government's action would prove futile. Second, they had contended that CERC did not possess *locus standi*—the legitimate standing to file a case—because it had cited the public interest, rather than its own, in making the appeal. Finally, the lawyers had proceeded to the crux of their case—an interpretation of the Commission of Inquiry Act of 1952. They had argued that the law's wording was unambiguous: the government could wind up a commission whenever it felt "of the opinion that the continued existence of the commission is unnecessary." Noting that the commission had not found faults in the dam's construction or floodgate operations, that the commission's work threatened to stretch on for years, and that Dr. Y. K. Murthy's one-man technical inquiry would prove far more efficient, the lawyers had maintained that the government had deemed the body unnecessary in good faith.[25]

Against this, the legal counsel for CERC had argued that the government had wound up the commission due to growing frustration with its questioning and its intrusions, rather than true feelings about the necessity of its work. The government had therefore acted in bad faith. According to CERC's argument, the government's intention to form a technical inquiry under Murthy betrayed its true position—that some kind of investigation was still necessary. The court needed to act to prevent the administration from overstepping its bounds.[26]

The High Court's ruling surprised all of Gujarat. In their lengthy opinion, the justices first affirmed CERC's *locus standi*:

> If the petitioners are not allowed to agitate this point, then, it would mean that the government is left free to violate the law. ... Under these circumstances, the petitioners are a public interest body ... trying to vindicate the rule of law, and hence they have sufficient interest to enable them to maintain this petition. They have the appropriate *locus standi* to file this petition.[27]

This technical decision alone made the ruling one for the ages; CERC's lawyer would call it an "epoch-making judgment."[28] The precedent it set—that advocacy organizations could bring legal action against corporations or the government on behalf of the general public—changed the face of litigation in Gujarat and in India at large.[29]

Moving on to the substance of the case, the court delivered the decision that CERC, the commission staffers, and the people of Morbi had long anticipated: the government's windup of the commission was tainted with unacceptable legal malice. The justices reasoned that, "since the legislature [had] not chosen to indicate under what circumstances the state government can form an opinion, or on what facts the state government can form an opinion that the continued existence of the commission is unnecessary," it fell to the judiciary to make that determination. They then asserted:

> If the purpose of making the inquiry into any definite matter of public importance still continues to exist as it existed at the time when the commission of inquiry was originally appointed. . . . It cannot be said that the continued existence of the commission is unnecessary. . . . To read the provisions otherwise would be to render a commission of inquiry a football or a plaything in the hands of the political executive.

The government's conclusion "that the collapse was due to natural causes" was "such as no reasonable person dealing with this matter could have arrived at." As such, the subsequent decision that the commission had become unnecessary was "vitiated." The court declared the government's decision "quashed."[30]

The High Court ruling, which ran to dozens of pages, revived the hopes of flood victims. On June 30, Dhirubhai Mehta wrote an effusive letter to CERC explaining his own connection to the flood and congratulating the organization for its victory. In his response, the center's director expressed sympathy for Mehta's loss and said, "My friends and I thank you on behalf of the center for the congratulations. . . . In truth, it is only because of the support and cooperation provided by the people of Morbi that we have been able to achieve this." In closing, the director issued a note of caution. "Much is left to be done," he explained. "We have won a small battle. The war is not yet over."[31]

By July 20, the government of Gujarat had lodged an appeal with India's Supreme Court. The drama of the Machhu dam disaster would have to play out to its conclusion on the country's grandest judicial stage.[32]

≋≋≋≋

While the legal gamesmanship surrounding the Machhu Dam-II Inquiry Commission shifted to India's highest court, the government of Gujarat pushed ahead with one of the most formidable irrigation projects in history. The Sardar Sarovar Dam, conceived by Prime Minister Jawaharlal Nehru in the late 1940s as one of the "temples of modern India," would impound the waters of the mighty Narmada River in rural central Gujarat. Championed by Babubhai Patel during his rule as chief minister, the project had stalled in the 1970s due to interstate water disputes. By the early 1980s, however, a central government tribunal had ruled in favor of Gujarat, and the state government was forging ahead with the sweeping project.[33]

Amid the excitement over the Sardar Sarovar project, the government of Gujarat had designated two esteemed engineers to advise it on matters related to damming the Narmada. In May 1982, the pair—known as the Narmada Dam Design Review Panel—received a somewhat surprising letter from Irrigation Department Chief Engineer J. F. Mistry, the man who had overseen the construction of the Machhu Dam-II and subsequently stymied the inquiry commission's work. Mistry wrote to the consultants:

> I furnish herewith a set of estimates, reports, designs, and drawings for restoration work of Machhu-II Dam at Morbi in Gujarat State. As you are already aware of the fact disaster which occurred in August 1979 by overtopping the dam due to unprecedented heavy rains in catchment for a period of 24 hours [sic].
>
> The government of Gujarat has, in view of the clearance given by [the] Supreme Court of India, decided to start the work and complete the same at the earliest so that the command of 18,000 acres which has been starving for water since 1979 can be flourished again. . . .[34]

Even as the fate of the inquiry commission remained uncertain, the government of Gujarat was eager to reconstruct the Machhu Dam-II. Approval from the prestigious Narmada Dam Design Review Panel would provide the state the necessary legitimacy to move ahead.

In truth, Irrigation Department engineers had long been keen to rebuild the broken structure. Planning for reconstruction had proceeded quietly while the inquiry commission carried on its investigation. In August 1981, one newspaper had reported:

> A senior official in the Gujarat state Irrigation Department reluctantly admits, "The government won't be able to tell you what it has done so far. But we have worked on new hydrology, the design work is advanced, plans and estimates are nearing completion. We are starting all preliminaries."[35]

One year later, when Mistry wrote to the Narmada consultants, a well-defined project proposal for the new Machhu Dam-II had taken form.

The two men dove into the new work. On June 22 and 23, 1982, one of them visited the dam site near Jodhpar, accompanied by Mistry and the supervising engineer in charge of the Central Designs Organization. The consultant surveyed the denuded concrete spillway, considered the proposed locations of the earthen embankments and the reservoir, and listened to the government engineers' presentations regarding the new design. One month later, the other consultant visited the dam site. Soon, the two men were meeting with Irrigation Department engineers every few months, driving the plans for reconstruction forward in spurts.[36]

Before long, B. J. Vasoya—the engineer who had overseen the construction of the original Machhu Dam-II—became an integral figure in the planning meetings. In late 1982, the government of Gujarat appointed him—apparently at the insistence of local legislators—as chief engineer for the entire Saurashtra Peninsula, charging him with the construction, maintenance, and investigation of dams from the Arabian Sea to the Gulf of Kutch. As one of his first tasks, he took up the redesign of the dam he had built a decade earlier.[37]

In light of the previous incarnation's catastrophic failure, the new Machhu Dam-II clearly needed a greater capacity to withstand large floods. The Irrigation Department estimated that the rains of August 1979 had delivered a peak inflow of 510,000 cubic feet per second (cusecs) to the dam, which had been designed to pass only about 200,000 cusecs. (By 1982, the government of Gujarat had apparently retreated from the idea of a 900,000-cusec flood, which it had endorsed in its official submission to the inquiry commission.) State engineers took the 510,000-cusec figure as a starting point for the new design flood, but they also incorporated data from smaller catchment areas and consulted railroad authorities, who had monitored small rivers since 1965 in order to protect crossings. Using a new method known as synthetic unit hydrograph, they derived a design flood of 739,000 cusecs and proposed a spillway outflow capacity of 691,000 cusecs. The difference between the maximum conceivable inflow and the outflow capacity would be permissible because the dam's freeboard—the distance between its crest and the highest allowable water level—would suffice to buffer excess water in a worst-case scenario.[38]

The consultants did not like the Irrigation Department's proposal. They felt that the river channel downstream of the dam could not safely pass much more than 350,000 cusecs without causing calamitous flooding in Morbi. Considering the possibility of "panicky operation of gates by the maintenance operators apprehending high floods coming from upstream," it seemed inadvisable to equip the new Machhu Dam-II to unleash catastrophic man-made flooding on the downstream area. The consultants proposed that the Irrigation Department reduce the spillway capacity and instead greatly augment the freeboard, thereby enabling the dam to store exceptionally heavy inflow and then release water gradually.[39]

The government of Gujarat raised various counterarguments to the consultants' position. Revising the Irrigation Department's design to create a dam with a lower maximum outflow "would limit, for all time to come, the spillway capacity and would thus not permit flexibility in operation when a flood higher than the design flood was encountered." Furthermore, a scheme that increased freeboard—and thereby, the reservoir's storage capacity—would be "extremely dangerous for the downstream areas if a breach in the dam unfortunately occurred in such a situation." There was also a logistical barrier: "raising of the dam would require large extension of the earth dam on both the flanks." Although the engineers did not cite economics in their arguments, it appears very likely that the additional construction required to increase the reservoir's buffering capacity would have rendered the project's ultimate cost-benefit ratio unfavorable. Whatever the reasons, the government of Gujarat seemed bent on reconstructing the Machhu Dam-II as it had been before, substantially modifying only the spillway outflow capacity.[40]

By the middle of the 1980s, a new normalcy had taken hold in the Machhu River Valley. Gangaram Tapu lived happily at home with his wife and children, working for the progress of his jati and entertaining visits from variegated characters on his front porch. Pratapbhai Adroja's Ghost Paan did brisk business amid an increasingly congested and hectic commercial zone. At the end of his term as Morbi's mayor, Ratilal Desai returned to private life, managing his paint factory and moving into a future without his firstborn. Retired statesman Gokaldas Parmar engrossed himself in social service activities. In New Lilapar, Bhagvanji Patel tended to his farm and, more often, his booming tile factory. As he had for three decades, T. R. Shukla dedicated himself to introducing college students to the joy of Gujarati literature.[41]

Over the course of the years, signs of the government officers who had resurrected Morbi slowly disappeared from daily life, though their legacy lived on in the public's memory. District Collector A. R. Banerjee, Special Secretary for Relief H. K. Khan, Home Guard Commander Ushakant Mankad, and Chief Minister Babubhai Patel had left the city long ago. After his time as district collector in Valsad, Banerjee was deputed to the Central Vigilance Commission, a national body dedicated to ensuring governmental integrity; after a few years in New Delhi, he returned to Gujarat to resume his climb up the state's civil service hierarchy. Khan oversaw the Gujarat Industrial Investment Corporation from 1980 until 1985, when he became Gujarat's Industry Secretary. Mankad—a native son of Morbi—disappeared from the city's gaze, throwing himself into journalism and political activity in the city of Rajkot. Babubhai had not returned to government since his 1980 ouster. Though he had held several important positions within the rapidly evolving Janata Party, he did not run for election in 1985, and it seemed that he had seen his last days as a member of the legislative assembly.[42]

Kanubhai Kubavat was among those whose return to a stable life took longest. In 1980, his wife and children came back to Morbi after living at his brother-in-law's house for a year. Around the same time, Kubavat, eager to rebuild his family's life, took a higher-paying job on the southern coast of Saurashtra. While he earned money, his family remained behind in the earthen hovel he had constructed on his plot in the Tiger Quarter. His father officiated at the temple, and his wife took care of the children and stepped in whenever her father-in-law could not lead a ceremony. For half a decade, Kubavat scraped together savings until, finally, he was able to build a spacious home, better than before, with concrete walls and modern floor tiles. By 1985, when he received an appointment as a government education administrator in the district where he had been working, the family was once again living in a proper house.[43]

For Khatijaben Valera and her clan, the restoration of normalcy left something to be desired; for them, the key to comfortable lives lay in a bygone era. Some members of the family would maintain that they never truly recovered from the structural, economic, and psychic damage they endured during the disaster. At any rate, the city seemed to leave the Valeras farther behind as it continued on its rapidly industrializing development trajectory. Khatijaben's husband and the other major partners in Valera Transport continued to fare well, but for other members of the family, the 1980s brought hard luck. Those who continued to rely on their musical gifts for income found that the new Morbi presented ever-tighter competition for the patronage of the middle class.[44]

To the north, Maliya sank back into oblivion. Husainbhai Manek, having abandoned fishing, toiled away on his ancestral farmland. Little by little, he expanded the land under cultivation.[45]

Abdulbhai Mor gradually extended his salt production. Though he did not produce the same quantities as the biggest out-of-town businessmen, he would make a very comfortable living for himself.[46]

Jashabhai Samani, unable to cultivate his ravaged fields, resigned himself to a lifetime of labor in the salt industry. From time to time, he walked past his forefathers' land. His blue eyes squinted as he glared at the scrub that had overgrown it, reclaiming it for the wasteland that would always lay siege to Maliya.[47]

For three years after the Gujarat High Court's 1981 ruling, the Machhu Dam-II Inquiry Commission's case languished on the Indian Supreme Court's docket. The commission, in a state of legal uncertainty, had remained inactive twice as long as it had once been active. The people of the Machhu River Valley—even those who had lost loved ones in the disaster—had largely put the matter out of their minds. "So far as our public memory is concerned," one lawyer for the commission would recall, "at the time the incident takes place, people are very keen to know and go into all the details. With the passage of time, everyone gets busy with some sort of thing, and they have their own problems."[48]

CERC, for one, could not forget the case. It scrambled to action when the Supreme Court abruptly took up the Machhu case in late July 1984. Nonetheless, the justices proceeded so quickly that CERC was not able to dispatch its star lawyer to New Delhi.[49]

In spite of the short notice, public attention in Gujarat rapidly fixed on the case. The court's decision would determine whether governments possessed absolute power over commissions of inquiry.[50]

After a brief hearing, the Supreme Court ruled that there was no evidence to suggest that the government of Gujarat had acted in bad faith:

> We are, therefore, unable to find any shred of legal malice in the order passed by the government. The government has rightly pointed out that [the] commission had already collected necessary materials which could be more effective and expeditiously examined by an expert officer for making necessary recommendations regarding reconstruction of the dam. . . . In these circumstances, we do not see any reason or justifiable cause to persuade us to come to a finding that the order of the government was influenced by collateral considerations. The High Court was entirely wrong in quashing the order of the government which was well grounded. . . . The government had ample discretion to discontinue the inquiry if it is of opinion that continuance of the said inquiry was wholly unnecessary.

Here, the writing justice paused to chide the Gujarati court: "It was not at all necessary for the High Court to have examined the pros and cons of the matter by a lengthy judgment running into more than one hundred pages which, in fact, amounted to all love's labour lost."

In closing, the court declared, "For these reasons, we allow the appeal, set aside the judgment of the High Court and restore the order of the government discontinuing the inquiry."[51]

With a ruling that barely filled one page, the Supreme Court had ended five years of struggle.

≋≋≋≋≋

In June 1985—nearly six years after the disintegration of the Machhu Dam-II—Dr. Y. K. Murthy completed his report on the disaster.[52] In finalizing his investigation, Murthy drew extensively on the documents and evidence collected by the original Machhu Dam-II Inquiry Commission. He also spoke at length with many of the engineers who had helped to design the dam; while they had bristled at the prospect of providing public testimony before a High Court judge, the men allowed their fellow engineer to "take them into confidence," according to Murthy's later recollection.[53]

The completion of the Murthy Report did not prompt any press coverage. Copies of the document found their way to the desks of engineers and bureaucrats and, soon thereafter, to the shelves of musty government storerooms. Though not strictly classified, the report never reached public view. Two decades after its completion, even former staffers from the original Machhu Dam-II Inquiry Commission remained unaware of its existence.[54]

The Murthy Report thus came to occupy a strange limbo. As a thorough and truthful explanation of the Machhu Dam-II's collapse, the document embodied the fulfilled wishes of thousands of flood survivors. Nonetheless, for nearly three decades after the flood, its findings would remain wrapped in burlap and tucked neatly away in the forgotten corners of state government archives, only remotely accessible to those who might have once sought them.

The 130-page document unfolded in a progression of logical steps, tracing the history of the dam's construction and considering possible explanations of its ultimate failure, from poor soil compaction to faulty floodgate operation, to inadequate spillway capacity, and beyond.

Murthy began by ruling out geologic shortcomings. Based on affidavits originally submitted to the inquiry commission, Murthy concluded that the government had undertaken adequate geological investigations before building the dam. Fears of a fault line running across the site had been appropriately addressed, and oversight from engineering geologists in the Irrigation Department had remained in place throughout the construction process.[55]

Next, Murthy examined the design and construction of the earthworks themselves, allowing for the possibility that structural failure, rather than catastrophic overtopping, had caused the earthen flanks to give way. In evaluating the integrity of the embankments, Murthy cited a study performed by two University of Roorkee professors at the behest of the inquiry commission; analysis of samples from the earthen dam—obtained during a 1980 visit to the dam site with commission secretary Dipankar Basu—had yielded "values of factors of safety well above the minimum recommended values," leading the professors to conclude that the earthworks were "safe for all critical conditions." Given the soil scientists' findings, Murthy concluded that the Machhu Dam-II's earthen flanks had been competent to withstand any force of water, short of complete overtopping.[56]

Given the available evidence, it seemed obvious that the earthen walls had disintegrated due to an overtopping reservoir, as might have been expected. Murthy's report examined three different scenarios for overtopping. The first corresponded to the dam workers' claims: though open, the floodgates simply could not pass enough water, resulting in the reservoir's inexorable and catastrophic rise. The second corresponded to the theory espoused by many citizens of Morbi and the surrounding villages: the gates had not been properly opened, and water accumulated in the reservoir as a result, eventually spilling over the earthworks. The third scenario involved a situation in which the reservoir remained below the maximum allowable water level while wind-driven waves overtopped the dam.[57]

Murthy quickly dismissed the third possibility. The flood had been so tremendous, he wrote, that the reservoir would have overtopped the embankments regardless of their height. Even if a few additional feet of freeboard had delayed the rush of initial waves over the embankments, they could not have prevented the dam's failure.[58]

Murthy's conviction regarding the inevitability of overtopping rested upon estimates of the peak inflow to the Machhu Dam-II's reservoir on August 11, 1979. In its "Statement of Facts and Opinions," the government of Gujarat had asserted the influx had been somewhere between 631,000 and 936,000 cusecs—three to four times the spillway's discharge capacity. Murthy, citing a unit hydrograph study conducted by University of Roorkee hydrologists at the commission's instigation, settled on an estimate of 460,000 cusecs. On the one hand, then, the state government had overstated the magnitude of the influx on the day of the disaster; the flood had been large, but not inconceivably so, as the Irrigation Department had hoped to suggest. On the other hand, the inflow rate—more than double the outflow capacity, sustained for several hours—had been more than sufficient to overfill the reservoir. Based on the numbers, Murthy concluded that the dam had been bound to fail by overtopping.[59]

Seeking to authenticate either the dam workers' version of events or the local villagers', Murthy reviewed the evidence regarding gate openings on the day of the disaster. As an appendix to the Murthy Report, he included the report issued by the steel company that had conducted a test of the dam's gate motors in 1980 with CERC's help. The investigating team had found all the gates in working order save for gates 9, 15, and 17; the motors of the latter three—precisely the gates cited by dam workers as the jammed ones—housed burnt brake coils, which had essentially caused them to lock. Overall, the gate test results strongly corroborated the crew members' accounts, suggesting that the gates had, in fact, been open on the fateful day.[60]

Murthy's painstaking consideration of the available evidence led him to a clear conclusion:

The spillway capacity was designed for a maximum flood discharge of 200,000 cusecs as per state-of-the-art of the subject
prevalent at that time. [It] was not able to pass the large peak
flood of 460,000 cusecs. The Machhu Dam-II was overtopped
and the flanking earth dams failed.[61]

With the Machhu Dam-II Inquiry Commission defunct and the
Murthy Report locked away in archives, flood survivors could
only speculate as to the causes of the calamity that had destroyed
their communities, livelihoods, and families.

A few would not bother to ask why the dam had failed. One
inhabitant of Morbi's Harijan Quarter would explain, "Among
people like us, no one talks of things like that. No one lays blame.
That is not for us to do. Big people take it upon themselves to
understand these things. . . . Poor people get saved by God."[62]

Some accepted the event as a natural disaster, like one Tiger
Quarter woman who asked, "Who would we blame? Nature
took its course. Who would we blame?"[63]

Nonetheless, most residents of the Machhu River Valley
refused to treat the dam failure as an act of nature or God.
Having sustained losses, often tremendous, in the flood, they
could not ignore questions of human agency and culpability.
Ratilal Desai, the former mayor, would explain, "This was a
great calamity. And what's worse, it was not a natural calamity.
This was a man-made disaster."[64]

Survivors searching for a blameworthy party would almost
universally settle on the dam's deputy engineer and crew members. According to Desai and thousands of others, the disaster
resulted directly from a failure to open the dam's floodgates in a
timely fashion. Some would claim that the employees responsible
for operating the gates had abandoned the dam; the purported
motivations varied among accounts, ranging from the Shravan
holidays to laziness to a fear about the rising water. Many would

contend that the dam workers had failed in their duties due to simple negligence.[65]

The general narrative of gate mismanagement, whatever its details, would gain almost universal acceptance in the flood-stricken area. As an explanation for the catastrophe, it possessed an alluring common-sense appeal. Desai would explain:

> If the gates are open, how can the dam burst? All the water that comes will leave! . . . If the gates are open, no matter what the inflow is, all the water can exit through just one gate. Dams are built with proper parameters, such that they can always release the water.[66]

Without public disclosure of the outflow deficiency that had led to overtopping, the dam's crew became an easy scapegoat, shielding Irrigation Department engineers and the government of Gujarat at large from scrutiny. Survivors would remain ignorant of the state design engineers' "gross bungling,"[67] as one lawyer for the aborted inquiry commission would call it. Directing their ire at the dam's operators, many would develop the attitude that former legislator Gokaldas Parmar voiced years later regarding Deputy Engineer A. C. Mehta: "This was really a crime. It should have been punished."[68] Few would think similar thoughts about the remote bureaucrats who had designed the dam.

Gate mismanagement became such a prevalent explanation for the flood that the public seemed prepared to reject any evidence suggesting that the gates had, in fact, been open. Asked about postdisaster photographs that showed fifteen of the eighteen gates open, Miyana industrialist Abdulbhai Mor would scoff: "What is the use of them being opened after the dam has burst? You can open them all you want after the fact. First, you didn't open the gates. Then, after the fact, you want to open them to protect yourself. What is the use of that?" Mor and many others would maintain that the government and dam workers had conspired to create the illusion of timely gate management after the emptying of the reservoir.[69]

Interestingly, the public's focus on alleged shortcomings in gate operations would overshadow questions falling within the old inquiry commission's second area of investigation—government disaster mitigation activities. With the dam workers' perceived lack of diligence providing a convenient, tangible target for survivors' anger, their actual failures to issue warnings would remain unexamined. For example, almost no one bothered to wonder about the fact that Lilapar, alone among the downstream communities, received a warning of an impending catastrophe. Similarly, although some newspapers had noted the blunder in the flood's immediate aftermath, Agriculture Minister Keshubhai Patel's bizarre failure to alert authorities to the unusual flooding near Morbi—well documented in the hidden Banerjee Report—would quickly fade from public awareness.

In the end, the windup of the inquiry commission, along with the restriction of the Murthy Report to engineering circles, allowed state engineers and administrative officials to skirt questions of culpability relating to the design of the Machhu Dam-II and to government vigilance on the day of the flood. Survivors adopted a more personal narrative of the disaster's causes; though fundamentally untrue, it proved convenient for the government of Gujarat, and it would continue to thrive for decades. While inhabitants of the Machhu River Valley blamed the dam's workers, the Irrigation Department could move ahead with the all-important work of tapping the state's water-wealth.

〰〰〰

Around the time Dr. Y. K. Murthy was completing his authoritative report on the failure of the old Machhu Dam-II, the Narmada Dam Design Review Panel submitted its report on the proposed design of the new dam. Over the course of four years, the panel's two consultants had held eight separate sessions with engineers from the government of Gujarat. They had watched the Irrigation Department revise the dam's probable maximum flood up from 739,000 cusecs to 941,000 cusecs in the wake of the unprecedented rains of June 1983, which had dwarfed even the flood of 1979. In early 1985, they had even witnessed the operation of a scale replica of the proposed dam at the Gujarat Engineering Research Institute.[70]

Throughout the process, the experts had disagreed with state engineers over the choice of a fundamental mechanism for dealing with heavy floods. The Irrigation Department wanted to build a spillway with colossal outflow capacity. The consultants, in contrast, favored the idea of giving the dam a moderate discharge capacity and buffering large inflows with the excess storage afforded by a large freeboard. These consultants repeatedly expressed concern that an unnecessarily high outflow capacity would create the potential for recurrent man-made floods; gate operators would avoid releasing water until as late as possible and would then release large volumes of water all at once. The state engineers offered a minor concession: some of the new dam's gates could be locked, with only senior officers possessing the authority to unlock and open them. The consultants roundly rejected the idea, noting that the scheme was "more likely to fail than operate successfully, under prevailing conditions in India." The dispute over the new dam's outflow capacity and freeboard dragged on for months.[71]

The state engineers ultimately prevailed. The consultants' role, they pointed out, was only to ensure that the design of the new dam was safe; the mechanism by which safety was assured remained the choice of the Irrigation Department. Minutes from one of the later meetings recorded the experts' helplessness:

> The panel of experts felt that though they would like to restrict the spillway capacity as suggested by the panel earlier, nevertheless this issue was a policy matter and as the Irrigation Department seems to have decided to provide additional gates as pro-

vided in the project after taking into consideration the various aspects, the panel of experts would not object. . . .[72]

The government had decided, and the government would build.

In 1985, the consultants of the Narmada Dam Design Review Panel granted their approval to the Irrigation Department's design. Directly adjacent to the original eighteen-gate spillway, the new Machhu Dam-II would sport an additional twenty spillway gates, each of which would measure forty-one feet in height and twenty-seven feet in width. At full opening, the dam would be capable of discharging 872,000 cubic feet of water into the riverbed every second. The consultants, who remained anxious about the possibility of unleashing sudden, massive floods on Morbi, insisted that workers operate the gates according to a "Rule-Curve" manual, which specified precisely how much water could be discharged under particular sets of circumstances. With the completion of the Murthy Report and the submission of the review panel's approval for the revised design, the government found all barriers to reconstruction of the Machhu Dam-II eliminated.[73]

J. F. Mistry considered the approval of the large-outflow design a personal victory. After overseeing the design of the original Machhu Dam-II and becoming chief engineer for irrigation projects, Mistry had been promoted to the post of Gujarat Irrigation Secretary—the highest rank in the state's irrigation engineering bureaucracy.

As irrigation secretary, Mistry came into direct conflict with Murthy. After more than half a decade of studying the Machhu Dam-II and its failure, the former chairman of the Central Water and Power Commission disagreed vehemently with the state government's plans for the new spillway. He would later remember, "I had a fight with the secretary: don't provide so many gates."

Like the Narmada Dam Design Review Panel consultants before him, Murthy believed that Mistry's insistence on an outflow capacity of nearly 900,000 cusecs was "a futile exercise." He would recall:

Now he has doubled the number of gates. . . . If that one million [cusecs] comes downstream, then Morbi is no more. So this
is a futile precautionary measure . . . . But he would not listen.

Attempting to assuage Murthy's anxiety, Mistry assured him,
"The keys to the gates will be in my pocket." Unlike the physical
gate locks proposed by project engineers as a concession to the
Narmada experts, the irrigation secretary's locking mechanism
was figurative. Still, Murthy shared the consultants' skepticism.
In later years, he would reflect on Mistry's idea with uncharac-
teristic bluntness, declaring simply, "That was absurd."

As an alternative, Murthy proposed remodeling the Machhu
Dam-II into an ungated structure, much like the upstream
Machhu Dam-I; once the reservoir filled, water would flow over
a solid concrete spillway into the riverbed below, and outflow
would match inflow. Mistry, however, would not be swayed. The
irrigation secretary had decided upon a large-outflow dam, and
the man who had once been India's most powerful irrigation
engineer could not change his opinion.[74]

Mistry left an unmistakable mark on the new Machhu Dam-II,
but he did not see it through to completion. Once the project was well
under way, he retired from public service. B. J. Vasoya—the man who
had supervised the construction of the original dam and had driven
forward its redesign as chief engineer for Saurashtra—succeeded
Mistry as irrigation secretary. From 1986 to 1987, Vasoya reigned
over all of Gujarat's irrigation activities, including the ongoing reconstruction of the Machhu Dam-II. Then, he too retired.[75]

Still, the dam continued to rise. An enormous new spillway
took shape next to the old one, and twenty shining Tainter gates
filled in its gaping maws. Piles of rocks and earth became long,
earthen embankments, replacements for those that had washed
away nearly ten years earlier. The World Bank funded the project,
even as it withdrew its support for the Sardar Sarovar Dam amid
controversy about the economic, environmental, and human
costs of a vast reservoir on the Narmada.[76]

In 1989, ten years after the disaster that ravaged Morbi, Maliya, and the surrounding villages, construction crews finished rebuilding the Machhu Dam-II.[77]

〰〰〰

In 1979, farmland had filled Morbi's southern reaches. From there, fields had stretched for miles outward. Every morning, Satwara farmers from Vajepar, Madhapar, and the Tiger Quarter would set out for their fields at 6:00 a.m., returning at 8:00 p.m. with bales of hay to feed their cattle.

Ten years later, an industrial revolution had drastically altered their daily routine. Some Satwaras still tilled the soil, but they would walk for well over an hour to reach their fields, passing by mounds of red tiling clay and numerous industrial complexes on the way. The transformation of cultivated fields into industrial land, paired with population growth within the jati, had forced the rest of Gokaldas Parmar's community out of agriculture. Like members of many other poorer jatis, they turned to the emerging master in Morbi's postflood economy: the factory.[78]

Morbi's industrial sector expanded rapidly in the decade after the Machhu dam disaster. The resulting metamorphosis produced a city in which old and new, traditional and modern, local and global constantly mixed together. Villagers herded their buffalo in front of gleaming corporate towers. Industrialists rode in luxury sedans down unpaved roads. Sari-clad women lined up each morning outside simple factories, seeking work manufacturing the clocks that were advertised on towering billboards near the Buffalo Bridge. In a short span, an industrial revolution—begun before 1979 but hastened by the disaster and its aftermath—thrust the City of the Peacock Flag squarely into modernity.[79]

Government measures for recovery after the flood played a key role in Morbi's economic transformation. Factory owners who reopened or started plants in the flood-affected area enjoyed access to generous loans from the State Bank of India, as well as substantial tax concessions. The state government's special treatment of the region's industries expedited the otherwise onerous process of attaining the permits necessary for establishing a new operation; would-be industrialists faced far fewer delays or demands for bribes than their counterparts elsewhere in Gujarat. The array of rehabilitation measures turned Morbi and Maliya subdistricts into ideal locales for fledgling enterprises.[80]

Patels from surrounding villages carried forward much of Morbi's postflood industrial development. As wealthy, land-owning farmers, they possessed substantial capital; as members of an influential jati, they also possessed social connections—to bankers and government officials, for instance—that would help them obtain more money, expedited processing, and favors large and small. Much as Bhagvanji Patel had in 1978, dozens of village Patels set out on the industrial path in the 1980s. They began producing clocks, ceramics, roofing tiles, floor tiles, sanitary fixtures, textiles, and electronics. As they witnessed the initial successes of postdisaster industrialists, other citizens of Morbi and the surrounding villages—Patels, but also members of other jatis and quoms—undertook similar efforts, leading to what journalists would refer to as "the Patel style of replicating success."[81]

The new factories operated at the threshold of modernity, playing host to a distinctively traditional industrial production. A typical tile factory occupied little more than an acre and comprised a single six- to seven-story brick smokestack, a warehouse, and perhaps small offices and laborer quarters. Given the relative cheapness of labor, machines made limited inroads; barefoot workers continued to serve as the primary drivers of productivity. Workforces remained fluid, with managers hiring labor on a daily basis.[82]

At the same time, Morbi's industrialization jostled the age-old social order. Women began seeking employment alongside men. Poor farmers, such as the Tiger Quarter Satwaras who attended Kanubhai Kubavat's temple services, shifted from agriculture to factory labor. Harijans and other low-jati citizens of Morbi, Lilapar, and numerous other communities abandoned cleaning, haircutting, leatherworking, and other traditional pursuits to work for high-jati industrialists. As the years wore on, the remnants of the preflood agrarian economy grew fainter, and Morbi became the epicenter of a thoroughly industrial region.[83]

〰〰〰

By 1990, new neighborhoods had fundamentally reshaped Morbi's visage. Large, previously barren tracts east of the Machhu River and southwest of downtown teemed with vast arrays of houses. In just a few years, the city's former outskirts had transformed into vibrant residential areas.[84]

In large part, the rising communities were populated by renters or homeowners who had lost their houses in the disaster. Abandoning the tin-and-earth hovels that had served as homes for several years, the flood survivors settled into boxy, concrete hulks painted in welcoming pastel colors. In many neighborhoods, such as the Rotary Nagar for which Principal T. R. Shukla had raised funds, all the houses followed a standard plan—two bedrooms, a kitchen, a bathroom, and a veranda. Over time, residents would add rooms and other modifications to fit their tastes and needs.[85]

Some of the neighborhoods also rose because of Morbi's burgeoning population, the influx of laborers from surrounding villages, and the increasing ability of the rising middle class to pay for more expansive housing. During the 1980s, the thick crescent of farmland between Madhapar and Vajepar began its metamorphosis into a sprawling residential zone. Members of the affluent new middle class—particularly Patels—filled up Morbi's southern reaches. As agriculture gave way to industry and commerce, the city gradually became urban from end to end.[86]

The changes in Morbi's housing landscape frayed the social tapestry that had persisted through centuries of royal rule. To be sure, the new neighborhoods did not escape recapitulating the city's age-old social divisions to a certain extent; low-jati flood survivors disproportionately received houses in the Gujarat Housing Board's meager projects, middle-class developments remained out of the reach of the poor, and the beneficiaries in "relief societies" segregated themselves by jati whenever they could. Nonetheless, the new residential order, shaped largely by the recovery from the Machhu dam disaster, thrust unprecedented mixing and novel social spaces upon Morbi in the span of just one decade. Harijans shared blocks with Patels, and Brahmins with goatherds. Muslims and Hindus took up residence next to one another. While many of the city's historical quarters continued to house fairly homogeneous populations, the rising neighborhoods created and fostered diverse new communities. In these emerging places, little pieces of the old order yielded to the growing identity of a modern Morbi.[87]

The date was February 9, 1990.[88] Former chief minister Babubhai Patel's car cruised through the mild winter air. The people of Morbi had radically transformed the surrounding landscape during the decade since the Machhu dam disaster. Babubhai had returned to the city on August 11, 1981, one year after missing the first annual memorial ceremony, and several times thereafter. He sometimes found it difficult to recognize the old royal city that he had personally shepherded through its most trying days.[89]

Large industrial plants flew past on both sides as Babubhai's car sped northward. Trucks laden with goods rumbled along the highway, just as they had rumbled along the streets of the main market eleven years earlier. Dozens of shining new communities—neighborhoods that had not existed even in concept at the time of Babubhai's long weeks of work—lined the car's path through eastern Morbi. As the leader marveled at the new city, the words of his former colleague, Gokaldas Parmar, hung in the air: "Are you coming or not?"

Ten years had passed since Babubhai's last appearance as a member of the Gujarat legislative assembly. After his defeat in the 1980 elections, he had not run for office in the 1985 elections. His previous stronghold—an Ahmedabad constituency known as Sabarmati—continued to elect Congress Party politicians. With the 1990 campaign approaching, Parmar had encouraged him to stand for election as an independent candidate in Morbi. The old legislator had said, "If you want to run again, run from Morbi, and we will elect you. We will pay for the costs and make the arrangements for your campaign." Babubhai had seriously contemplated running from Morbi, but he had not made a firm commitment.[90]

Then, one morning, Parmar called him. Less than a week remained until the deadline for submitting nominations.

"Are we to fill out this form or not? Are you coming or not?"

"I will send someone to fill out the form on my behalf. I will fill out the form in Sabarmati and in Morbi, and then I will decide."

"Well, then, no. If that is the case, I will not leave the Congress Party and give you my support. . . . Only if you agree to come to Morbi. Otherwise, just say no. And if you want to see the support you have here, come here in person and see."

A heavy silence hung over both men. Then Babubhai spoke.

"I want to talk to Ratilal."[91]

Parmar readily agreed. Explaining the situation to Ratilal Desai, he asked the former mayor to prevail upon his old friend. Desai called Babubhai and carried on the briefest of conversations; in his typically blunt style, he told the former chief minister to come to Morbi as quickly as possible. A short time later, Babubhai's car was approaching the Machhu River.[92]

Fifty of the city's most prominent residents gathered together at the old guesthouse where Babubhai had stayed during the relief work of 1979. There, behind closed doors, the men exhorted him to declare his candidacy in Morbi. Parmar would recall:

Everyone told him, "We are immensely grateful to you for the work you did during the Machhu disaster. And as a sign of our gratitude, we will give you our votes. We will elect you. . . ." So we told Babubhai to stay in Morbi, to leave thoughts of Sabarmati. That was my condition.

And he said that he would run from Morbi. We went to fill out the form. I submitted his nomination. I resigned from Congress to give him support. And then he stayed here until the election.[93]

Parmar, Desai, and a few other citizens raised money for Babubhai's effort, and the old statesman campaigned tirelessly, walking the streets of Morbi and riding out to dusty villages.[94]

On February 27, 1990, the people of Morbi and the surrounding villages resoundingly elected Babubhai as their representative to the state government; he garnered sixty percent of all votes—twenty-two percent more than his nearest competitor. Five days later, he began his final term as a member of the legislative assembly.[95]

On August 11 of that year, Babubhai and the people of Morbi commemorated the disaster's eleventh anniversary.[96] As it had for a decade, the city shut down for a day. Survivors offered prayers and remembrance at the riverside memorial outside the Mani Mandir.

At 3:30 p.m., twenty-one sirens echoed across the city.

Epilogue

"Can Any Page of History Be Forgotten?"

"Seven generations from now, neither your lineage nor your city will remain!"

Two centuries and eight generations after the Vaniyan hurled her infamous curse at King Jiyaji Jadeja, neither subject nor monarch would recognize the City of the Peacock Flag. The wave of industrialization that followed in the flood's wake has endowed Morbi with a prosperity that makes the city, once again, the envy of many throughout Saurashtra.

When we traveled to Morbi during the monsoon season of 2006, we encountered a transformed city—one whose face and character were increasingly defined by its place in the global economy. Although residents still took pride in the city's crumbling monuments and royal past, a frenetic energy pervaded the urban atmosphere. The modern and the industrial reigned supreme. In the snarl of morning traffic crossing the newly widened Buffalo Bridge, young men raced their scooters to new electronics factories, passing beneath signs advertising GRE test preparation for those aspiring to attend graduate school in the United States.

We found Morbi in the aftermath of another devastating disaster. In 2001, an earthquake centered just north of the Gulf of Kutch wrecked much of the northern Saurashtra Peninsula. In Morbi, many died as entire neighborhoods crumbled. The tremors cracked some of the most characteristic monuments of the Paris of Saurashtra—Nehru Gate, the Mani Mandir, and the marble arcades of the Royal Court. When we visited, much of the earthquake's damage remained visible in the form of scattered rubble, unstable buildings, and broken families. For some citizens—particularly those belonging to younger generations—the 2001 disaster felt much more vivid than its 1979 counterpart.[1]

We were surprised, then, to find, as we carried on our fieldwork, that the Machhu dam disaster remained *the* disaster for the city's inhabitants. Survivors drew a clear distinction between "the earthquake" and "The Disaster." In the streets of Morbi, the Gujarati word *honaarat*—"disaster"—could only mean the events of August 11, 1979. Citizens of the Machhu River Valley used the flood as a milestone for dating important events, from births to deaths to weddings. Although the region had transformed radically in the intervening decades, the disaster of 1979 remained a definitive event in the local consciousness.

We paid several visits to the new Machhu Dam-II in 2006. We walked across the original concrete spillway, marveling at the colossal radial floodgates, touching the motors that jammed just before the disaster, and looking into the tiny control room where six terrified men huddled while the floodwaters rushed past. The supplementary spillway—its outflow capacity sufficient to devastate Morbi if fully utilized—stood just to the east, a tragically belated monument to the power of impounded water. On our first visit, we scrambled up one of the earthen embankments to look out at Jog Bapu's Hummock, which rose just slightly above the vast, dry, flat expanse behind the dam. On our last visit, we stood atop the earthen walls and stared at an enormous store of precious water-wealth, deposited in the reservoir by the monsoon of 2006.

By 2006, many survivors of the Machhu dam disaster had long since left the area. T. R. Shukla retired as principal of Morbi's arts college in 1985. That year, he and his family emigrated to the United States. Shukla and his wife would spend the next two decades recounting their experiences during the 1979 flood and singing the duet "This Monsoon Descends" for their oldest grandchild, Utpal Sandesara, who would spend his undergraduate years living with one Tom Wooten. On December 31, 2005, the Shuklas became the first of the 148 interviewees whose stories form the backbone of this book.

Like the Shukla family, Gangaram Tapu had left Morbi several years before we arrived; we were fortunate to catch him during a brief return to the city. We met Tapu at his house in Kabir Hill. A crowd of men sat on his front porch, speaking in hushed voices. He invited us into his sitting room and offered us cola, recounting his feats before walking us through his neighborhood and describing the flood's destruction. Although twenty-seven years had passed since his heroic swim through Morbi's flooded streets, he had not lost his youthful vigor. He laughed convulsively as he spoke of the past, his mouth grinning widely below a thick, black mustache. He had gained an ample paunch, which rumbled with every bout of laughter.

We managed to speak with Tapu because he was free on a two-week parole. In 2004, after two and a half decades of life as a free man, he had been sentenced to life in prison. According to the court, Tapu had conspired with Morbi's member of the legislative assembly—the man who occupied Gokaldas Parmar's former seat—to arrange the murder of a prominent local politician.[2]

The year after our interview, Tapu died in prison. A few months later, the Gujarat High Court exonerated him posthumously, explaining that insufficient evidence had existed to declare him guilty.[3]

West of Tapu's Kabir Hill, Khatijaben Valera discussed the flood with us on the first floor of her clan's decaying bungalow. The years since the disaster had witnessed a divergence of for-

tunes within the Valera family. Some of the men, such as Khatijaben's husband, enjoyed substantial prosperity on the basis of
Valera Transport and other business ventures. By contrast, those
who continued to rely on music lessons for their livelihoods—
such as Khatijaben's youngest brother-in-law Shaukatbhai,
whose vocal chords had been seared in his youth by maliciously
placed vermilion—struggled to make ends meet. Indigence and
comfort shared quarters within the cramped family compound,
with the clan of former court musicians torn between the nineteenth century and the twenty-first.

Khatijaben's eyes lit up as she recounted the events of the disaster and its aftermath with humor and poignancy. With many of
her relatives present, she was able to introduce us to two or three
of the small children who had nearly fallen prey to the floodwaters; they were now adults, with small children of their own.

Elsewhere in southern Morbi, Kanubhai Kubavat welcomed
us into his house and his temple in the Tiger Quarter. After
spending much of the decade after the flood working to rebuild his
family's home, he had become Rajkot District's chief government
administrator for primary education in 1990. Upon his retirement
in 2000, he had settled into a leisurely life full of temple services,
conversations with his wife, and large wads of paan.

We met Pratapbhai Adroja late on a muggy August night at
Ghost Paan. He had carried on his business uninterrupted since
the shop's resurrection five days after the flood. While his hair had
grayed, his personality remained energetic and friendly. Of late, he
had begun to collect plastic toys from the United States Halloween
industry to enhance the shop's ghoulish atmosphere. He proudly
exhibited one of his most recent acquisitions, a cloaked ghost that
vibrated, glowed, and howled when activated. As we watched the
unexpected show, several waiting customers laughed along with
us; more than three decades after its founding, Ghost Paan
remained a fixture of Morbi's commercial scene.

In the Mahendra Quarter, Dhirubhai Mehta invited us into
Mehta Machinery and led us behind the counter where he had sat

on the afternoon of August 11, 1979. There, quietly stowed away, a portfolio of carefully arranged documents—newspaper clippings, legal notices, and letters to leading Indian politicians—served as a bitter reminder of the Machhu Dam-II Inquiry Commission's ultimate futility. Mehta and his wife led us through the house where they and their children had struggled against the raging waters. Their voices choked as they held up a framed photograph of their son Vimal, the lost heir of the Mehta lineage.

Outside Morbi, we encountered Bhagvanji Patel at his office in the Sri Lilapar Potteries plant. Sweating in the July heat, he widened his eyes as he described the utter destruction of his village. He then led us on a tour of New Lilapar, proudly noting the village's model character. Within a few years, he would sell off his farmland and his factory, happily retiring to a quiet rural life.

The Harijans of Lilapar, who witnessed the disintegration of the Machhu Dam-II from the shadow of its western flank, had not fared as well as Bhagvanji. We interviewed them in the village's Harijan Quarter, a slightly disarrayed settlement located just outside the edges of New Lilapar's neat grid. After the 2001 earthquake, we learned, the village council had refused aid from the government of Gujarat, claiming that the community had suffered little damage and did not need help. Like the high-jati villagers' refusal of the Ramakrishna Ashrama temple's housing reconstruction aid in the aftermath of the 1979 flood, the village council's denial greatly handicapped the community's Harijans, who possessed weaker homes and more meager financial resources. One man would lament:

> The council gave it in writing that there was no damage in the village. They wanted to show that there was no riff-raff here: "We do not have any poor in our village. No one is needy here."
>
> This village does not want to see its poor. "There are no poor"—that is what they wrote! . . . The officials do not consider us to be of the village. They consider us outside the village.[4]

Much like the Harijans of Lilapar, the Miyanas found 2006 as difficult as 1980. When we traveled to Maliya on the morning after the twenty-seventh anniversary of the disaster, days of heavy rains had covered the northern town in more than a foot of water. The rocky fields surrounding the community had become inundated paddies, and the dusty streets looked like muddy canals. We sat under an awning in the main market with Abdulbhai Mor, Husainbhai Manek, and Jashabhai Samani, sipping milky chai and listening to their stories.

By the time we met him, Mor had successfully consolidated his salt-manufacturing business. Nonetheless, he had never abandoned the sense of persecution that haunted the Miyana tribe. He remarked, "Say seven of our generations have gone by. They have done their work and died. Now we will die too. So what if we die? That will be eight generations."[5]

For his part, Manek had fared well as a farmer. After starting cultivation on his ancestral lands in the immediate aftermath of the disaster, he had acquired more fields and expanded his agricultural output. All the same, he recalled with great bitterness the lack of postdisaster aid to fishermen from the government of Gujarat, which had provided such generous relief to Morbi's artisans.

Samani continued to toil as a salt-industry laborer. In the twenty-seven years since the loss of his six children in the Machhu's raging waters, he had not managed to resume farming on his lands. His forefathers' fields, like many others in Maliya's blighted landscape, sat fallow as a direct consequence of the 1979 disaster.

In our travels beyond the Machhu River Valley, we met with several of the bureaucrats and lawyers who had participated in the inquiry commission's work, including secretary Dipankar Basu. All had continued on to distinguished government careers, with two becoming justices on the Gujarat High Court. Nonetheless, twenty-two years after the Supreme Court's final decision quashing the commission, the disappointment still felt raw for all the men.

Dr. Y. K. Murthy remained remarkably sharp when he welcomed us to his home office in New Delhi. He had spent three decades consulting on some of South Asia's most technically challenging and controversial hydro-engineering projects, including the massive Sardar Sarovar Dam on the Narmada River. Our conversation was interrupted several times as Murthy fielded phone calls from government officials in Gujarat, who were struggling to contend with widespread flooding downstream of a major dam in the southern part of the state.

Madhavsinh Solanki—the man who demanded the Machhu Dam Inquiry Commission, wound it up, and appointed Murthy as a one-man technical commission—became the first chief minister of Gujarat to complete a five-year term, serving through the legislative assembly elections of 1985.[6] When we contacted him in 2006, he declined to offer comment on the Machhu dam disaster and its aftermath.

Solanki's predecessor and longtime rival, Babubhai Patel, served one five-year term as Morbi's representative to the state government. During this period, he became the cabinet minister in charge of the Sardar Sarovar dam project. Describing him as "an ardent pro-Narmada activist" and the "prime 'opponent'" of those agitating against the dam, a 1993 article reported:

> The moment the Narmada issue is raised, soon he starts reeling off figures and making cogent arguments showing a surprising alertness for an octogenarian. Mr. Patel strongly justifies the Narmada project, saying its cost is nothing compared to the loss of crops . . . [and] drought relief. . . . The environmental benefits would far outweigh the losses, he believes . . . Far from violating human rights, the project would help the project-affected people lead a much better quality of life. . . . Mr. Patel said the irrigation project would help wipe out Gujarat's food deficit and make it a surplus state. . . . Big dams are, in the ultimate analysis, economically more advantageous, he claims.[7]

In his last years of public service, the man who inspired thousands to rebuild Morbi after one of history's deadliest dam failures became a vociferous advocate for one of history's most controversial dams.

Babubhai retired from the legislative assembly in 1995, at the end of his term as Morbi's representative. He passed away in 2002, at the age of ninety-one.[8]

Following years of political maneuvering, Keshubhai Patel—the former agriculture minister who had turned back from the outskirts of a devastated Morbi—became chief minister of Gujarat in 1995 as a member of the Bharatiya Janata Party, the Hindu nationalist successor to the Janata Party. He would serve two stints in the position; both were plagued by conflict with Congress and Bharatiya Janata leaders.[9] We sought him out but were unable to establish contact.

In 2006, after spending much of our first week in India floundering amid the corruption and inefficiency of Gujarat's engineering bureaucracy, we somehow secured a four-minute audience with Keshubhai's successor, Narendrabhai Modi. A rival from within the Bharatiya Janata Party, Modi had ruled the state with an iron fist since supplanting Keshubhai in 2000. Upon entering his stately office, we learned that the stern Modi—widely revered and reviled as a radical Hindu nationalist[10]—had performed relief work in Morbi as a young member of the Rashtriya Swayamsevak Sangh. After listening to a minute-long description of our project and contemplating quietly for what felt like an interminable twenty seconds, the chief minister—a self-styled anticorruption, protransparency crusader—granted us access to the broad range of formerly inaccessible government documents that would come to inform much of our narrative.

A. R. Banerjee—the district collector in Rajkot at the time of the disaster—spent the rest of his career battling the aftereffects of the controversial report he had penned in the days following the flood. When we spoke with him, he noted wearily:

I have been made to suffer. Because Keshubhai became chief minister later on. . . . I was harmed. My career was harmed. You could say that there was some vindictiveness. . . .

I was a very senior officer. I was in the central vigilance commission, a post reserved for men of very high integrity. In spite of this and my earlier record, I was ignored for many important postings. At the time of Mr. Patel, I was sidelined. . . .

It was not a very wise thing to do, to go against the government. But I wrote a report. And I told the truth.[11]

Rajkot District Collector Pradeep Sharma released the long-hidden Banerjee Report to us on a rainy August day in 2006, allowing us to incorporate its understated but damning contents into our work.

Banerjee's fellow Indian Administrative Service officer, H. K. Khan, enjoyed a smoother career trajectory. After serving as Gujarat's industry secretary, Khan accepted a top central government position in the late 1980s. He returned to Gujarat in 1990 for a two-year stint as the chief secretary—the highest-ranking civil servant in the state. He acted as the chief minister's personal adviser for two more years before retiring from public service in 1994.

A. C. Mehta—the deputy engineer in charge of the Machhu Dams-I and -II at the time of the disaster—was a figure shrouded in mystery. Many vaguely recalled him; none could describe him or pinpoint his whereabouts. We did not find him.

We met Lakshmanbhai Mohan—the Machhu Dam-II's mechanic in 1979—at his house in the village of Jodhpar. His grandchildren scurried about, playing boisterously, as we talked with him in his dusty front yard. He recapitulated the events surrounding the dam failure, corroborating his affidavit before the inquiry commission in the minutest details.

By the time we met him in 2006, former member of the legislative assembly Gokaldas Parmar was an octogenarian. Age had replaced his teeth with dentures and bloated his small feet, but he remained as keen as ever. Over a series of rainy July afternoons, sitting atop a cot in his quiet Shakti Plot home, the retired legislator offered recollections that matched his immediate postflood testimony to a remarkable degree. He spoke proudly of the social welfare activities to which he had devoted his life since 1980, most of which centered on education for girls and for members of historically disadvantaged jatis.

Former mayor Ratilal Desai—Morbi's greatest advocate and "the government's son-in-law"—met us at the Nilesh Paint factory in southern Morbi. His body was ailing, but his spirit had not weakened. Although Desai had long ago retreated to private life, he continued to meticulously clip newspaper articles about governance in India and rail against the deterioration of civic spirit in the republic.

Like Dhirubhai Mehta, he showed us a picture of his lost son with tears in his eyes. After many years of fasting on August 11, he had grudgingly begun eating one meal on the anniversary due to his ill health. Over the decades, he had maintained warm relations with Babubhai, Banerjee, Khan, and the other men he had come to know in the flood's aftermath. He remained unabashed in his criticism of the government's practices and of the inquiry commission windup, raging against the death of the memory of the Machhu dam disaster.

In early 2010—nearly thirty-one years after losing his city and his son to the Machhu Dam-II's raging waters—Ratilal Desai passed away.

With every passing year, the number of those who remember dwindles, and the Machhu dam disaster inches toward oblivion. The state government's windup of the inquiry commission, containment of the Murthy and Banerjee Reports, and lack of subsequent transparency over the past three decades have shrouded the events of August 11, 1979, in considerable mystery, leaving the lay public ignorant and flood victims discontented. Aside from listings in old editions of *The Guinness Book of World*

Records and occasional references in the academic and engineering literatures, the Machhu dam disaster has largely disappeared from the public awareness.

Even as the 1979 flood remains "The Disaster" in the Machhu River Valley, its vividness has diminished markedly. We witnessed the August 11, 2006, memorial ceremony in the sunken garden in front of the Mani Mandir. The era of citywide closures and awe-inspiring parades through the Nehru Gate plaza had long since ended. The commemoration had slowly diminished in its extent, becoming a program of just a few minutes by the time we visited. Under a gray sky and a light drizzle, some of the city's leading politicians and sundry other residents—a few dozen, in total—stood uncomfortably in front of the memorial plaque. After some generic words and muttered prayers, the crowd dispersed.

Few survivors could be seen at the ceremony; most had remained at home or gone to work, whether from indifference or from avoidance. A few years earlier, a journalist had collected this explanation from one man:

> For years, on the day of the disaster, the city of Morbi observed a shutdown. . . . But for the last three years, with business proceeding as per usual, I have been going to work as well. . . . I do not even feel like going to the memorial, because from there I can see the Machhu's waters, and everything becomes fresh.[12]

While slowly slipping out of the public memory, the disaster remains a source of great private pain for many citizens of the Machhu River Valley.

During our fieldwork, one interviewee issued a critique of our project that has never left our minds. He asked:

> So why have you taken the time to do this now, twenty-five years later? . . . The work of recording the story is the government's, isn't it? The government is always doing that work; history is always being written. Can any page of history be for-

gotten? Haven't the details of this event been properly recorded? The government does not need to publish. You speak of things being forgotten—nothing is being forgotten. The events are recorded someplace.[13]

The government of Gujarat did, indeed, record the tragic events of August 11, 1979, albeit in fragmentary form. The narrative of the Machhu dam disaster was written in the Banerjee Report and in the Murthy Report, in Irrigation Department memoranda and in Revenue Department telegraphs, in the government's "Statement of Facts and Opinions" and in the affidavits before the inquiry commission. The events are recorded someplace.

But that is not enough. Any page of history can be forgotten if it is not read, scrutinized, questioned, and debated. Any page of history can be forgotten if it is not actively remembered.

Until now, the full story of the Machhu dam disaster—its antecedents, its terror, and its consequences—has remained inaccessible. The state government's lack of transparency—the windup of the inquiry commission, the suppression of documents, the willful public silence—has, coupled with the natural diminishment in survivors' righteous anger, kept the truth from public scrutiny. Flood survivors have lived and died for thirty-one years without answers as to why they became embroiled in one of history's deadliest flash floods, all while such answers have been meticulously pursued and recorded inside government offices. Dhirubhai Mehta has spent a lifetime of mourning without ever learning the full causes of his son's death. Ratilal Desai died without that knowledge. Thousands of survivors suffered twice—once through the disaster, and once through the injustice of being denied answers that existed.

It is with great satisfaction that we have watched the residents of the Machhu River Valley struggle against the slow ravages of oblivion. In 2006, during our stay in India, we befriended Dilipbhai Barasara, a journalist of Morbi. He had come to know of our project through his ample connections; having been born after the flood, he desired to join us in learning about the great tragedy in his city's past. Over the course of our fieldwork in the Machhu River Valley, Dilipbhai became a dear friend and an invaluable collaborator.

On August 11, 2006, his newspaper printed a full-page spread commemorating the disaster, including photographs from the time and interviews with survivors. Since then, Dilipbhai has persuaded all Saurashtra's major newspapers to run a memorial story each year on the anniversary of the flood. In the aftermath of our fieldwork, which became a small press sensation of its own, the efforts of Dilipbhai and other dedicated journalists have revived the memory of the Machhu dam disaster in Morbi, Maliya, and the surrounding villages. From the Machhu Dam-II to the Gulf of Kutch, the events that led to the destruction of a dam and a region are slowly reentering the public consciousness.

As we turn from the past toward the future, we hope that the story of the Machhu dam disaster will not disappear from the public eye. Despite thirty-one years of silence, the narrative of August 11, 1979, and its aftermath remains alive, strengthened by the recent infusion of long-suppressed information. This book is a testament to flood survivors' tenacity, resilience, and memory, and to the enduring tragedy of one of history's deadliest floods. We firmly believe that, if people choose to remember, this page of history will not be forgotten.

Resources

NOTES

Foreword: Disasters Natural and Unnatural

1. Adriana Petryna's book *Life Exposed: Biological Citizens after Chernobyl* (Princeton: Princeton University Press, 2002) investigates the new subjectivities and state-citizen power relationships produced in the aftermath of the Chernobyl disaster. On Haiti, see, for example, the book that came out of my doctoral work in anthropology, *AIDS and Accusation: Haiti and the Geography of Blame* (Berkeley: University of California Press, 1992). Chapters 2–3 explore how the construction of the Péligre Dam—hailed as a beacon of modernity—displaced and dehumanized the rural communities living in the river valley.

2. On the effects of malaria and yellow fever during efforts to build the Panama Canal, see Marcos Cueto, *Missionaries of Science: The Rockefeller Foundation and Latin America* (Bloomington: Indiana University Press, 1994), especially the introduction and chapter 4. See also Marcos Cueto, *The Value of Health: A History of the Pan American Health Organization* (Washington, DC: PAHO, 2007), chapters 1–3. On the forces behind the decline of cholera in nineteenth-century American cities, see Charles Rosenberg's *The Cholera Years: The United States in 1832, 1849, and 1866* (Chicago: University of Chicago

319

Press, 1962). See also *Cholera, Chloroform, and the Science of Medicine: A Life of John Snow* (Oxford: Oxford University Press, 2003) by Peter Vinten-Johansen et al. on the origins of the sanitation movement in England and the associated claims of causality about disease transmission. "The sanitary reform movement was driven," the authors write, "by the medical opinion that poisonous vapors, whether miasmas rising from marshes or from decomposing organic matter near human dwellings, were the main cause of disease, including epidemic cholera, which had killed tens of thousands of people in England since 1831" (Vinten-Johansen et al., p. 7).

3. Robert Merton. "The Unanticipated Consequences of Purposive Social Action," *American Sociological Review* 1, no. 6 (1936): 894–904.

4. These "late Victorian holocausts" totaled fifty million deaths. Davis concludes that "we are not dealing, in other words, with 'lands of famine' becalmed in stagnant backwaters of world history, but with the fate of tropical humanity at the precise moment (1870–1914) when its labor and products were being dynamically conscripted into a London-centered world economy. Millions died, not outside the 'modern world system,' but in the very process of being forcibly incorporated into its economic and political structures." Mike Davis, *Late Victorian Holocausts: El Nino Famines and the Making of the Third World* (London: Verso, 2001), p. 9.

5. See Amartya Sen's *Resources, Values, and Development* (Cambridge: Harvard University Press, 1984); *Development As Freedom* (New York: Anchor Books, 1999); and *Identity and Violence: The Illusion of Destiny* (New York: Norton, 2006).

6. See Paul Farmer, *Infections and Inequalities: The Modern Plagues* (Berkeley: University of California Press, 1999). On "contested claims of causality," see especially chapter 2 ("Rethinking 'Emerging Infectious Diseases'") and chapter 9 ("Immodest Claims of Causality: Social Scientists and the 'New' Tuberculosis").

7. Dave Eggers, *Zeitoun* (New York: Vintage Books, 2009).

Prologue: "A Vaniyan of Morbi Goes to the Machhu's Waters"

1. The legend in this vignette is reconstructed from "The Vaniyan Rebuffed the King" in *Aaspaas*, "Special Edition"; Dave, *History of Morbi State*, 15; and Neelimaben Shukla, interview, May 17, 2006.

2. For a review of Morbi's royal history, see Dave, *Glory of Morbi*, 9–40; Dave, *History of Morbi State*; Playne, "State of Morvi"; and Shah, "Morvi." For an account of the city's development after Indian independence, see Dave, *Glory of Morbi*, 41–376.

3. For biographical information on King Jiyaji Jadeja, see Dave, *History of Morbi State*, 12–13.

4. "The Vaniyan Rebuffed the King" in *Aaspaas*, "Special Edition."

5. An alternative account of a curse placed on a Jadeja king by a chaste woman can be found in "The Curse of the Sati and the Destruction of Morbi," in *Aaspaas*, "Special Edition."

6. Dave, *Glory of Morbi*; "Morbi: The Paris of Saurashtra," in *Aaspaas*, "Special Edition"; and Interviewee 26.

Chapter 1: On the Banks for the Machhu River

1. This vignette's portrayal of Pratapbhai Adroja's biography, attitudes, and daily routine relies on Pratapbhai Adroja, interview, August 3, 2006.

2. For information on the rainfall pattern of June and July 1979, see Murthy, *Report on Failure of Machhu Dam-II*, 1:15; and Parthasarathy et al., *Before the Machhu Dam-II Inquiry Comission*, 1:106. Government officials' preoccupations with the drought are evident in H. K. Khan, interview, August 14, 2006; and A. R. Banerjee, interview, August 16, 2006.

3. For information on the Buffalo Bridge, see Bhandari, *Western Railway Metre Gauge System*, 158–59; and T. R. Shukla and Ushaben Shukla, interview, December 31, 2005.

4. For general discussions of Morbi's monuments, see Dave, *Glory of Morbi*, 69–75; "Spectacular Monuments," in *Aaspaas*, "Special Edition"; and Playne, "State of Morvi." Details about the Royal Court can

be found in Dave, *Glory of Morbi*, 72. Details about the Mani Mandir can be found in Dave, *Glory of Morbi*, 69–72; and Dave, *History of Morbi State*, 39.

5. For a sense of Morbi's growth during the mid-twentieth century, see Chhaya, *Census 1981*; Doctor, *Census 1971*; and Trivedi, *Census 1961*.

6. For some sense of the practice of paan consumption, see Sivaramakrishnan, *Tobacco and Areca Nut*.

7. For discussions of Morbi's infrastructure in the mid-twentieth century, see Dave, *Glory of Morbi*; MRF, "Summary of Jadeja Reigns" [inferred title]; MRF, "Summary of Royal Achievements" [inferred title]; Playne, "State of Morvi"; and Singh, "Progressive Administration."

8. For more on commercial prosperity in Morbi in the mid-twentieth century, see Dave, *Glory of Morbi*, 185–257.

9. This vignette's portrayal of Khatijaben Valera's biography, attitudes, and daily routine relies on Khatijaben Valera, interview, July 25, 2006.

10. For a discussion of the Valera family's ancestors and their place in Morbi's history, see Dave, *Glory of Morbi*, 139–47.

11. For description of a typically opulent Jadeja royal function, see Chitaliya, "Morbi Coronation Issue."

12. For biographical information on King Lakhdhirji Jadeja, see Dave, *Glory of Morbi*, 27–34; Dave, *History of Morbi State*, 35–47; and Singh, "Progressive Administration."

13. "Mayurdhvaj to Mayurdhvaj," in *Aaspaas*, "Special Edition"; Dave, *Glory of Morbi*, 10; and Dave, *History of Morbi State*, 3.

14. Dave, *Glory of Morbi*, 11; and Dave, *History of Morbi State*, 5–6.

15. For subjects' attitudes toward the Jadeja kings, consider Shah, *Addresses to His Highness*. For favorable accounts of Jadeja beneficence, see Chitaliya, "Morbi Coronation Issue"; Dave, *Glory of Morbi*, 9–40; Dave, *History of Morbi State*; and Singh, "Progressive Administration."

16. Dave, *Glory of Morbi*, 34–46; Dave, *History of Morbi State*, 48–52; and Neelimaben Shukla, interview, May 17, 2006.

17. T. R. Shukla and Ushaben Shukla, interview, December 31, 2005; and Neelimaben Shukla, interview, May 17, 2006.

18. This vignette's portrayal of Bhagvanji Patel's biography, attitudes, and daily routine relies on Bhagvanji Patel, interview, July 21, 2006.

19. For accessible introductions to the concepts of jati and quom, see Mandelbaum, *Society in India*, 13–30, 151–324; Nazir, "Social Structure, Ideology, and Language"; and Sharma, *Caste*.

20. For ethnologic accounts of Patels, see Pocock, *Kanbi and Patidar*; and Singh, *People of India*, 1094–98. For accounts of the Patels' rise to power, see Pocock, *Kanbi and Patidar*; and Sinha, "Divided Loyalties." For further information on Sardar Vallabhbhai Patel and the Patel jati, see Gandhi, *Patel*.

21. For Satwaras, see Singh, *People of India*, 1273–77. For Kolis, see ibid., 693–97. For examples of pastoralist jatis found in the Machhu River Valley, see ibid., 46–50, 194–200, 1158–62. For Vaniyas, see ibid., 1419–28. For Brahmins, see ibid., 445–86. Information on various other jatis and quoms may be found in ibid.

22. For Bhangis, see ibid., 181–84. For Chamars, see ibid., 276–80. For Hajaams, see ibid., 1414–18. For Mochis, see Tripathy and Chokshi, *Rajkot District Gazetteer*, 138. For more on "untouchable" jatis, see Singh, *People of India*; Tripathy and Chokshi, *Rajkot District Gazetteer*, 142–47; Trivedi, *Gazetteer of India: Gujarat State Gazetteer*, 1:335–40; and Yadav, *Encyclopaedia of Backward Castes*.

23. For more on discrimination against "backward" groups, see Yadav, *Encyclopaedia of Backward Castes*, 177–310.

24. For more on the layout of a typical Gujarati village, see Trivedi, *Gazetteer of India: Gujarat State Gazetteer*, 1:353. For scholarly accounts of spatial separation of jatis, see Béteille, *Caste, Class, and Power*, 19–44; and Ghurye, "Features of the Caste System," 41–42.

25. The importance of agriculture in the kingdom of Morbi—and the role of the Jadeja kings in protecting and promoting it—may be gleaned from the sheer volume of references to agriculture in the Morbi Royal Family Papers.

26. Dave, *Glory of Morbi*, 207–9.

27. For postindependence industrial growth in Morbi, including the crucial role of clocks, see Dave, *Glory of Morbi*, 205–69; Interviewee 25, July 22, 2006; and Interviewee 25, July 23, 2006.

28. Interviewee 25, July 22, 2006.

29. Pocock, *Kanbi and Patidar*; Singh, *People of India*, 1094–98; and Sinha, "Divided Loyalties."

30. For information on the tile-manufacturing process, see Interviewee 25, July 23, 2006.

31. This vignette's portrayal of Kanubhai Kubavat's biography, attitudes, and daily routine relies on Kanubhai Kubavat, interview, August 12, 2006.

32. Chatterjee, *Indian Calendric System*.

33. One has only to survey Gujarati folk songs to see the associations of Shravan with sacredness and heavy rain.

34. Gokhale, *Book of Shiva*, 53–58; and Turner and Coulter, *Dictionary of Ancient Deities*, 281.

35. For one survey of the religious practices of Gujarati Hindus during Shravan, see Gopalan, "Vrat," 109–11.

36. For Dipping Fourth, see Crooke and Enthoven, *Religion and Folklore of Northern India*, 365. For Cobra Fifth, see Trivedi, *Gazetteer of India: Gujarat State Gazetteer*, 1:360–61. For Cooking Sixth, see ibid., 1:360. For Smallpox Seventh, see Raval, *Gujarat State Gazetteer: Rajkot District*, 156–57; and Trivedi, *Gazetteer of India: Gujarat State Gazetteer*, 1:360–61. For an alternative account of these four holidays, see Gopalan, "Vrat," 111, 117–18.

37. For Birth Eighth, see Raval, *Gujarat State Gazetteer: Rajkot District*, 157. For one survey of Krishna's importance in Gujarati culture, see Shukla-Bhatt, "Gujarat," particularly 256–57.

38. Bryant, *Krishna*, 19–31; and Haberman, *Journey through the Twelve Forests*, 3–4.

39. For more on the Tiger Quarter's social fabric, see Gokaldas Parmar, interview, July 26, 2006; Interviewee 87 and Interviewee 88; and Kanubhai Kubavat, interview, August 12, 2006.

40. This vignette's portrayal of Ratilal Desai's biography, attitudes, and daily routine relies on Ratilal Desai and Interviewee 30, interview, July 20, 2006; Ratilal Desai, interview, July 24, 2006; and Ratilal Desai, interview, July 25, 2006.

41. Tripathy and Chokshi, *Rajkot District Gazetteer*, 63. According to Trivedi, *Gazetteer of India: Gujarat State Gazetteer*, 363, fifty-one carnivals take place at various sites in Gujarat on Smallpox Seventh.

42. In addition to Ratilal Desai, interview, July 24, 2006; and Ratilal Desai, interview, July 25, 2006; see Dave, *Glory of Morbi*, 241.

43. Gandhi grew up on the Saurashtra Peninsula and spent the majority of his life in Gujarat, using his *ashrama* in Ahmedabad as the base for his *satyagraha* independence movement. He wrote much of his work in Gujarati, and his writings are replete with references to Gujarat. For an analysis of the influence of Gujarat on Gandhi, see Spodek, "On the Origins of Gandhi's Political Methodology."

44. For a sense of the turmoil engulfing Gujarati government in the 1970s, see Kohli, *Democracy and Discontent*, 248–52; and Sanghavi, "Dissolution and After."

45. This vignette's portrayal of Gangaram Tapu's biography, attitudes, and daily routine relies on Ganagaram Tapu, interview, July 29, 2006.

46. Ibid.

47. Playne, "State of Morvi," 594.

48. Watson, *Gazetteer of the Bombay Presidency*, 166.

49. Playne, "State of Morvi," 594.

50. Dave, *Glory of Morbi*, 13; and Tambs-Lyche, *Good Country*, 264.

51. Dave, *Glory of Morbi*, 13; Tambs-Lyche, *Good Country*, 264; and Watson, *Gazetteer of the Bombay Presidency*, 166.

52. Dave, *Glory of Morbi*, 13–14; and Dave, *History of Morbi State*, 7–12. Quote from Dave, *History of Morbi State*, 10.

53. Dave, *History of Morbi State*, 12; and "King Kayaji, Founder of the Morbi Throne," *Sandesh*, August 12, 2006.

54. This vignette's portrayal of Adulbhai Mor, Jashabhai Samani, and Husainbhai Manek's biographies, attitudes, and daily routines relies on Adulbhai Mor, interview, August 12, 2006; Husainbhai Manek, interview, August 12, 2006; and Jashabhai Samani, interview, August 12, 2006.

55. For Ramadan in Gujarat, see Trivedi, *Gazetteer of India: Gujarat State Gazetteer*, 1:361.

56. Playne, "State of Morvi," 594; and Tambs-Lyche, *Good Country*, 264.

57. Tambs-Lyche, *Good Country*, 264.

58. Abdulbhai Mor, interview, August 12, 2006; and Jashabhai Samani, interview, August 12, 2006.

59. Accounts of a desolate Maliya may be found in Tambs-Lyche,

Good Country, 82; "A Small Town Seeks Justice," *Indian Express,* August 30, 1981; and Abdulbhai Mor, interview, August 12, 2006.

60. Abdulbhai Mor, interview, August 12, 2006.

61. Ibid.

62. For salt production, see Interviewee 25, July 23, 2006; and Abdulbhai Mor, interview, August 12, 2006. For seasons in India, see Tripathy and Chokshi, *Rajkot District Gazetteer,* 8–10.

63. Watson, *Gazetteer of the Bombay Presidency,* 166.

64. Husainbhai Manek, interview, August 12, 2006.

65. For more on fishing in Gujarat, see Trivedi, *Gazetteer of India: Gujarat State Gazetteer,* 1:418–19.

Chapter 2: "The Government Decides, and the Government Builds"

1. For Nehru's visit, see Varma and Saxena, *Modern Temples of India,* 1–2. For the Hirakud Dam, see Baboo, "State Policies and People's Response"; Baboo, *Technology and Social Transformation,* 23–38; and Baboo, "Politics of Water." For subsequent dam construction, see Bajaj, *National Register of Large Dams.* For a narrative account of this dam construction, see Khagram, *Dams and Development,* 33–64.

2. Varma and Saxena, *Modern Temples of India,* 1.

3. For Nehruvian development, see Guha, *India after Gandhi,* 213–32. Quote from Varma and Saxena, *Modern Temples of India,* 1. For further evidence of Nehru's views on hydro-engineering projects, see other speeches in ibid.

4. Varma and Saxena, *Modern Temples of India,* 2. For a survey of the rhetoric surrounding the nexus of hydro-engineering projects, the greater common good, and personal sacrifice, see Roy, *Greater Common Good.*

5. For Nehru's visit, see Varma and Saxena, *Modern Temples of India,* 40–41. For the Hirakud Dam, see Baboo, "State Policies and People's Response"; Baboo, *Technology and Social Transformation*; and Baboo, "Politics of Water." For the land area of Sri Lanka, see CIA, "Sri Lanka."

6. Varma and Saxena, *Modern Temples of India,* 41. Other

speeches in ibid. are replete with further examples of Nehru's rhetoric on dams.

7. For ongoing dam construction, see Bajaj, *National Register of Large Dams*; and Khagram, *Dams and Development*, 33–64.

8. This vignette's account of the Machhu River's geography draws on Murthy, *Report on Failure of Machhu Dam-II*, 1:13; Raval, *Gujarat State Gazetteer: Rajkot District*, 37–49; Tripathy and Chokshi, *Rajkot District Gazetteer*, 8–10; and Trivedi, *Gazetteer of India: Gujarat State Gazetteer*.

9. This vignette's portrayal of Bhagvanji Patel's attitudes toward water and toward the Machhu Dam-II relies on Bhagvanji Patel, interview, July 21, 2006.

10. Gujarati folk songs abound with references to the joyous advent of the monsoon. For one formalized account of the monsoon in Indian culture, see Wolpert, *India*, 13–17.

11. For information on the rainfall pattern of June and July 1979, see Murthy, *Report on Failure of Machhu Dam-II*, 1:15; and Parthasarathy et al., *Before the Machhu Dam-II Inquiry Commission*, 1:106.

12. Parthasarathy et al., *Before the Machhu Dam-II Inquiry Commission*, 2:5–6.

13. Interviewee 32; Bhagvanji Patel, interview, July 21, 2006; and Jashabhai Samani, interview, August 12, 2006.

14. For an overview of the planning process that led to the completion of the Machhu Dam-II, see GOG, "Machhu Irrigation Project-II"; and Parthasarathy et al., *Before the Machhu Dam-II Inquiry Commission*, 1:7–66.

15. For information on the proposal, see GOG, "Machhu Irrigation Project-II," 2; Jathal, "Administrative Approval"; and Murthy, *Report on Failure of Machhu Dam-II*, 1:6.

16. For the rationale for the dam's construction, see Parthasarathy et al., *Before the Machhu Dam-II Inquiry Commission*, 1:7. For an analysis of Nehruvian socialism's tendency to reduce nature to manipulable resources, see Appadorai, "Recent Socialist Thought."

17. Parthasarathy et al., *Before the Machhu Dam-II Inquiry Commission*, 1:7; Ratilal Desai and Interviewee 30, interview, July 20, 2006; and Ratilal Desai, interview, July 25, 2006.

18. Parthasarathy et al., *Before the Machhu Dam-II Inquiry Commission*, 1:8.

19. Ratilal Desai and Interviewee 30, interview, July 20, 2006; and Ratilal Desai, interview, July 25, 2006.

20. For the formation of Saurashtra State, see Raval, *Gujarat State Gazetteer: Rajkot District*, 404; and Trivedi, *Gazetteer of India: Gujarat State Gazetteer*, 1:iii, 272, 311. For the Machhu Dam-I, see Murthy, *Report on Failure of Machhu Dam-II*, 1:5–6.

21. Parthasarathy et al., *Before the Machhu Dam-II Inquiry Commission*, 1:7; and MRF, "Summary of Royal Achievements" [inferred title].

22. Murthy, *Report on Failure of Machhu Dam-II*, 1:6.

23. For ongoing dam construction, see Bajaj, *National Register of Large Dams*; and Khagram, *Dams and Development*, 33–64.

24. For a general discussion of dams and risk, see Hartford and Baecher, *Risk and Uncertainty in Dam Safety*.

25. Murthy, *Report on Failure of Machhu Dam-II*, 1:41–42; Parthasarathy et al., *Before the Machhu Dam-II Inquiry Commission*, 1:52, 59; and Lee Wooten, interview, May 23, 2006.

26. Murthy, *Report on Failure of Machhu Dam-II*, 1:7, 10; and Parthasarathy et al., *Before the Machhu Dam-II Inquiry Commission*, 1:8, 71–72.

27. Lee Wooten, interview, May 23, 2006; and Y. K. Murthy, interview, August 12, 2006.

28. Parthasarathy et al., *Before the Machhu Dam-II Inquiry Commission*, 1:15; and Y. K. Murthy, interview, August 12, 2006.

29. For surface hydrology, see Interviewee 20. For the paucity of rainfall data, see Murthy, *Report on Failure of Machhu Dam-II*, 1:10; and Parthasarathy et al., *Before the Machhu Dam-II Inquiry Commission*, 1:16–18.

30. Interviewee 20.

31. Parthasarathy et al., *Before the Machhu Dam-II Inquiry Commission*, 1:16–17, 19–20.

32. Murthy, *Failure of Machhu Dam-II*, 1:6.

33. Ibid.

34. Parthasarathy et al., *Before the Machhu Dam-II Inquiry Commission*, 1:20–21.

35. Ibid., 1:21.

36. GOG, "Machhu Irrigation Project-II," 23–25.

37. Raval, *Gujarat State Gazetteer: Rajkot District*, 404; Tripathy and Chokshi, *Rajkot District Gazetteer*, 33–36; and Trivedi, *Gazetteer of India: Gujarat State Gazetteer*, 1:iii, 311–12.

38. Parthasarathy et al., *Before the Machhu Dam-II Inquiry Commission*, 1:21.

39. Ibid.

40. Ibid., 1:23.

41. For the spillway design, see Murthy, *Report on Failure of Machhu Dam-II*, 1:6. For more information on Tainter gates, see Tainter, "Sluiceway-Gate"; and Erbisti, *Design of Hydraulic Gates*.

42. GOG, "Machhu Irrigation Project-II," 23–25.

43. This vignette's account of villagers' early knowledge of the Machhu Dam-II project draws on Bhagvanji Patel, interview, July 21, 2006; and Interviewees 63–65.

44. Interviewees 63–65.

45. GOG, "Machhu Irrigation Project-II," 23–25; and Trivedi, *Census 1961*, 66–67.

46. This vignette's portrayal of B. J. Vasoya's biography and work relies on Interviewee 145.

47. For details of the construction hierarchy, see Parthasarathy et al., *Before the Machhu Dam-II Inquiry Commission*, 2:41.

48. For allegations of favoritism, see Ratilal Desai and Interviewee 30, interview, July 25, 2006. Quote from Vasoya, "Machhu-2 Dam Works and Construction of Outlet."

49. Parthasarathy et al., *Statement of Facts and Opinions*, 1:26.

50. Ibid., 1:72–76, 85.

51. Bhagvanji Patel, interview, July 21, 2006.

52. Interviewees 63–65.

53. This account of Jog Bapu draws on Hemiben Devda, Interviewee 85, and Interviewee 86, interview, July 26, 2006; and Interviewee 126. Quote from Interviewee 126.

54. Bhagvanji Patel, interview, July 21, 2006; and Interviewees 63–65.

55. Interviewees 63–65.

56. For lawsuits, see Interviewee 119. Quote from Bhagvanji Patel, interview, July 21, 2006.

57. For spillway construction, see Parthasarathy et al., *Before the Machhu Dam-II Inquiry Commission*, 1:76–79; and Interviewee 145. For the quality control protocol, see Parthasarathy et al., *Before the Machhu Dam-II Inquiry Commission*, 1:84.

58. Parthasarathy et al., *Before the Machhu Dam-II Inquiry Commission*, 1:26.

59. Ibid., 1:21.

60. For information on unit hydrograph, see Gupta, *Hydrology and Hydraulic Systems*, 339–73.

61. Parthasarathy et al., *Before the Machhu Dam-II Inquiry Commission*, 1:26.

62. Ibid., 1:25–26. Quote from ibid., 1:26.

63. Murthy, *Report on Failure of Machhu Dam-II*, 1:10; and Parthasarathy et al., *Before the Machhu Dam-II Inquiry Commission*, 1:28–32.

64. Parthasarathy et al., *Before the Machhu Dam-II Inquiry Commission*, 1:29.

65. Murthy, *Report on Failure of Machhu Dam-II*, 1:10.

66. Ibid.

67. "A Small Town Seeks Justice," *Indian Express*, August 30, 1981.

68. Murthy, *Report on Failure of Machhu Dam-II*, 1:10.

69. Parthasarathy et al., *Before the Machhu Dam-II Inquiry Commission*, 1:70.

70. This vignette's portrayal of Ratilal Desai's attitudes relies on Ratilal Desai and Interviewee 30, interview, July 25, 2006; Ratilal Desai, interview, July 24, 2006; and Ratilal Desai, interview, July 25, 2006.

71. Murthy, *Report on Failure of Machhu Dam-II*, 1:33.

72. For the fall of the Morarji government, see Metcalf and Metcalf, *Concise History of Modern India*, 257–58. For the political turmoil of the 1970s, see Guha, *India after Gandhi*, 446–543.

73. For a sense of the turmoil engulfing Gujarati government in the late 1970s, see Kohli, *Democracy and Discontent*, 248–52; and Sanghavi, "Dissolution and After." For information on Babubhai, see GOG, "Shri Babubhai Jashbhai Patel"; and Pandit et al., *Leader of Rock-Hard Principles*. For information on Madhavsinh, see GOG, "Shri Madhavsinh Fulsinh Solanki."

74. For the functioning of the canal, see Murthy, *Report on Failure of Machhu Dam-II*, 1:33.

75. Ratilal Desai and Interviewee 30, interview, July 25, 2006.

76. Cullet, *Sardar Sarovar Dam Project*, 1–76; Fisher, *Toward Sustainable Development?*; Khagram, *Dams and Development*, 65–100; Prabhakarbhai Khamar, interview, June 30, 2006; and Prabhakarbhai Khamar, interview, July 4, 2006.

77. For Mistry, see Parthasarathy et al., *Before the Machhu Dam-II Inquiry Commission*, 2:54. For Vasoya, see Interviewee 145.

78. This vignette's account of H. K. Khan's experience on August 1, 1979, draws on H. K. Khan, interview, August 14, 2006.

79. Arora and Goyal, *Indian Public Administration*, 317–408; and Maheshwari, "Indian Administrative Service."

80. McAllister, *Legend in Her Time*.

81. For a discussion of cloud seeding, see Dennis, *Weather Modification by Cloud Seeding*.

82. H. K. Khan, interview, August 14, 2006.

83. Ibid.

Chapter 3: "This Monsoon Descends"

1. Dhar et al., "Rainstorm which Caused the Morvi Dam Disaster," 77.

2. Ibid., 76. For further information on the rainfall patterns of August 1–10, 1979, see ibid.; Murthy, *Report on Failure of Machhu Dam-II*, 1:15–17; and Parthasarathy et al., *Before the Machhu Dam-II Inquiry Commission*, 1:107–9.

3. "On the Ninth Day, Still Rain and Cold in Saurashtra; Prediction of Clearing Proven Wrong," *Phulchhab*, August 8, 1979.

4. For the collapse of buildings, see Banerjee, "Report on the Flood Situation"; "In Rajkot, the Cloud-Lord's Mischief: Two Inches of Water in One Hour; Building Falls in Junction Plot," *Phulchhab*, August 11, 1979; and "Two of Bhavnagar's Reservoirs Overflow," *Phulchhab*, August 11, 1979. For the violent seas, see "Warning of a Terrible Storm in Saurashtra-Kutch; Winds Will Blow at Speeds of 80 KMH in Kutch," *Phulchhab*, August 8, 1979. For disrupted communications, see "The Cloud-Lord Wallops Saurashtra for the Twelfth Day

in a Row; 109 Villages of Ghed Cut Off: Lots of Earthen Buildings Have Been Leveled," *Phulchhab*, August 11, 1979.

5. For Home Guard mobilization, see "Home Guards in Every Town with a Population of Five Thousand," *Phulchhab*, August 11, 1979. For public health concerns, see "Two of Bhavnagar's Reservoirs Overflow," *Phulchhab*, August 11, 1979. For rescues, see "Entire Ghed Area Turned into Gulf: Water on All Four Sides; Two Corpses Exposed," *Phulchhab*, August 11, 1979.

6. Banerjee, "Report on the Flood Situation"; and "Warnings of Gales of 50–80 KMH in Saurashtra and Kutch; Warning to Downstream Areas with Overflow of the Bhadar Dam; Water in the Low-Lying Areas of Gondal," *Phulchhab*, August 11, 1979.

7. This vignette's portrayal of Lakshmanbhai Mohan's routine relies on Parthasarathy et al., *Before the Machhu Dam-II Inquiry Commission*, 1:80–81, 94; Interviewee 33, July 16, 2006; Interviewee 116; Lakshmanbhai Mohan, interview, July 29, 2006; and Interviewee 33, July 29, 2006.

8. Joshi, "Voluntarily Given Statement"; Parthasarathy et al., *Before the Machhu Dam-II Inquiry Commission*, 1:94; and Lakshmanbhai Mohan, interview, July 29, 2006. For the gate operations manual, see GOG, *Detailed Notes on the Operation of the 18 30 × 20 Steel Gates.*

9. For the delay, see Kothari, "Superintending Engineer's Report." For inflow calculation, see Joshi, "Voluntarily Given Statement."

10. GOG, *Detailed Notes on the Operation of the 18 30 × 20 Steel Gates.* Quote from Joshi, "Voluntarily Given Statement."

11. Murthy, *Report on Failure of Machhu Dam-II*, 1:18, 21.

12. Parthasarathy et al., *Before the Machhu Dam-II Inquiry Commission*, 1:80–81.

13. Ibid., 1:94.

14. Lakshmanbhai Mohan, interview, July 29, 2006.

15. This vignette's portrayal of Machhu River Valley residents' activities on the evening of August 10, 1979, relies on Bhagvanji Patel, interview, July 21, 2006; Khatijaben Valera, interview, July 25, 2006; Ratilal Desai, interview, July 25, 2006; Pratapbhai Adroja, interview, August 3, 2006; Abdulbhai Mor, interview, August 12, 2006; and Kanubhai Kubavat, interview, August 12, 2006.

16. For the rainfall pattern of the evening of August 10, 1979, see "The Cloud-Lord Wallops Saurashtra for the Twelfth Day in a Row; 109 Villages of Ghed Cut Off: Lots of Earthen Buildings Have Been Leveled," *Phulchhab*, August 11, 1979; and "Army Troops Called for Relief of the Disaster Descending from the Ripped Sky on Friday Night," *Phulchhab*, August 12, 1979.

17. For more on the Raga tradition and Raga Malhar, see Bor, *Raga Guide*.

18. T. R. Shukla and Ushaben Shukla, interview, December 31, 2005.

19. *Proceedings of the Gujarat Legislative Assembly* 66, no. 2:196; and Gokaldas Parmar, interview, July 21, 2006.

20. Murthy, *Report on Failure of Machhu Dam-II*, 1:21, 22.

21. Joshi, "Voluntarily Given Statement"; Murthy, *Report on Failure of Machhu Dam-II*, 1:22; and Interviewee 116.

22. Mohan, "Voluntary Statement"; Patel, "Voluntary Statement"; and Trivedi, "Voluntary Statement."

23. Mohan, "Voluntary Statement"; and Murthy, *Report on Failure of Machhu Dam-II*, 1:21, 22; Parthasarathy et al., *Before the Machhu Dam-II Inquiry Commission*, 1:112; and Trivedi, "Voluntary Statement."

24. Mohan, "Voluntary Statement"; Murthy, *Report on Failure of Machhu Dam-II*, 1:21, 22; Parthasarathy et al., *Before the Machhu Dam-II Inquiry Commission*, 1:113; and Trivedi, "Voluntary Statement."

25. Mohan, "Voluntary Statement." See also Trivedi, "Voluntary Statement."

26. For gate operations, see Mohan, "Voluntary Statement"; Murthy, *Report on Failure of Machhu Dam-II*, 1:21, 22; Parthasarathy et al., *Before the Machhu Dam-II Inquiry Commission*, 1:113; Patel, "Voluntary Statement"; and Trivedi, "Voluntary Statement." Quote from Mohan, "Voluntary Statement."

27. Parthasarathy et al., *Before the Machhu Dam-II Inquiry Commission*, 1:113.

28. Banerjee, "Report on the Flood Situation," 2.

29. For the role of the collector, see Arora and Goyal, *Indian Public Administration*, 243–58; Raval, *Gujarat State Gazetteer: Rajkot District*, 405–7; and Trivedi, *Gazetteer of India: Gujarat State Gazetteer*, 2:108, 112–13. For the population of Rajkot District, see

Doctor, *Census 1971*, xi. For the enumeration of subdistricts, see Tripathy and Chokshi, *Rajkot District Gazetteer*, 1–2.

30. Banerjee, "Report on the Flood Situation," 1–2.

31. Banerjee, "Report on the Flood Situation," 2–3; and Parthasarathy et al., *Before the Machhu Dam-II Inquiry Commission*, 1:143.

32. Dave, "Regarding the Flooding in Morbi"; and Parthasarathy et al., *Before the Machhu Dam-II Inquiry Commission*, 1:114.

33. Murthy, *Report on Failure of Machhu Dam-II*, 1:21.

34. Mehta, "Deputy Engineer's Report."

35. Dave, "Regarding the Flooding in Morbi."

36. Ibid.; and Parthasarathy et al., *Before the Machhu Dam-II Inquiry Commission*, 1:115–16.

37. Joshi, "Voluntarily Given Statement."

38. Murthy, *Report on Failure of Machhu Dam-II*, 1:22; and Parthasarathy et al., *Before the Machhu Dam-II Inquiry Commission*, 1:120.

39. This vignette's account of the events in Jodhpar and of the Jodhpar villagers' trip to the dam draws on Joshi, "Voluntarily Given Statement"; Mohan, "Voluntary Statement"; Murthy, *Report on Failure of Machhu Dam-II*, 1:22; Trivedi, "Voluntary Statement"; Parthasarathy et al., *Before the Machhu Dam-II Inquiry Commission*, 1:115, 120; Interviewee 31; and Interviewee 99, July 25, 2006.

40. Mohan, "Voluntary Statement."

41. This vignette's account of the morning of August 11, 1979, in Lilapar draws on Bhagvanji Patel, interview, July 21, 2006; Interviewees 95–103; and Interviewee 104.

42. Interviewee 104.

43. Bhagvanji Patel, interview, July 21, 2006.

44. Khatijaben Valera, interview, July 25, 2006.

45. Interviewee 30.

46. Parthasarathy et al., *Before the Machhu Dam-II Inquiry Commission*, 1:144–46, 2:110–17.

47. Interviewee 45; Interviewee 48; Interviewees 49–51; Interviewee 52 and Interviewee 53; Interviewees 54–57; Interviewee 75; Interviewee 77; Interviewee 79; and Interviewee 80.

48. Kanubhai Kubavat, interview, August 12, 2006.

49. Khatijaben Valera, July 25, 2006.

50. This vignette's portrayal of A. R. Banerjee's attitudes relies on A. R. Banerjee, interview, August 16, 2006; and A. R. Banerjee, interview, August 18, 2010.

51. Banerjee, "Report on the Flood Situation"; and GOG, "Details of Happenings from 10.8.1979."

52. Banerjee, "Report on the Flood Situation," 2. For information on Keshubhai Patel, see GOG, "Shri Keshubhai Patel."

53. For the Agriculture Department's scope, see Trivedi, *Gazetteer of India: Gujarat State Gazetteer*, 2:111–12.

54. Banerjee, "Report on the Flood Situation," 2–3.

55. Ibid., 2.

56. Ibid., 4.

57. Ibid.

58. This vignette's account of Gangaram Tapu's attitudes and actions draws on Gangaram Tapu, interview, July 29, 2006.

59. This vignette's account of the Shuklas' experiences draws on "A Fearsome Cobra Saved the Lives of an Entire Family in the Morbi Flood Disaster," *Gujarat Mitra*, August 30, 1979; T. R. Shukla and Ushaben Shukla, interview, December 31, 2005; and Neelimaben Shukla, interview, May 17, 2006.

60. Abdulbhai Mor, interview, August 12, 2006; Husainbhai Manek, interview, August 12, 2006; and Jashabhai Samani, interview, August 12, 2006.

61. Parthasarathy et al., *Before the Machhu Dam-II Inquiry Commission*, 1:147.

62. GOG, "Radio Announcement."

63. This vignette's portrayal of Dhirubhai Mehta's biography, attitudes, and activities on August 11, 1979, relies on Dhirubhai Mehta, interview, July 23, 2006.

64. Pratapbhai Adroja, interview, August 3, 2006.

65. For evacuations, see Parthasarathy et al., *Before the Machhu Dam-II Inquiry Commission*, 2:110–17.

66. Hemiben Devda, Interviewee 85, and Interviewee 86, interview, July 26, 2006; and Kanubhai Kubavat, interview, August 12, 2006.

67. Dave, "Regarding the Flooding in Morbi"; and Parthasarathy et al., *Before the Machhu Dam-II Inquiry Commission*, 1:144–46.

68. For information on Parmar, see Parmar, *Memorable Events*.

69. *Proceedings of the Gujarat Legislative Assembly* 66, no. 2:197; and Gokaldas Parmar, interview, July 21, 2006.

70. *Proceedings of the Gujarat Legislative Assembly* 66, no. 2:196.

71. Gokaldas Parmar, interview, July 21, 2006.

72. Dave, "Regarding the Flooding in Morbi"; and Parthasarathy et al., *Before the Machhu Dam-II Inquiry Commission*, 1:149–50. Quote from Dave, "Report on Flooding and Evacuations."

73. Parthasarathy et al., *Before the Machhu Dam-II Inquiry Commission*, 1:151–52.

74. Banerjee, "Report on the Casualties Occurred," 1–2; and Banerjee, "Report on the Flood Situation."

75. Banerjee, "Report on the Flood Situation," 5.

76. A. R. Banerjee, interview, August 18, 2010.

77. Ibid.

78. Kothari, "Superintending Engineer's Report," 4–5.

79. Banerjee, "Report on the Flood Situation," 5–6.

80. Ibid., 6.

81. Pratapbhai Adroja, interview, August 3, 2006; and Interviewee 127.

82. "A Fearsome Cobra Saved the Lives of an Entire Family in the Morbi Flood Disaster," *Gujarat Mitra*, August 30, 1979; T. R. Shukla and Ushaben Shukla, interview, December 31, 2005; and Neelimaben Shukla, interview, May 17, 2006.

83. Bhagvanji Patel, interview, July 21, 2006; Interviewees 95–103; and Interviewee 104.

84. For Tapu, see Gangaram Tapu, interview, July 29, 2006. For evacuations, see Parthasarathy et al., *Before the Machhu Dam-II Inquiry Commission*, 2:110–17.

85. Pratapbhai Adroja, interview, August 3, 2006.

86. For Mehta, see Dhirubhai Mehta, interview, July 23, 2006. For Parmar, see *Proceedings of the Gujarat Legislative Assembly* 66, no. 2:197; and Gokaldas Parmar, interview, July 21, 2006. For Desai, see Ratilal Desai and Interviewee 30, interview, July 20, 2006. For highlying neighborhoods, see ibid.; and Interviewee 30.

87. Abdulbhai Mor, interview, August 12, 2006.

Chapter 4: "Something out of the Ordinary"

1. This vignette's account of events at Sanala draws on Banerjee, "Report on the Flood Situation"; Kothari, "Superintending Engineer's Report"; Parthasarathy et al., *Before the Machhu Dam-II Inquiry Commission*, 1:119–20; and *Proceedings of the Gujarat Legislative Assembly* 66, no. 2:293–94.

2. *Proceedings of the Gujarat Legislative Assembly* 66, no. 2:293–94.

3. Kothari, "Superintending Engineer's Report," 7.

4. This vignette's account of events on Morbi's western periphery draws on Interviewee 134.

5. Ibid.

6. This vignette's account of events on the Machhu River's eastern bank draws on T. R. Shukla and Ushaben Shukla, interview, December 31, 2005; and Neelimaben Shukla, interview, May 17, 2006.

7. This exchange from T. R. Shukla and Ushaben Shukla, interview, December 31, 2005.

8. Ibid.

9. Ibid.

10. This vignette's account of A. C. Mehta's day draws on GOG, "Detailed Report on the Breaches"; Mehta, "Deputy Engineer's Report"; and Parthasarathy et al., *Before the Machhu Dam-II Inquiry Commission*, 1:118, 121–22.

11. Interviewee 116.

Chapter 5: "Not a Single Brick Will Survive"

1. This vignette's account of events on the Machhu Dam-II draws on Harilal, "Statement"; Joshi, "Voluntarily Given Statement"; Mohan, "Voluntary Statement"; Patel, "Voluntary Statement"; Rajapara, "Statement"; Trivedi, "Voluntary Statement"; Interviewee 33, July 16, 2006; Interviewee 116; Lakshmanbhai Mohan, interview, July 29, 2006; Interviewee 33, July 29, 2006; and Parthasarathy et al., *Before the Machhu Dam-II Inquiry Commission*, 1:120–21.

2. Interviewee 116.

3. Mohan, "Voluntary Statement."

4. Joshi, "Voluntarily Given Statement."

5. Ibid.

6. Lakshmanbhai Mohan, interview, July 29, 2006.

7. GOG, "NK-01/08 R 2EQ1 DID082130."

8. Joshi, "Voluntarily Given Statement."

9. Mohan, "Voluntary Statement."

10. This vignette's account of events in Jodhpar draws on Interviewee 31; and Interviewee 32.

11. Interviewee 31.

12. Interviewee 32.

13. Interviewee 31.

14. This vignette's account of events in Lilapar and Lakhdhirnagar draws on Bhagvanji Patel, interview, July 21, 2006; Interviewees 63–65; Interviewee 66 and Interviewee 67; Interviewees 95–103; Interviewee 99, July 28, 2006; and Interviewee 104.

15. Bhagvanji Patel, interview, July 21, 2006.

16. This vignette's account of events in Vajepar draws on Gokaldas Parmar, interview, July 26, 2006; Hemiben Devda, Interviewee 85, and Interviewee 86, interview, July 26, 2006; Interviewee 87 and Interviewee 88; Interviewee 91; Interviewee 92; and Interviewee 93 and Interviewee 85.

17. Hemiben Devda, Interviewee 85, and Interviewee 86, interview, July 26, 2006.

18. Interviewee 91.

19. Interviewee 92.

20. Interviewee 93.

21. Hemiben Devda, Interviewee 85, and Interviewee 86, interview, July 26, 2006.

22. Interviewees 52 and 53.

23. Khatijaben Valera, interview, July 25, 2006.

24. This vignette's account of events in Kabir Hill draws on Gangaram Tapu, interview, July 29, 2006. The account of events on the Police Line draws on Interviewee 43; Interviewee 89 and Interviewee 90; Gangaram Tapu, interview, July 29, 2006; and Interviewee 105.

25. This vignette's account of events in the Tiger Quarter draws on Kanubhai Kubavat, interview, August 12, 2006.

26. Ibid.

27. This vignette's account of events in Shakti Plot draws on Gokaldas Parmar, interview, July 21, 2006; Gokaldas Parmar and Mrs. Parmar, interview, July 24, 2006; and *Proceedings of the Gujarat Legislative Assembly* 66, no. 2:197–208.

28. *Proceedings of the Gujarat Legislative Assembly* 66, no. 2:197.

29. Gokaldas Parmar, interview, July 21, 2006.

30. *Proceedings of the Gujarat Legislative Assembly* 66, no. 2:197–98.

31. Ibid., 198.

32. This vignette's account of events in Morbi's riverside neighborhoods draws on Interviewee 34; Interviewee 107; Interviewees 108–110; Interviewee 121 and Interviewee 122; and Interviewee 132 and Interviewee 133. The account of events at the northern evacuation sites draws on Interviewee 45; Interviewee 48; Interviewees 49–51; Interviewee 52 and Interviewee 53; Interviewees 54–57; Interviewee 75; Interviewee 77; Interviewee 79; and Interviewee 80.

33. Interviewee 34.

34. Interviewees 49–51.

35. This vignette's account of events in Morbi's main market area draws on Ratilal Desai and Interviewee 30, interview, July 20, 2006; and Ratilal Desai, interview, July 25, 2006.

36. Ratilal Desai and Interviewee 30, interview, July 20, 2006.

37. Ratilal Desai, interview, July 25, 2006.

38. This exchange from Ratilal Desai and Interviewee 30, interview, July 20, 2006.

39. Ibid.

40. This vignette's account of events in the Mahendra Quarter draws on Shah, "Twenty-Fifth Anniversary"; Dhirubhai Mehta, interview, July 23, 2006; and Pratapbhai Adroja, interview, August 3, 2006.

41. Pratapbhai Adroja, interview, August 3, 2006.

42. Ibid.

43. Dhirubhai Mehta, interview, July 23, 2006.

44. Ibid.

45. Ibid.

46. This vignette's account of events on the Machhu River's eastern bank and of the breaking of the Buffalo Bridge draws on T. R.

Shukla and Ushaben Shukla, interview, December 31, 2005; Interviewee 34; and Interviewee 70.

47. Interviewee 34.

48. Interviewee 70.

49. Interviewee 34.

50. This vignette's account of Ratilal Desai and the subdistrict magistrate's experience draws on Dave, "Regarding the Flooding in Morbi"; Ratilal Desai and Interviewee 30, interview, July 20, 2006; and Ratilal Desai, interview, July 25, 2006.

51. Ratilal Desai, interview, July 25, 2006.

52. This exchange from Ratilal Desai and Interviewee 30, interview, July 20, 2006.

53. Ibid.

54. Ibid.

55. This vignette's account of Gangaram Tapu's experience draws on Interviewee 89 and Interviewee 90; and Gangaram Tapu, interview, July 29, 2006.

56. Gangaram Tapu, interview, July 29, 2006.

57. Ibid.

58. This vignette's account of events downstream of Morbi draws on Interviewee 68; Abdulbhai Mor, interview, August 12, 2006; Husainbhai Manek, interview, August 12, 2006; Jashabhai Samani, interview, August 12, 2006; Interviewee 140; and Interviewee 141.

59. Harilal, "Statement"; Joshi, "Voluntarily Given Statement"; Mohan, "Voluntary Statement"; Parthasarathy et al., *Before the Machhu Dam-II Inquiry Commission*, 1:120–21; Patel, "Voluntary Statement"; Rajapara, "Statement"; Trivedi, "Voluntary Statement"; Interviewee 33, July 16, 2006; Interviewee 116; Lakshmanbhai Mohan, interview, July 29, 2006; and Interviewee 33, July 29, 2006.

60. Bhagvanji Patel, interview, July 21, 2006; and Interviewees 63–65. Quote from Bhagvanji Patel, interview, July 21, 2006.

61. Hemiben Devda, Interviewee 85, and Interviewee 86, interview, July 26, 2006.

62. Khatijaben Valera, interview, July 25, 2006.

63. Gokaldas Parmar, interview, July 21, 2006; Gokaldas Parmar and Mrs. Parmar, interview, July 24, 2006; and *Proceedings of the Gujarat Legislative Assembly* 66, no. 2:197–208.

64. Gangaram Tapu, interview, July 29, 2006.

65. Kanubhai Kubavat, interview, August 12, 2006.

66. T. R. Shukla and Ushaben Shukla, interview, December 31, 2005; and Neelimaben Shukla, interview, May 17, 2006.

67. Dave, "Regarding the Flooding in Morbi."

68. Interviewee 45; Interviewee 48; Interviewees 49–51; Interviewee 52 and Interviewee 53; Interviewees 54–57; Dhirubhai Mehta, interview, July 23, 2006; Interviewee 75; Interviewee 77; Interviewee 79; Interviewee 80; and Pratapbhai Adroja, interview, August 3, 2006.

69. Interviewee 81.

70. Ibid.

Chapter 6: "Even the Pests Were Dead"

1. Banerjee, "Report on the Flood Situation," 1–2, 7; and Banerjee, "Report on the Casualties Occurred," 3.

2. A. R. Banerjee, interview, August 18, 2010.

3. Ibid.; and Banerjee, "Report on the Flood Situation," 7.

4. Banerjee, "Report on the Flood Situation," 8.

5. Ibid., 13.

6. Ibid., 8.

7. This vignette's account of Ushakant Mankad's biography and experiences on August 12, 1979, draws on Ushakant Mankad, interview, July 7, 2006.

8. Ibid.

9. "After Death Strikes, the Reign of Criminal Thievery in Morbi," *Gujarat Samachar*, August 17, 1979; T. R. Shukla and Ushaben Shukla, interview, December 31, 2005; Neelimaben Shukla, interview, May 17, 2006; Interviewee 21, July 7, 2006; Interviewee 23; Interviewee 30; Ratilal Desai and Interviewee 30, interview, July 20, 2006; Bhagvanji Patel, interview, July 21, 2006; Interviewee 70; Interviewee 71; Gokaldas Parmar and Mrs. Parmar, interview, July 24, 2006; Naseemben Valera, July 25, 2006; and Interviewee 105.

10. Ratilal Desai and Interviewee 30, interview, July 20, 2006.

11. Ushakant Mankad, interview, July 7, 2006.

12. Banerjee, "Report on the Flood Situation," 8; Interviewee 23; and A. R. Banerjee, interview, August 16, 2006.

13. Banerjee, "Report on the Flood Situation," 8.

14. Ibid.

15. Interviewee 23.

16. Ibid.

17. Banerjee, "Report on Salvage and Relief," 2; Banerjee, "Report on the Casualties Occurred," 3; and Banerjee, "Report on the Flood Situation," 8–9.

18. Banerjee, "Report on the Flood Situation," 9.

19. Ibid., 23.

20. Patel, *Diaries*, August 12, 1979; and Prabhakarbhai Khamar, interview, June 30, 2006.

21. Details of Babubhai's biography from GOG, "Shri Babubhai Jashbhai Patel"; Pandit et al., *Leader of Rock-Hard Principles*; Prabhakarbhai Khamar, interview, June 30, 2006; and Prabhakarbhai Khamar, interview, July 4, 2006.

22. Patel, *Diaries*, August 12, 1979.

23. Ibid.; and Prabhakarbhai Khamar, interview, June 30, 2006.

24. Prabhakarbhai Khamar, interview, June 30, 2006.

25. Patel, *Diaries*, August 12, 1979.

26. This vignette's account of H. K. Khan's experiences draws on H. K. Khan, interview, August 14, 2006.

27. Interviewee 16; and Interviewee 18.

28. Interviewee 21, July 7, 2006. For Keshubhai's connection to the RSS, see GOG, "Shri Keshubhai Patel."

29. Interviewee 124.

30. Interviewee 10.

31. Interviewee 16; and Interviewee 18.

32. H. K. Khan, interview, August 14, 2006.

33. Joshi, "Voluntarily Given Statement"; Lakshmanbhai Mohan, interview, July 29, 2006; and Interviewee 116.

34. "The Greatest Destruction in the History of Saurashtra," *Gujarat Samachar*, August 13, 1979.

35. For representative experiences, see Interviewee 34; Gokaldas Parmar, interview, July 21, 2006; and Interviewee 131.

36. Pratapbhai Adroja, interview, August 3, 2006.

37. Interviewee 45; Interviewee 48; Interviewees 49–51; Interviewee 52 and Interviewee 53; Interviewees 54–57; Interviewee 75; Interviewee 77; Interviewee 79; and Interviewee 80.

38. Gangaram Tapu, interview, July 29, 2006.

39. "The Machhu Becomes Death and Attacks Morbi" in *Aaspaas*, "Special Edition"; "The Speaking Deaths of Dumb Morbi" in *Aaspaas*, "Special Edition"; "All of Morbi City Waterlogged, Corpses Everywhere: The Relief Effort That the Army Has Taken on Its Shoulders," *Gujarat Samachar*, August 13, 1979; "The Paris of Saurashtra Turned into a Tomb," *Gujarat Samachar*, August 14, 1979; "Morvi a City of Dead; Bodies Lie Submerged; All Communications Disrupted," *Indian Express*, August 14, 1979; and "Morvi Looks a Ruined Desolate Tract," *Indian Express*, August 14, 1979. This section also draws on photographs from the T. R. Shukla Photographs and the Phulchhab Photographic Archive.

40. Interviewee 81.

41. Hemiben Devda, Interviewee 85, and Interviewee 86, interview, July 26, 2006.

42. Banerjee, "Report on Salvage and Relief," 2–3.

43. Dhirubhai Mehta, interview, July 23, 2006.

44. Interviewee 69; and Interviewee 131.

45. Khatijaben Valera, interview, July 25, 2006.

46. Ibid.

47. T. R. Shukla and Ushaben Shukla, interview, December 31, 2005.

48. Gokaldas Parmar, interview, July 21, 2006.

49. Gokaldas Parmar and Mrs. Parmar, interview, July 24, 2006.

50. Gokaldas Parmar, interview, July 21, 2006.

51. This vignette's account of Kanubhai Kubavat's experiences on August 12, 1979, draws on Kanubhai Kubavat, interview, August 12, 2006.

52. For examples of such speculation, see T. R. Shukla and Ushaben Shukla, interview, December 31, 2005; Ratilal Desai and Interviewee 30, interview, July 20, 2006; Gokaldas Parmar, interview, July 21, 2006; and Kanubhai Kubavat, interview, August 12, 2006.

53. Ratilal Desai and Interviewee 30, interview, July 20, 2006.

54. Ibid.

55. Gokaldas Parmar, interview, July 21, 2006.

56. Ibid. Quote from *Proceedings of the Gujarat Legislative Assembly* 66, no. 2:200.

57. Gokaldas Parmar, interview, July 21, 2006.

58. Ibid.

59. For Banerjee's account of Keshubhai's work, see Banerjee, "Report on the Casualties Occurred," 5.

60. Bhagvanji Patel, interview, July 21, 2006.

61. *Proceedings of the Gujarat Legislative Assembly* 66, no. 2:43; Interviewee 68; and Interviewee 140.

62. "A Fear That the 10,000 People of Maliya Are Sunk," *Gujarat Samachar*, August 13, 1979.

63. This portrayal of the exodus from Morbi relies on photographs from the T. R. Shukla Photographs, the Prabhakarbhai Khamar Photographs, and the Phulchhab Photographic Archive.

64. Ratilal Desai and Interviewee 30, interview, July 20, 2006.

65. For exodus on foot, see Interviewee 29; Interviewee 47; and Interviewee 91. For exodus by private vehicle, see Interviewee 59; and Interviewee 69. For exodus by bus, see Interviewee 36; Interviewee 74; Pratapbhai Adroja, interview, August 3, 2006; Interviewee 131; and Kanubhai Kubavat, interview, August 12, 2006.

66. For information on bus services, see Banerjee, "Report on Salvage and Relief," 5. For the inadequacy of the number of buses, see *Proceedings of the Gujarat Legislative Assembly* 66, no. 2:215, 313. For chaos and rumors, see H. K. Khan, interview, August 14, 2006.

67. Dhirubhai Mehta, interview, July 23, 2006; Khatijaben Valera, interview, July 25, 2006; Pratapbhai Adroja, interview, August 3, 2006; and Kanubhai Kubavat, interview, August 12, 2006.

68. T. R. Shukla and Ushaben Shukla, interview, December 31, 2005; Gokaldas Parmar and Mrs. Parmar, interview, July 24, 2006; Gangaram Tapu, interview, July 29, 2006; and Kanubhai Kubavat, interview, August 12, 2006.

69. Ratilal Desai and Interviewee 30, interview, July 20, 2006.

70. Ratilal Desai, interview, July 25, 2006.

71. Banerjee, "Regarding the Coordination of Relief" [inferred title].

72. Banerjee, "Report on Salvage and Relief," 2.

73. H. K. Khan, interview, August 14, 2006.

74. For eastern Morbi, see T. R. Shukla and Ushaben Shukla, interview, December 31, 2005. For evacuation sites, see Interviewee 45; Interviewee 48; Interviewees 49–51; Interviewee 52 and Interviewee

53; Interviewees 54–57; Interviewee 75; Interviewee 77; Interviewee 79; and Interviewee 80.

75. Banerjee, "Report on Salvage and Relief," 2.

76. Interviewee 125.

Chapter 7: "They Would Work and Cry, Cry and Work"

1. "1,000 Feared Dead in Indian Dam Burst," *Karachi Dawn*, August 13, 1979; "India Dam Toll May Be 25,000," *London Telegraph*, August 13, 1979; and "Hundreds Die in India as Dam Break Frees 20-Foot Water Wall," *New York Times*, August 13, 1979.

2. For television coverage, see *ABC World News*, August 13, 1979, in Vanderbilt Television News Archive; *CBS Evening News*, August 13, 1979, in Vanderbilt Television News Archive; and *NBC Nightly News*, August 13, 1979, in Vanderbilt Television News Archive. For representative examples of the spy satellite suspicion, see "America Found Out First," *Gujarat Samachar*, August 17, 1979; and Neelimaben Shukla, interview, May 17, 2006.

3. T. R. Shukla and Ushaben Shukla, interview, December 31, 2005.

4. "The Greatest Destruction in the History of Saurashtra," *Gujarat Samachar*, August 13, 1979; "In Morbi, the Death of Four Thousand by Water-Annihilation: Upon the Breaking of the Machhu Dam, the Biggest Human Disaster Seen in Gujarat in Centuries," *Gujarat Samachar*, August 13, 1979; and "In a Disaster Unlike Any Saurashtra Has Seen in a Thousand Years, 1,000 Die as the Machhu Dam Bursts Near Morbi: 250 Corpses Found," *Sandesh*, August 13, 1979.

5. "Fear of 3000 Deaths: 60% of Buildings Ruined," *Phulchhab*, August 13, 1979.

6. "The Tearful Sights of Morbi's Earth," *Phulchhab*, August 13, 1979; and "Even People Who Climbed up onto Roofs and Trees Were Dragged away by the Raging Flood; The Police and Military Have Started Rescue Efforts; More Bodies Expected to Emerge from the Debris," *Sandesh*, August 13, 1979.

7. "Scenes That Would Make Even the Toughest Cry," *Gujarat Samachar*, August 13, 1979.

8. The examples of suffering stories are drawn from "A Daughter Who Came Home for the Seventh-Eighth Holidays Drowned in the Water with Her Daughter: As the Shock of Death Cools Down, The Pain Increases," *Phulchhab*, August 17, 1979. The examples of hopeful stories are drawn from "Wondrous Are Nature's Whimsies: With Destruction Unfolding All Around, Two Children Were Born on the Balcony of the Maternity Hospital," *Phulchhab*, August 16, 1979; and "A Convicted Murderer of Morbi Saves 35," *Phulchhab*, August 17, 1979.

9. *ABC World News*, August 17, 1979, in Vanderbilt Television News Archive.

10. This vignette's account of H. K. Khan's attitudes and experiences draws on H. K. Khan, interview, August 14, 2006.

11. Banerjee, "Regarding Distribution of Work."

12. Banerjee, "Regarding the Coordination of Relief" [inferred title].

13. Ibid.

14. Banerjee, "Report on Salvage and Relief," 2.

15. H. K. Khan, interview, August 14, 2006.

16. Ibid.

17. Interviewee 18.

18. Banerjee, "Report on Salvage and Relief," 2–3.

19. Ushakant Mankad, interview, July 7, 2006.

20. Banerjee, "Report on the Casualties Occurred," 4; and Banerjee, "Report on Salvage and Relief," 3.

21. Banerjee, "Report on Salvage and Relief," 3; Interviewee 16; Interviewee 18; Interviewee 21, interview, July 6, 2006; Ushakant Mankad, interview, July 7, 2006; Ratilal Desai and Interviewee 30, interview, July 20, 2006; Interviewee 81; Interviewee 125; and H. K. Khan, interview, August 14, 2006.

22. Interviewee 21, July 6, 2006.

23. H. K. Khan, interview, August 14, 2006.

24. Ushakant Mankad, interview, July 7, 2006.

25. Interviewee 18.

26. Ratilal Desai, interview, July 25, 2006.

27. Ushakant Mankad, interview, July 7, 2006.

28. Ibid.

29. Interviewee 36; Interviewees 37–41.

30. Interviewee 18.
31. Ibid.
32. Interviewee 36.
33. Ibid.
34. Interviewee 107.
35. Patel, *Diaries*, August 13, 1979.
36. Prabhakarbhai Khamar, interview, June 30, 2006.
37. Patel, *Diaries*, August 13, 1979; and Prabhakarbhai Khamar, interview, June 30, 2006.
38. Ratilal Desai and Interviewee 30, interview, July 20, 2006.
39. Patel, *Diaries*, August 13, 1979. Also see GOG, *Tale of Woe*, 13; Ratilal Desai and Interviewee 30, interview, July 20, 2006; and Gokaldas Parmar, interview, July 21, 2006. Quote from Gokaldas Parmar, interview, July 21, 2006.
40. Nishubhai Sedani, interview, July 6, 2010. For some of these photographs in context, see "Aftermath of Dam Burst," *Indian Express*, August 17, 1979.
41. Banerjee, "Report on Salvage and Relief," 3.
42. Interviewee 125.
43. Banerjee, "Report on Salvage and Relief," 3.
44. T. R. Shukla and Ushaben Shukla, interview, December 31, 2005; and Neelimaben Shukla, interview, May 17, 2006.
45. Interviewee 29; Interviewee 36; Interviewee 47; Interviewee 59; Interviewee 69; Interviewee 74; Interviewee 91; Pratapbhai Adroja, interview, August 3, 2006; Interviewee 131; and Kanubhai Kubavat, interview, August 12, 2006.
46. *Proceedings of the Gujarat Legislative Assembly* 66, no. 2:48; Interviewee 35; Interviewee 45; Interviewees 49–51; Interviewees 54–57; Dhirubhai Mehta, interview, July 23, 2006; Khatijaben Valera, interview, July 25, 2006; Interviewee 106; and Interviewee 131.
47. Ratilal Desai and Interviewee 30, interview, July 20, 2006.
48. Pratapbhai Adroja, interview, August 3, 2006.
49. Kanubhai Kubavat, interview, August 12, 2006.
50. Gangaram Tapu, interview, July 29, 2006.
51. Gokaldas Parmar and Mrs. Parmar, interview, July 24, 2006. Quote from *Proceedings of the Gujarat Legislative Assembly* 66, no. 2:199.

52. Bhagvanji Patel, interview, July 21, 2006; Interviewees 95–103.

53. Pratapbhai Adroja, interview, August 3, 2006.

54. For national turmoil, see Guha, *India after Gandhi*, 446–543; and Metcalf and Metcalf, *Concise History of Modern India*, 257–58. For state turmoil, see Kohli, *Democracy and Discontent*, 248–52; and Sanghavi, "Dissolution and After."

55. H. K. Khan, interview, August 14, 2006.

56. "Madhavsinh Asking for a Judicial Inquiry for the Morbi Disaster: Accusations of Failed Government Administration," *Phulchhab*, August 15, 1979.

57. "Calls for Irrigation Minister's Resignation," *Gujarat Samachar*, August 18, 1979; and "Vallabhbhai: The Machhu Dam Disaster Happened Because of the Earthen Dam's Faulty Underdesign; A Warning Had Been Given Two Years Ago," *Phulchhab*, August 13, 1979.

58. "All Possible Surveillance Steps Were Taken to Avoid Destruction," *Gujarat Samachar*, August 13, 1979; "Morvi Got 'Adequate' Warning," *Indian Express*, August 19, 1979; and "Why Did the Machhu Dam Break? The Gujarat Government's Explanation," *Phulchhab*, August 14, 1979.

59. "Madhavsinh Asking for a Judicial Inquiry for the Morbi Disaster: Accusations of Failed Government Administration," *Phulchhab*, August 15, 1979.

60. *ABC World News*, August 17, 1979, in Vanderbilt Television News Archive; "Indians Still Disagree on Number of Deaths Caused by Dam Break," *New York Times*, August 15, 1979; "Babubhai: Not More than a Thousand Deaths in Morbi," *Phulchhab*, August 15, 1979; "Estimates of Deaths: Workers Say 4,000 to 5,000, Chief Minister Says 1,000," *Phulchhab*, August 15, 1979; "After Unprecedented Water-Destruction, A Fear of Thousands of Deaths in Communities from Morbi to Maliya: Popular Estimates of 5,000 Dead in Morbi and 25,000 Dead in the Villages," *Sandesh*, August 14, 1979; and "Morvi Death Toll 20,000, Says Solanki," *Western Times*, August 14, 1979.

61. "Madhavsinh Asking for a Judicial Inquiry for the Morbi Disaster: Accusations of Failed Government Administration," *Phulchhab*, August 15, 1979; and H. K. Khan, interview, August 14, 2006.

62. "Chief Minister Babubhai Announces that There Will Be a Judicial Inquiry into the Machhu Dam Disaster," *Phulchhab*, August 15, 1979.

63. Patel, *Diaries*, August 12, 1979.

64. "Chief Minister Babubhai Announces that There Will Be a Judicial Inquiry into the Machhu Dam Disaster," *Phulchhab*, August 15, 1979.

65. H. K. Khan, interview, August 14, 2006.

66. "Indira Gandhi's Aerial Survey of the Flood-Affected Area: Everyone Set Aside Partisanship and Start Working to Get Morbi Back to Normal," *Phulchhab*, August 17, 1979.

67. Ratilal Desai and Interviewee 30, interview, July 20, 2006.

68. Kanubhai Kubavat, interview, August 12, 2006.

69. "Indira Gandhi's Aerial Survey of the Flood-Affected Area: Everyone Set Aside Partisanship and Start Working to Get Morbi Back to Normal," *Phulchhab*, August 17, 1979.

70. H. K. Khan, interview, August 14, 2006.

71. "Morarji Desai Visiting Morbi," *Akila*, August 25, 1979; "Estimates of Deaths: Workers Say 4,000 to 5,000, Chief Minister Says 1,000," *Phulchhab*, August 15, 1979; "Chandrashekhar and Advani Dedicating Themselves to Service," *Phulchhab*, August 17, 1979; and Ratilal Desai and Interviewee 30, interview, July 20, 2006.

72. "The Queen Mother before the Citizens: I Will Loot All of My Wealth to Help Morbi," *Akila*, August 15, 1979. Also see "The Queen Mother Cried upon Seeing the State of Morbi," *Sandesh*, August 17, 1979.

73. For detailed information on the relief work undertaken during the week after the disaster, see Banerjee, "Report on Salvage and Relief"; GOG, "Notes on the Suggestions Made during the Voluntary Planning Meeting"; GOG, "Proceedings of Meeting Held on 19.8.1979"; GOG, "Proceedings of the Meeting Convened at 10:00 A.M. on 16-8-79"; GOG, "Proceedings of the Meeting Convened at 4:00 P.M. on 15-8-79"; and GOG, "Proceedings of the Meeting Convened at 4:00 P.M. on 16-8-79." Our account is also informed by daily issues of *Akila*, *Phulchhab*, and *Sandesh* from August 13, 1979, to August 20, 1979.

74. For information on cleaning, see Banerjee, "Report on Salvage

and Relief"; Ushakant Mankad, interview, July 7, 2006; Interviewee 25, July 11, 2006; Interviewee 44; Interviewees 49–51; Interviewee 52 and Interviewee 53; Interviewees 54–57; Interviewee 59; Interviewee 71, July 22, 2006; Interviewee 79; and Interviewee 81.

75. Banerjee, "Report on Salvage and Relief," 4; "115,000 Tons of Mud Moved," *Akila*, September 23, 1979; and Interviewee 18.

76. GOG, *Tale of Woe*, 14; Banerjee, "Report on Salvage and Relief," 4.

77. Banerjee, "Report on Salvage and Relief," 19–25, 29–31, 41–42; Interviewee 10; Interviewee 19; Ushakant Mankad, interview, July 7, 2006; and Interviewee 81.

78. Banerjee, "Report on Salvage and Relief," 19–25, 29–31, 41–42; and "Rajkot Has Become the Kerchief to Wipe Morbi's Tears: The Flow of Food Packets and Clothes," *Phulchhab*, August 14, 1979. For more on donations, see daily issues of *Akila*, *Phulchhab*, and *Sandesh* from August 13, 1979 to August 20, 1979.

79. Banerjee, "Report on Salvage and Relief," 5.

80. Interviewee 30.

81. Ratilal Desai and Interviewee 30, interview, July 20, 2006.

82. Compare with "A Fear That the 10,000 People of Maliya Are Sunk," *Gujarat Samachar*, August 13, 1979. Also see "15–17 Towns of the Maliya Area Still Cannot Be Contacted," *Gujarat Samachar*, August 14, 1979; "As of Monday, No Aerial Survey of Maliya Possible," *Sandesh*, August 14, 1979; and "Contact Could Not Be Established with Maliya Even by Railway," *Gujarat Samachar*, August 14, 1979.

83. Banerjee, "Report on Salvage and Relief," 6; and "Maliya Did Not Experience Loss of Life," *Phulchhab*, August 14, 1979.

84. "Contact with Maliya Established," *Gujarat Samachar*, August 14, 1979; and "Maliya Did Not Experience Loss of Life," *Phulchhab*, August 14, 1979.

85. "Because the Waters Spread out for Miles, Maliya Was Spared," *Phulchhab*, August 15, 1979.

86. "Maliya-Miyana Was Not Saved Either: 190 Corpses Found: 90% of Buildings Destroyed; More Details Coming Out: Need for Food, Medicine," *Phulchhab*, August 17, 1979.

87. "300 People Lost Their Lives in Maliya-Miyana," *Gujarat Samachar*, August 18, 1979.

88. Banerjee, "Report on Salvage and Relief," 6.

89. For further examples of official skepticism, see Banerjee, "Report on a Tour of Maliya" [inferred title]; *Proceedings of the Gujarat Legislative Assembly* 66, no. 2: 395.

90. Abdulbhai Mor, interview, August 12, 2006; Husainbhai Manek, interview, August 12, 2006; and Jashabhai Samani, interview, August 12, 2006.

91. This vignette's account of the recovery of Ghost Paan draws on Interviewee 23; and Pratapbhai Adroja, interview, August 3, 2006.

Chapter 8: "Everyone Was a Beggar"

1. This vignette's portrayal of Babubhai Patel's early morning routine in Morbi relies on Patel, *Diaries*, August 16, 1979, to September 9, 1979; Prabhakarbhai Khamar, interview, June 30, 2006; and Prabhakarbhai Khamar, interview, July 4, 2006. The account of Babubhai Patel's biography draws on GOG, "Shri Babubhai Jashbhai Patel"; and Pandit et al., *Leader of Rock-Hard Principles*; Prabhakarbhai Khamar, interview, June 30, 2006; and Prabhakarbhai Khamar, interview, July 4, 2006.

2. This vignette's account of morning meetings in the Mani Mandir draws on Patel, *Diaries*, August 16, 1979, to September 9, 1979; GOG, "Meeting Convened at 10:00 A.M. on 16-8-79"; Prabhakarbhai Khamar, interview, June 30, 2006; Prabhakarbhai Khamar, interview, July 4, 2006; Ushakant Mankad, interview, July 7, 2006; Ratilal Desai and Interviewee 30, interview, July 20, 2006; Gokaldas Parmar, interview, July 21, 2006; Gokaldas Parmar and Mrs. Parmar, interview, July 24, 2006; Ratilal Desai, interview, July 25, 2006; H. K. Khan, interview, August 14, 2006; and A. R. Banerjee, interview, August 16, 2006. For full proceedings of one such meeting, see GOG, "Meeting Convened at 10:00 A.M. on 16-8-79."

3. H. K. Khan, interview, August 14, 2006.

4. Ibid.

5. Photographs from the era, such as those from the Prabhakarbhai Khamar Photographs or the Phulchhab Photographic Archive, provide a sense of the composition of these meetings.

6. Ratilal Desai, interview, July 25, 2006.

7. Ratilal Desai and Interviewee 30, interview, July 20, 2006.

8. Ratilal Desai, interview, July 25, 2006.

9. This vignette's account of relief provision draws on Banerjee, "Report on Salvage and Relief"; GOG, *Tale of Woe*; Trivedi, "Morbi Flood Disaster"; T. R. Shukla and Ushaben Shukla, interview, December 31, 2005; Interviewee 18; Interviewee 19; Interviewees 37–41; Interviewee 43; Interviewee 44; Interviewees 49–51; Interviewees 54–57; Ratilal Desai and Interviewee 30, interview, July 20, 2006; Bhagvanji Patel, interview, July 21, 2006; Gokaldas Parmar, interview, July 21, 2006; Interviewee 66 and Interviewee 67; Interviewee 68; Interviewee 77; Interviewee 79; Interviewee 80; Interviewee 81; Ratilal Desai, interview, July 25, 2006; Interviewees 111–113; Interviewee 124; and Kanubhai Kubavat, interview, August 12, 2006. It also draws on daily newspaper accounts in the August and September 1979 issues of *Akila* and *Phulchhab* and on photographs from the Prabhakarbhai Khamar Photographs and the Phulchhab Photographic Archives.

10. Interviewee 43.

11. GOG, "Meeting Convened at 4:00 P.M. on 15-8-79."

12. For the Harijan Quarter, see Interviewee 77; and Interviewee 80. For the Leatherworker Quarter, see Interviewees 111–113.

13. Interviewees 37–41.

14. For the Ahmedabad function, see photograph on the front cover of *Phulchhab*, September 17, 1979. For the London function, see "An Indian Dance Program in London for Morbi," *Akila*, September 28, 1979. An announcement of Mother Theresa's visit to Morbi can be found in "Mother Theresa." For personal accounts of interactions with Mother Theresa and the Missionaries of Charity, see T. R. Shukla and Ushaben Shukla, interview, December 31, 2005; Ratilal Desai and Interviewee 30, interview, July 20, 2006; and Ratilal Desai, interview, July 25, 2006.

15. For allegations of corruption, see "Machhu Dam Disaster: Butter and Bananas for the Volunteers in Relief Collection," *Akila*, September 4, 1979. For Babubhai Patel's reaction, see Ushakant Mankad, interview, July 7, 2006.

16. This quote and the previous one from Interviewee 19.

17. Interviewee 18.

18. Gokaldas Parmar, interview, July 21, 2006.

19. Interviewee 68.

20. T. R. Shukla and Ushaben Shukla, interview, December 31, 2005.

21. Kanubhai Kubavat, interview, August 12, 2006.

22. GOG, "Proceedings of Meeting Held on 19.8.1979."

23. Interviewee 66 and Interviewee 67.

24. Ratilal Desai and Interviewee 30, interview, July 20, 2006.

25. This vignette's portrayal of Babubhai Patel's attitudes and late-morning routine in Morbi relies on Patel, *Diaries*, August 16, 1979, to September 9, 1979; Prabhakarbhai Khamar, interview, June 30, 2006; and Prabhakarbhai Khamar, interview, July 4, 2006.

26. Ushakant Mankad, interview, July 7, 2006.

27. Banerjee, "Report on Salvage and Relief," 2.

28. Interviewee 127.

29. This vignette's account of relief provision in Maliya draws on Abdulbhai Mor, interview, August 12, 2006; Husainbhai Manek, interview, August 12, 2006; Jashabhai Samani, interview, August 12, 2006; and Interviewee 141. It also draws on newspaper accounts in the August 1979 issues of *Gujarat Samachar* and the August and September 1979 issues of *Akila* and *Phulchhab*.

30. Husainbhai Manek, interview, August 12, 2006.

31. Abdulbhai Mor, interview, August 12, 2006.

32. Ibid.

33. Ibid.

34. Patel, *Diaries*, August 14, 1979; and GOG, "Meeting Convened at 10:00 A.M. on 16-8-79."

35. Banerjee, "Report on a Tour of Maliya" [inferred title].

36. "Request for Forgiveness of Flood-Affected Farmers' Debts: Presentation Made to Governor on Her Visit to Maliya," *Phulchhab*, September 5, 1979.

37. Jashabhai Samani, interview, August 12, 2006.

38. Ibid.

39. For this vignette, in addition to the below-cited sources, see "Morbi's Startled Populace Is Still Silent," *Phulchhab*, September 1, 1979.

40. T. R. Shukla and Ushaben Shukla, interview, December 31, 2005. For the article on the family's experience during the flood, see "A

Fearsome Cobra Saved the Lives of an Entire Family in the Morbi Flood Disaster," *Gujarat Mitra*, August 30, 1979.

41. Khatijaben Valera, interview, July 25, 2006; and Naseemben Valera, interview, July 25, 2006. Spiritual leader's quote from Khatijaben Valera, interview, July 25, 2006.

42. Bhagvanji Patel, interview, July 21, 2006.

43. Interviewee 52 and Interviewee 53; and Interviewee 71.

44. Kanubhai Kubavat, interview, August 12, 2006.

45. Amrutia, "Notice Under Sec. 80."

46. "A Commission of Inquiry Named to Investigate the Machhu Dam Disaster: Naming of Justice B. K. Mehta; The Report Will Be Received in Six Months: Two Assessors Will Aid," *Phulchhab*, September 11, 1979. For the inquiry commission's notice inviting statements, see Basu, "Public Notice."

47. Dhirubhai Mehta, interview, July 23, 2006.

48. Gangaram Tapu, interview, July 29, 2006.

49. This vignette's account of the relief kitchens and Babubhai Patel's participation in them draws on Patel, *Diaries*, August 16, 1979, to September 9, 1979; Interviewee 10; Prabhakarbhai Khamar, interview, June 30, 2006; Interviewee 18; Prabhakarbhai Khamar, interview, July 4, 2006; Ushakant Mankad, interview, July 7, 2006; Interviewee 34; Interviewee 81; Kanubhai Kubavat, interview, August 12, 2006; and H. K. Khan, interview, August 14, 2006.

50. Interviewee 10.

51. Ibid.

52. Interviewee 81.

53. This vignette's account of Gokaldas Parmar and his family's experiences draws on *Proceedings of the Gujarat Legislative Assembly* 66, no. 2:197–208; Gokaldas Parmar, interview, July 21, 2006; and Gokaldas Parmar and Mrs. Parmar, interview, July 24, 2006.

54. Gokaldas Parmar and Mrs. Parmar, interview, July 24, 2006.

55. Ibid.

56. Ibid.

57. Ibid.

58. This vignette's account of infrastructural recovery and Babubhai Patel's role in it draws on Patel, *Diaries*, August 16, 1979, to September 9, 1979; Interviewee 10; Prabhakarbhai Khamar, interview,

June 30, 2006; Interviewee 18; Prabhakarbhai Khamar, interview, July 4, 2006; and Ushakant Mankad, interview, July 7, 2006. It also draws on daily newspaper accounts in the August and September 1979 issues of *Akila* and *Phulchhab*. For a favorable account of government infrastructural improvements, see GOG, *Tale of Woe*. For some of the controversies surrounding government infrastructural work, see *Proceedings of the Gujarat Legislative Assembly* 66, no. 2:42–83, 171–298, 308–97.

59. For concrete examples of infrastructural advances, see "All of Morbi's Government Offices Are Running Again Starting Today," *Akila*, August 29, 1979; "Growing Electrical Supply in Morbi," *Phulchhab*, September 2, 1979; "Trunk Call Telephone Arrangements in Morbi: Roads Are Ready for 26 Towns," *Phulchhab*, September 3, 1979; and "Cleaning Work in Morbi; Electric Arrangements; Water Arrangements," *Akila*, September 20, 1979.

60. This anecdote from Ushakant Mankad, interview, July 7, 2006.

61. This anecdote from ibid.

62. Guha, *India after Gandhi*, 536–38; "At Last, the Resignation of the Charan Singh Government," *Akila*, August 20, 1979; and "Chief Minister's Decision to Hold Gujarat Legislative Assembly Elections Simultaneously with Parliamentary Elections," *Phulchhab*, September 13, 1979.

63. "More Unfortunate Than Unfortunate," *Jai Hind*, August 26, 1979.

64. "Morvi Death Toll 20,000 Says Solanki," *Western Times*, August 14, 1979.

65. Ibid.

66. "MLA's Doubts over RSS's Role in Morbi," *Times of India*, August 25, 1979.

67. "Collector Says Half of Morvi Population Killed," *Hindustan Times*, August 22, 1979.

68. "Rajkot Collector Collars Irrigation Engineers," *Indian Express*, September 9, 1979.

69. The relevant paragraph is in Banerjee, "Report on the Flood Situation," 7.

70. This vignette's account of Babubhai Patel's evening routine in

Morbi draws on Patel, *Diaries*, August 16, 1979, to September 9, 1979; Prabhakarbhai Khamar, interview, June 30, 2006; and Prabhakarbhai Khamar, interview, July 4, 2006.

Chapter 9: "But Courage and Strength Remain"

1. For Babubhai's exit from Morbi, see Patel, *Diaries*, August 29, 1979, to September 9, 1979.

2. Specific instances of the acrimonious political climate in Gandhinagar may be found in "Madhavsinh Solanki: Dissolution of the Gujarat Legislative Assembly before the 17th," *Phulchhab*, September 2, 1979; "Babubhai's Specification: We Won't Ask for Dissolution before the Legislative Assembly Meets," *Phulchhab*, September 4, 1979; and "Chief Minister's Decision to Hold Gujarat Legislative Assembly Elections Simultaneously with Parliamentary Elections," *Phulchhab*, September 13, 1979.

3. The entirety of the debate may be found in *Proceedings of the Gujarat Legislative Assembly* 66, no. 2:34, 36–42, 42–83, 171–298, 308–97.

4. For a representative example of the controversy over the *sub judice* issue, see ibid., 65–83.

5. Ibid., 182–83.

6. Ibid., 209–13.

7. Ibid., 176–78, 308–19.

8. Ibid., 197–208.

9. Ibid., 173–76. For an account of this speech, see "Government Hit Hard over Machhu Disaster; Asking for Keshubhai's Resignation, Palkhiwala Suggests the Disaster Was Man-made," *Phulchhab*, September 20, 1979.

10. *Proceedings of the Gujarat Legislative Assembly* 66, no. 2:190.

11. Ibid., 293–94.

12. Ibid., 336. For another example of an aggressive line of argument from a Janata leader, see ibid., 189–95.

13. Ibid., 370. For the entirety of Babubhai's statement, see ibid., 360–92.

14. For further information on Diwali, see Raval, *Gujarat State*

Gazetteer: Rajkot District, 154, 157; Trivedi, *Gazetteer of India: Gujarat State Gazetteer*, 1:359–360.

15. "The Chief Minister Will Spend New Year's Day with Morbi's People," *Akila*, October 15, 1979; and Ushakant Mankad, interview, July 7, 2006. Quote from Ushakant Mankad, interview, July 7, 2006.

16. For accounts of the concerns presented to the chief minister, see "After Two Months, a Sad State Persists in Lilapar: A Presentation before the Chief Minister," *Phulchhab*, October 26, 1979; "Twenty Questions That Must Be Addressed Immediately for Morbi: A Presentation before the Chief Minister," *Phulchhab*, October 26, 1979; and "A Presentation for Saving Morbi's Clock Industry: An Open Letter to the Chief Minister," *Phulchhab*, October 27, 1979.

17. For accounts of the day in Lilapar, see Patel, *Diaries*, October 21, 1979; "Sweets Distributed in Lilapar, by the Chief Minister's Hand," *Akila*, October 23, 1979; and "For Diwali, Sweets from the Chief Minister's Hand for Lilapar," *Phulchhab*, October 24, 1979.

18. The account of Babubhai's morning in Morbi, including all quotes, is drawn from "Let Us Strive Mightily to Fill Morbi with Even Greater Grandeur: A Warm Gathering in the Chief Minister's Presence," *Phulchhab*, October 23, 1979. For additional accounts, see Patel, *Diaries*, October 22, 1979; and "The Chief Minister Gives the People of Morbi Patience; Rain Falls and Thunder Sounds," *Akila*, October 22, 1979.

19. This vignette's account of the Machhu Dam-II Inquiry Commission's staffers and activities draws on Bhimjiani, *Government Delays Commission, Denies Justice*; R. A. Mehta, interview, June 24, 2006; B. R. Shah, interview, June 27, 2006; and Dipankar Basu, interview, August 14, 2006.

20. For the formal notice, see Patel, "Notification under Commissions of Inquiry Act (1952)." For more on the powers of the inquiry commission, see Bhaskarbhai Tanna, interview, June 15, 2006.

21. For discussion of the November 11 deadline and its significance, see Bhimjiani, *Government Delays Commission, Denies Justice*, 7.

22. B. R. Shah, interview, June 27, 2006.

23. For the figures in this paragraph and other official tallies of the disaster's toll, see GOG, *Tale of Woe*, 2–8.

24. For the August 31, 1979, milestone, see "Not Even One

Corpse Has Been Found in Morbi City or the Surrounding Rural Area Today," *Phulchhab*, September 1, 1979. For discussion of issues in counting deaths, see Interviewee 30; Interviewee 48; Gokaldas Parmar, interview, July 21, 2006; Interviewee 66 and Interviewee 67; Gokaldas Parmar and Mrs. Parmar, interview, July 24, 2006; and Ratilal Desai, interview, July 25, 2006.

25. For representative examples of the ongoing political debate over the disaster's death toll, see *Proceedings of the Gujarat Legislative Assembly* 66, no. 2:207, 215–16, 229–32, 238–42, 258–69, 314, 341–43, 380; "Certainly Not Less Than Fifteen Thousand Deaths: Chimanbhai's Challenge," *Phulchhab*, August 22, 1979; and "More Unfortunate Than Unfortunate," *Jai Hind*, August 26, 1979.

26. *Proceedings of the Gujarat Legislative Assembly* 66, no. 2:207; and Gokaldas Parmar, interview, July 26, 2006.

27. GOG, *Tale of Woe*, 33; *Proceedings of the Gujarat Legislative Assembly* 66, no. 2:54; and Ratilal Desai, interview, July 25, 2006.

28. MOM, *Book of Deaths Registered*.

29. For discussion of these issues, see Interviewee 30; Interviewee 48; Gokaldas Parmar, interview, July 21, 2006; Interviewee 66 and Interviewee 67; Gokaldas Parmar and Mrs. Parmar, interview, July 24, 2006; and Ratilal Desai, interview, July 25, 2006.

30. The account of Mehta's brother-in-law's experience, including all quotes, is drawn from Interviewee 30; and Ratilal Desai and Interviewee 30, interview, July 20, 2006.

31. Jashabhai Samani, interview, August 12, 2006.

32. Kanubhai Kubavat, interview, August 12, 2006.

33. Interviewee 68; Interviewee 72.

34. Representative government accounts of this process in GOG, *Tale of Woe*, 33; *Proceedings of the Gujarat Legislative Assembly* 66, no. 2:55; and Trivedi, "Morbi Flood Disaster." Representative voluntary organization perspectives in Interviewee 16; Interviewee 18; Interviewee 21, July 7, 2006; and Interviewee 28. Representative homeowner perspectives in Interviewee 52 and Interviewee 53; Interviewee 59; and Interviewee 128. For reconstruction of the railway, see "Morbi–Maliya–Navlakhi Department: A Happy Ending to the Agitation to Restart the Railway," *Akila*, November 19, 1979.

35. Kanubhai Kubavat, interview, August 12, 2006.

36. Khatijaben Valera, interview, July 25, 2006; and Naseemben Valera, interview, July 25, 2006.

37. For accounts of Morbi's commercial recovery, see GOG, *Tale of Woe*, 29; *Proceedings of the Gujarat Legislative Assembly* 66, no. 2:54–55, 57; Trivedi, "Morbi Flood Disaster"; "Morbi's Vegetable Market Restarted," *Akila*, September 26, 1979; "In the Morbi-Maliya Area, Relief Will Be Given for Damaged Vehicles," *Phulchhab*, October 6, 1979; "Editorial: Morbi's Commerce and Banks," *Phulchhab*, October 10, 1979; "Work Instruments Given to Twelve Hundred of Morbi's Flood Affected," *Phulchhab*, October 18, 1979; "Morbi's Merchants Need Loans, Not Aid; If the Problems Are Not Addressed, Merchants Will Agitate: Creation of the Morbi Merchants Association," *Phulchhab*, October 19, 1979; Interviewee 118; Interviewee 120; Interviewee 121 and Interviewee 122; Interviewee 123; Interviewee 127; Interviewee 129; and Interviewee 132 and Interviewee 133. For Dhirubhai Mehta, see Dhirubhai Mehta, interview, July 23, 2006. For movie theaters, see "2 Lakhs of Economic Aid to Morbi's Cinema Houses: Gujarat State Industrial Investment Corporation's Work," *Phulchhab*, November 2, 1979. For T. R. Shukla, see T. R. Shukla and Ushaben Shukla, interview, December 31, 2005. For Kanubhai Kubavat, see Kanubhai Kubavat, interview, August 12, 2006.

38. This vignette's account of the Machhu Dam-II Inquiry Commission's staffers, ongoing activities, and difficulties draws on Bhimjiani, *Government Delays Commission, Denies Justice*; and Dipankar Basu, interview, August 14, 2006.

39. For discussion of this delay and various others in the course of the Machhu Dam-II Inquiry Commission's work, see Bhimjiani, *Government Delays Commission, Denies Justice*.

40. Kothari, "Machhu-2 Dam Disaster."

41. Dipankar Basu, interview, August 14, 2006.

42. Ibid.

43. Information on Murthy from Murthy, "Bio-Data"; and Y. K. Murthy, interview, August 12, 2006.

44. Information on Matthai from Rangarajan, "Obituary: Ravi Matthai."

45. Interviewee 6.

46. GOI, *Statistical Report on General Election, 1980 to the Seventh Lok Sabha*. For further background on the national political climate and the parliamentary elections of 1980, see Guha, *India after Gandhi*, 446–543; and Metcalf and Metcalf, *Concise History of Modern India*, 257–58.

47. Representative examples of the Janata Party's woes may be found in "Protest at Keshubhai Patel's Residence," *Akila*, October 5, 1979; "Chimanbhai Shukla: Asking for Keshubhai's Resignation Is Ridiculous," *Akila*, October 29, 1979; and "Gujarat Chief Minister Babubhai Patel's Ill Health; Unable to Attend the Last Day of the Ongoing Janata Event in Kheda District," *Akila*, November 5, 1979. We have also consulted newspaper accounts from the September and October 1979 daily issues of *Phulchhab* and *Akila* and from the November 1979, December 1979, January 1980, and February 1980 daily issues of *Akila*. For dissolution and presidential rule, see GOG, "Chief Ministers of Gujarat"; and Sanghavi, "Dissolution and After." For more information on the political climate in Gujarat during late 1979 and early 1980, see Kohli, *Democracy and Discontent*, 248–52; and Sanghavi, "Dissolution and After."

48. GOG, "Chief Ministers of Gujarat"; and GOI, *Statistical Report on General Election, 1980 to the Legislative Assembly of Gujarat*.

49. Parmar, *Memorable Events*; and Gokaldas Parmar, interview, July 21, 2006.

50. A. R. Banerjee, interview, August 16, 2006; and A. R. Banerjee, interview, August 18, 2010.

51. Parthasarathy et al., *Before the Machhu Dam-II Inquiry Commission*, 1:1.

52. Bhimjiani, *Government Delays Commission, Denies Justice*, 10.

53. Y. K. Murthy, interview, August 12, 2006.

54. Parthasarathy et al., *Before the Machhu Dam-II Inquiry Commission*, 1:6.

55. Ibid.

56. Ibid., 1:20–21, 126.

57. Ibid., 1:167.

58. Y. K. Murthy, interview, August 12, 2006.

59. Bhimjiani, *Government Delays Commission, Denies Justice*, 9–11.

60. Parthasarathy et al., *Before the Machhu Dam-II Inquiry Commission*, 1:104–54.

61. Ibid., 1:111, 120–22.

62. Abdulbhai Mor, interview, August 12, 2006.

63. "569 of Morbi-Maliya's Industrial Units Closed Because of the Flood," *Phulchhab*, September 27, 1979; and Interviewee 134.

64. "Morbi-Maliya's Industrial Units Will Receive Interest-Free Loans of up to 25 Thousand," *Phulchhab*, September 3, 1979; "Sewing Machines for Morbi and Maliya's Tailors," *Phulchhab*, September 20, 1979; and "Work Instruments Given to Twelve Hundred of Morbi's Flood-Affected," *Phulchhab*, October 18, 1979.

65. Ratilal Desai, interview, July 25, 2006.

66. Bhagvanji Patel, interview, July 21, 2006.

67. Interviewee 31; Interviewee 32; Bhagvanji Patel, interview, July 21, 2006; Interviewees 63–65; Jashabhai Samani, interview, August 12, 2006; and Interviewee 140.

68. For the government compensation scheme, see *Proceedings of the Gujarat Legislative Assembly* 66, no. 2:56. For nongovernmental donations, see "Efforts to Get Farming back on Its Feet in Morbi and Maliya's Villages," *Phulchhab*, September 3, 1979; "Distribution of Seeds in Flood-Affected Towns," *Akila*, Ocober 14, 1979; and "Mumbai's Charitable Organizations Will Send Cows and Oxen for the Morbi Department," *Akila*, October 15, 1979. For government bulldozing of land, see "A Start to the Restoration of Farmland in Morbi Subdistrict," *Akila*, November 7, 1979.

69. Interviewee 31; Interviewee 32; and Interviewees 63–65, July 21, 2006.

70. Interviewees 63–65, July 21, 2006.

71. Interviewee 31; and Interviewee 32.

72. Jashabhai Samani, interview, August 12, 2006.

73. Husainbhai Manek, interview, August 12, 2006.

74. Abdulbhai Mor, interview, August 12, 2006.

75. Harilal, "Statement"; Mohan, "Voluntary Statement"; Patel, "Voluntary Statement"; Trivedi, "Voluntary Statement"; and Rajapara, "Statement."

76. Mohan, "Voluntary Statement"; Trivedi, "Voluntary Statement"; and Rajapara, "Statement."

77. Murthy, *Report on Failure of Machhu Dam-II*, 1:21; and ibid., 2:37–74. The authors corroborated this account by examination of photographs from the Rajkot Ramakrishna Ashrama Photographic Archive.

78. Y. K. Murthy, interview, August 12, 2006. For examples, see Interviewee 31; Interviewees 95–103; Interviewee 104; and Interviewee 99, July 28, 2006.

79. Interviewee 31.

80. Interviewees 95–103; and Interviewee 104.

81. Y. K. Murthy, interview, August 12, 2006.

82. Ibid.

83. Murthy, *Report on Failure of Machhu Dam-II*, 2:37–74.

84. Y. K. Murthy, interview, August 12, 2006.

85. Murthy, *Report on Failure of Machhu Dam-II*, 1:11; and Dipankar Basu, interview, August 14, 2006.

86. For an account of the ongoing delays, see Bhimjiani, *Government Delays Commission, Denies Justice*, 11–13.

87. Bhagvanji Patel, interview, July 21, 2006. For the Ramakrishna Ashrama perspective, see Interviewee 124.

88. Bhagvanji Patel, interview, July 21, 2006.

89. Interviewees 95–103; and Interviewee 104.

90. Interviewee 107.

91. Interviewees 111–113. For the Sadvichar Parivar perspective, see Interviewee 16.

92. GOG, "Correspondence on the Construction and Allotment of Gujarat Housing Board L.I.G.H. and M.I.G.H. Buildings" [inferred title]; GOG "Correspondence on the Construction and Allotment of Gujarat Slum Clearance Board Buildings" [inferred title]; GOG, "Correspondence on the Construction and Allotment of Phulchhab Colony" [inferred title]; T. R. Shukla and Ushaben Shukla, interview, December 31, 2005; Interviewee 21, July 6, 2006; Interviewee 24; Interviewee 29; and Dhirubhai Mehta, interview, July 23, 2006.

93. T. R. Shukla and Ushaben Shukla, interview, December 31, 2005.

94. GOG, "Correspondence on the Construction and Allotment of Gujarat Housing Board L.I.G.H. and M.I.G.H. Buildings"; GOG "Correspondence on the Construction and Allotment of Gujarat Slum Clearance Board Buildings"; GOG, "Correspondence on the Construc-

tion and Allotment of Phulchhab Colony"; GOG, "File on the Distribution of Gujarat Housing Board Buildings" [inferred title]; GOG, "File on the Activities of the Lions Club" [inferred title]; GOG, "File on the Activities of the Rashtriya Swayamsevak Sangh's Flood-Affected Relief Committee" [inferred title]; and Maniyar and Doshi, *Nature's Fury and Destruction*.

95. This vignette's account of the Machhu Dam-II Inquiry Commission's ongoing work draws on Bhimjiani, *Government Delays Commission, Denies Justice*. Its portrayal of Dipankar Basu's attitudes relies on Dipankar Basu, interview, August 14, 2006.

96. Bhimjiani, *Government Delays Commission, Denies Justice*, 12.

97. Ibid.

98. Ibid., 12–13.

99. Bhimjiani, *Government Delays Commission, Denies Justice*, 13–14; Verghese, "Something to Hide?"; and Manubhai Shah, interview, June 24, 2006.

100. Manubhai Shah, interview, June 24, 2006.

101. Dipankar Basu, interview, August 14, 2006.

102. Bhimjiani, *Government Delays Commission, Denies Justice*, 12.

103. This vignette's account of the memorial ceremony draws on "In Remembrance of Those Lost in Machhu Disaster: Today Will Be a Day of Mourning in the Morbi-Maliya Area," *Phulchhab*, August 11, 1980; Ratilal Desai and Interviewee 30, interview, July 20, 2006; and Ratilal Desai, interview, July 25, 2006. It also draws on photographs from the Ratilal Desai Photographs.

104. For perspectives on the return to normalcy, and on the first anniversary as a milestone, see Interviewee 34; Interviewees 37–41; Interviewee 47; Interviewee 48; Interviewee 52 and Interviewee 53; Interviewee 106; Khatijaben Valera, interview, July 25, 2006; Interviewee 107; Pratapbhai Adroja, interview, August 3, 2006; Kanubhai Kubavat, interview, August 12, 2006; and H. K. Khan, interview, August 14 2006.

Chapter 10: "Justice Was Not Done"

1. For an overview of the process, see Bhimjiani, *Government Delays Commission, Denies Justice*.

2. Ibid.; and Rahul Bhimjiani, interview, June 7, 2006.

3. Dipankar Basu, interview, August 14, 2006.

4. Y. K. Murthy, interview, August 12, 2006.

5. This portrayal relies on "Morvi Town up in Arms: Probe Panel Issue," *Times of India*, April 24, 1981; and photographs from the Ratilal Desai Papers.

6. "Morbi's City Hall Opposes the Decision to Wind up the Machhu Dam Commission of Inquiry," *Phulchhab*, March 23, 1981; "Morvi Town up in Arms: Probe Panel Issue," *Times of India*, April 24, 1981; and "A Small Town Seeks Justice," *Indian Express*, August 30, 1981.

7. "Morvi Town up in Arms: Probe Panel Issue," *Times of India*, April 24, 1981.

8. Oza, letter to Sanatbhai Mehta.

9. "Morvi Town up in Arms: Probe Panel Issue," *Times of India*, April 24, 1981.

10. Oza, letter to Sanatbhai Mehta.

11. Tanna, "Machhu Ado about Nothing?"; and Manubhai Shah, interview, June 24, 2006.

12. "A Small Town Seeks Justice," *Indian Express*, August 30, 1981; and Manubhai Shah, interview, June 24, 2006.

13. Bhimjiani, *Government Delays Commission, Denies Justice*. For the report, see Murthy, *Report on Failure of Machhu Dam-II*, 2:37–74.

14. Shah, "Government Privilege Claim Rejected"; Manubhai Shah, interview, June 24, 2006; and Dipankar Basu, interview, August 14, 2006.

15. Tanna, "Machhu Ado about Nothing?"

16. GOI, "Commissions of Inquiry Act"; and Manubhai Shah, interview, June 24, 2006.

17. Tanna, "Machhu Ado about Nothing?"; and Shah, "Winding up Machhu Enquiry Commission Quashed."

18. This vignette's account of Dhirubhai Mehta's attitudes draws on Dhirubhai Mehta, interview, July 23, 2006.

19. Ibid.

20. Mehta, "A Protest"; and Mehta, "List: Put in the Mail." For the ultimate futility of Mehta's quest, see Desai, letter to Dhirubhai Mehta; Paswan, letter to Dhirubhai Mehta; Private secretary to the prime minister, letter to Dhirubhai Mehta; and Roy, letter to Dhirubhai Mehta.

21. "Was the Machhu Dam-II Built on the Basis of Only Three Years of Rain and Storm Data?" *Sandesh*, May 31, 1981.

22. "After Dam Breaks, Go to a Technical Committee before Creating a Judicial Inquiry: President Mistry's Request at the Engineers Conference," *Sandesh*, June 1, 1981.

23. Mehta, "Letter to the Editor."

24. Shah, "Winding up Machhu Enquiry Commission Quashed."

25. Ibid., 6–7.

26. Ibid., 9.

27. "Consumer Education & Research Centre & Ors.," 713.

28. Tanna, "Machhu Ado about Nothing?"

29. Ibid.; and Manubhai Shah, interview, June 24, 2006.

30. "Consumer Education & Research Centre & Ors.," 714–16.

31. Shah, letter to Dhirubhai Mehta.

32. "State of Gujarat v. Consumer & Education Research Centre and Ors.," 492.

33. Cullet, *Sardar Sarovar Dam Project*, 1–76, 82–93; Fisher, *Toward Sustainable Development?*; and Khagram, *Dams and Development*, 65–100.

34. Mistry, "Submission of the Plans."

35. "A Small Town Seeks Justice," *Indian Express*, August 30, 1981.

36. For the first consultant's visit to the dam site, see Purohit, "Notes regarding the Visit of Mr. P. M. Mane." For the second consultant's visit, see Mane, "Panel of Experts to Review the Designs of Machhu-2 Dam: Notes of Discussion regarding Machhu-2 Dam—Vadodara, 13th July, 1982." For subsequent meetings, see Mane, "Decisions Taken about the Spillway Capacity"; Mane, "Panel of Experts to Review the Designs of Machhu-II Dam: Note of Discussions at the Meeting Held at Bombay on 9.10.1982"; and Mane, "Panel of Experts to Review the Designs of Machhu Dam.II. Note of Discussions at the Meeting Held at Rajkot on 7/6/1983."

37. Interviewee 145. For examples of Vasoya's involvement, see Mane, "Decisions Taken about the Spillway Capacity"; Mane, "Panel of Experts to Review the Designs of Machhu-II Dam: Note of Discussions at the Meeting Held at Bombay on 9.10.1982"; and Mane, "Panel of Experts to Review the Designs of Machhu Dam.II: Note of Discussions at the Meeting Held at Rajkot on 7/6/1983."

38. Mane, "Panel of Experts to Review the Designs of Machhu-2 Dam: Notes of Discussion regarding Machhu-2 Dam—Vadodara, 13th July, 1982"; Mane, "Panel of Experts to Review the Designs of Machhu-II Dam: Note of Discussions at the Meeting Held at Bombay on 9.10.1982"; and Interviewee 20.

39. Mane, "Panel of Experts to Review the Designs of Machhu-II Dam: Note of Discussions at the Meeting Held at Bombay on 9.10.1982"; and Mane, "Panel of Experts to Review the Designs of Machhu Dam.II: Note of Discussions at the Meeting Held at Rajkot on 7/6/1983." Quote from Mane, "Panel of Experts to Review the Designs of Machhu-II Dam: Note of Discussions at the Meeting Held at Bombay on 9.10.1982."

40. Mane, "Decisions Taken about the Spillway Capacity." For speculation on the issue of cost-benefit ratio, see Y. K. Murthy, interview, August 12, 2006.

41. For Tapu, see Gangaram Tapu, interview, July 29, 2006. For Adroja, see Prataphbhai Adroja, interview, August 3, 2006. For Desai, Ratilal Desai and Interviewee 30, interview, July 20, 2006; and Ratilal Desai, interview, July 25, 2006. For Parmar, see Gokaldas Parmar, interview, July 21, 2006. For Bhagvanji, see Bhagvanji Patel, interview, July 21, 2006. For Shukla, see T. R. Shukla and Ushaben Shukla, interview, December 31, 2005.

42. For Banerjee, see A. R. Banerjee, interview, August 16, 2006; and A. R. Banerjee, interview, August 18, 2010. For Khan, see H. K. Khan, interview, August 14, 2006. For Mankad, see Ushakant Mankad, interview, July 7, 2006. For Babubhai, see GOI, *Statistical Report on General Election, 1985 to the Legislative Assembly of Gujarat*; Prabhakarbhai Khamar, interview, June 30, 2006; and Prabhakarbhai Khamar, interview, July 4, 2006.

43. Kanubhai Kubavat, interview, August 12, 2006.

44. Khatijaben Valera, interview, July 25, 2006.

45. Husainbhai Manek, interview, August 12, 2006.

46. Abdulbhai Mor, interview, August 12, 2006.

47. Jashabhi Samani, interview, August 12, 2006.

48. R. A. Mehta, interview, June 24, 2006; and B. R. Shah, interview, July 27, 2006. Quote from B. R. Shah, interview, July 27, 2006.

49. Bhaskarbhai Tanna, interview, June 15, 2006; and R. A. Mehta, interview, June 24, 2006.

50. For one example of such public interest in the court's decision, see "A Small Town Seeks Justice," *Indian Express*, August 30, 1981.

51. "State of Gujarat v. Consumer & Education Research Centre and Ors.," 483.

52. Murthy, *Report on Failure of Machhu Dam-II*.

53. Y. K. Murthy, interview, August 12, 2006.

54. For examples, see R. A. Mehta, interview, June 24, 2006; B. R. Shah, interview, June 27, 2006; and Dipankar Basu, interview, August 14, 2006.

55. Murthy, *Report on Failure of Machhu Dam-II*, 1:7–10, 34–36, 45, 65–66. For the full text of the study that informed this conclusion, see ibid., 2:9–18.

56. Ibid., 1:10–12, 31–32, 38–40, 47, 66; and ibid., 2:19–35. Quotes from ibid., 2:31. For the full text of the Roorkee soil study, see ibid., 2:19–35.

57. Ibid., 1:31–32.

58. Ibid., 1:70.

59. For the government's figures, see Parthasarathy et al., *Before the Machhu Dam-II Inquiry Commission*, 1:126. For Murthy's figures, see Murthy, *Report on Failure of Machhu Dam-II*, 1:52. For the report informing Murthy's figures, see ibid., 2:85–182.

60. For the report of the gate tests, see ibid., 2:37–74.

61. Ibid., 1:64.

62. Interviewees 49–51.

63. Interviewee 43.

64. Ratilal Desai, interview, July 24, 2006.

65. For failure to operate gates in a timely fashion, see Ratilal Desai and Interviewee 30, interview, July 20, 2006; and Bhagvanji Patel, interview, July 21, 2006. For abandonment, see T. R. Shukla and Ushaben Shukla, interview, December 31, 2005; Interviewee 4; Interviewee 26; and Interviewee 126. For negligence, see Gokaldas Parmar, interview, July 21, 2006.

66. Ratilal Desai and Interviewee 30, interview, July 20, 2006.

67. R. A. Mehta, interview, June 24, 2006.

68. Gokaldas Parmar, interview, July 21, 2006.

69. Abdulbhai Mor, interview, August 12, 2006. Many other interviewees espoused this theory.

70. For the text of the appraisal report, see Saldanha and Mane, "Appraisal Report." For records of the meetings held, see Mane,

"Decisions Taken about the Spillway Capacity"; Mane, "Panel of Experts to Review the Designs of Machhu-2 Dam: Notes of Discussion regarding Machhu-2 Dam—Vadodara, 13th July, 1982"; Mane, "Panel of Experts to Review the Designs of Machhu-II Dam: Note of Discussions at the Meeting Held at Bombay on 9.10.1982"; Mane, "Panel of Experts to Review the Designs of Machhu Dam.II: Note of Discussions at the Meeting Held at Rajkot on 7/6/1983"; Purohit, "Notes regarding the Visit of Mr. P. M. Mane"; Saldanha and Mane, "Minutes of the Meeting for machhu-II Dam Held by the Consultants on 8.8.1984 at Gandhinagar"; Saldanha and Mane, "Minutes of the Meeting for Machhu-II Dam Held by the Consultants on 29/11/1983 at Vadodara"; and Saldanha and Mane, "Notes of Consultants for the Machhu-II Dam During Visit to the Hydraulic Model at GERI on 13-3-1985." For the revision of the design flood, see Saldanha and Mane, "Appraisal Report"; and Interviewee 20. For the scale replica, see Saldanha and Mane, "Notes of Consultants for the Machhu-II Dam During Visit to the Hydraulic Model at GERI on 13-3-1985."

71. For the ongoing disagreement, see Mane, "Panel of Experts to Review the Designs of Machhu-II Dam: Note of Discussions at the Meeting Held at Bombay on 9.10.1982"; and Mane, "Panel of Experts to Review the Designs of Machhu Dam.II: Note of Discussions at the Meeting Held at Rajkot on 7/6/1983." Quote from Mane, "Decisions Taken about the Spillway Capacity."

72. Ibid.

73. Saldanha and Mane, "Appraisal Report."

74. Y. K. Murthy, interview, August 12, 2006.

75. Interviewee 145.

76. Interviewee 20.

77. Interviewee 119.

78. Interviewee 87 and Interviewee 88.

79. Interviewee 25, July 23, 2006; Gokaldas Parmar, interview, July 26, 2006; and Interviewee 134.

80. GOG, *Tale of Woe*, 23–29; *Proceedings of the Gujarat Legislative Assembly* 66, no. 2:57–59; Interviewee 19; Interviewee 25, July 23, 2006; and Interviewee 134.

81. Interviewee 25, July 22, 2006; Interviewee 25, July 23, 2006; and Gokaldas Parmar, interview, July 26, 2006. Quote from "Ceramic Tile Makers Look to Middle East," *Economic Times*, September 16, 2006.

82. Interviewee 25, July 23, 2006; Bhagvanji Patel, interview, July 21, 2006; and Interviewees 95–103.

83. For women, see "Where Women Have the Time of Their Lives," *Hindu Business Line*, January 2, 2004; and Gokaldas Parmar, interview, July 26, 2006. For Satwaras, see Interviewee 87 and Interviewee 88; and Gokaldas Parmar, interview, July 26, 2006. For Harijans and other members of low-status jatis, see Interviewee 75; and Interviewees 95–103. For a recent view of Morbi's industry, see "In a New India, an Old Industry Buoys Peasants," *New York Times*, June 3, 2007.

84. For examples of the new neighborhoods, see GOG, "Correspondence on the Construction and Allotment of Gujarat Housing Board L.I.G.H. and M.I.G.H. Buildings" [inferred title]; GOG, "Correspondence on the Construction and Allotment of Gujarat Slum Clearance Board Buildings" [inferred title]; GOG, "Correspondence on the Construction and Allotment of Phulchhab Colony" [inferred title]; GOG, "File on the Distribution of Gujarat Housing Board Buildings" [inferred title]; GOG, "File on the Activities of the Lions Club" [inferred title]; and GOG, "File on the Activities of the Rashtriya Swayamsevak Sangh's Flood-Affected Relief Committee" [inferred title].

85. Interviewee 29; Interviewee 70; Interviewee 71; Gokaldas Parmar and Mrs. Parmar, interview, July 24, 2006; Interviewee 106; and Interviewee 124.

86. Interviewee 25, July 23, 2006; and Ratilal Desai, interview, July 25, 2006.

87. For examples of social dynamics in flux, see GOG, "Correspondence on the Construction and Allotment of Gujarat Housing Board L.I.G.H. and M.I.G.H. Buildings"; GOG "Correspondence on the Construction and Allotment of Gujarat Slum Clearance Board Buildings"; GOG, "Correspondence on the Construction and Allotment of Phulchhab Colony"; GOG, "File on the Distribution of Gujarat Housing Board Buildings"; GOG, "File on the Activities of the Lions Club"; GOG, "File on the Activities of the Rashtriya Swayamsevak Sangh's Flood-Affected Relief Committee; and Interviewee 71.

88. This vignette's account of the events of February 9, 1990, draws on Patel, *Diaries*, February 9, 1990.

89. For Babubhai's return to Morbi on August 11, 1981, see Patel, *Diaries*, August 11, 1981.

90. For the 1985 election, see GOI, *Statistical Report on General*

Election, 1985 to the Legislative Assembly of Gujarat. For the interaction with Parmar, see Gokaldas Parmar, interview, July 21, 2006.

91. This conversation is drawn from ibid.

92. Ratilal Desai and Interviewee 30, interview, July 20, 2006.

93. Gokaldas Parmar, interview, July 21, 2006.

94. Patel, *Diaries*, February 9, 1990, to February 27, 1990; Ratilal Desai and Interviewee 30, interview, July 20, 2006; and Gokaldas Parmar, interview, July 21, 2006.

95. GOI, *Statistical Report on General Election, 1990 to the Legislative Assembly of Gujarat*; and Patel, *Diaries*, March 4, 1990.

96. Patel, *Diaries*, August 11, 1990.

Epilogue: "Can Any Page of History Be Forgotten?"

1. For more on the 2001 earthquake, see Mistry, Dong, and Shah, "Interdisciplinary Observations"; and Reddy, *Pain and Horror.*

2. "Life for BJP Morbi MLA in Murder Case," *Indian Express,* August 24, 2004.

3. "Poll-Time Gift: HC Acquits Amrutiya in Murder Case," *Indian Express,* October 26, 2007; and "Morbi MLA Acquitted in Murder Case," *Times of India,* October 26, 2007.

4. Interviewees 95–103.

5. Abdulbhai Mor, interview, August 12, 2006.

6. GOG, "Shri Madhavsinh Fulsinh Solanki."

7. "At Eighty-Three, an Ardent Pro-Narmada Activist," *Times of India,* July 19, 1993.

8. Pandit et al., *Leader of Rock-Hard Principles.*

9. GOG, "Chief Ministers of Gujarat." For glimpses of key moments in Keshubhai's career as Chief Minister, see Dasgupta, "Is Keshubhai up to It?"; Mahurkar, "Man Overboard"; and Mahurkar, "Sweet Revenge."

10. For one account that considers the various aspects of Modi's character, see Kaplan, "India's New Face."

11. A. R. Banerjee, interview, August 18, 2010.

12. Shah, "Twenty-Fifth Anniversary."

13. Interviewee 120.

BIBLIOGRAPHY

Aaspaas. "Special Edition: Becoming Death, the Machhu Attacks Morbi." [In Gujarati.] Special issue, *Aaspaas* 31 (1979).

Amrutia, P. M. "Notice under Sec. 80 of the Code of Civil Procedure: Failure of Dam Machchoo-2, Claim Arising From." Letter to Secretary, Government of Gujarat. Morbi, August 5, 1980. Dhirubhai Mehta Papers.

Appadorai, Arjun. "Recent Socialist Thought in India." *Review of Politics* 30 (1968): 349–62.

Arora, Ramesh Kumar, and Rajni Goyal. *Indian Public Administration: Institutions and Issues.* New Delhi: Wishwa Prakashan, 1995.

Baboo, Balgovind. "Politics of Water: The Case of the Hirakud Dam in Orissa, India." *International Journal of Sociology and Anthropology* 1, no. 18 (2009): 139–44.

———. "State Policies and People's Response: Lessons from Hirakud Dam." *Economic and Political Weekly*, October 12, 1991, 3273–79.

———. *Technology and Social Transformation: The Case of the Hirakud Multipurpose Dam in Orissa.* Delhi: Concept, 1992.

Bajaj, A. K. *National Register of Large Dams 2009.* New Delhi: Central Water Commission (Government of India), 2009. http://www.cwc.nic.in/main/downloads/National%20Register%20of%20Large%20Dams%202009.pdf.

Banerjee, A. R. "Regarding Distribution of Work." Rajkot: Revenue Department (Government of Gujarat), 1979. A. R. Banerjee Papers.

———. "Regarding the Coordination of Relief." [Inferred title.] Rajkot: Revenue Department (Government of Gujarat), 1979. A. R. Banerjee Papers.

———. "Report of the Happenings Since Early Morning of 12.8.79" [Draft]. Rajkot: Revenue Department (Government of Gujarat), 1979. A. R. Banerjee Papers.

———. "Report on a Tour of Maliya and the Surrounding Areas, 22-8-1979." [Inferred title.] Rajkot: Revenue Department (Government of Gujarat), August 22, 1979. A. R. Banerjee Papers.

———. "A Report on Salvage and Relief Operations at Morvi and

Maliya from 12.8.79 and Onwards." Rajkot: Revenue Department (Government of Gujarat), September 3, 1979. A. R. Banerjee Papers.

———. "Report on the Casualties Occurred Due to Heavy Rains and Floods in Morvi of Rajkot District on 11th Aug. 1979." Rajkot: Revenue Department (Government of Gujarat), 1979. A. R. Banerjee Papers.

———. "Report on the Flood Situation at Rajkot Between 10th and 12th Aug. 79." [Parts in Gujarati.] Rajkot: Revenue Department (Government of Gujarat), 1979. A. R. Banerjee Papers and Rajkot Collectorate Papers.

Basu, Dipankar. "Public Notice: Machhu Dam-II Inquiry Commission." Ahmedabad: 1979. Rajkot Irrigation Circle Papers.

Béteille, André. *Caste, Class, and Power: Changing Patterns of Stratification in a Tanjore Village.* Berkeley: University of California Press, 1971.

Bhandari, R. R. *Western Railway Metre Gauge System.* Bombay: Western Railway Printing Press, 1987.

Bhimjiani, Rahul. *Government Delays Commission, Denies Justice.* Ahmedabad: Consumer Education and Research Centre, 1981. Consumer Education and Research Centre Library.

Bor, Joep, ed. *The Raga Guide.* Monmouth: Wyastone Estate, 1999.

Bryant, Edwin F., trans. *Krishna: The Beautiful Legend of God (Srimad Bhagavata Purana Book X).* New York: Penguin Books, 2004.

Central Intelligence Agency (CIA). "Sri Lanka." *The CIA World Factbook 2009.* Central Intelligence Agency, 2009. https://www.cia.gov/library/publications/the-world-factbook/geos/ce.html.

Chatterjee, S. K. *Indian Calendric System.* New Delhi: Ministry of Information and Broadcasting (Government of India), 1998.

Chhaya, R. S, ed. *Census 1981, Gujarat: District Census Handbook, Rajkot District.* New Delhi: Government of India, 1981.

Chitaliya, K. K., ed. *Morbi Coronation Issue.* Special issue, *Jaybharat Magazine* 11 ([1950?]). Morbi Royal Family Papers.

"Consumer Education & Research Centre & Ors. v. State of Gujarat & Ors." *Gujarat Law Reporter* 22 (1981): 712–72. Gujarat High Court, June 23, 1981.

Crooke, William, and Reginald Edward Enthoven. *Religion and Folklore of Northern India.* Oxford University Press, 1926.

Cullet, Philippe, ed. *The Sardar Sarovar Dam Project: Selected Documents*. Aldershot: Ashgate Publishing, 2007.

Dasgupta, Swapan. "Is Keshubhai up to It?" *India Today*, February 12, 2001.

Dave, Mahendra. *The Glory of Morbi*. [In Gujarati.] Morbi: Gujarat State Cultural Museum, 1972. Morbi Flood Museum Library.

———. *A History of Morbi State*. [In Gujarati.] Morbi: Morbi Royal Family, 2006. Morbi Royal Family Papers.

Dave, S. S. "Regarding the Flooding in Morbi on 11-8-79." [In Gujarati.] Morbi: Revenue Department (Government of Gujarat), August 12, 1979. In *Before the Machhu Dam-II Inquiry Commission: The Statement of Facts and Opinions* by R. Parthasarathy, C. S. S. Rao, K. V. Bhanujan, and R. B. Sudiwala, 2:118–19. Gandhinagar: Government of Gujarat, 1980. Central Designs Organization Papers and Morbi Flood Museum Library.

———. "Report on Flooding and Evacuations." [In Gujarati.] Morbi: Revenue Department (Government of Gujarat), 1979. In "Report on the Flood Situation at Rajkot Between 10th and 12th Aug. 79" by A. R. Banerjee, 20–22. Rajkot: Revenue Department (Government of Gujarat), 1979. A. R. Banerjee Papers.

Dennis, Arnett S. *Weather Modification by Cloud Seeding*. New York: Academic Press, 1980.

Desai, Morarji. Letter to Dhirubhai Mehta. New Delhi, May 7, 1981. Dhirubhai Mehta Papers.

Dhar, O. N., P. R. Rakhecha, B. N. Mandal, and R. B. Sangam. "The Rainstorm Which Caused the Morvi Dam Disaster in August 1979." *Hydrological Sciences Bulletin* 26, no. 1 (1981): 71–81.

Doctor, C. C., ed. *Census 1971, Gujarat: District Census Handbook, Rajkot District*. Ahmedabad: Government of Gujarat, 1972.

Erbisti, Paulo C. *Design of Hydraulic Gates*. Lisse: Swets & Zeitlinger, 2004.

Fisher, William F., ed. *Toward Sustainable Development? Struggling over India's Narmada River*. Armonk: M. E. Sharpe, 1995.

Gandhi, Rajmohan. *Patel: A Life*. Ahmedabad: Navajivan Publishing House, 1990.

Ghurye, G. S. "Features of the Caste System." In *Social Stratification*, edited by D. Gupta, 35–48. New York: Oxford University Press, 1992.

Gokhale, Namita. *The Book of Shiva*. New York: Penguin, 2010.

Gopalan, Gopalan V. "Vrat: Ceremonial Vows of Women in Gujarat." *Asian Folklore Studies* 37, no. 1 (1978): 101–29.

Government of Gujarat (GOG). "Annual Administrative Report on Natural Disasters for the Year 1979." [In Gujarati.] Gandhinagar: Revenue Department (Government of Gujarat), 1986. Revenue Department Papers.

———. "Chief Ministers of Gujarat." Gujarat Legislative Assembly (Government of Gujarat). http://www.gujaratassembly.gov.in/pastcm.htm.

———. "Correspondence on the Construction and Allotment of Gujarat Housing Board L.I.G.H. and M.I.G.H. Buildings." [Inferred title. Parts in Gujarati.] Morbi: Revenue Department (Government of Gujarat), [1990?]. Mani Mandir Archives.

———. "Correspondence on the Construction and Allotment of Gujarat Slum Clearance Board Buildings." [Inferred title. Parts in Gujarati.] Morbi: Revenue Department (Government of Gujarat), [1986?]. Mani Mandir Archives.

———. "Correspondence on the Construction and Allotment of Phulchhab Colony." [Inferred title. Parts in Gujarati.] Morbi: Revenue Department (Government of Gujarat), [1984?]. Mani Mandir Archives.

———. *Detailed Notes on the Operation of the 18 30 × 20 Steel Gates on the Machhu-II Irrigation Dam*. [In Gujarati.] Gandhinagar: Public Works Department (Government of Gujarat), 1973. Rajkot Irrigation Circle Papers.

———. "A Detailed Report on the Breaches in the Earthworks of the Machhu-II Dam on 11-8-79." [In Gujarati.] Rajkot: Irrigation Department (Government of Gujarat), 1979. Rajkot Irrigation Circle Papers.

———. "Details of Happenings from 10.8.1979." Rajkot: Revenue Department (Government of Gujarat), 1979. Rajkot Collectorate Papers.

———. "File on Relief and Other Details." [Parts in Gujarati.] Morbi: Revenue Department (Government of Gujarat), 1985. Mani Mandir Archives.

———. "File on the Activities of the Lions Club." [Inferred title. Parts in Gujarati.] Morbi: Revenue Department (Government of Gujarat), [1985?]. Mani Mandir Archives.

———. "File on the Activities of the Rashtriya Swayamsevak Sangh's Flood-Affected Relief Committee." [Inferred title. In Gujarati.] Morbi: Revenue Department (Government of Gujarat), [1986?]. Mani Mandir Archives.

———. "File on the Distribution of Gujarat Housing Board Buildings." [Inferred title. Parts in Gujarati.] Morbi: Revenue Department (Government of Gujarat), 1985. Mani Mandir Archives.

———. "Machhu Irrigation Project-II: Compliance Report on Preliminary Comments of Central Water and Power Commission." Ahmedabad: Central Designs Organization (Government of Gujarat), 1962. Rajkot Irrigation Circle Papers.

———. "Memorandum to the Central Team regarding Floods, 1979." Gandhinagar: Government of Gujarat, 1979. Revenue Department Papers.

———. "NK-01/08 R 2EQ1 DID082130." Morbi: Irrigation Department (Government of Gujarat), 1979. Rajkot Irrigation Circle Papers.

———. "Notes on the Suggestions Made During the Voluntary Planning Meeting of Leading Citizens and Organizations in the Rajkot Collectorate Meeting Room." [In Gujarati.] Rajkot: Revenue Department (Government of Gujarat), August 18, 1979. A. R. Banerjee Papers.

———. "Proceedings of Meeting Held on 19.8.1979." Morbi: Revenue Department (Government of Gujarat), August 19, 1979. A. R. Banerjee Papers.

———. "Proceedings of the Meeting Convened at 10:00 A.M. on 16-8-79 by the Hon. Revenue Minister to Discuss the Undertaking of Work on a War Footing for the Disaster Befalling the City of Morbi after Dam Failure." [In Gujarati.] Morbi: Revenue Department (Government of Gujarat), 1979. A. R. Banerjee Papers.

———. "Proceedings of the Meeting Convened at 4:00 P.M. on 15-8-79 by the Hon. Revenue Minister to Discuss the Undertaking of Work on a War Footing for the Disaster Befalling the City of Morbi after Dam Failure." [In Gujarati.] Morbi: Revenue Department (Government of Gujarat), August 15, 1979. A. R. Banerjee Papers.

————. "Proceedings of the Meeting Convened at 4:00 P.M. on 16-8-79 by the Hon. Revenue Minister to Discuss the Disaster Befalling the City of Morbi after Dam Failure." [In Gujarati.] Morbi: Revenue Department (Government of Gujarat), 1979. A. R. Banerjee Papers.

————. "Radio Announcement Made over All-India Radio [Akash-vani], Rajkot on 11 August 1979." Rajkot: Revenue Department (Government of Gujarat), 1979. Rajkot Irrigation Circle Papers.

————. "Shri Babubhai Jashbhai Patel." Gujarat Information Bureau (Government of Gujarat). http://www.gujaratinformation.net/gallery/Chief_Minister/Babubhai.htm.

————. "Shri Keshubhai Patel." Gujarat Information Bureau (Government of Gujarat). http://www.gujaratinformation.net/gallery/Chief_Minister/Keshubhai.htm.

————. "Shri Madhavsinh Fulsinh Solanki." Gujarat Information Bureau (Government of Gujarat). http://www.gujaratinformation.net/gallery/Chief_Minister/Madhavsinh.htm.

————. *A Tale of Woe in Morvi*. Gandhinagar: Directorate of Information (Government of Gujarat), 1979.

Government of India (GOI). "The Commissions of Inquiry Act." New Delhi: Parliament (Government of India), August 14, 1952.

————. *Statistical Report on General Election, 1980 to the Legislative Assembly of Gujarat*. New Delhi: Election Commission of India (Government of India). http://eci.gov.in/eci_main/Statistical Reports/SE_1980/Statistical%20Report%201980%20Gujarat.pdf.

————. *Statistical Report on General Election, 1980 to the Seventh Lok Sabha*. Vol. 2, *Constituency Data, Summary*. New Delhi: Election Commission of India (Government of India). http://eci.nic.in/eci_main/StatisticalReports/LS_1980/Vol_II_LS_80.pdf.

————. *Statistical Report on General Election,1985 to the Legislative Assembly of Gujarat*. New Delhi: Election Commission of India (Government of India). http://eci.nic.in/eci_main/StatisticalReports/SE_1985/Statistical%20Report%20Gujarat%201985.pdf.

————. *Statistical Report on General Election, 1990 to the Legislative Assembly of Gujarat*. New Delhi: Election Commission of India (Government of India). http://eci.nic.in/eci_main/StatisticalReports/SE_1990/StatRep_GJ_90.pdf.

Guha, Ramachandra. *India after Gandhi: The History of the World's Largest Democracy*. New York: Harper, 2008.

Gupta, Ram S. *Hydrology and Hydraulic Systems*. Long Grove: Waveland Press, 2008.

Haberman, David. *Journey through the Twelve Forests*. New York: Oxford University Press, 1994.

Harilal. "Statement." [In Gujarati.] Rajkot: Irrigation Department (Government of Gujarat), August 23, 1979. Rajkot Irrigation Circle Papers.

Hartford, Desmond N. D., and Gregory B. Baecher. *Risk and Uncertainty in Dam Safety*. London: Thomas Telford Books, 2004.

Jathal, M. N. "Administrative Approval to the Machhu-II Irrigation Project: Correspondence Resting with Government Letter No. IPM 2364-K Dt. 21-5-64." Ahmedabad: Central Designs Organization (Government of Gujarat), 1964. Rajkot Irrigation Circle Papers.

Joshi, G. J. "Voluntarily Given Statement." [In Gujarati.] Rajkot: Irrigation Department (Government of Gujarat), August 23, 1979. Rajkot Irrigation Circle Papers.

Kaplan, Robert. "India's New Face." *Atlantic Monthly*, April 2009.

Khagram, Sanjeev. *Dams and Development: Transnational Struggles for Water and Power*. Ithaca: Cornell University Press, 2004.

Kohli, Atul. *Democracy and Discontent: India's Growing Crisis of Governability*. New York: Cambridge University Press, 1990.

Kothari, V. M. "Machhu-2 Dam Disaster: Appointment of Judicial Inquiry Commission." Letter to Chief Engineer (I) and Joint Secretary, Department of Irrigation (Government of Gujarat). Rajkot: Irrigation Department (Government of Gujarat) October 17, 1979. Rajkot Irrigation Circle Papers.

———. "The Superintending Engineer's Report on the Period of Extremely Heavy Rain from 9-8-1979 to 12-8-1979." [In Gujarati.] Rajkot: Irrigation Department (Government of Gujarat), 1979. Rajkot Irrigation Circle Papers.

Maheshwari, S. R. "Indian Administrative Service." In *Indian Administration*, 6th ed., 315–21. New Delhi: Orient Longman, 2004.

Mahurkar, Uday. "Man Overboard." *India Today*, October 15, 2001.

———. "Sweet Revenge." *India Today*, March 16, 1998.

Mandelbaum, David Goodman. *Society in India: Continuity and Change*. Berkeley: University of California Press, 1970.

Mane, P. M. "Decisions Taken about the Spillway Capacity of Machhu Dam-II and Relevant Design Aspects at the Meeting of the Panel of

Experts with the Officers of the Govt. of Gujarat, at Bombay on 16.9.1983." Gandhinagar: Central Designs Organization (Government of Gujarat), 1983. Central Designs Organization Papers.

———. "Panel of Experts to Review the Designs of Machhu Dam.II: Note of Discussions at the Meeting Held at Rajkot on 7/6/1983 for Machhu Dam.II." Gandhinagar: Central Designs Organization (Government of Gujarat), August 9, 1983. Central Designs Organization Papers.

———. "Panel of Experts to Review the Designs of Machhu-II Dam: Notes of Discussions at the Meeting Held at Bombay on 9.10.1982 for Machhu-II Dam." Gandhinagar: Central Designs Organization (Government of Gujarat), November 6, 1982. Central Designs Organization Papers.

———. "Panel of Experts to Review the Designs of Machhu-2 Dam: Notes of Discussions regarding Machhu-2 Dam—Vadodara, 13th July, 1982." Gandhinagar: Central Designs Organization (Government of Gujarat), July 17, 1982. Central Designs Organization Papers.

Maniyar, Pravin, and P. V. Doshi. *Nature's Fury and Destruction: Striving and Rehabilitation*. [In Gujarati.] Ahmedabad: Rashtriya Swayamsevak Sangh, 1980.

McAllister, Bruce. *DC-3: A Legend in Her Time; A 75th Anniversary Photographic Tribute*. Boulder: Roundup Press, 2009.

Mehta, A. C. "The Deputy Engineer's Report on His Activities from 10-8-79 to 12-8-79." [In Gujarati.] Morbi: Irrigation Department (Government of Gujarat), 1979. Rajkot Irrigation Circle Papers.

———. *Diary of Deputy Engineer A. C. Mehta, July–September 1979*. Irrigation Department (Government of Gujarat), 1979. Rajkot Irrigation Circle Papers.

Mehta, A. P. "Report of the Machhu Irrigation Scheme." Rajkot: Public Works Department (Government of Saurashtra), n.d. Rajkot Irrigation Circle Papers.

Mehta, Dhirubhai. "Letter to the Editor of *Sandesh*." [In Gujarati.] Morbi, June 5, 1981. Dhirubhai Mehta Papers.

———. "List: Put in the Mail, 30 April 1981." [In Gujarati.] Morbi, April 30, 1981. Dhirubhai Mehta Papers.

———. "A Protest against the Winding up of the Judicial Commission regarding Machhu-2 Dam Disaster by Govt. of Gujarat." Letter to various recipients. Morbi, April 30, 1981. Dhirubhai Mehta Papers.

Mehta, R. A. "List of Critical Areas: Machhu Dam-II Inquiry Commission." Ahmedabad: Government of Gujarat, September 19, 1980. Rajkot Irrigation Circle Papers.

Metcalf, Barbara D., and Thomas R. Metcalf. *A Concise History of Modern India.* 2nd ed. New York: Cambridge University Press, 2001.

Mistry, J. F. "Submission of the Plans and Estimates and Project Report of Restoration of Machhu-II Dam and Canals etc." Letter to P. M. Mane and E. C. Saldanha. Gandhinagar: Irrigation Department (Government of Gujarat), May 21, 1982. Central Designs Organization Papers.

Mistry, Ravi, Weimin Dong, and Haresh Shah. "Interdisciplinary Observations on the January 2001 Bhuj, Gujarat Earthquake." World Seismic Safety Initiative, 2001. http://www.rms.com/ publications/Bhuj_EQ_Report.pdf.

Mohan, Lakshmanbhai. "Voluntary Statement." [In Gujarati.] Rajkot: Irrigation Department (Government of Gujarat), August 23, 1979. Rajkot Irrigation Circle Papers.

Morbi Royal Family (MRF). "A Summary of Jadeja Reigns." [Inferred title.] Morbi: Morbi Royal Family, [2000?]. Morbi Royal Family Papers.

———. "A Summary of Royal Achievements." [Inferred title. In Gujarati.] Morbi: Morbi Royal Family, [1990?]. Morbi Royal Family Papers.

"Mother Theresa" [Poster]. [In Gujarati.] Morbi: 1980. Ratilal Desai Papers.

Municipality of Morbi (MOM). *Book of Deaths Registered in the Municipality Death Register after the Flood Disaster.* [In Gujarati.] 2 vols. Morbi: Municipality of Morbi, 1980. Municipality of Morbi Archives.

Murthy, Y. K. "Bio-Data of Dr. Y. K. Murthy." New Delhi, 2010. Y. K. Murthy Papers.

———. *Report on Failure of Machhu Dam-II, Gujarat.* 2 vols. N.p.: Government of Gujarat, 1985. Central Designs Organization Papers.

Nazir, Pervaiz. "Social Structure, Ideology, and Language: Caste among Muslims." *Economic and Political Weekly*, December 25, 1993, 2897–2900.

Oza, Manubhai. Letter to Sanatbhai Mehta. [In Gujarati.] Morbi, May 7, 1981. Dhirubhai Mehta Papers.

Pandey, G. "The Human Response to Natural Disaster: The Case of the Morvi Floods." *Disaster Management* 4, no.1 (1991): 15–20.

Pandit, Manu, Prabhakar Khamar, Vinubhai D. Patel, Geeraben S. Patel, and Satishbhai B. Patel, eds. *A Leader of Rock-Hard Principles: Babubhai Jashbhai Patel; A Book of Memories.* [In Gujarati.] Nadiyad: Shri Babubhai J. Patel Memorial Trust, 2005.

Pandit, U. P., J. Joshi, P. Joshi, G. Doshi, S. Mehta, and G. Jani. "Impressions from a Visit to Morbi on 20 September 1979." Rajkot: Morbi Flood Relief Coordination Committee, September 26, 1979. Rajkot Collectorate Papers.

Parmar, Gokaldas. *The Memorable Events of My Life.* [In Gujarati.] Morbi: Gokaldas Parmar Timeless Celebration Welcome Committee, 1997. Gokaldas Parmar Papers.

Parthasarathy, R., C. S. S. Rao, K. V. Bhanujan, and R. B. Sudiwala. *Before the Machhu Dam-II Inquiry Commission: The Statement of Facts and Opinions.* [Parts in Gujarati.] 2 vols. Gandhinagar: Government of Gujarat, 1980. Central Designs Organization Papers and Morbi Flood Museum Library.

Paswan, Ram Vilas. Letter to Dhirubhai Mehta. New Delhi, June 20, 1981. Dhirubhai Mehta Papers.

Patel, Babubhai Jashbhai. *Diaries.* [In Gujarati.] Consulted 1979, 1981, 1990. Babubhai Jashbhai Patel Papers.

Patel, Bhagvanji Nanji. "Voluntary Statement." [In Gujarati.] Rajkot: Irrigation Department (Government of Gujarat), August 23, 1979. Rajkot Irrigation Circle Papers.

Patel, N. B. "Notification under Commissions of Inquiry Act (1952)." Gandhinagar: Legal Department (Government of Gujarat), 1979. Rajkot Irrigation Circle Papers.

Playne, Somerset. "The State of Morvi." In *Indian States: A Biographical, Historical, and Administrative Survey*, 586–96. London: Foreign and Colonial Compiling and Publishing, 1921. Morbi Royal Family Papers.

Pocock, David Francis. *Kanbi and Patidar: A Study of the Patidar Community of Gujarat.* Oxford: Clarendon Press, 1972.

Private secretary to the prime minister. Letter to Dhirubhai Mehta. New Delhi, May 14, 1981. Dhirubhai Mehta Papers.

Proceedings of the Gujarat Legislative Assembly (Official Record) 66, no. 2. [In Gujarati.] Gandhinagar: Gujarat Legislative Assembly Secretariat (Government of Gujarat), 1979. Gujarat Legislative Assembly Archives.

Purohit, M. U. "Notes regarding the Visit of Mr. P. M. Mane, Chairman, Panel of Experts to Review the Dam Safety to the Machhu Dam Site on 22nd and 23rd June 1982." Gandhinagar: Central Designs Organization (Government of Gujarat), July 5, 1982. Central Designs Organization Papers.

Rajapara, Vanubhai. "Statement." [In Gujarati.] Rajkot: Irrigation Department (Government of Gujarat), August 23, 1979. Rajkot Irrigation Circle Papers.

Rakhecha, P. R., and B. N. Mandal. "Estimation of Peak Flow at Machhu-2 Dam on the Day of the Disaster in 1979." *Vayu Mandal*, 13 (1983): 71–73.

Rangarajan, C. "Obituary: Ravi Matthai." *Economic and Political Weekly*, March 20, 1984, 413–14.

Raval, Manoj, ed. *Gujarat State Gazetteer: Rajkot District*. [In Gujarati.] Gandhinagar: Government of Gujarat, 2001.

Reddy, L. R. *The Pain and Horror: Gujarat Earthquake*. New Delhi: APH Publishing, 2001.

Roy, Arundhati. *The Greater Common Good*. Bombay: India Book Distributor, 1999.

Roy, R. N. Letter to Dhirubhai Mehta on behalf of George Fernandes. New Delhi, May 5, 1981. Dhirubhai Mehta Papers.

Saldanha, E. C., and P. M. Mane. "The Appraisal Report of the Consultants to Govt. of Gujarat for Review of the Design of Machhu-II Irrigation Scheme." Gandhinagar: Central Designs Organization (Government of Gujarat), 1985. Central Designs Organization Papers.

———. "Notes of Consultants for the Machhu-II Dam during Visit to the Hydraulic Model at GERI on 13-3-1985." Gandhinagar: Central Designs Organization (Government of Gujarat), 1985. Central Designs Organization Papers.

———. "Minutes of Meeting for Machhu-II Dam Held by the Consultants on 8.8.1984 at Gandhinagar." Gandhinagar: Central Designs Organization (Government of Gujarat), September 5, 1984. Central Designs Organization Papers.

———. "Minutes of Meeting for Machhu-II Dam Held by the Consultants on 29/11/1983 at Vadodara." Gandhinagar: Central Designs Organization (Government of Gujarat), December 7, 1983. Central Designs Organization Papers.

Sanghavi, Nagindas. "Dissolution and After." *Economic and Political Weekly*, March 22, 1980, 587–88.

———. *Gujarat: A Political Analysis*. Surat: Centre for Social Studies, 1996.

Shah, Laxmichand Dossabhai. "Morvi." In *The Prince of Wales and the Princes of India*, 236–39. Rajkot: Kathiawar Printing Works, 1923. Morbi Royal Family Papers.

Shah, Maneklal H., ed. *Addresses to His Highness the Maharaja Shri Sir Lakhdhirsinhji Saheb Bahadur*. Nadiad: *Gujrat-Times* Printing Press, 1934. Morbi Royal Family Papers.

Shah, Manubhai. "Government Privilege Claim Rejected." Ahmedabad: Consumer Education and Research Centre, 1980. Consumer Education and Research Centre Library.

———. "Gujarat Government Directed to Release Withheld Grant to Consumer Education and Research Centre, Ahmedabad." Ahmedabad: Consumer Education and Research Center, 1983. Consumer Education and Research Centre Library.

———. Letter to Dhirubhai Mehta. [In Gujarati.] Ahmedabad, July 7, 1981. Dhirubhai Mehta Papers.

———. "Winding up Machhu Enquiry Commission Quashed." Ahmedabad: Consumer Education and Research Center, 1981. Consumer Education and Research Centre Library.

Shah, Naresh. "The Twenty-Fifth Anniversary of the Machhu Disaster: Even If I Wanted to, How Could I Forget You?" [In Gujarati.] *Abhiyaan*, August 28, 2004.

Sharma, Ursula. *Caste*. Philadelphia: Open University Press, 1999.

Shukla-Bhatt, Neelima. "Gujarat: Govinda's Glory: Krishna-*Lila* in the Songs of Narsinha Mehta." In *Krishna: A Sourcebook*, edited by E. F. Bryant, 255–84. New York: Oxford University Press, 2007.

Singh, K. S., ed. *People of India: Gujarat*. 3 vols. Mumbai: Anthropological Survey of India, 2002.

Singh, Makhan. "Progressive Administration of Morvi State: Achievements of H. H. Maharaja Shri Sir Lakhdhir Ji Wagh Ji. Bahadur,

K. C. S. I., G. C. B. E." In *Special Morvi Number of the* Naresh. Special issue, *Naresh*, March 12, 1942. Morbi Royal Family Papers.

Sinha, Aseema. "Divided Loyalties: The Regional Politics of Divergence." In *The Regional Roots of Developmental Politics in India: A Divided Leviathan*, 160–211. Bloomington: Indiana University Press, 2005.

Sivaramakrishnan, V. M. *Tobacco and Areca Nut*. Hyderabad: Orient Blackswan, 2001.

Spodek, Howard. "On the Origins of Gandhi's Political Methodology: The Heritage of Kathiawad and Gujarat." *Journal of Asian Studies* 30, no. 2 (1971): 361–72.

"State of Gujarat v. Consumer & Education Research Centre and Ors." *Gujarat Law Reporter* 25, no. 1 (1984): 492–93. Supreme Court of India, February 8, 1984.

Tainter, Jeremiah Burnham. Sluiceway-Gate. US Patent 344,876, filed November 16, 1865, and issued July 6, 1886.

Tambs-Lyche, Harald. *The Good Country: Individual, Situation, and Society in Saurashtra*. New Delhi: Manohar Publishers and Distributors, 2004.

Tanna, Bhaskar. "Machhu Ado about Nothing?" *Consumer Confrontation*, September 1981, 2–3. Consumer Education and Research Centre Library.

Tripathy, S., and C. M. Chokshi, eds. *Gazetteer of India: Gujarat State Gazetteer Supplement; Rajkot District Gazetteer*. Ahmedabad: Government of Gujarat, 1982.

Trivedi, M. K. "Morbi Flood Disaster, 11-8-79: Sheet Showing Progress up to 24-1-80." Morbi: Revenue Department (Government of Gujarat), January 25, 1980. A. R. Banerjee Papers.

Trivedi, M. R., ed. *Gazetteer of India: Gujarat State Gazetteer*. 2 vols. Gandhinagar: Government of Gujarat, 1989.

Trivedi, R. K., ed. *Census 1961, Gujarat: District Census Handbook, Rajkot*. Ahmedabad: Government of Gujarat, 1964.

Trivedi, V. P. "Voluntary Statement." [In Gujarati.] Rajkot: Irrigation Department (Government of Gujarat), August 23, 1979. Rajkot Irrigation Circle Papers.

Turner, Patricia, and Charles Russell Coulter. *Dictionary of Ancient Deities*. New York: Oxford University Press, 2001.

Varma, C. V. J., and K. R. Saxena, eds. *Modern Temples of India: Selected Speeches of Jawaharlal Nehru at Irrigation and Power Projects and Various Technical Meetings of Engineers & Scientists.* New Delhi: Central Board of Irrigation and Power (Government of India), 1989.

Vasoya, B. J. "Machhu-2 Dam Works and Construction of Outlet for Water Supply to Kandla: Inquiry." Letter to Superintending Engineer, Rajkot Irrigation Circle. Morbi: Public Works Department (Government of Gujarat), June 8, 1972. Rajkot Irrigation Circle Papers.

Verghese, B. G. "Something to Hide?" *India Today*, May 16, 1981.

Watson, John W., ed. *Gazetteer of the Bombay Presidency: Kathiawar.* Bombay: Government Central Press, 1884.

Wolpert, Stanley. *India.* 3rd ed. Berkeley: University of California Press, 2005.

Yadav, Neelam, ed. *Encyclopaedia of Backward Castes.* New Delhi: Anmol Publications, 2005.

NEWSPAPERS

English

Dawn (Karachi)
Economic Times (Online)
Hindu (Chennai)
Hindu Business Line (Online)
Hindustan Times (New Delhi)
Indian Express (New Delhi)
New York Times (New York)
Telegraph (London)
Times of India (Ahmedabad)
Western Times (Ahmedabad)

Gujarati

Akila (Rajkot)
Gujarat Mitra (Surat)
Gujarat Samachar (Ahmedabad)
Jansatta (Ahmedabad)
Jai Hind (Ahmedabad)
Phulchhab (Rajkot)
Prabhat (Ahmedabad)
Sandesh (Rajkot)

ARCHIVES

Documents

A. R. Banerjee Papers (Ahmedabad)
Babubhai Jashbhai Patel Papers (Gandhinagar)
Central Designs Organization Papers (Gandhinagar)
Consumer Education and Research Centre Library (Ahmedabad)
Dhirubhai Mehta Papers (Morbi)
Gokaldas Parmar Papers (Morbi)
Gujarat Legislative Assembly Archives (Gandhinagar)
Kasperson Research Library (Worcester)
Mani Mandir Archives (Morbi)
Morbi Flood Museum Library (Morbi)
Morbi Royal Family Papers (Morbi)
Municipality of Morbi Archives (Morbi)
Rajkot Collectorate Papers (Rajkot)
Rajkot Irrigation Circle Papers (Rajkot)
Ratilal Desai Papers (Morbi)
Revenue Department Papers (Gandhinagar)
Y. K. Murthy Papers (New Delhi)

Audiovisual

Phulchhab Photographic Archive (Rajkot)
Prabhakarbhai Khamar Photographs (Ahmedabad)
Rajkot Ramakrishna Ashrama Photographic Archive (Rajkot)
Ratilal Desai Photographs (Morbi)
T. R. Shukla Photographs (Fort Wayne)
Vanderbilt Television News Archive (Nashville)

INTERVIEWS

December 31, 2005	T. R. Shukla And Ushaben Shukla, former residents of eastern Morbi
May 17, 2006	Neelimaben Shukla, former resident of eastern Morbi
May 23, 2006	Lee Wooten, geotechnical engineering expert
June 7, 2006	Rahul Bhimjiani, former chief operating officer of the Consumer Education and Research Centre [telephone]
June 8, 2006	Interviewee 4, professor at the University of Roorkee [telephone]
June 8, 2006	Bhaskarbhai Tanna, former counsel for the Consumer Education and Research Centre [telephone]
June 15, 2006	Bhaskarbhai Tanna, former counsel for the Consumer Education and Research Centre
June 16, 2006	Interviewee 6, professor at the Indian Institute of Management–Ahmedabad
June 17, 2006	Interviewee 7, Ahmedabad journalist
June 17, 2006	Interviewee 8, Ahmedabad disaster expert
June 19, 2006	Interviewee 9, officer of the Rashtriya Swayamsevak Sangh
June 23, 2006	Interviewee 10, officer of the Santram Mandir temple
June 24, 2006	Manubhai Shah, director emeritus of the Consumer Education and Research Centre
June 24, 2006	R. A. Mehta, former counsel for the Machhu Dam-II Inquiry Commission

June 26, 2006	Interviewee 13, Gujarat Revenue Department official
June 26, 2006	Interviewee 14, member of the Gujarat chief minister's staff
June 27, 2006	B. R. Shah, former counsel for the Machhu Dam-II Inquiry Commission
June 28, 2006	Interviewee 16, former officer of the Sadvichar Parivar
June 28, 2006	Interviewee 14, member of the Gujarat chief minister's staff
June 30, 2006	Prabhakarbhai Khamar, former personal secretary to Babubhai Patel
July 2, 2006	Interviewee 18, former officer of the Sadvichar Parivar
July 2, 2006	Interviewee 19, former officer of the State Bank of India
July 4, 2006	Interviewee 20, former engineer for the government of Gujarat
July 4, 2006	Prabhakarbhai Khamar, former personal secretary to Babubhai Patel
July 6, 2006	Interviewee 21, former officer of the Rashtriya Swayamsevak Sangh
July 7, 2006	Ushakant Mankad, former Rajkot District Home Guard commander
July 7, 2006	Interviewee 23, Rajkot Directorate of Information official
July 7, 2006	Interviewee 21, former officer of the Rashtriya Swayamsevak Sangh
July 10, 2006	Interviewee 24, Gujarat Revenue Department official
July 11, 2006	Interviewee 25, industries expert
July 11, 2006	Interviewee 26, Officer of the Morbi Flood Museum
July 11, 2006	Interviewee 27, Morbi social activist
July 12, 2006	Interviewee 28, Gujarat Revenue Department official
July 12, 2006	Interviewee 29, former Gujarat Revenue Department official
July 13, 2006	Interviewee 30, resident of the main market area

July 16, 2006	Interviewee 31, resident of Jodhpar
July 16, 2006	Interviewee 32, resident of Jodhpar
July 16, 2006	Interviewee 33, former Machhu Dam-II laborer
July 17, 2006	Interviewee 34, resident of Mochi Gali
July 18, 2006	Interviewee 35, resident of the crematorium area
July 18, 2006	Interviewee 36, resident of the crematorium area
July 18, 2006	Interviewees 37–41, residents of the crematorium area
July 18, 2006	Interviewee 42, former resident of the crematorium area
July 18, 2006	Interviewee 43, former resident of the Tiger Quarter
July 18, 2006	Interviewee 44, resident of the crematorium area
July 18, 2006	Interviewee 45, former resident of the Shepherd Quarter
July 18, 2006	Interviewee 46, former resident of Lati Plot
July 18, 2006	Interviewee 47, former resident of the main market area
July 19, 2006	Interviewee 48, resident of the Harijan Quarter
July 19, 2006	Interviewees 49–51, residents of the Harijan Quarter
July 19, 2006	Interviewee 52 and Interviewee 53, residents of the Harijan Quarter
July 19, 2006	Interviewees 54–57, residents of the Harijan Quarter
July 19, 2006	Interviewee 58, resident of Ravapar
July 19, 2006	Interviewee 59, resident of the Harijan Quarter
July 20, 2006	Ratilal Desai and Interviewee 30, former mayor of Morbi and resident of the main market area
July 21, 2006	Bhagvanji Patel, resident of Lilapar
July 21, 2006	Gokaldas Parmar, former member of the legislative assembly from Morbi
July 21, 2006	Interviewees 63–65, residents of Lakhdhirnagar
July 21, 2006	Interviewee 66 and Interviewee 67, residents of Lilapar
July 22, 2006	Interviewee 68, resident of Juna Sadulka
July 22, 2006	Interviewee 69, resident of Rotary Nagar
July 22, 2006	Interviewee 70, resident of Rotary Nagar

July 22, 2006	Interviewee 25, industries expert
July 22, 2006	Interviewee 71, resident of Relief Nagar
July 22, 2006	Interviewee 30, resident of the main market area
July 22, 2006	Interviewee 72, former resident of eastern Morbi
July 23, 2006	Dhirubhai Mehta, resident of the Mahendra Quarter
July 23, 2006	Interviewee 25, industries expert
July 23, 2006	Interviewee 74, former officer of the National Cadet Corps
July 24, 2006	Interviewee 75, resident of the Harijan Quarter
July 24, 2006	Gokaldas Parmar and Mrs. Parmar, former member of the legislative assembly from Morbi and his wife
July 24, 2006	Interviewee 76, former resident of the Shepherd Quarter
July 24, 2006	Interviewee 77, resident of the Harijan Quarter
July 24, 2006	Interviewee 78, resident of the Shepherd Quarter
July 24, 2006	Interviewee 79, resident of the Harijan Quarter
July 24, 2006	Interviewee 80, resident of the Harijan Quarter
July 24, 2006	Ratilal Desai, former mayor of Morbi
July 24, 2006	Interviewee 81, former member of the Home Guards
July 25, 2006	Khatijaben Valera, resident of southern Morbi
July 25, 2006	Naseemben Valera, resident of southern Morbi
July 25, 2006	Ratilal Desai, former mayor of Morbi
July 26, 2006	Gokaldas Parmar, former member of the legislative assembly from Morbi
July 26, 2006	Hemiben Devda, Interviewee 85, and Interviewee 86, residents of Vajepar
July 26, 2006	Interviewee 87 and Interviewee 88, residents of Vajepar
July 26, 2006	Interviewee 89 and Interviewee 90, police officers of Morbi
July 26, 2006	Interviewee 91, resident of Vajepar
July 26, 2006	Interviewee 92, resident of Vajepar
July 26, 2006	Interviewee 93 and Interviewee 85, residents of Vajepar
July 27, 2006	Interviewee 94, resident of the main market area

July 27, 2006	Interviewees 95–103, residents of the Lilapar Harijan Quarter
July 27, 2006	Interviewee 104, resident of the Lilapar Harijan Quarter
July 27, 2006	Interviewee 105, resident of the Gujarat Slum Clearance Board neighborhood on Lilapar Road
July 27, 2006	Interviewee 106, resident of the Gujarat Labor Board neighborhood on Lilapar Road
July 28, 2006	Interviewee 107, resident of Mochi Gali
July 28, 2006	Interviewees 108–10, residents of Mochi Gali
July 28, 2006	Interviewees 111–13, residents of the Leatherworker Quarter
July 28, 2006	Interviewee 99, resident of the Lilapar Harijan Quarter
July 29, 2006	Gangaram Tapu, resident of Kabir Hill
July 29, 2006	Interviewee 116, former Machhu Dam-II laborer
July 29, 2006	Lakshmanbhai Mohan, former Machhu Dam-II mechanic
July 29, 2006	Interviewee 33, former Machhu Dam-II laborer
July 30, 2006	Bhaskarbhai Tanna, former counsel for the Consumer Education and Research Centre [telephone]
July 31, 2006	Interviewee 118, tailor of the main market area
July 31, 2006	Interviewee 119, engineer for the government of Gujarat
July 31, 2006	Interviewee 120, jeweler of the main market area
July 31, 2006	Interviewee 121 and Interviewee 122, paint merchants of the main market area
July 31, 2006	Interviewee 123, cobbler of the main market area
August 1, 2006	Interviewee 124, officer of the Rajkot Ramakrishna Ashrama temple
August 1, 2006	Interviewee 125, Rajkot journalist
August 3, 2006	Interviewee 126, resident of Madhapar
August 3, 2006	Interviewee 127, resident of the main market area

August 3, 2006	Interviewee 128, resident of the main market area
August 3, 2006	Interviewee 129, electronics merchant of the main market area
August 3, 2006	Pratapbhai Adroja, resident of Madhapar
August 3, 2006	Interviewee 131, former resident of the main market area
August 3, 2006	Interviewee 132 and Interviewee 133, watch merchants of the main market area
August 4, 2006	Interviewee 134, former factory owner
August 12, 2006	Y. K. Murthy, former engineering adviser for the Machhu Dam-II Commission of Inquiry
August 12, 2006	Abdulbhai Mor, resident of Maliya
August 12, 2006	Husainbhai Manek, resident of Maliya
August 12, 2006	Jashabhai Samani, resident of Maliya
August 12, 2006	Kanubhai Kubavat, resident of the Tiger Quarter
August 13, 2006	Interviewee 140, resident of Sarvad
August 13, 2006	Interviewee 141, resident of Maliya
August 14, 2006	Dipankar Basu, former secretary for the Machhu Dam-II Inquiry Commission
August 14, 2006	H. K. Khan, former Gujarat special secretary for relief
August 16, 2006	A. R. Banerjee, former Rajkot district collector
August 18, 2006	Interviewee 145, former engineer for the government of Gujarat
July 6, 2010	Nishubhai Sedani, son of photographer Gunvantbhai Sedani
August 18, 2010	A. R. Banerjee, former Rajkot district collector [telephone]

Index

393